MANUAL OF DIGITAL MUSEUM PLANNING

MANUAL OF DIGITAL MUSEUM PLANNING

Edited by Ali Hossaini and Ngaire Blankenberg

ROWMAN & LITTLEFIELD
Lanham • Boulder • New York • London

Published by Rowman & Littlefield
A wholly owned subsidiary of The Rowman & Littlefield Publishing Group, Inc.
4501 Forbes Boulevard, Suite 200, Lanham, Maryland 20706
www.rowman.com

Unit A, Whitacre Mews, 26-34 Stannary Street, London SE11 4AB

Copyright © 2017 by Rowman & Littlefield

All rights reserved. No part of this book may be reproduced in any form or by any electronic or mechanical means, including information storage and retrieval systems, without written permission from the publisher, except by a reviewer who may quote passages in a review.

British Library Cataloguing in Publication Information Available

Library of Congress Cataloging-in-Publication Data Available

ISBN 978-1-4422-7895-0 (cloth : alk. paper)
ISBN 978-1-4422-7896-7 (pbk. : alk. paper)
ISBN 978-1-4422-7897-4 (electronic)

∞™ The paper used in this publication meets the minimum requirements of American National Standard for Information Sciences—Permanence of Paper for Printed Library Materials, ANSI/NISO Z39.48-1992.

Printed in the United States of America

Contents

List of Figures and Tables	ix
Foreword	xiii
Gail Dexter Lord and Barry Lord, *Co-Presidents, Lord Cultural Resources*	
Acknowledgments	xv
Introduction	xvii
Ngaire Blankenberg and Ali Hossaini	

Section 1: A New Value Proposition for Museums in the Digital Age — 1

CHAPTER 1: Discovering a New Kind of Dialogue — 3
Chris Michaels, *Head of Digital and Publishing, The British Museum*

CHAPTER 2: The Omnichannel Museum — 13
Ali Hossaini, *CEO, Cinema Arts Network, and Associate, Lord Cultural Resources*

CHAPTER 3: Making It Personal: Putting Data at the Heart of Your Museum — 27
Rob Stein, *Executive Vice President and Chief Program Officer, American Alliance of Museums*

Section 2: Transforming the Way We Relate to Our Community — 43

CHAPTER 4: Social Media and Audience Development — 45
Ngaire Blankenberg, *Principal Consultant, European Director, Lord Cultural Resources*

FOLLOW ME: GROWING YOUR TWITTER COMMUNITY:
INTERVIEW WITH ALEX ESPINÓS AND GLORIA CASTELLVÍ,
Founder, and Web Media Analyst, LaMagnética   54

CHAPTER 5: Analytics   61

    Katie Moffat, *Head of Digital, The Audience Agency*

A HEAD FOR NUMBERS: INTERVIEW WITH MARK PAJAK,
Head of Digital, Bristol Culture   71

CHAPTER 6: Museum Learning in the Digital Age   77

    Ngaire Blankenberg, *Principal Consultant, European Director, Lord Cultural Resources*

CHAPTER 7: New Frontiers in the Visitor Experience   109

    Lisa Wright, *Senior Consultant, Lord Cultural Resources*

DIGITAL PEN AT THE COOPER HEWITT MUSEUM:
INTERVIEW WITH JAKE BARTON, Principal and Founder, Local Projects   121

PLANNING NEW TECHNOLOGIES: INTERVIEW WITH JESSICA DOIG,
Vice President and Executive Producer, NGX Interactive   124

Section 3: Transforming the Way We Work   131

CHAPTER 8: Content for Every Channel   133

    Ali Hossaini, *CEO, Cinema Arts Network, and Associate, Lord Cultural Resources*

CHAPTER 9: The Pursuit of Efficient Relevance: An Enterprise
Content Management System   161

    Corey Timpson, *Vice President, Exhibition, Research and Design, Canadian Museum of Human Rights*

CHAPTER 10: Digital Collections Management   175

    Edward Purvis, *Head of Collections, Services, National Portrait Gallery*

USING VOLUNTEERS FOR DIGITIZATION PROJECTS: INTERVIEW WITH
PAM BABES, Collections Information Manager, National Museums of Scotland   197

CHAPTER 11: Digital Project Management   201

Rachel Clements Walker, *Senior Manager of Ecommerce and Systems, Metropolitan Museum of Art*

DIGITAL PROJECTS IN MUSEUMS: INTERVIEW WITH EILEEN WILLS, Editorial Director, Lincoln Center for Performing Arts   238

AGILE PROJECTS AT THE METROPOLITAN MUSEUM OF ART: INTERVIEW WITH ADAM PADRON, Senior Manager, Application and Data Services   239

CHAPTER 12: Visitor Experience Design   245

Marco Mason, *Marie Curie Fellow at University of Leicester School of Museum Studies and University of Cambridge Fitzwilliam Museum*

Section 4: Resilience and Sustainability   269

CHAPTER 13: Museum Organization for the Future   271

Ngaire Blankenberg, *Principal Consultant, European Director, Lord Cultural Resources*

CHAPTER 14: Planning for IT Infrastructure   289

Ali Hossaini, *CEO, Cinema Arts Network, and Associate, Lord Cultural Resources*

DEVELOPING FLEXIBLE INFRASTRUCTURE FOR THE TWENTY-FIRST-CENTURY MUSEUM: INTERVIEW WITH KEVIN CUNNINGHAM, Founder and Executive Artistic Director, 3-Legged Dog Media and Theater Group and 3LD Art & Technology Center   332

CHAPTER 15: Planning for Digital Revenues   341

Ngaire Blankenberg and Ali Hossaini

AFTERWORD: Digital Placemaking   355

Ali Hossaini, *CEO, Cinema Arts Network, and Associate, Lord Cultural Resources*

Glossary	359
Bibliography	369
Index	377
About the Authors	385

List of Figures and Tables

List of Figures

FIGURE 2.1	The Omnichannel Stack	20
FIGURE 3.1	Comment Card of Utagawa Kunisada Block Print	28
FIGURE 3.2	Comment Card of Bill Viola Video	29
FIGURE 3.3	The OODA Loop	32
FIGURE 5.1	Digital Metrics Dashboard Template	70
FIGURE 6.1	Connected Learning	79
FIGURE 6.2	Learning for Change	80
FIGURE 6.3	Multiliteracies	82
FIGURE 6.4	Evaluating Social Media for Learning	91
FIGURE 6.5	Teaching Network	100
FIGURE 6.6	A Learning Network	102
FIGURE 9.1	An Early Sketch of Canadian Museum of Human Rights' ECMS	162
FIGURE 9.2	ECMS Diagram	170
FIGURE 10.1A	Cataloging Data Fields	183
FIGURE 10.1B	Cataloging Data Fields	184
FIGURE 10.2	Guidelines for Naming	189
FIGURE 10.3	Data Processing Workflow for Primary Users	190
FIGURE 10.4	Workflow Diagram for Secondary Users	190

FIGURE 11.1	The Triple Constraint	203
FIGURE 11.2	Sample Agenda	214
FIGURE 11.3	Outline Project Schedule	218
FIGURE 11.4	Tips for Building a Gantt Chart	220
FIGURE 11.5	Example of a Risk Log Entry for an Exhibition-Related Product	226
FIGURE 11.6	Example of How to Start Building a Test Script	230
FIGURE 12.1	Visitor Experience Design	249
FIGURE 12.2	The Visitor Experience Design Process	250
FIGURE 12.3	Examples of Personas	253
FIGURE 12.4	Example of a Visual Scenario	255
FIGURE 12.5	Sample Storyboard	258
FIGURE 12.6A	Wireframe Example	259
FIGURE 12.6B	Final Results	259
FIGURE 12.7	Flowchart Example	260
FIGURE 12.8	Low-Fidelity Prototype	262
FIGURE 12.9	Low-Fidelity Interactions Created with the POP App	263
FIGURE 12.10	Frames Extracted from a Video Step-Through	263
FIGURE 13.1	Traditional Organogram	272
FIGURE 13.2	Visitor-Centered Organogram	273
FIGURE 14.1	Basic Network Architecture	293
FIGURE 14.2	Physical Topology	294
FIGURE 14.3	Network Termination Device	298
FIGURE 14.4	Patch Panel	299
FIGURE 14.5	Server Rack	300
FIGURE 14.6	RJ-45 Ethernet Cable	303
FIGURE 14.7	WiFi Access Point, Example 1	305
FIGURE 14.8	WiFi Access Point, Example 2	306
FIGURE 14.9	Logical Topology	311

FIGURE 14.10 Router   312

FIGURE 14.11 Switch   313

FIGURE 14.12 MAC Address   314

FIGURE 14.13 Rack Server   315

FIGURE 14.14 Rack Server in situ   315

List of Tables

TABLE 4.1 Tips for Shareable Content on Social Media   48

TABLE 5.1 Commonly Used Analytics Tools   64

TABLE 6.1 New Media Literacies   81

TABLE 8.1 Sample List of Digital Channels and Relevant Information   146

TABLE 10.1 CMS Users and Their Requirements   179

TABLE 10.2 Inward Loan and Outward Loan Information   186

TABLE 10.3 Public Engagement with Collections: Challenges and Solutions   196

TABLE 11.1 Project Roles and Decision Making   212

TABLE 11.2 Comparing Waterfall and Agile Development Methods   216

TABLE 11.3 Typical Activities and Deliverables during Each Project Phase   219

TABLE 11.4 Sample Test Plan for Ecommerce Website   229

TABLE 14.1 PCI DSS Guidelines   330

Foreword
Planning the Digital Museum

**Barry Lord and
Gail Dexter Lord**

Museums are about real things—original works of art, historic artifacts, specimens of natural history, and the tangible records of human achievement. Museums are about real people, those who visit and those who work inside and the many who pass by wondering what is contained within those impressive walls. At first glance the digital world of images and data seems to be a very different and unrelated place. Yet two basic human impulses bring them together: communication and storage.

From our invention of language and music some 150,000 years ago, human beings have continued to develop tools for communicating with each other. We now see the many forms of print from stone to scroll to book and e-book as an evolutionary process. Museums in one form or another have been there for all of these. The increasing miniaturization of communications tools—cameras, the telegraph, telephone, movies, radio, TV, and the Internet—speaks to the human need for better and faster communication. Museums are themselves a form of communication, but one that has grown ever bigger with more monumental buildings until now when the digital revolution provides museums with the opportunity to be transferable and transportable, thereby better meeting human needs for communication.

Storage is another basic human need, starting with storage of food. The granary that stored grains was the center of civic life and the center of power. Museums collect and display containers—always different for each culture—while themselves being the great container. The storage, conservation, and use of collections in museums anticipate the storage, conservation, and use of data in the digital world. And the digital world enhances, accelerates, and shares the somewhat primitive capacity of museums to store, analyze, and disseminate their information and wisdom.

We are therefore delighted to welcome this newest book in the Lord museum planning series: *Manual of Digital Museum Planning*. Here coauthors and editors Ngaire Blankenberg and Ali Hossaini have assembled the core concepts on how to plan for the digital museum—the museum for our times and future generations. Some of us will turn to the glossary every page; many more will find that the language of digital fits your world perfectly.

As Blankenberg and Hossaini explain in the following pages, planning for digital in museums and other cultural institutions is not just about understanding new technology, it is about understanding how such technologies change our values, the way we relate to our community, the way we work, and our ability to be resilient and sustainable. The chapters in this manual aim to establish a balance between the why and the how. It is written for students seeking to understand museum practice, policy makers, museum directors, boards, and funders who are working to be prepared and responsive in the digital age and professionals aiming to integrate new technologies within their work and museums. They have incorporated different approaches—from the technical to the theoretical—to be interesting and, most importantly, to be useful. Keywords are highlighted to enable readers to become familiar with the most prevalent terms, while sidebars provide more detail on unfamiliar concepts. Interviews with practitioners who reflect on their own experiences enliven the chapters, offering readers new insights when it comes to implementing change in their own organizations.

Acknowledgments

We would like to thank Cinema Arts Network and the member organizations that made much of this research possible. Labyrinth Technology, Ltd., of London provided generous advice on the creation of technical diagrams. Finally we would like to acknowledge—and reflect upon—the generosity of the hundreds of bloggers, lecturers, research agencies, and conferences who freely share stories of success, failure, and the learning that goes with both. One of the most profound qualities of digital culture is the way it enables cooperation, spontaneous kindness, and a common striving for improvement. It is in this spirit that this book has been written.

Introduction
A Changing Value Proposition for Museums

Ngaire Blankenberg and Ali Hossaini

The public museum, by which is meant an institution that collects and displays ideas, artifacts, works of art, and specimens in the public interest, has been evolving for 250 years, and will continue to do so far into the future. Recent estimates tell us there are eighty thousand museums in the world, mainly in Europe and the Americas, and the number keeps growing as Asia and Africa develop their museums. Continuous growth in the number of new museums being built around the world and increasing global museum audiences attest to the fact that, on the whole, the museum is a successful institution. Nonetheless, many people predict the end of museums in the Digital Age. This argument typically rests on the notion that museums are redundant as sources of information, given the Internet; outdated as forms of public education and engagement, given their reluctance to share content and authority; and ineffective as sources of entertainment. These arguments are not entirely without merit.

The Digital Age has created new power dynamics, new forms of authority, and new communities with shifting expectations, motivations, and behavior. Where once there were a limited number of credible knowledge providers—with museums being among the most accessible—the Internet throws open an expanding universe of facts, relationships, and experiences. Knowledge and creative production have been integrated into a new machinery that has radically shifted avenues for exhibition and distribution. Artists, scientists, historians, and the interested public have new and rapidly evolving options through which to communicate their work and ideas.

Yet, museums continue to have value. As Chris Michaels points out in chapter 1 using the example of the British Museum, museums still occupy a privileged place in people's quest for knowledge and experience. He argues that there is not necessarily a disconnect between user-centricity and a curator-led model of didactic knowledge. The challenges lie rather in transforming museums to embrace three core ideas: "disintermediation" (i.e., removing the barriers between audience and museum experts), "informalization (a change in tone and communication), and audience participation (creating avenues for conversation). The example of the British Museum is a powerful case study to demonstrate how changes in the way in which museums and their communities relate to one another underpin changes in the role of museums in the broader society. Museums are no longer regarded as fixed entities with a "take it or leave it" attitude toward visitors, but rather are expected to be proactive members of multiple communities of geography and interest. They need to demonstrate their value for the long term as they preserve our "treasures" in perpetuity, but also in the short term as they inspire and empower us all to create them.

The Digital Age has created new opportunities for people to enjoy exclusive museum content that used to only be accessed by a visit to an exhibition. People can connect virtually and physically with one another and with the museums on various platforms—social media, mobile apps, a website, an exhibition, a public program, a learning resource, the shop. This approach is described by Ali Hossaini in chapter 2 as *omnichannel*. Omnichannel museums place visitors at the center of their activities, and they ensure visitors encounter content and experiences whenever and wherever they are. The points through which people encounter the museum are called "channels," which can be understood equally as platforms or programs in that each channel is an opportunity for museums to publish content and people to respond to it.

The far-reaching implications of the omnichannel approach are explored throughout this book. They include freeing and developing museum content such as collection documentation, exhibition media, learning resources, and curatorial research to be scaled, served, distributed, and repurposed via an integrated content management system; activating virtual platforms such as social networks and mobile web; ensuring supportive and flexible IT infrastructure; and changes in the museum's organization, staff, and roles.

Data is the driving force behind user-centricity, argues Rob Stein in chapter 3. The ability to know rather than intuit the behavior, expectations, and motivations of a museum's community is one of the fundamental transformations afforded by digital technology. Data-driven systems are the lifeblood of the omnichannel museum because they distinguish individuals, measure success and enable accountability across an organization. Data also enables rational decision making, and it is key to forming a responsive organization that responds quickly and effectively to feedback. In chapter 5, Katie Moffatt gives practical guidelines for introducing data-driven analytics into evaluation and decision making. She interviews Mark Pajak, Head of Digital at Bristol Museums, Galleries and Archives, about the way in which Bristol Museums uses analytics across five museums and a records office in order to inform concrete decision making. This includes prioritizing "what's on" and "how to find us" as they develop their website, considering whether or not to decommission an older website, and design a new audio tour.

New Relationships with Our Community

Data provides us with the ability to relate to individuals, not groups, which is a necessity as people expect personalization and agency in all their experiences. However, one can identify three groups with similar motivations that museums have a special relationship with: those who connect with the museum via social media, which is a new and growing community; learners and teachers, the foundation of visitors for many museums; and those who visit museum exhibitions and participate in public programs.

Rather than being a marketing vehicle for the "real experience," social media are channels and programs that are an end in and of themselves. Social media platforms have their own culture and norms that museums do not originate or control, and they require particular kinds of content, tone, and invitations for engagement that museums need to adapt to in order to participate. It is interesting to note a recent study that found that US millennials prefer discovering new art on Instagram rather than going to museums[1]—a trend that may soon be global and expand to include history, science, archaeology, and other disciplines. As Ngaire Blankenberg explores in chapter 4, museums hold a rich trove of unique content perfectly adaptable to social media channels, and social media provides an opportunity to engage with new people who do not, cannot, or will not visit the physical museum. Museums that wish to reach out to new audiences and to maintain a responsive and accessible value proposition need to devote the right resources to delivering programs to their varied and distinct social media communities. Strong content, however, is not the only variable.

Museums need to also understand the mechanics of social media algorithms and how they impact on their ability to grow their followers and friends. This is the subject of an interview between Ngaire Blankenberg and Alex Espinós and Gloria Castellví, speaking about their intensive research into how 1,250 museums use Twitter. Museums need to keep abreast of how the controllers of these algorithms (commercial companies such as Facebook and Snapchat) may be moving closer to "pay to play" requiring museums to think about the overall benefits and "returns on investment" of paying for access to such platforms.

Museums contain some of society's most valuable knowledge resources, yet, despite museums being positioned as informal learning institutions, much of this content is too locked inside the museum to support sustained and equitable learning. In chapter 6, Ngaire Blankenberg looks at new pedagogies for the digital age and their impact on museum learning and teaching. She explores such questions as: "How can new technologies enable museum content to be retrieved, annotated, and adapted by learners themselves or teachers from outside the museum? How can museum programs equip learners with twenty-first-century skills? And how can museums recognize and be recognized as a node within a network of teaching and learning that includes schools, other informal learning institutions, peers, and the Internet?" As with all transformations catalyzed by technology, learning in the digital age can also be supported by analytics enabling teachers and learners to track progress, adapt techniques and improve constantly, provided aspects of learning are included within the museum's strategic goals and key performance indicators.

New technologies are also creating new aspects of the visitor experience on site, many of which are designed to find new ways of connecting people with art objects and ideas and each other. Lisa Wright's chapter 7 on the visitor experience explores new developments such as mobile engagement, VR/AR and the Internet of Things. In Wright's interview with Jake Barton—principal and founder of Local Projects, the designers of the "pen" at the Cooper Hewitt Smithsonian Design Museum, and Gallery One at the Cleveland Museum of Art, among others—he speaks of how emotional engagement through storytelling is the underlying motivation for many of his team's projects. Enabling visitors to be creators is a powerful way to connect them to the museum's mission, as evidenced by the success of the pen that allows visitors to gather and self-curate objects from the galleries.

Such experiences need to be planned carefully, ensuring that the thematic goals, desired visitor experience, and learning objectives are considered alongside the technology, advises experience designer Jessica Doig, of NGX Interactive, also interviewed by Lisa Wright in chapter 7.

Changing How We Work in Museums

Planning for every content and experience channel is a critical component of creating powerful new experiences for visitors, and the third section of this book looks at how museum staff, contractors, and even volunteers can develop such experiences through preparing the appropriate content for the right channels, instituting supporting content and collection management systems and managing and designing projects efficiently and effectively.

In chapter 8, Ali Hossaini provides an overview of how museum content can be adapted and distributed to the museum's multiple channels by understanding user behavior and expectations, transforming content into digital assets, having an integrated software system in place and ensuring a robust technology and performance plan. These elements help us to engage the public through open access, personalization, and other user-centric principles described in section 1.

An integrated content management system is a critical interface between content and users, and in chapter 9, Corey Timpson reflects on his experience spearheading the development of such a universal system for content management at the Canadian Museum for Human Rights. The enterprise content management system (ECMS) was a response to three imperatives—an incessant and continued evolution in audience expectation, rapid media and technological advancement, and data ubiquity. The ECMS functions as an information utility that pushes experiences to the various points of engagement between visitor and museum. It brings together various systems for content management of collections, digital assets, copyright management, and others and works on a number of guiding principles including separation of content from presentation, store once and reference often, complete modularity and scalability, and standards compliance.

For many museums, the collections are the richest resource of content that they have, and ensuring that collections and their documentation can be accessed easily within and outside the physical museum by scholars, learners, creators, and members of the public is a mammoth undertaking facing tens of thousands of museums worldwide. In chapter 10, Edward Purvis provides precise guidelines on how to implement core collections management systems in new and legacy museums. He interviews Pam Babes at National Museums Scotland about the use of volunteers in digitization projects in order to support this labor-intensive but critically important work.

Volunteers are a good example of a museum's community that can play a crucial role in the workings of the museums—whether they are inputting records in a collections management system, taking part in a citizen science research project (chapter 4), or participating in a crowdsourcing campaign (see chapter 15). Having new relationships with visitors means blurring the lines between who works in museums and who is a beneficiary of it.

Contractors and consultants are part of this blurred category, and play a particularly important and often overlooked role when it comes to understanding how museums work and how museums transform. In digital projects, museums often use contractors who also do work in other sectors, and they are able to bring best practices from these into the museums. Agile development is one such practice initiated from software development; the other is user experience design—an approach used widely in industrial and digital design and human-computer interaction.

In chapter 11, as part of her eminently useful chapter on project management, Rachel Walker interviews her colleague Adam Padron, at the Metropolitan Museum of Art, about how agile methodology represents a new way of working within established museums. In agile development, a minimum viable product, or MVP, gets to its end users as quickly as possible in order for it to be tested and then for the team to adapt and improve iteratively. Not only does this mean trusting your visitors to accept participation over perfection, but this way of working shifts authority among staff. As Padron points out, product owners come from all departments at the museum, and they are empowered to make quick tactical decisions about resources, a quality that ultimately leads to a useful sense of ownership among team members.

Agile projects, like all projects, are successful if there is clear communication among all team members and the stakeholder relationships are well managed, relates Eileen Willis, director at the Lincoln Center for the Performing Arts in her interview with Rachel Walker (chapter 11). Communication and relationship management are skills of project managers in balancing time, scope, cost, and quality, but are also essential attributes in the day-to-day practice of the "digital" and omnichannel museum.

User experience design for exhibitions is the focus of chapter 12, in which Dr. Marco Mason also advocates agile methodology. He describes a process that starts with empathy based on qualitative research into the expected audience for an exhibition. A series of low-fidelity prototypes are tested on three levels—experience, interaction and interface—and they are gradually improved by an iterative design process. The final product is the definition of user-centric: it has been informed by visitor requirements at every stage.

Supporting Sustainability and Resilience

A sustainable museum is one that is able to operate within the carrying capacity of its community and the broader world—including the natural world. Resilience refers to a museum's capacity to adapt to changing conditions and recover quickly from problems.

How can museums today ensure that their key resources—their collections, knowledge base, people, and buildings—are not overloaded by the collective expectations of society? How can museums be prepared for the inevitability of change from funding cuts, terrorism, war, natural disaster, or competition from digital disruptors?

It is clear that digital technologies can empower museums and the individuals who care about them. They can enhance the sustainability and resilience of museums by helping them deliver their mission more efficiently and by broadening the scope, accessibility, and impact of their programs.

The desire to introduce new technologies into existing museums requires planning, but it also requires methodologies to judge the worthiness of projects. Both are supplied in this manual. Our goal is to help museums become responsive to the opportunities of digital technologies and to the changing expectations of their visitors, but be nimble enough to avoid costly investments in technical platforms that become unpopular or obsolete. Our approach to planning emphasizes the importance of flexibility and collaboration during the development process, two qualities that enhance sustainability in an uncertain world.

There is a perception that new technologies are out of reach for many museums. It is certainly true that many projects for enhancing visitor experience come with a hefty price tag. But some changes are unavoidable, and museums need to develop best practices that support sustainable yet effective progress. The fourth and final section of the book focuses on ensuring that a museum's human resources, its physical infrastructure, and its ability to secure funding remain strong and competitive in the digital present and future. Many digital investments require innovations in management, or they will create more, not less, work. However, many organizations have made the mistake of replicating functional divisions of the past when they adopt digital networks. Experience has shown that digital technologies demand new forms of organization, but these need not come as a shock. In chapter 13, Ngaire Blankenberg advises a gradualist approach to change, in which new ways of working evolve as people are hired, museum staff acquire new skills, and people practice change on a smaller scale by working on a project basis. The drive for digital transformation may mellow into an expectation that digital maturity happens in measured increments.

One of these measures is the growing importance of IT departments. Since the turn of the millennium, IT has gone from being a sideline within operations to a critical element of every activity. The stakes around IT get higher every year, driven by the demands of audiences and the imaginations of content creators, and in chapter 14 Ali Hossaini describes the basics of information technology for managers who are making critical decisions about their building's infrastructure. He interviews Kevin Cunningham about the IT infrastructure required to do groundbreaking immersive artistic work. Cunningham eschews hardwiring and proprietary software for flexible, open source systems that can adapt to new forms of expression—such as video-mapping and large-scale holographic projections.

Digital technologies have transformed many aspects of society, and the pace of innovation shows no sign of slowing. At the same time, adoption of digital technologies presents huge challenges with no easy solution. Revenues from digital platforms are elusive, and the contradiction between what people want—and often get—and what they will financially support has led to the decline of established industries. Who would have predicted the radical changes in journalism or music a few years ago? Thriving in the omnichannel digital world where people expect everything freely on demand requires rethinking the value chain. Museums will need to act creatively in years to come, but as community relationship builders par excellence, there are already bright spots. Digital channels allow for much more accurate reporting of public engagement, and hard evidence that proves the value of museums as destinations for learning, engagement, and experience can bolster existing funding streams while opening new ones—as discussed in chapter 15.

When pondering how technological change will affect museums, it is worth keeping Roy Amara's famous statement in mind: *We tend to overestimate the effect of technology in the short run and underestimate it in the long run.* Time and again, inventions that seem like a sideshow become engines of disruption—in no small part because established players are complacent.

This book hopes to help you avoid complacency and embrace those aspects of technology that will help you do what you want to do and what you need to do better, more collaboratively, and more creatively than you have done before. With the confidence that comes with understanding, and applying technology to the museum environment, we look forward to innovation coming from within.

Note

1. "Study: U.S. Millennials Prefer Instagram to Museums; Purchase and Discover Art Online," Invaluable, http://news.invaluable.com/press-release/art-fine-art-antiques/study-us-millennials-prefer-instagram-museums-purchase-discover-.

Section 1: A New Value Proposition for Museums in the Digital Age

Discovering a New Kind of Dialogue

Chris Michaels

In January 2015, The British Museum launched its first digital strategy. The purpose of this five-year program is to take the museum's founding vision, borne out of Enlightenment ideals, and illuminate them in new ways through the potential for global scale that the Internet brings. The strategy is a process of discovery, guided by a vision, themes, and large goals. But it is really about iteration: about continuously trialing and testing new approaches in partnership with our audiences, until the right path emerges. That kind of inquiry might seem at odds with the kinds of didactic knowledge sharing a great institution like the British Museum might be easily associated with.

This chapter will tell the real story of what happens when digital culture, and a culture of user-centricity, comes into contact with a place as diverse, surprising, and shifting as the British Museum, and the unexpected results this has brought about so far. It is a story that might appear to be about conflict, but is actually about new models of accommodation, and the changing forms of social dialogue the Internet makes possible.

The Museum's Digital Strategy

The British Museum was founded in 1753 following the bequest of Sir Hans Sloane of his collection of antiquities, books, and natural historical pieces to the British nation. He made the bequest on a single condition: that his collection be made available to all "studious and curious personnes" forever, for free. The British government took that bequest and made something great and new with it, a National Museum, which it placed in Montague House, up in what was then the outskirts of London in Bloomsbury.

That notion of sharing knowledge and enabling study for all was a new idea, made possible by a combination of economic, political, and philosophical circumstances in a country fast emerging as the dominant global-colonial power. In the 1700s universal knowledge didn't really apply to *everyone*—children, for example, were explicitly banned from visiting the nascent Museum. But the principle, that here was a place where you could come and experience the whole history of the world, all under one roof, was one that became enshrined in law, and in the common imagination of the world—it took only a few decades for other "universal" museums to be established in Paris at the Louvre and in St Petersburg at the Hermitage.

Fast forward 250 years and that original idea of the British Museum would be forcefully amplified again under the directorship of Dr. Neil MacGregor. Dr. MacGregor's thirteen-year tenure, which ended in December 2015, would see the museum establish a preeminent place in the culture of world museums through public engagement work, which made clear the capacity of the museum's collection to be for everyone, everywhere. This liberal, universal principle is clear in projects such as *A History of the World in 100 Objects*, a project that crossed radio, exhibitions, and publishing to tell a complete history of human activity through objects. It was seen in exhibitions such as *Pompeii, The First Emperor* and *Vikings* in the way their narratives showed how human advancement comes from intercultural encounter. And it was shown in acts of cultural diplomacy that demonstrated the way museum collections can cross complex political and economic borders to unite people through shared history in the loans of the Cyrus Cylinder to Iran in 2008 and of part of the controversial Parthenon sculptures to the Hermitage in 2015.

Out of this culture of openness and universality emerged the possibility of an ambitious approach to digital in 2014. Strongly supported by former chairman, Niall Fitzgerald KBE, the museum's digital strategy was developed and approved by the museum's trustees in summer 2014. This strategy was presented as a framework rather than a definitive document, outlining an approach the museum could take to explore different areas and establish and quantify opportunity. It was based on a clear assumption, however, that huge growth of the size, quality, and value of the museum's digital audience was both possible and *necessary*.

Why necessary? Exactly because of those founding principles established in the 1750s and amplified so strongly under Neil MacGregor's directorship. If the role of the museum, the reason it exists, is to tell the story of the history of humankind to all of humankind, then you need a way of *doing* that act of telling. In simple terms, the

Internet is that way. Sometime in the next twenty or thirty years all of the world will get access to the Internet. Four billion people are expected to be online by 2020 alone. When that happens, the museum will be uniquely enabled to do the very thing it was set up to do. Its digital strategy is therefore the things it needs to do to go along that path to Internet-facilitated universalism.

That's too big an idea in many ways to be meaningful, and so the near term is about taking a set of concrete steps to move the museum rapidly along a path to that aim, establishing the operational, fiscal, and creative structures in which the work the museum creates can flourish. Anchoring those are a set of key metrics that qualify scale. As an example, if the Museum's ultimate job is to communicate to billions of people about the history of humankind, then its initial job should be to understand how to talk consistently to hundreds of millions of people through its digital channels, as opposed to the tens of millions achieved today. By taking these quantified exponential leaps forward, the museum can thereby establish the right positioning to make those huge next steps in the 2020s and 2030s.

At the heart of all this, however, is a thorny principle: that none of this growth will be achieved without encountering our audience in a specific way. The principle of user-centricity is one that cannot be decoupled from the growth of digital—it's closely aligned with the successes of all the great digital corporations who so occupy the shared behavior of the world. It is ultimately by putting the audience at the heart of the digital strategy that the British Museum intends to achieve its goals. So how is it doing that, and what does that mean for the way the museum has historically worked?

User-Centricity as the Core of Digital Practice

Whatever incredible universalism the Internet achieves, it has proven almost beyond doubt that audiences are more subtle, more complex in their behavior, and "smarter" than any designer or design group's ability to foreguess their wants and needs. When the economic stakes of multibillion-dollar valuations, of hundred-million-dollar investment rounds, and the use of digital services by tens or hundreds of millions or even billions of people (and the loud complaint they can make if they don't like something) are at stake, undertaking a design process that involves, engages, and reflects their view is crucial.

This has led over the last twenty years to an increasingly sophisticated discipline of user experience design (see chapter 12), and the emergence of digital product management (see chapter 11) as something primarily focused on revealing the "true" value of a digital proposition through a relentless process of testing with audiences.

The British Museum is not alone in integrating these practices into its approach to digital. Similar models are emergent across the sector, from Silvia Filippini-Fantoni's approach to interpretation and experience design at the Indianapolis Museum of Art to Seb Chan's innovations at the Smithsonian's Cooper Hewitt Design Museum.[1] It is inevitable perhaps that as the overall digital sector evolves, and its methods saturate all organizations, that the museum and gallery sector will adopt these habits and behaviors.

What is not inevitable is that this process of coadaptation will be a simple one. Museums, and an old museum like the British Museum more than most, are organized around a model of expert knowledge that goes deep into their culture and public perception. The museum curator, that dusty, charming idea of an expert wrestling with the mysteries of Babylonian archaeology, is an exemplar of the kind of individual genius that the enlightenment, and later the Romantic period, put at the center of our culture.

This stereotype of an expert-led culture meant it was very easy to foretell failure for the museum's approach to digital.

But it's a false idea, nonrepresentative of how museums work today, and of how curatorial practice has evolved.

The Assumed Negative Encounter of User-Centricity vs. Didactic Knowledge

It's too easy to assume that a new-world model of thought like the user-centricity at the heart of digital experience design would sit uncomfortably with the way a place like the British Museum would work. Too easy and also, so it has turned out so far, untrue. It is worth exploring where that false assumption comes from though.

The digital model of knowledge, of user-centricity and "'test, test, test" behavior, has its ultimate roots in scientific inquiry, and its specific roots in the practices of iterative product and service design emergent since the release of Eric Ries's *Lean Startup* blog and book in 2011.[2] Ries has voiced with great acuity that when creating digital products that might be used by huge audiences and that have both high complexity and subtlety of use, that you can only begin the design process with an idea and a set of assumptions, and keep adapting your ideas through user testing, often out in the wilds of the open market, until you either find a true and valid opportunity or give up.

This would seem in immediate conflict with the stereotype of the curator—individual genius on an individualized quest for the truth in their particular corner of a great collection. But the truth of a museum now is very different, due in part to changes in the model of academic research and in part to the working model serving huge global audiences like the British Museum brings.

Academic work is now rarely the pursuit of lone individuals, but rather is driven by inter-institutional, pan-global networks of researchers working together to share aims.

This intensely collaborative approach is being intensified in the Humanities as technology (in what is called **digital humanities**) becomes a more central part of the academic process.

This collaborative approach dissipates the notion of individual genius, resetting expectations among curators of how they should work, and how best to uncover new insight. This model of collaboration makes it easier for the kinds of new working practice digital brings into an institution to be accommodated. At the British Museum, the largest research institution in the UK outside the university system, with over thirty simultaneous research projects taking place, and over 190 papers published in 2014, that spirit of intense collaboration sets a context for bringing the audience into the dialogue, and a spirit of open scientific inquiry that "fits'" with what a user-centric digital approach needs to do.

Additional to that are the processes of user-testing and research already present in museums before "digital" really starts as a discipline. In the public engagement process, from the interpretation work that goes into the creation of a gallery to the formative qualitative research present in exhibition development, inquiry about visitor opinion, and the use of that in content development, is an ever-present factor. What digital user-centricity is doing here, then, is not introducing something utterly new, but intensifying its presence—pulling the voice of the audience further toward the center of museum experience, but not bringing it into the dialogue in the first place.

If this simplistic and binary expectation of conflict between old world and new has not proven true, then what new truth is emerging out of the act of bringing digital and the British Museum together?

> **KEY TERMS**
>
> **DIGITAL HUMANITIES**
>
> "A diverse and still emerging field that includes the practice of humanities research in and through information technology. It also includes the development of digital educational/research/teach/archival/publishing resources for the specific use and study of the humanities and interconnected disciplines. The digital humanities is also concerned with an exploration of how humanities may evolve through their engagement with technology."[1]
>
> ---
>
> [1] From Ernesto Priego, "How Do You Define DH?" Day of DH 2012, http://archive.artsrn.ualberta.ca/Day-of-DH-2012/dh/index.html#comment-94.

The Unexpected Truth: Desire for Knowledge in a New Way

The first year of implementation of the digital strategy has uncovered a different circumstance from the clash of sensibilities between user-centricity and traditional didactic knowledge that many assumed as the museum started on this strategic journey.

What it has begun to uncover is an unmet need in the audience in the way the Museum provides content to the public, which is, I believe, ultimately down to a changing sociological model in how knowledge is consumed. What we seem to be uncovering through the work of the museum in digital is that the audience does not want the type of expert knowledge provided by curators to disappear and be replaced by some alternative model, whether user-generated, automated, or otherwise. Rather, what they want is that knowledge in a new way, which museums have up to now been unable to provide at scale with the huge audiences they serve.

This new way of consuming the knowledge curators hold is based on three principles:

- A "disintermediation" of the way curatorial knowledge has been historically packaged, and the emergence of new formats that place the expert in closer dialogue with the audience
- An "informalization" of the way knowledge is shared, replacing formal academic tonalities with idiomatic conversation
- A role of "participation" by the audience, playing an active and defined part in the digital product, content or service

These three principles have combined to enable the emergence of new kinds of content and new ways of sharing knowledge in the first year of the digital strategy's implementation. There are many examples of this already, but one story captures all three behaviors in one piece of social media.

In February 2015, Twitter launched a new service called Periscope. Periscope is a live-streaming video app, allowing anyone, anywhere with a smartphone to tell their story live to the Internet. The welter of media noise around this suggested an opportunity—that the British Museum become the first to launch programming on the site. Over an intense two weeks of planning a format emerged, with TV presenter and historian Dan Snow (himself an instant adopter of Periscope) fronting a tour of the exhibition of Greek sculpture *Defining Beauty* taking place in the Museum's Sainsbury Exhibition Galleries.

At 6:30 p.m. on Thursday, May 28, 1015, the show went live, and instantly the audience began to participate and react. "Reaction" on Periscope means two things—making comments and "hearting" what you watch. Both comments and hearts float up the screen as you watch, evaporating like steam over the image to show the public thinking and feeling out loud. As the show moved round the gallery, the numbers started to build—within minutes of launching its first show the museum had gained forty thousand followers.

But it was as Dan reached toward the end of the exhibition that the process of disintermediation-informalization-participation really crystallized. Waiting for Dan at the exhibitions' end, next to the magnificent Belvedere Torso left tantalizingly off screen due to rights clearance issues, was Ian Jenkins, venerable curator in the department of Greece and Rome. His presence on screen seemed to galvanize something in the audience—the volume of questions intensified, the number of hearts flying up the screen became a dense thicket. Ian—a masterful raconteur of the intensity being lived by the Greeks, their roving sexuality, and veneration of the human as God-made-flesh—kept being asked to say more about specific objects. One questioner kept asking about a statue of two people wrestling.

Behind the camera, Patricia Wheatley, head of broadcasting at the museum and producer of the show, asked Ian the question about the wrestlers. And at that moment something changed. Suddenly Dan was no longer the presenter, and Ian no longer the expert. The audience was no longer a remote passive entity. Instead they were all equal participants in an act of exploration and discovery. What was the object, where was it? What story did it tell? Ian, Dan, and crew took off around the exhibition, looking for the mysterious wrestlers.

When they found it, it was something else—not wrestlers, but two lovers mid-copulation—a discovery both comic and profound, allowing Ian to tell one of his famed anecdotes about sex in the ancient world. But it was an important moment, a point when the fabric of a well-produced "show," a legacy of television, fell away and the pure, Dionysian form of social media really came out—audience, expert, presenter, and crew engaged together in an act of making that is both light and profound. In my time at the museum it was the first thing that felt truly new—when a new structural behavior came about that didn't rely on a separation between audience and expert, but put them together in a heady brew.

That crystallized a sense that these three concepts were the critical ones:

- Disintermediation, because at the point where the audience and Ian were in dialogue, exploring the exhibition together, Dan, a living symbol of "TV" and its packaged approach to meaning, was no longer important, and the highly produced visual format of the show became more live and chaotic.
- Informalization, not just because the tone and voice of this moment took place outside that of an academic register, but because there was uncertainty. For a brilliant moment no one knew what it meant.
- Participation, because what happened then could only happen because the audience was part of the show and were sharing in the act of discovery and exploration.

It was a crucial point of coalescence that has enabled the Museum to go on and refine its content offer for digital. Over the course of the year since this first broadcast, five more live shows happened, and each time another layer of intermediation and of formality was removed. After Dan Snow's participation in the first two broadcasts, each one thereafter has been curators only—giving the public what they really seem to want most:

unrestricted dialogue with the expert. And in each show we've progressively built more dialogue in—folding the act of questioning and conversation evermore into the fabric of the show.

This has gone on to influence other video-based programming. In November 2015, the Museum relaunched its YouTube channel. To do that, four different video formats were created—from a BuzzFeed-style listicle format, to a behind-the-scenes view of conservation science. The winning format though was no surprise based on the learnings to date: a format called Curator's Corner that took the "YouTube bedroom" concept that's launched vloggers to stardom and remade it for curators sharing their own passions and preoccupations directly. Fully disintermediated, and wildly informal, it demonstrates the power of a new structure of relationship between museum and public.

The question, in a larger sense, is what does that mean, and what do we do about it?

A Brighter Tomorrow

This is a time of existential crisis in museums around the world. As the onward impacts of the recession are felt, pressures on funding, whether governmental or philanthropic, are growing. Around the UK, museums dependent on local council funding have "flipped" from free entry to paid, making them sustainable as businesses, but slashing their total potential visitor numbers. In the United States, an emerging crisis in visitorship is becoming ever clearer as report after report shows a stark drop-off in visits by millennials, asking hard questions of short-term legitimacy and long-term sustainability. And while this is happening, the changing socioeconomic patterns of global tourism are seeing a major influx of Asian tourists into museums that are ill equipped to provide services for a new audience with few of the local-language skills that make a visit even barely comprehensible.

All this change makes life uncertain, but what we are seeing in this process of disintermediation, informalization and participation is a potential path to a new, brighter, sustainable future.

If the early truth emergent here is right, then the threat to museums is not their people, the focus of their knowledge, or their internal process. It is instead the way they present the knowledge they hold, and the channels of distribution they prioritize. There is much to work through here, but one simple directive seems important: treat social media with deadly seriousness.

Social Media: Disintermediation, Informalization, and Extended Participation

Social—the place where digital audiences exist at the largest scale, and where the public voice is most broadly held is the place where this exploration of disintermediation, informalization, and extended participation can play out. It's a channel that's available, at global scale, and free to use.

So use it.

For museums to be meaningful tomorrow, when the turbulence of media, economic, and audience change has settled, if it ever settles at all, they should dive deep into the social stream now. They should find out what layers of intermediation, what baggage of obsolescent models of communication, what older modes of doing things they can move past. They should learn to speak without formality among a community of followers and friends, and learn to let those followers and friends shape the question, "What is it, and what does it mean?" with the brilliant experts who actually know.

It won't save the future now, but it will define the path toward it, and there's no other space where you'll learn more along the way.

 KEY TAKEAWAYS

1. User-centricity is the core of digital practice and of institutional transformation.
2. Social media supports user-centricity through enabling:
   - Disintermediation: Removing the 'mediating' elements in museums in order to place the expert in closer dialogue with the audience.
   - Informalization: Sharing knowledge through informal conversation rather than through academic publications or an academic tone.
   - Participation: The audience plays an active and defined part in the digital product, content, or service.

Notes

1. Dana Allen-Griel, "Silvia Filippini-Fantoni, Director of Interpretation, Media, and Evaluation at the Indianapolis," *Musete.ch*, September 14, 2013, accessed September 20, 2016. http://www.musete.ch/2013/09/14/silvia-filippini-fantoni-director-of-interpretation-media-and-evaluation-at-the-indianapolis-museum-of-art/; "Meet the Staff: Sebastian Chan," *Cooper Hewitt*, September 9, 2013, accessed September 20, 2016. http://www.cooperhewitt.org/2013/09/09/meet-the-staff-sebastian-chan/ .

2. Eric Ries, *The Lean Startup: How Today's Entrepreneurs Use Continuous Innovation to Create Radically Successful Businesses* (New York: Crown Business, 2011).

The Omnichannel Museum

Ali Hossaini

Digital technologies are permeating society, and museums are no exception. Yet the pace of change in museums and the cultural sector has been much slower than other parts of society. Technical progress has profoundly transformed industries as diverse as music, banking, and newspapers. In many cases, digital transformation has been disruptive, even revolutionary, and it has eliminated organizations that were unwilling or unable to evolve. Experience has taught us to ignore digital change at our own peril, and although the sector is stable for now, we should not assume museums will never be threatened by disruptive upstarts. Like any new frontier, the digital world offers unbeaten paths, and entering it demands experimentation and tolerance for failure. Best practices are still in the making, and, once accepted, they are likely to be discarded by rapidly evolving markets.

Museums can benefit from their comparatively slow adoption of digital processes by drawing lessons from other sectors. Media companies, sports franchises, retail establishments and government have discovered broad truths about people's digital behavior, expectations, and phobias, and museums can learn from these.

One concept stands out, and much of this volume is devoted to following its implications. It is *customer-centrism*, which for museums means being visitor-centric or

KEY TERMS

USER-CENTRIC

User-centrism puts visitors, audiences, or customers at the center of organizational planning and operations.

DIGITAL DISRUPTION

Digital disruption happens when technologies enable new processes, services, or products to radically change existing organizations.

PROPRIETARY VS. OPEN SOURCE

As the name implies, proprietary databases are owned. If your museum operates a proprietary database, you likely own the content, or data, but the templates and code that make the database function are owned by a software company which charges for its use. In contrast, open source code is freely available for anyone to use to create their own database, although modifications can be owned by the developers who write them.

INTERNET OF THINGS (IoT)

Internet of Things is a network of physical items that are connected using digital sensors, software, and the Internet to exchange and collect data.

user-centric. It might seem obvious that stores service customers, sport franchises cater to fans, museums offer their programs to visitors, and governments serve citizens. But many organizations operate by internal imperatives while leaving the client experience to front-line staff.

Digital disruption happens when new entrants use technology to "super-serve" neglected constituencies, unlock new markets, or otherwise circumvent older systems. The rise of Amazon, Airbnb, and Uber is a prime example of how digital innovators shocked established industries by changing fundamental relationships with shoppers, travelers, and riders.

User-Centrism and Omnichannel

User-centrism is a value, and it is also an organizing principle. What happens when this principle is applied within museums? How do we describe a user-centric museum? For this we might adopt the term *omnichannel* from retail. Like museums, stores have been the ultimate brick-and-mortar institutions. Mail order has been around since the nineteenth century when Sears pioneered remote sales, but the discipline became more vibrant in the 1990s when Amazon and others took the catalog online. Today online media form a major sales channel, but the Internet is a double-edged sword for retailers. Price comparison has never been easier, and shoppers use mobile Internet to bring competition within a retailer's walls. Rather than resist the trend, stores have decided to embrace new behaviors by offering public WiFi to customers. Anyone is free to compare prices or even buy from competitors, but WiFi also enables spontaneous deal-making. It captures fine-grained data on customer interests, and it can be used to build long-term relationships with shoppers. Strategists coined the term omnichannel to describe the new approach: *give customers what they want, when they want it, and how they want it*, through every possible channel. But for retailers omnichannel means more than

24/7 service on the Internet. It also means a relentless focus on ever-changing individual customers or, in the case of museums, the visitor, and digitally driven companies are reorganizing departments to achieve that goal. From R&D to sales, digital technologies address people as individuals. Omnichannel has moved from retail into sports and entertainment. Both sectors generate large amounts of media that have moved from distinct channels like radio, television, and print onto a converged Internet. They also produce live events that increasingly engage audiences digitally over arena-based WiFi. Omnichannel organizations move people seamlessly from computer to mobile to physical locations. Content publishing systems are context aware, and they structure experiences according to user profiles.

Visitors and other museum users like researchers and educators have much to gain from the omnichannel approach. Smartphones and mobile networks give visitors the freedom to access museum content anywhere, and omnichannel planning strives to include every possible avenue of engagement, including ones that have not been invented. The foundation of omnichannel is open content and open organizations serving dynamic audiences. Content should not be locked in **proprietary** databases. Instead it should be freed, that is, managed by standards that let it be scaled, served, and repurposed across any digital platform. A similar evolution is happening in operational structure. People want to get behind the scenes, and everyone in your organization should be responsive to visitors and their interests. Social networks, Wikipedia, and other content sites are important points of contact with your museum, and

DISRUPTING MUSEUMS

In the museum sector, one can anticipate two technologies that may have a similar impact. The **Internet of Things**, commonly called IoT, will vastly simplify access to collections. Digitization is a monumental task, but once accomplished finding objects becomes a simple online search. Data—contextual information—can be quickly retrieved, and like any other online object, items can easily accrue communities of interest where expertise is accessed, shared or sold.

Another technology that holds great promise and possible disruption for museums is virtual reality. VR has been making headlines for decades, but the newest headsets deliver on the promise of high-quality immersion—the feeling you really are in a place. VR goggles will likely go farther than replacing most of the screens in use today. They may also function as a substitute or replacement for galleries, studios, theaters and architecture itself. VR or something like it could alter the business and social models of museums. Some of the ingredients for disruption are already in place: high travel costs, crowds, and the inaccessibility of collections. Conceptually it is not a major step to reconstitute collections within virtual spaces, and it is worthwhile for museums to explore and, more importantly, to control this eventuality.

Museums are secure in their mission. With planning horizons that span centuries, they are surely safe from disruptive upstarts. Yet vulnerability comes in many forms. Entire sectors are being overturned by rapid advances in technology because they refused or were unable to recognize vulnerabilities, and museums should examine the digital landscape for opportunities that let them evolve with the changing expectations of society.

a new breed of professionals can lead conversations about your content, collections, and events. Social media experts are the front line of public engagement, but in an omnichannel world, everyone in the museum faces the public.

Omnichannel engagement benefits museums. In the commercial sector, superior service is rewarded by sales, and equally museums can use online campaigns to enhance sales of tickets and merchandise. But a deeper engagement also serves a social purpose. By liberating content and letting people into the organization, museums can convert visitors into stakeholders who see the vital role they play in their community. Open organizations can build powerful membership and donation campaigns by tailoring messages to a supporter's individual interests. Omnichannel delivers value, but it also quantifies it in personal, social and financial terms.

This chapter is organized into three sections. The first lays out the principles for omnichannel planning. These principles are emotional as well as cognitive. They can guide your vision, and they can be used to manage desires, expectations, and frustrations. The second applies those principles to planning at the strategic and operational levels. The third section is practical. It supplies processes for applying omnichannel principles, implementing digital plans and developing twenty-first-century organization.

Principles of Omnichannel

Digital technologies are transforming society, but change is happening at different rates depending on sector, organization, and even department. There's no way to create a distinct recipe for creating a digital organization, but the following principles animate the omnichannel approach.

- Change is inevitable, so plan for change.
- Everything is networked.
- Build a nimble, responsive organization.
- Projects should be driven by strategy.
- Experiment constantly.
- Use data to validate and communicate.
- Online visitors are equivalent to physical visitors.

As we discuss in chapter 13, omnichannel thinking catalyzes certain kinds of change in your staffing and organization. Planning horizons shift closer to the present because linear processes become iterative. Traits we first noticed in software development, which is always between versions, are becoming characteristic of organizations. Change is always happens constantly in dynamic, technology-driven markets. For the foreseeable future there will be a constant flow of new hardware, new software and new behavior punctuated by disruptions that throw aside assumptions. Expect cycles of change and reivision in projects.

Because change is constant, multidisciplinary teams are becoming the most effective way of quickly responding to markets. This approach, called agile development in engineering circles, emphasizes small steps with rapid evaluation. Agile development principles for project management, exhibition design, and management can be found respectively in chapters 11, 12, and 13. Each step of agile development assesses whether a particular approach is worth pursuing. Limited ambition and resources means more risk can be built into the system without the possibility of catastrophic failure. This raises the rate, or productivity, of innovation because an agile team can both afford and learn from failure. In an agile environment, departmental barriers erode, and informal staff networks—knowledge sharing—are increasingly important. For some processes, interdepartmental cooperation at the team level is complementing, or even replacing, linear management that runs from the top.

As you implement omnichannel processes, research and development (R&D) becomes part of operations. Experimentation becomes more acceptable, and the appetite for risk grows because small failures prevent larger ones. You may set aside a certain percentage of your budget for risk and reward staff who engage in fruitful failure—that is, projects that deliver useful information, whether or not they accomplish their original objectives. Generalists who understand multiple arenas will become more important, and you will begin creating career paths that move diagonally through the organization to cultivate them.

Planning for Omnichannel

Transforming your organization in one pass is neither possible nor desirable. Instead count on deploying change in phases. It is important to remember that you are engaged in engineering. Technical installations should be implemented systematically, and they proceed with the least grief when professionally planned and managed. Even the best planners require strategic oversight that is firmly rooted in organizational vision. You need to know what you are trying to accomplish, why you are doing it, and who is benefitting. Everything else follows. And bear in mind: *Digital technologies are being adopted so rapidly that it is unlikely that digital planning will be treated as a separate topic for more than a few years.*

Planning for omnichannel starts with ensuring that connectivity is part of the foundation of your museum experience and continues to ensure that projects, infrastructure, and architecture are planned with the visitor at the center. When reviewing the mission

> **KEY TERMS**
>
> **PERSONALIZATION**
>
> Personalization is when an organization addresses users as individuals by understanding their preferences, special needs, and history.

statement, keep in mind that a key element of omnichannel is a shift in focus. Omnichannel institutions organize themselves around the needs of constituents—the individual people they serve. In retail, sports and entertainment, and even government, forward-looking initiatives are giving people maximum information and maximum choice. As shop owners know, one size does not fit all, and smart data technologies are making **personalization** the norm. When reviewing your mission statement, consider:

- Does your strategic plan meet evolving visitor expectations?
- Does it promote current best practices in the cultural sector?
- What are the areas in acute need of revision?
- Where can change be easily effected?
- What projects give the largest return on investment?

Secondly, planning includes incorporating digital practices wherever they can improve your organization. Virtually every activity can be performed more efficiently or more robustly with digital intervention, and much of your future infrastructure will be handled by information technology (IT). Key points to consider are covered in this book starting with collections management and working to exhibitions and global visitor engagement.

Thirdly, when embarking on digital projects, it is important to view them holistically. Interdependencies between digital projects are no less critical than the dependencies you encounter in managing plumbing, electricity

PRIORITIZING DIGITAL PROJECTS

1. **How does the project advances your strategy?** Every digital project should advance some element of your organization's mission, vision, values or strategic plan. Answer the following questions.
   - How does this project advance your mission?
   - Does the project support your values?
   - What strategic aims does the project achieve?
   - Does the project support other initiatives?

2. **How does the project fits into your current and planned infrastructure?** It is important to consider how your project fits into current and planned infrastructure. Review its full requirements, including connectivity and operations, to ensure you have accounted for its future demands. Does it—or can it—utilize existing resources? Will new investments enhance current resources?

3. **Who are the stakeholders or the internal constituents for your project?** Form a committee of interested parties to review, discuss, and revise the proposal. Convene your panel at key stages of completion.

4. **Coordinate the project with other initiatives.** Create a chart that projects the progress of current technical projects on a timeline. Identify resources required to execute, test and launch project to discover dependencies, bottlenecks or conflicts.

and the many activities that rely on them. Yet digital projects are often pursued on an ad hoc basis with no connection to senior manager or a strategic plan. Prioritizing projects according to their impact and resources are a key component of planning for omnichannel.

The importance of integrated planning can be likened to the familiar processes of designing the infrastructure and architecture of your facilities. Architecture can be many things: a symbol of your mission, a physical shelter for your collection, a dwelling place for your organization, a lab for scientists and scholars, and an environment that shapes the experience of the visiting public. Digital channels are starting to fill all these roles, and it might be easiest to think of them as a parallel universe that reflects, affects, and converges with the physical world. We are in stages of a major social transition in which more activities will take place in virtual environments, and museums should start planning digital environments that augment their physical venues.

Information technology is the bedrock of the omnichannel approach. IT is the discipline that incorporates computing, networking, and telecommunication resources into an integrated system that supports human activities. It follows, therefore, that an important component of planning for omnichannel is to ensure you have a plan for IT service management (ITSM) within your museum. The complexity of IT management grows with our reliance on digital systems, and an ITSM plan details how these systems will be maintained into the future.

Chapter 14 discusses IT planning in depth, but before any planning exercise museums must make a fundamental choice about how to develop the technical resources that support omnichannel. Organizations have a choice of developing a full IT department, outsourcing IT, or developing a mix of in-house and outsourced activity. Cloud services and remote access tools enable organizations to acquire sophisticated services at relatively low thresholds of cost and expertise. However, unless an organization possesses internal capacity, it is difficult to manage outsourcing firms. Evaluation of budgets, impact, and the necessity of proposed work is best managed by an internal advocate who is firmly in the museum's camp.

The Omnichannel Stack

The stack is a useful way to visualize your organization will need to implement an omnichannel approach. Digital services perform distinct functions that are nonetheless interrelated from the standpoint of planning, maintenance, and operations. You can draw this yourself. Each layer of the stack depends on the layers below for vital services, so a stack diagram helps planners evaluate the resources and consequences of technical initiatives.

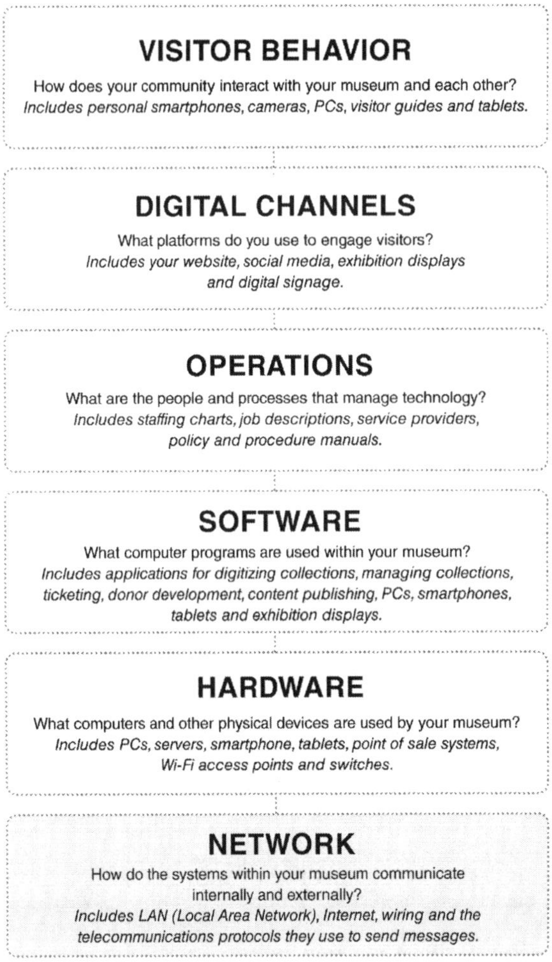

VISITOR BEHAVIOR
How does your community interact with your museum and each other?
Includes personal smartphones, cameras, PCs, visitor guides and tablets.

DIGITAL CHANNELS
What platforms do you use to engage visitors?
Includes your website, social media, exhibition displays and digital signage.

OPERATIONS
What are the people and processes that manage technology?
Includes staffing charts, job descriptions, service providers, policy and procedure manuals.

SOFTWARE
What computer programs are used within your museum?
Includes applications for digitizing collections, managing collections, ticketing, donor development, content publishing, PCs, smartphones, tablets and exhibition displays.

HARDWARE
What computers and other physical devices are used by your museum?
Includes PCs, servers, smartphone, tablets, point of sale systems, Wi-Fi access points and switches.

NETWORK
How do the systems within your museum communicate internally and externally?
Includes LAN (Local Area Network), Internet, wiring and the telecommunications protocols they use to send messages.

FIGURE 2.1 The Omnichannel Stack.
Ali Hossaini and Lord Cultural Resources

Laying the Technical Foundation for Omnichannel

What does an omnichannel museum look like in practice? We have seen that omnichannel strives to reach visitors where they are. In principle the omnichannel museum does not discriminate between online visitors and visitors to its physical exhibitions. For now, there is a clear difference between digital exhibitions on a website and physical objects in a collection, but advances in technology are shifting the balance. In some cases digital exhibition is superior. For instance, even specialists with direct access to paintings have gained new insights by zooming into ultra-high resolution images commissioned by Google Art Project.

Omnichannel means projecting your museum's entire range of activities onto a coherent digital platform. As the name implies, omnichannel integrates previously separate services. For example, processes in collections management, interpretation, marketing, ticketing, and analytics can be combined to create more efficient operations and superior visitor experience. It takes architects and a host of planners, engineers, and designers to create a building. If they are successful, your building is a coherent whole composed of rooms, passages and functions that host the many activities of your museum. Your digital infrastructure should do no less, and, to plan digital organization effectively, you need to treat it as an architectural whole.

To adopt an omnichannel mindset, it may be helpful to think of your museum building as a website. Consider the features that make browsing the web compelling. Well-designed websites recognize you as an individual. They remember your preferences, make recommendations, and enable sharing with family, friends, interest groups, and the wider public. You can activate your museum with these same features by creating points of contact that transition from the Internet into physical places. Powerful opportunities for visitor engagement begin with WiFi, smartphones and visitor-centric planning that gradually introduce omnichannel practices to your museum.

WIFI

Contemporary WiFi systems do far more than link visitors to the Internet. They enable omnichannel by offering dedicated media channels, location awareness, and location analytics that benefit visitors and host organizations. These services can be packaged into new forms of audience engagement.

The basic function of WiFi is to provide Internet access to radio-enabled devices. Originally developed for computers, demand for WiFi grew alongside the tremendous growth of smartphones, which use it as an alternative to expensive cellular data. It is also a fixture in cafes and public spaces where digital nomads use it to work on notebook computers. Many people now expect free WiFi in public spaces even though it is costly to support. At the same time, WiFi has evolved features that offset the cost of providing it.

CONTENT EVERYWHERE

With WiFi you can make sure every device in your building receives content. Already visitors use public WiFi for their own purposes. Without interfering with their intentions, you can foreground content when they are definitely paying attention: as they log into WiFi on their smartphone.

WiFi has the capacity to launch a splash screen, also known as captive portal, when someone logs in. This is the Terms and Services screen that pops up on many public WiFi services. Rather than offer generic messages, why not use this page as a content channel that gets people excited? It can also serve as a hub for audio tours and deeper information

> **KEY TERMS**
>
> **LOCATION AWARENESS**
>
> Location awareness and analytics is the use of digital systems such as beacons or WiFi to identify the location and movements of individuals through buildings or other public spaces. It is combined with analytics to optimize wayfinding, circulation management, security, and visitor engagement.

about exhibitions. See chapter 8 for guidance about developing digital content inside and outside your museum.

LOCATION AWARENESS

Any mobile device that has WiFi turned on will signal its presence even when not logged into an access point. Advanced WiFi systems can track the movement of devices to generate a heat map that shows the density of visitors within galleries, corridors, and other spaces.

LOCATION ANALYTICS

Heat maps and other tracking functions can be analyzed for circulation management. By observing the movement of visitors across time, museums can judge the popularity of exhibits, the effectiveness of signage and wayfinding, and the placement of bottlenecks and other impediments to visitor flow.

COMMON INFRASTRUCTURE

Separation among digital services originates in departmental specialization. Organizations that have not integrated omnichannel thinking into their planning tend to handle digital projects separately. But each project relies on infrastructure, and running common infrastructure is far more efficient than maintaining multiple, conflicting standards. It also enables coordination, and possibly innovation, among departments whose functions overlap from the visitor standpoint.

THE SMARTPHONE

Smartphones are well established, and their potential for growth seems unlimited. For now it is inconceivable not to plan around the use of smartphones in every environment. And virtual reality has been promised for decades, but the appearance of effective, affordable systems is finally delivering a mass medium that works on smartphones.

Mobile phones provide a disembodied presence for users, but they will increasingly be used to interact with place. The afterword to this volume gives a detailed discussion of how visitors may interact with places via smartphones.

Personalization and analytics can provide additional layers of service. (For guidance on how analytics deepen engagement, see chapters 3 and 5.) The latter can assist circulation management by routing visitors around crowded areas or timing entry into popular exhibits. Registered visitors can transmit their identity automatically or by swiping their phone over sensors. Membership schemes build relationships while gathering valuable data about visitor interests. They also provide a clear opt-in to personalization that addresses privacy and security concerns.

Visitors increasingly expect their phone to be location aware by serving content relevant to where they are. Museums are well positioned to take advantage of this trend. Studies commissioned by the V&A Museum, the Museum of Natural History (London), and the UK Museums Association discovered that the majority of visitors carry mobile phones in museums.[1] People wield phones freely in museums, and use them mostly to take photographs or conduct independent searches. Museums can guide this behavior by engaging visitors through WiFi. In some cases, selfies and photographs serve as valuable channels for further engagement of visitors. However, where photography proves disruptive, museums can offer high-resolution images for immediate download. Future interfaces will include swipes and other gestures that minimize stopping and poking. While allowing people to search for information independently, extended interpretation and resources can also be offered over WiFi. This superior service has the added benefit of directing visitors toward educational channels.

DIGITAL EXPRESSION

For museums that commission art, WiFi may become a new medium of expression. As digital technology permeates society, creative interventions will become a regular feature of mobile engagement. Many artists are already creating mobile apps as art, and the smartphone is becoming a natural extension of physical gallery galleries.

Virtual reality takes digital media to their logical extreme. The best systems track movements of head, body, and hands to transport individuals into simulated environments. Nature, architecture, and even screens appear in virtual reality. Like museum architecture, virtual reality is placemaking par excellence, and, as television has done since the 1950s, it will likely provide many people the majority of their experience outside daily life. As VR becomes a mass medium, the pressure on museums to create virtual environments will become intense, and, without stopping progress, management should be careful about giving outside organizations rights to their buildings and collections. Licenses should not cede control that will be vital to future engagement.

Conclusion

Omnichannel practices will change over time, but its principles will remain consistent. It is important to bear these in mind even as you plan for change. To the greatest degree possible, combine digital services onto the same operational and management infrastructure. It is easiest to give people a seamless experience when there are no seams. To achieve this, transcend departmental silos when planning digital projects. Develop a unified, interoperable specification for databases and online publishing systems and make sure everyone has a voice in planning and operations. Closely monitor what standards are evolving for museums, especially those that share your community or mission. This makes for huge efficiencies in operations and allows you to closely coordinate engagement with visitors and partner organizations.

People will have better experiences if they automatically know how to use your services. To achieve this goal, press for standards in your museum, in your community and around the world. Exercise leadership by participating in committees, councils and conferences that promote best practices. Adopt those practices and spread your learning through articles, conference, and, of course, online publications. As with everything else in the digital world, omnichannel engagement relies on networks, and networks begin with you.

💡 KEY TAKEAWAYS: OMNICHANNEL

1. Omnichannel is a term derived from retail to describe a visitor-centric approach that ensures customers what they want, when they want it and how they want it through every possible channel.

2. Principles of omnichannel include:
   - Change is inevitable, so plan for change.
   - Everything is networked.
   - Build a nimble, responsive organization.
   - Projects should be driven by strategy.
   - Experiment constantly.
   - Use data to validate and communicate.
   - Online visitors are equivalent to physical visitors.

3. Planning for omnichannel should start with integrating a visitor-centric approach into your museum's vision and mission statements. Your museum should then incorporate digital practices wherever it can to maximize interdependencies and prioritize projects in keeping with your mission and resources.

4. The omnichannel stack visualizes the interdependent layers of the omnichannel approach: visitor behavior, digital channels, operations, software, hardware, and IT infrastructure.

5. The digital foundation for omnichannel includes WiFi, content everywhere; location awareness and analytics, common infrastructure, the smartphone, WiFi as medium of expression, and common standards.

Note

1. Fusion Research & Analytics LLC, and Frankly, Green + Webb Ltd., *Understanding the Mobile V&A Visitor: Autumn 2012*, accessed October 7, 2016. https://www.vam.ac.uk/__data/assets/pdf_file/0009/236439/Visitor_Use_Mobile_Devices.pdf; Fusion Research & Analytics, *Natural History Museum: Understanding the Mobile Visitor*, July 2013, accessed October 7, 2016. http://www.nhm.ac.uk/resources-rx/files/nhm-mobile-report-july-2013-127910.pdf; Fusion Research & Analytics, *Mobile Survey May 2012: Museums Association*, accessed October 7, 2016. https://www.museumsassociation.org/download?id=731198.

Making It Personal
Putting Data at the Heart of Your Museum

Rob Stein

Museums are personal. Ask a friend someday to tell you a story about the last time they visited a museum and chances are they will recount for you a vivid memory of their visit. As museum professionals, this is not surprising. Many of us see amazing things in the galleries each and every week. We can tell terrific stories of how our specific museum is impacting the lives of our visitors. These are the stories that inspire us to keep working hard so that our museum truly makes a difference in the world. More than that, life-changing encounters with museums are the best path to future sustainability for the sector. Museums mean so much to so many people, but our ability to improve—and prove—community impact is the key to securing the long-term future of our museums.

Consider these two comments we received while I was at the Indianapolis Museum of Art (see figures 3.1 and 3.2).

What if we could uncover the secrets to making peak experiences more frequent and less serendipitous? What if museums could harness tools to give them insights into how to change their work to ensure successful encounters? What if I told you that how you

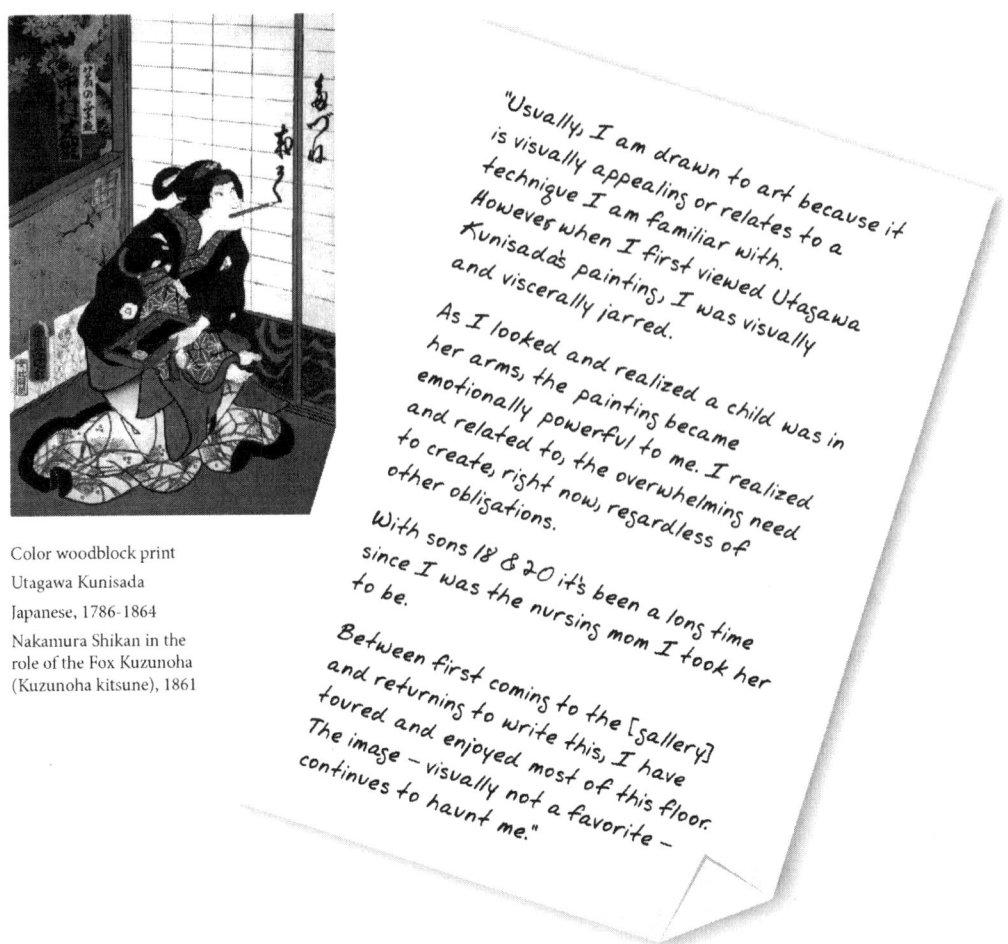

Color woodblock print
Utagawa Kunisada
Japanese, 1786-1864
Nakamura Shikan in the role of the Fox Kuzunoha (Kuzunoha kitsune), 1861

"Usually, I am drawn to art because it is visually appealing or relates to a technique I am familiar with. However when I first viewed Utagawa Kunisada's painting, I was visually and viscerally jarred.

As I looked and realized a child was in her arms, the painting became emotionally powerful to me. I realized and related to, the overwhelming need to create, right now, regardless of other obligations.

With sons 18 & 20 it's been a long time since I was the nursing mom I took her to be.

Between first coming to the [gallery] and returning to write this, I have toured and enjoyed most of this floor. The image — visually not a favorite — continues to haunt me."

FIGURE 3.1 Comment card of Utagawa Kunisada block print.
Lord Cultural Resources

use data will determine whether you succeed or fail to deliver on the promise of personal impact?

Let's be honest, there is a philosophic gap between the aspirations of a museum's mission and the measured world of data. Museums are intimate, emotional, and inspirational. Data and analysis feel distant, impersonal, and clinical. Most museum professionals did not seek their current career paths from a love for statistics. Cultural professionals are the intellectual equals of any profession, and museum administration requires diverse and ever-expanding bodies of knowledge. That said, the cultural sector is relatively inexperienced when it comes to collecting, analyzing, and applying data. Compared to other sectors, it lacks a sophisticated market for tools and services based on data analysis.

Despite our desire to transform lives, museum professionals know relatively little about the people who visit museums. Like museums, companies like Netflix, Amazon,

MAKING IT PERSONAL

Video

"American, 1951
The Quintet of the Silent"
by Bill Viola,

DVD, Panasonic Plasma screen,
line doubler, surge supressor,
DVD player

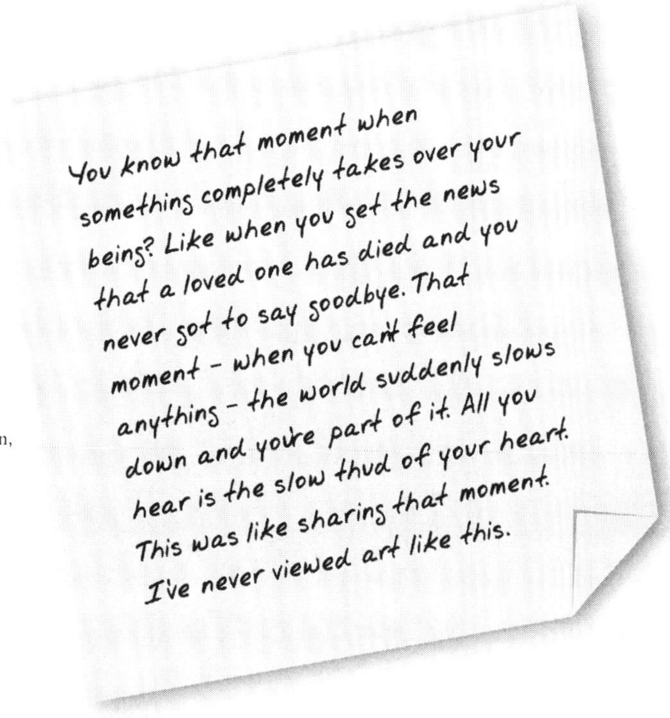

> You know that moment when something completely takes over your being? Like when you get the news that a loved one has died and you never got to say goodbye. That moment – when you can't feel anything – the world suddenly slows down and you're part of it. All you hear is the slow thud of your heart. This was like sharing that moment. I've never viewed art like this.

FIGURE 3.2 Comment card of Bill Viola video.
Lord Cultural Resources

and Facebook offer entertaining, educational, social, and life-changing encounters with creative content. Unlike museums they recognize that the key to their business is in showing just as much interest in their visitors as their products, and, in the past twenty years they have revolutionized the way that personal data can guide customers to new diverse experiences while serving them with what they want.

Companies use data to capitalize on the loyalty and patronage of their customers. Their goal is to maximize revenue, but they also generate positive social effects such as better-informed citizens and support for creative industry. Museums share many of the same goals, including sustainability, as proved by the willingness of their visitors to financially support them. Purchases and donations are not simply economic indicators. They effectively gauge the relevance of a museum's services to the lives of its constituency.

Overcoming Challenges of Using Data in Museums

While it's easy to say that all museums should take cues from the corporate likes of Amazon and Netflix, the reality is that very few of us would agree with that approach on a wholesale basis. Even if we did, it's unlikely that doing so would lead to the kind of sustaining change that museums will need to perpetuate themselves in the coming decades. In reality, the factors that influence why museums are not currently taking advantage of data and analysis are quite complex. In chapter 1, Chris Michaels reflects on the experience of implementing a digital strategy at the British Museum and the unexpected challenges and rewards of doing so. I have also observed a range of other factors.

First, museums deal with conflicting timescales in their operations that make adapting to change notoriously difficult. Many museums are caring for objects that are hundreds of years old, if not millennia. We furthermore intend to keep and care for those objects for the foreseeable future. Many museums have existed more than a century by relying on business models that have remained mostly unchanged since founding. Exhibitions are a staple feature of museums, and they require several years to gestate before blossoming for just a few months. With a project cycle measured in years, museums are geared toward long-term planning. The rapid changes required by digital technology undermine well-established practices that have been highly successful over lifetimes.

It can take many years for museums to develop workflows and practice to deliver projects. This makes it very difficult for museums to adapt to change rapidly. As our public lives continue to change more and more rapidly, it is imperative that museums become more agile and able to respond at a similar pace.

Secondly, the nature of museums as mission-driven nonprofit businesses sometimes conflicts with the laws of supply and demand that govern other sectors. Museums have a point of view and a responsibility to advocate for their subject area, and they are not free to adjust their mission when the zeitgeist of public attention shifts in a different direction. For example, historic house museums cannot suddenly decide to start displaying contemporary installation art without first considering carefully whether or not this decision will ultimately support their mission. Art museums cannot simply determine that an "Art of *Star Wars*" exhibit would be the best thing to do, even though it would likely make money and be popular with the public. In the cultural sector, the tail cannot wag the dog without compromising the mission and primary objective of the museum.

This is not to say that the desires of the public are not important as we plan the best strategies for our museums' future. Rather, museums must determine the best way to communicate the interest, meaning, and passions we hear and see in our galleries every day to a broad public that has no idea why they should care about us.

For this reason, data is all the more important. Data about public opinions, behaviors, desires, and participation is the map by which today's cultural organizations can find their way toward reliably communicating the meaning we long to see in a larger and more diverse audience of visitors. This goes far beyond simply counting attendance at our doors and reporting box office revenues. I'm talking about becoming as sophisticated as any Amazon or Netflix about the individual preferences of cultural consumers and about building long-term relationships with audiences that matter. At the end of the day, we have a better product than any commercial sector company can easily replicate, and we need these relationships to support the long-term viability of museums as an endeavor worth keeping.

If at First You Don't Succeed . . . Introducing the OODA Loop

The shadow is always darkest beneath the lamp.

A friend shared this proverb with me a few years ago as we talked about how museums should be prepared to change in order to better serve future audiences. It has come back to mind so many times since then as I think about what it will really take for us to shape and adapt museums into organizations that are truly visitor centered.

As institutions that seek to create environments for learning, it sometimes surprises me that museums place so little emphasis on their own systems of learning. What would it look like for an active learning culture to become embedded among the museum's staff from the janitor to the director's office? One of the major consequences of having such long planning cycles in museums is that the pace of iterative learning is constrained to those same time scales. There is no one-size-fits-all formula for the cultural sector to use that will ensure its success delivering mission impact to its audiences. Therefore, it is key that today's cultural organizations figure out how to break these inherently long-term cycles into series of small and fast iterations that we can learn from. A museum that learns is a museum that can change, adapt, respond, and succeed.

John Boyd was born in Erie, Pennsylvania, just before the stock market crash of 1929. He enlisted in the U.S. Army and served in the Army Air Forces from 1945–1947. For someone who would eventually become one of the most important military strategists his country had ever known, Boyd's career began with an inauspicious post as a swimming instructor in occupied Japan. After the war, Boyd returned to the United States and attended the University of Iowa. He joined the U.S. Air Force after graduation and served as a fighter pilot and officer until his retirement in 1975.

During the Korean War, Boyd flew very few missions, never fired a shot, and never downed a single enemy aircraft. Despite these facts, he rose to become a successful instructor of other pilots and developed theories of aerial combat that are still important today.

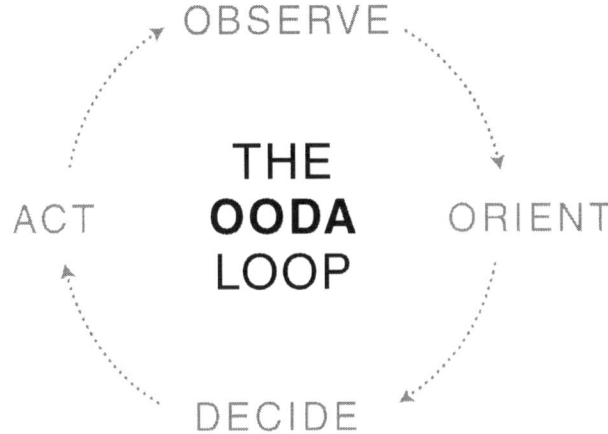

FIGURE 3.3 The OODA loop.
Lord Cultural Resources

One of those theories is called the OODA loop (Observe, Orient, Decide, Act) and has had an important impact on many fields that are far removed from aerial combat. Boyd observed that fighter pilots, locked in a dogfight, face a series of uncertain, ambiguous, and changing factors that can dramatically alter the course of the encounter. He postulated that the pilot who accurately *observes* the evolving situation, *orients* himself to the information he is seeing, *decides* on the appropriate next steps, and then *acts* on those decisions the quickest will be the most likely victor.

While Boyd's theories go much further to explain the psychology of decision making, the key point for museums to consider is that in the face of an environment that is changing, uncertain, and ambiguous, the museum that can iterate its process the most quickly gains the most information and experience necessary to deal with an evolving cultural landscape. The learning that results from each cycle can be used in each subsequent cycle, thereby accelerating progress and improving our chances of success.

This same idea of iterative learning as a way of working is at the heart of today's most successful software technology companies. This agile approach to software development zeros in on a repeated series of short sprints, or work cycles, during which a team adds or creates new features, joining them to a continuously growing software product. This accretion of new and expanded features is key to growing very large and complex software platforms that are sometimes difficult to specify and whose behaviors are sometimes difficult to diagnose.

A cyclical approach has the benefit of allowing the team to adjust the direction of their efforts incrementally as time marches on. How many times have we all worked on a project for the museum in which we needed to change direction in midstream? Probably every time if your work is anything like my own! The iterative process specifically anticipates and allows for this evolution to take place and embraces it as part of improving the product and becoming smarter over time.

I would propose that the same method of teamwork can be effective at helping museums become more self-aware and progressive about their own performance and learning, as we will see in the next sections.[1]

Measure What Matters

In 2004, Maxwell Anderson wrote what was to become a well-known paper proposing a new set of "Metrics of Success in Art Museums."[2] While widely read and discussed in the field, there are still very few museums that have succeeded in shifting their focus to include these more mission-directed measures of success. While many of us will agree that attendance and box office successes are not the ultimate arbiters of a healthy museum program, it's also hard to imagine how we could meet our practical day-to-day needs without a robust effort in those areas. I believe there is a logical fallacy that is at work here that needs to be addressed.

In the museum, it is tempting to think that once a visitor arrives and pays for a ticket, that in a certain respect we've done our job. We've scored a point, crossed the finish line, checked the box. It feels good to know that our attendance has risen and our coffers are incrementally fuller than they were before. Many times it has taken so much work to prepare the galleries, execute the marketing, and open the doors themselves, that when the visitor finally arrives, we feel a rush of relief. It's normal to feel that we've crested the first hill of the rollercoaster, but this is in fact where the fallacy lies.

If we shift our focus to a long-term view that sees the overall relationship of the museum to its visitor, it becomes clear that this single visit is really part of a much larger cycle. While attendance and box office revenue is of practical importance to the daily operations of the museum, each visit also signifies a choice made by the visitor. This choice reflects, to some degree, what the visitor finds to be important, fun, and worth their time. The experience of that same visitor once they enter the doors of the museum will determine their likelihood to visit again and may represent the single chance we have to pique their curiosity and jump-start their learning process.

In reality, measurement of attendance and box office revenues is simply the first step in determining more mission-oriented metrics of success. Relevance to our community is difficult to determine without members of that community first having attended the museum. Education, engagement, and meaning making are the desired outcomes of having first shown up. Much of the work in preparing the museum and activating the visitor is leading up to this opportunity to make an experience for them that will fulfill the museum's mission.

By stopping at recording just the most obvious factors of attendance, we're missing the chance to understand what drove that attendance in the first place. Furthermore, we're also missing the chance to get to the heart of why the museum matters at all. Why settle for the skin-deep signifiers of success when we might in fact use them as a starting point to better understand and address the root causes of success or failure as mission-driven cultural organizations?

Let's Get Serious about Knowing Our Visitors

At the heart of every museum is a core belief that museums matter to real people. While mission statements invariably focus on collecting, preserving, and interpreting—collecting for whom, preserving for whom, and interpreting for whom are questions that are commonly asked, but with too little specificity.

Even in today's age of hyper-personalized online services, one-hour delivery, and ad retargeting magic, it is still fairly common to hear museums talk about *the audience* as one large homogeneous group. We often talk about how *the audience* did or didn't respond to specific exhibitions, programs, or online campaigns, which exhibitions were *popular* and which were not. Doing so neglects the fact that each museum's overall audience is composed of many smaller sub-audiences and, in fact, those sub-audiences are composed of individuals who may or may not fit the characteristics of any particular box we might want to put them in.

Though this is the case, it is also true that there are incredibly few museums in the world that know very much about their individual visitors at all. *Customer relationship management* is the term used for the tools and processes that businesses use to track the connection, engagement, and transactions of their audiences.

In the cultural sector, this is a discipline that has historically been associated mainly with fundraising and membership. Furthermore, the skills museums do possess in this area often revolve around how best to optimize the specific transactional relationships of being a member. Most museums have no system or skills in place to begin to collect any data at all about how the general visitor participates and engages with the museum once they are inside the doors.

What would happen if the cultural sector began building knowledge—based in data—that could inform us about our visitors' participation, preferences, and personal needs? Isn't this exactly the kind of information we need to encourage long-term engagement and learning among a broad audience? Isn't it also the kind of knowledge we could use effectively to ensure that our patrons and members feel known and appreciated by the museum, thereby securing their long-term support and goodwill?

Questions we would normally ask visitors if we bumped into them in the gallery could be incredibly valuable if we were systematic about collecting and recording them over time. Who are they? Where do they come from? Do they have family or friends they like to visit with? What kind of art do they like? Did their family immigrate here? What kinds of things make them curious? What social causes do they think are important? What is it that they dream of doing someday? What's on their bucket list? Did they have a good time today? What could we do better? Did they have a favorite part of the visit? Would they plan to come back?

While these conversations are common and probably already occurring in one-on-one interactions with visitors, we would quickly exhaust ourselves if we tried to have this level of conversation with the entire audience. Furthermore, anecdotes from conversations such as these cannot be aggregated and analyzed efficiently to tell us—in real time—how the museum is doing today. In order to achieve this, we will have to redesign our ways of working and begin to prioritize and capture this information alongside more basic statistics like attendance and cash transactions.

How to Begin

Now that we've thoroughly discussed the many reasons why putting data at the heart of your visitor experience could help the museum succeed, what is the best way to start what can appear to be such a daunting task?

STEP 1: ESTABLISH THE TEAM

First, let's recognize that this is a foreign concept for many in the cultural sector. It's likely that this practice will feel very strange to some members of your team. Remember from our earlier discussions that the iterative process itself is as important as the metrics you choose. Your goal is to create a team that learns together, not one that can quote the most detailed statistics. Teams should include members from different departments and people with enough seniority to integrate the practice and findings into the museum workflow. The team should be manageable in size.

STEP 2: CHOOSING KEY METRICS

Choosing those first few metrics is the most important place to start. These are often referred to as key performance indicators (KPIs), and the best ones serve as bedrock information that can illustrate the basics tenets of your business. After spending a good many words in this chapter bemoaning how inadequate attendance and box office

LINKING KPIS TO YOUR MISSION

Questions to consider for mission-linked KPIs.

1. How about some measure of visit satisfaction? Did visitors enjoy their time at the Museum? Did it meet their expectations? What percentage of visitors report high satisfaction, and how does this change during high-attendance weeks? Think of how to solicit this question from hundreds of visitors each day instead of waiting for the results of an intercept survey administered once every few months.

2. School visitors as a percentage of overall attendance. How do teachers rate their experience in the museum and their likelihood of returning with another class? Do they feel that the museum supported the learning that happens in the classroom? Does the museum support the acquisition or practice of key twenty-first-century skills? Are its resources accessible for teachers and learners before, during and after the visit? Rather than surveying teachers with these questions once per year, what if we knew this information for every class that visits the museum? What would the trends look like?

3. Which neighborhoods did our visitors come from this week? How balanced is the visitation across the city? How does it compare to last week? What could we do to connect with neighborhoods that didn't come this week?

revenues are to represent whether your museum is successful, I am now going to contradict myself. For many organizations attendance and box office revenue may in fact be the best place to start.

Here's why:

- Your staff is probably already collecting these statistics. By starting here, you can spend less time putting systems in place to collect a more esoteric KPI.

- You are probably already required to report on these numbers, but perhaps not as frequently. Taking an existing process and increasing the frequency with which you analyze and report is a simple way to jumpstart an iterative OODA loop.

- These are statistics your staff is already familiar with, and many departments across the museum will already be heavily invested in seeing them succeed. Using these as a place to start will be clear and easy for the team to understand, allowing you to spend time with them establishing a process of review and learning.

The problem will be if you simply stop at collecting these two statistics and never go any further. If you do, you will have missed the boat entirely. Attendance and revenue are precursors for more mission-driven impacts that will ultimately propel your museum into succeeding in terms of your mission as well as financially.

Once you've established a comfortable rhythm with your team, iterating and learning from these simple KPIs, try branching out toward KPIs that are intrinsically tied to achieving your mission, or are explicitly driven by educational objectives (see chapter 4).

STEP 3: ESTABLISH A BASELINE

This is perhaps the most important step in the entire process. A baseline of data tells you what your current performance is prior to beginning a process of change. Establishing a solid baseline that the team has confidence in will allow you to notice when you hit on a success and will alert you more quickly when things go awry.

Many KPIs you might collect will follow some kind of seasonal pattern. In fact, there may be more than one pattern at work. Imagine that your attendance is higher on weekends than weekdays and more active in the summer than in the winter. These are two overlapping seasonal variances for attendance. They are predictable and need to be defined as you seek to understand how your performance is improving.

To establish your baseline, you must first collect enough data to represent one of these seasonal cycles. To continue the example—you must first collect one week's worth of data to understand to what degree Saturday has higher attendance than Tuesday and to compare the following Tuesday against a fair benchmark. Likewise, you must first collect one year's worth of attendance in order to understand whether your performance in July exceeds last year.

In reality, these baseline statistics will be continually updated. Consider the case of a KPI you've never tracked before, like visitor satisfaction. It's not clear whether there is any seasonality at all in this metric. We will need to discover it over time. As we will see in the next section, the frequency you choose to review visitor satisfaction will drive how much data you need to establish your baseline.

As time goes forward, plan to continually improve your baseline accuracy by incorporating new data on a rolling basis. For example, once you have collected several weeks of visitor satisfaction data, you can improve a one-week baseline by continuously averaging the prior four weeks. This is sometimes called a rolling average or a sliding window—meaning that the new baseline is continually updated to reflect your most recent performance.

STEP 4: FREQUENCY, PROJECTIONS, AND TRENDS

Now that you've primed the team, chosen some initial KPIs, and established some early baselines it's time to begin the process of analysis.

The first step is to determine a natural frequency that makes sense for each KPI. While something like attendance and revenue may naturally fall into weekly reporting, other KPIs like press mentions or grants awarded may naturally change on a less frequent basis. Encourage the team to choose a reporting frequency that seems most natural based on how often the KPI changes and how difficult the reporting process is.

Remember, a learning museum needs many iterative loops in the course of a year to learn quickly and adapt.

Next, make a projection for each KPI. This is a guess about the value of that KPI for the next reporting cycle and for other cycles in the future. Encourage the team to have a basis for why they think this will be the outcome. By making guesses, you are fine-tuning your intuition about how the museum really works and giving yourself a chance to better understand the factors that truly impact performance. Being wrong about your guess and *recognizing* it is just as important as being right in the first place.

Finally, be sure to track the trends. In chapter 5, Katie Moffat provides a detailed approach to analytics that results in deeper insights rather than raw numbers. These include calculating how far above or below the baseline your actual performance was last week. Do the same for your projection—how far off was your guess? Use these trends to try to make a better guess next week.

STEP 5: BEGIN THE LOOP

Now you've established all the basics of becoming an agile and data-driven cultural machine. Congratulations! Once you've gotten this far, the team should be getting a bit more comfortable seeing this kind of data on a regular basis. It's important at this point to find a regular and consistent time when this data is naturally in front of them. This could be sent in email on a regular basis and then be discussed during a few minutes of a regular weekly meeting.

Building an expectation that the institution's collective performance will be discussed on a regular basis can help establish accountability and at the same time reinforce learning. Doing so can help diffuse the sting of failure and channel it into adaptable and resilient teamwork. Remember why we're doing all this work in the first place. We hope to create a passion and skill for learning among our staff that is based on data and performance, not opinion. The result will be a team that is empowered to innovate their own work on behalf of the museum.

Let's return for a moment to Boyd's OODA loop and examine how it applies in this case.

Observe: Your team has developed the capacity to capture and record consistent data, with appropriate baselines, for KPIs that are critical to the museum's long-term success. Reports summarizing these KPIs are developed and delivered to the larger team on a regular and consistent basis.

Orient: The team will gather together to examine these KPI reports in person. They will orient themselves to the trends in the data and how actual performance compared to what they thought would happen.

Decide: Having made sense of the data, the team will decide what actions can be taken during the next cycle to try to improve performance. It is key at this point to create and adjust projections that can be used as a goal and a way to document our own thought process.

Act: Having a clear understanding of what our current performance and challenges are and also having agreed to what we can do about them gives each team member a clear path to execute on their tasks for the next cycle.

It's important to understand and reinforce that this loop itself is a process of learning. The goals are to improve and sustain performance over a long period by better understanding our audiences and ourselves so that we can make better choices.

A Word about Qualitative Methods

Because this chapter has focused deeply on establishing an iterative practice and has emphasized quantitative data collection and analysis, I think it's important to highlight the important role that qualitative methods should continue to play in museums.

TIPS FOR PUTTING DATA AT THE HEART OF YOUR MUSEUM

- Simplicity: Select two or three very simple KPIs to start. Any more can lead to analysis paralysis as you're just getting started.

- Frequency: Pick a regular time each week to look at this data with your team. This can take just two or three minutes from another regular meeting.

- Training: Plan opportunities for training. This way of working is new for most staff in cultural institutions. Even experienced staff can develop their skills in statistics and prediction.

- Consistency: Be consistent. Consistent measurement over time helps you to see trends. In this case, consistency trumps accuracy.

- Personality: Plan for regular qualitative studies to validate what your quantitative data is telling you. Being data-driven but visitor-centered requires talking to real people in addition to collecting lots of data.

There are many museums that have devoted significant time and effort toward the thorough research and study of the qualitative aspects of their audience—its makeup, motivations, participation, and preferences. This is immensely important work that is crucial to maintain and even expand as we head into the iterative approach we've been discussing.

In truth, there is an important balance museums must strike between the pursuit of high-frequency quantitative reporting and the kind of in-person qualitative research that has been more common across the cultural sector. While quantitative reporting can provide near real-time feedback about your museum's performance, it can never take the place of talking to real people about their experience and opinions.

While quantitative reporting on KPIs can help us see and discover trends in the data, it's often the case that the root causes of the patterns we see in the data are difficult to discern. This is where qualitative evaluation can shine a light on what's really going on within our audiences.

By pairing both qualitative and quantitative methods, museums can balance the best of both worlds. As we discussed in the opening of this chapter, museums are personal places, and data analysis often seems cold and clinical. By keeping real people and real visitors in the center of the museum's vision through qualitative evaluation techniques, it's possible to achieve a more balanced, visitor-centered but data-driven process.

Conclusion

It's clear that there has never been a better time for museums to move towards a more analytical approach for putting data at the heart of their connection to visitors. Changes in technology and data science have lowered many of the barriers that used to exist for museums that wanting to begin this process.

As many museums move in this direction, it is critical to keep the core values of the cultural sector in place and ensure that the tools and insights we can gain from these methods are ultimately used to further the mission of the organization over the long term. Those museums that succeed in motivating a team of staff to pursue this approach will stand the best chance of becoming true learning institutions both inside the museum and in the galleries.

> **KEY TAKEAWAYS: PUTTING DATA AT THE HEART OF YOUR MUSEUM**
>
> 1. The OODA loop (Observe, Orient, Decide, Act) is a process that helps museums to iterate quickly in order to gain the most information and experience necessary to deal with an evolving cultural landscape.
> 2. Establishing key performance indicators that are missioned aligned help museums to measure what matters.
> 3. Five steps to placing data at the heart of the visitor experience:
>   - Step 1: Establish the team.
>   - Step 2: Choosing key metrics.
>   - Step 3: Establish a baseline.
>   - Step 4: Establish frequency of measurement, make projections, and observe trends.
>   - Step 5: Begin the loop.

Notes

1. David Ellis et al., "The Service Oriented Museum Web," *Museums and the Web 2007*, accessed September 28, 2016. http://www.museumsandtheweb.com/mw2007/papers/ellis-d/ellis-d.html.

2. Maxwell L. Anderson, "Metrics of Success in Art Museums," The Getty Leadership Institute, 2004.

SECTION 2: TRANSFORMING THE WAY WE RELATE TO OUR COMMUNITY

Social Media and Audience Development

Ngaire Blankenberg

Social media is an important channel between museums and their existing and potential communities. It is a tool to "push" content, as well as a platform to "pull" in new communities and new community-generated content, networks, and conversation. Through social media, museums have a strong opportunity to reach new people and engage their existing community in ways other than from inside the physical museum.

Increasingly people are accessing social media through smartphones, and within the next few years, one can assume that mobile phones will be the main channel for social media almost anywhere in the world. A discussion of social media in museums, therefore, should assume that it is accessed "on the go" through a mobile device and through a data plan or WiFi—as discussed in chapter 14 on infrastructure.

Preferred social media platforms are different depending on countries, demographics, and WiFi access, and most people use more than one platform. In the United States, for example, average social network users sixteen-to-twenty-four-years-old access at least five different social platforms per week.[1] Although the social media world is stabilizing—with the dominance of Facebook in most countries (with the notable exception of China and Russia)—there continues to be the possibility for new disruptive platforms to emerge. Messenger apps such as WhatsApp have created group features that operate in a similar although more closed way to social media, and these can also be considered to work on similar principles.

Each social media platform has a slightly different function and works with different media, and it is important that once museums decide to use a particular platform they research and observe the conduct and activity of that community to act accordingly. On the whole, however, museums can consider social media as a program or channel (see the discussion of omnichannel programming in chapters 2 and 8) that provides digital content, supports conversation, and facilitates or drives action.

In this chapter we do not focus on one particular platform but rather examine in general how museums can use social media to reach new audiences, as well as to engage existing communities through content discovery, conversation and participation. We speak to Alex Espinós and Gloria Castellví about what they found out about how to grow followers from their study of 1,250 museums on Twitter. Finally we touch on metrics associated with social media (also in chapter 5) and some of the implications of social media for a museum's staffing and operations (also see chapter 13).

Reaching New Audiences

Social media becomes particularly important as a strategy when considering audience development among the hard-to-reach millennials. This segment of visitors, representing people who were born between the early 1980s and the early 2000s, are a challenge for many museums. They are digital natives—in that they were born into a world of ubiquitous communication technology, and they are major users of smartphones and social media. In the United States, millennials are not visiting cultural organizations as much as other generations,[2] a trend predicted to lead to long-term declining visitor numbers to the museum's physical location. A recent study in the United States found that millennials discover art through social media[3] rather than visiting museums—although the opposite is true for baby boomers.[4]

Of course, millennials are not the only people using social media—LinkedIn's main demographic in the United States is adults thirty to forty-nine years of age, and on Facebook—the most popular social media site in the world—there are almost the same percentage of users ages thirty to forty-nine as there are eighteen to twenty-nine.[5] Nevertheless, it would be prescient for museums to plan for social media as a key point of entry for millennials.

The Digital Divide

Access to the Internet via either desktop or smartphone is not universal. In advanced economies over three-fourths of the population is likely to have access to the Internet, which most access via a smartphone,[6] but in emerging/developing economies as little as one-tenth of the population have similar access. Social media follows a similar pattern—with 59 percent of the North American population on social media, but only 6 percent in central Asia and 11 percent in Africa and South Asia.[7] Although most predict that smartphone growth will continue at a faster pace than anything else and will become the primary means for most of the world to access Internet and social media, at present it is far from a level playing field. Uneven access for technical and economic reasons is further compounded by countrywide bans on particular social media platforms—which in some places is more of an impediment than individuals not having devices or being able to afford Internet access.

For museums, it is important to bear in mind that despite the divide social media is probably one of the best ways to reach people that do not connect in any other way with the museum. For many, social media may also be the *only* way they connect with the museum, and therefore should be seen not only a marketing tool to drive people to the "real" museum experience (i.e., a visit to the physical location) but also an experience in and of itself.

Social Media as a Channel for Content

Museums that wish to engage people through publishing their content on social media should consider carefully the requirements of each of their chosen platforms. Instagram, for example, requires strong images; YouTube depends on engaging videos; Facebook users prefer personal and emotive stories; LinkedIn centers around professional information; and Twitter thrives on images and/or pithy text; and Snapchat is based on short high impact video and photos. Like other channels social media requires an integrated but distinct content strategy, as explored by Ali Hossaini in chapter 8. Social media is different from exhibitions, for example, in that its community expects to be able to share content, and content sharing is at the heart of its success.

In general, the more people are engaged (inspired, amused, entertained, informed) the more they share. However, museums must also make sure they technically enable sharing, by:

- Making sure the digital content they share on social media is rights free or owned by the museum,
- Including a share option to digital content, and
- Displaying the number of people who have already shared content as an encouragement (or form of peer pressure).

The table below summarizes some basic ingredients for shareable content across four common social media platforms used by museums, focusing in particular on tone, form, and frequency—the three elements that change most frequently depending on the format. Note that tips are constantly being updated with new and frequent research done primarily by marketers, and the platforms regularly introduce new features and constraints:

TABLE 4.1 TIPS FOR SHAREABLE CONTENT ON SOCIAL MEDIA[1]

	FACEBOOK	INSTAGRAM AND PINTEREST	TWITTER	SNAPCHAT
Tone	Chatty	Considered Conversational Embody your brand	Simple and direct Have an opinion Be personal	Irreverent Informal "Human"
Form	Text, video, and images. Live video via Facebook Live. Long form trustworthy content Use lists and infographics Re-promote successful old content Make sure your video works without sound (most watch without sound) Be entertaining, surprising, and helpful (people love tips)	High-quality photos that tell a story Front-load captions as they can cut off in a feed after 3–4 lines of text Updates of what's new at the institution New views and images that can't be seen elsewhere (behind the scenes) Connect to campaigns and events happening in community Post personal photos Create Pinterest boards for campaigns, special exhibitions, or events Use hashtags for people to find you, but not too many (don't forget #museum).	140-character text + links, photos, GIFs, or videos Use images Follow influencers and encourage them to follow you back Stay on point and become the "go to" source for specific content or approach Share valuable content (with shortened links) Ask questions, respond to answers Learn the language (there are key abbreviations that the community uses—Google "glossary for twitter" to learn some)	Video and photos of "right now"—1–10 seconds for a chat; stories—25 seconds–24 hours Create first browse second Tell a story— beginning, middle (drama), and resolution Share your snapchat QR code on other platforms

	FACEBOOK	INSTAGRAM AND PINTEREST	TWITTER	SNAPCHAT
Frequency[2]	1–2 x a day; 10 x a week Don't "clog" feeds with too much posting	2 x a day on Instagram 4–10 x day for Pinterest	3–5 x a day Be responsive to others	1–5 x a day Stories only exist on the platform for 24 hours

[1] This list drew from a number of sources—including Noah Kagan, "Why Content Goes Viral: What Analyzing 100 Million Articles Taught Us," April 21, 2014, *OkDork* (blog), http://okdork.com/2014/04/21/why-content-goes-viral-what-analyzing-100-millions-articles-taught-us/; "Data-Backed Tips for Getting Your Content Shared on Facebook," *kissmetrics* (blog), https://blog.kissmetrics.com/data-backed-facebook-tips/; "How to Use Twitter: Critical Tips for New Users," *Wired*, https://www.wired.com/2016/05/twitter-onboarding-tips-for-new-users; Tom Roy, "4 Ways to Build a Cool Snapchat Audience for Brands," April 11, 2016, *Digital Marketing Strategy 101*, http://tomroychoudhury.blogspot.com.es/2016/04/4-ways-to-build-cool-snapchat-audience.html; Lindsay Devos, "5 Tips from Museums Who Kill It on Instagram," *Museum Revolution*, http://museumrevolution.com/5-tips-museums-instagram/.

[2] Tips for frequency draw on a number of research-based blogs: "How Often You Should Post to Social Media" [Infographic] Shortstack, http://www.shortstack.com/how-often-you-should-post-to-social-media-infographic/; "How Often to Post to Twitter, Facebook, Instagram and Pinterest," May 6, 2016, Adobe Spark, https://spark.adobe.com/blog/2016/05/06/how-often-to-post-to-twitter-facebook-instagram-and-pinterest/.

Understanding the Algorithms

Content is a critical consideration when it comes to creating an engaging museum experience, but the quality of the content is secondary when it comes to the likelihood of someone receiving that content. Museum content "pops up" within an individual's social media feed not because it's "good" but because of how its **algorithm** works.

Social media platforms value relevance over chronology. The success of each platform is predicated on how often they give you content you care about, so they each constantly change their algorithms to try to make sure they personalize your content with as much nuance as possible and as often as possible in order to control what goes into your feed.

KEY TERMS

ALGORITHM

An algorithm is a routine or process for performing a calculation. All social media latforms work according to an ever changing and "secret" algorithm that aims to optimize user news feeds.

Social Media as Forum for Conversation

Some social media, such as Twitter and Facebook, are an excellent platform for dialogue or conversation between the museum and its community or among the museum's community. This can be done in a number of ways, including creating social media "live" events and launching a hashtag chat or campaign. It is also possible for museums to track conversations on social media through social media monitoring (also called social listening) and engage in them if appropriate.

LIVESTREAMED EVENTS ON SOCIAL MEDIA

Twitter, Facebook, and YouTube all provide a "live" option, and it is likely that the other platforms will follow suit. In chapter 2, Chris Michaels describes the experience at the British Museum with Periscope—a Twitter app that enables anyone on Twitter to watch a live video and simultaneously like it and make comments or ask questions to be answered in real time.

People can watch an event such as a tour or a curator's talk "live" on social media in real time and can contribute comments and questions that can be addressed "live." After the event the museum can save the video and make it accessible on YouTube, for example, and can also get information about how many people saw the video, how long they watched and how often the video was replayed later. On Facebook Live, you can "narrowcast" the event to a specific group, and YouTube Live offers a preview option and the ability to stop and start the stream.

Livestreaming an event on social media has the same benefits of any museum-related event—it encourages people to visit for a special value add they wouldn't get with a normal visit, and it allows people to meet someone they may not otherwise have the opportunity to.

Considerations for livestreamed events include:

- Charisma and approachability of the host: The main speaker doesn't need to be a celebrity (as discussed in Chapter 2, direct access to curators may in fact be preferable to a typical "host"); however, this person should be fairly charismatic, speak in a dynamic way and be knowledgeable about the subject matter. He or she should also be able to speak in a conversational tone rather than give a more formal presentation.

- Visuals: A person talking against a black background can be interesting, but it is far more interesting to push the medium and bring attendees into a new world—showing them parts of the museum, or a neighborhood, or of an artwork that they wouldn't necessarily have access to anywhere else.

- Acknowledgment of the audience: Although attendees can make comments and their profiles show up, the speaker doesn't actually see or meet them and therefore does not know what language they speak, how old they are, or even what time or season they are experiencing. Nevertheless it is polite for the speaker to acknowledge people from everywhere and make everyone feel welcome at the event.

- Clarity of expectation. Just like any live event, the host can explain to the participants what is expected of them and encourage them to participate by inviting them to make a comment or by asking them to answer a specific question. The host should do this several times, as people may come in and out during the event.

HASHTAG CHATS AND CAMPAIGNS

A social media campaign solicits comments and contributions for a particular duration of time, under a particular heading, for example #askacurator or #nationaldesignweek. A hashtag chat may be of a shorter duration (for example, an hour on a specific day), and a campaign may last a couple of days or weeks. People who want to contribute just add the hashtag to their comments and it becomes part of the conversation.

Hashtag chats can be part of a live event—like a talk at the museum or a concert. This becomes a way for people not attending the event to still feel connected to it.

The #askapp at the Brooklyn Museum is an app offered to museum visitors to enable them to ask the museum's audience engagement staff—comprised of experienced art historians, researchers, and educators—a question directly, at the time of their visit. Staff can then give a personal answer as to what to see and do, or to give more information, rather than a prepackaged recommendation.

Here are some considerations for museums wanting to launch a hashtag chat:

- Know what your visitors want to talk about. This can be identified through interviews, focus groups or through reviewing data analytics. A campaign is stronger if it builds on what your visitors are interested in or passionate about.
- Come up with a clever campaign name—it should be short, catchy, unique, and only involve one hashtag.
- Tie it to other media—a hashtag campaign gains more traction if it is supported by other marketing material such as posters or brochures at the museum, billboards or other social media.

SOCIAL LISTENING

Social listening is making use of social monitoring tools that can track specific keywords, locations, and hashtags across social media platforms. These can be tracked on a single dashboard to get a snapshot of the museum's reputation on social media. These tools can also help the museum's social media team (or person) to connect with others in a particular location who use specific keywords (for example, a museum may reply to a question about What to do in Brandon? with the suggestion to visit a museum event).

Social Media to Drive Action

Most social media is consumed "passively"—which means that someone just reads or sees it but doesn't do anything further than that (also considered lurking). Second to passive engagement is when people like or share and then comment. In some instances, however, social media is used to catalyze even greater levels of engagement by getting people to take action—like visit an exhibition, donate money, upload a creative project, or participate in research. Using social media to drive people to visit an exhibition is relatively common and follows a number of marketing conventions mainly focused on providing exciting reasons why a visit will benefit a particular market segment. Crowdsourcing and competitions are two other ways that social media can promote participation.

CROWDSOURCING

Crowdsourcing is a version of the hashtag campaign in which a greater degree of action is invited. In chapter 15, crowdsourcing is discussed as a fundraising tool for museums.

Crowdsourcing can also be used to engage the public in research projects. *Citizen science* is the term given to a project, usually supported by social media, that solicits the help of the general public in collecting and analyzing data related to the natural world. Zooniverse is an online platform for Internet-powered citizen science projects. People can go and select a project, download an app, or log into a website and contribute their research. They can also read the publications arising from their contribution.

Crowdsourcing is also used for archaeological and historical research. For example, the MicroPasts website is a collaboration between the UCL Institute of Archaeology and the British Museum. It focuses on research projects in archaeology, history, and heritage such as creating 3D models of archaeological artifacts, enriching old photographic archives, or transcribing old archaeological or historical records.

COMPETITIONS

Social media can also be used for competitions. In this instance, people are encouraged through social media to either upload something that itself is shared on social media (for example, a video, photograph, a poem) or to do something that takes place at a physical location like the museum. The Rijksmuseum, for example, encourages users of its Rijksstudio—an online repository of high-resolution, rights-free images—to create something out of these images and then enter into the competition.

Competitions are a way of museums to acknowledge that social media is a valued program or platform and its followers are part of a museum community. It's a way of valuing and encouraging deep and active engagement with the museum among a broad spectrum of people who may or may not find equal enjoyment visiting the physical building.

Operations

Maintaining social media programs is a challenge that needs to be planned for like any other program. It requires skills in content creation and publishing, as well as in analyzing analytics to be able to identify what works and doesn't work with a particular user segment. Given the importance of social media as the primary engagement channel with many museum visitors and potential visitors, it is important that museums appoint or hire someone with specific skills in social media to be able to do this work. If they do social media as part of other responsibilities, it is equally important that the time needed to create and maintain a social media account is not underestimated. Other staff can also be trained to support them with preparing content for the platforms the museum chooses to invest in. Chapter 13 explores organizational requirements of social media as well as other aspects of digital operation.

In addition to investing in a staff person to program social media, museums may also consider paying for advertising on social media platforms. Increasingly, social media platforms are moving towards a "pay-to-play" model, in which their algorithms make it more and more restrictive for organizations to get the content they want to the people they want. In this instance, a paid advertisement may be worth the investment given the importance of social media as a programming channel equal in importance to exhibitions.

Metrics

Social media requires an investment of time and resources. It requires skilled staff to maintain the museum's accounts—publishing quality content frequently and being responsive to community conversation—and it requires appropriate content to be prepared for publishing—whether clearing rights or ensuring interesting images and videos. Such an investment needs to be measured against specific key performance indicators identified at the outset (see chapter 3). These social media KPIs could include:

- Reaching new audiences not served by other channels;
- Engaging existing audiences in new, sustained ways;
- Gaining community contributions;
- Catalyzing important and relevant conversations; and
- Increasing engagement with other channels.

In chapter 5, Katie Moffat examines analytics, which includes social media and explores how to set up and analyze data to support decision making.

Conclusion

Social media is about relationships, detail, and algorithms. There are no magic ingredients to determine what will "go viral" and what will receive no interest; however, museums that have committed, sustained, data-driven insights into their communities will be able to discover which platforms and content stimulate the greatest interest and response. Each platform needs attention to different details, and each requires a particular publishing schedule. And while content is important for social media as a channel for engagement, it is not the only thing that matters when it comes to audience development. Algorithms have their own logic, and understanding how they work for the museum's chosen platform is as important as making sure the content and conversations reflect the museum's vision and mission.

FOLLOW ME: GROWING YOUR TWITTER COMMUNITY
Ngaire Blankenberg Interviews Alex Espinós and Gloria Castellví

Alex Espinós and Gloria Castellví are principals at LaMagnética, a Barcelona-based online consulting agency that works mainly for museums and tourism authorities.

> **NB:** You recently completed a major research project on how museums use Twitter. What did you find out?
>
> **AE & GC:** First of all, there are several distinctive factors that impact on a museum's ability to build a social media following. The museum sector is quite collaborative.

Museums are prone to share other museums' posts on social media, and that allows the museums whose post has been reposted to access the other museum's community. Museums also have high levels of follower engagement: cultural content and particularly museum content is shared and commented on quite often. And thirdly, museums have small advertising budgets—if at all. Most museums do not have enough budget to base their online strategy on paid campaigns. So newcomers and museums with small social media communities need to build a social media following based on the help of their community and other museums.

NB: So how do museums build a following on Twitter?

AE & GC: The most important way for museums to grow their followers is through recommendations. A new user signs up on Twitter and is asked about the topics he or she is interested in. After setting a location and choosing "museums" or "culture" among their topics of interest, Twitter presents the new user with a list of museums' profiles to follow. After choosing several museums, other museums are going to show as suggested Twitter accounts to follow.

Secondly, the Twitter algorithm continuously offers account holders new profiles to follow based on their past behavior—that is, who they follow, mention, favorite, and retweet.

Thirdly are mentions or retweets. When a museum's follower mentions the museum in a tweet or retweets a post, this follower's followers can see this interaction and may choose to follow the museum from which the post originates.

We found out that these three mechanisms actually account for 70–90 percent of new followers for museums.

NB: Why are the recommendations so effective?

AE & GC: We were really interested in this question and studied it further. The mechanism that underlies the three main sources of new followers is called *triadic closure*. Triadic closure works in a similar fashion across most social media—including Facebook or LinkedIn, although some details may differ.

The underlying idea of triadic closure is quite simple: if two people are connected through a third person, chances are they too will be connected in the future. It is the way we have gotten to know many of our acquaintances and friends in the "real world." The chances that these two people or two Twitter accounts connect may still be small, yet they are much higher than those of two random users among the half a billion Twitter users or 1.4 billion Facebook users.

If a museum is connected with another museum (mutual following) or if they share a significant number of followers, it is likely Twitter will suggest the first museum to the followers of the second one. For instance, a user that follows several contemporary art museums is going to get other contemporary art museums as recommendations.

Through our research we found that when museums gain new followers at a path of five hundred to several thousand new followers a week, the main source of new followers are Twitter recommendations. Being among the choice of tailored recommendations for new users from a certain location or within a topic of interest allows for a much faster growth.

NB: What about mentions and retweets?

AE & GC: Mentions and retweets allow only for a slow growth and account for a small share of growth in fast-growing museums. But they are important because they are a good measure of engagement and because without them it is very unlikely a museum gets into Twitter recommendations. In our analysis we have not found a single fast-growing museum that does not receive mentions and retweets and that does not get part of their new followers through them.

NB: So what does this mean for museums that want to grow their social media followers quickly?

AE & GC: We give museums a few tips about this. Firstly—connect with the big players. Each time you gain a new follower you have the opportunity to grow your community among his/her followers. A connection—reciprocal following and reciprocal mentions or retweets—with a big player will create thousands of new triadic relationships that for a smaller museum are thousands of opportunities for growth and word spread. The big players that are more useful for a small or medium-sized museum are those nearby and those focused on similar themes.

NB: How do you get big museums to follow you back?

AE & GC: The big museums are like celebrities. It is impossible for them to manage all the mentions they receive or to engage in all conversations about them. You need to strengthen the bond slowly, and for that it is useful to use not only Twitter but also professional conferences, a more personalized social media connection through LinkedIn, etc.

NB: What are the limits of followers' growth based on these mechanisms?

AE & GC: Our research on Twitter showed that there is a clear increase in the probability to get a user as a new follower when there are three to five paths connecting the user to the museum. One can assume that the frequency with which people are being encouraged to follow a new account within the Twitter algorithm increases the likelihood that people will likely do so, and that users to whom we are connected through several paths have a greater affinity with the museum.

It is interesting to note, however, that when people are connected to one another from six paths onward that likelihood declines—indicating perhaps a saturation point, as these users have had many chances to follow us and they have chosen not to.

NB: Can you elaborate on the idea of a saturation point? What are its consequences for museums' growth on social media?

AE & GC: Stagnation in follower growth is a common challenge for Twitter—and also for other social media. In many cases, the museum starts slowly, and then its growth path speeds up, but after a threshold the growth is increasingly slower. Sometimes the stagnation is complete and the museum gains only a few followers a month but also loses a few; sometimes it leads to very slow growth.

Diversity within the set of our followers and the set of our followers' followers helps ensure both growth and information spread. The same number of followers split in different geographic and topic-centered communities will lead to a greater growth and word spread than the same number of followers in a single local community.

Stagnation is most often related to lack of diversity. Museums that have communities in several countries and around different topics do not usually have this problem and may grow at a healthy rate of 40 percent to 80 percent a year.

Language diversity for museums outside of English-speaking countries is also important, as it allows you to engage with people interested in your museum worldwide and keep in touch with tourists who have visited your museum.[9] Even for museums in the United States, it may sometimes be wise to use other languages in areas with significant linguistic minorities.

Being active in initiatives such as #askacurator or #museumweek is a good way to increase diversity, as it allows you to gain new followers out of your community—along with advertisement it is one of the few sources not based on triadic closure.

NB: Are there other ways?

AE & GC: Yes. They do not generate as many followers as the recommendations and mentions and retweets but they are still important. In some cases Twitter tracks websites you have visited during the last ten days and bases its recommendations on this. However, certain restrictions apply depending on your settings, devices, and location.

Of course there are people with previous knowledge of the museum or who have visited its website then decide to follow the museum on Twitter, and finally there are paid adverts, which are a good option if museums can afford it.

And there is also the profile information. An appealing avatar and a clear and short name increase the probability of being chosen when appearing in a tailored recommendation piece. Your profile on social media may seem like a small thing—but it is really important that it be catchy and appealing but also reflect your brand.

NB: Is it worth it to pay for advertising?

AE & GC: In most cases growth of followers is proportional to initial number of followers. The quality of the work of the different museums' community managers—along with other variables such as brand awareness, collection appeal—influence the growth percentage, but in most cases do not change the fact that growth is proportional to the initial number of followers. Advertisement, however, is one of the few strategies that help to break this rule and to diversify our community.

The cost per new follower of a Twitter campaign depends on the country, month of the year, and target. For a well-targeted and designed campaign, they may be in the range of $0.30 to $1.00. If the campaign is not properly designed, the cost may increase up to tenfold or even more. Facebook costs per fan are usually lower.

Most museums lack the budget to base their growth on campaigns, but many have small budgets that can be used wisely as a seed for allowing future growth. If campaigns are used to get to key influential users in new communities, our potential growth through the triangulation process described before can increase greatly even with a small investment. If we think about the resources devoted to social media and the size of our audience, it is an idea worth considering.

Twitter campaigns allow different forms of advanced segmentation, including targeting a campaign to another museum's followers. Facebook also allows advanced targeting. Both have re-marketing campaigns, which help to enroll website visitors on social networks. As this kind of campaign targets only visitors to our website, they are inexpensive and effective for small and medium-sized museums.

> As the expected follower's growth within a certain time span is usually directly proportional to the initial number of followers, it is wise to use campaigns for followers' growth as early as possible in your social media strategy, as their effects will increase over time.

The research mentioned in the above interview was published as a paper at Museums and the Web, *both on the website and the written proceedings: Alex Espinós, "Museums on Social Media: Analyzing Growth through Case Studies," MW2016: Museums and the Web 2016, January 31, 2016, accessed September 26, 2016, http://mw2016.museumsandtheweb.com/paper/museums-on-social-media-analyzing-growth-through-case-studies/.*

💡 KEY TAKEAWAYS: SOCIAL MEDIA AND AUDIENCE DEVELOPMENT

1. Social media (likely accessed through mobile) is an important way for museums to reach new audiences. For younger audiences, it will likely become the main channel of discovery of a museum's resources.
2. Social media is a channel and a program of the museum—not just a marketing tool—and should be resourced accordingly. Maintaining social media accounts requires time and skill.
3. As a program social media has its own community and culture—some of these may visit the physical museum, but not all.
4. Social media is a channel for content, a forum for conversation, and a drive to action. Livestreamed events, hashtag chats and campaigns, and crowdsourcing are all ways to encourage engagement.
5. Social media growth is in large part attributed to algorithms that do not evaluate content.

Notes

1. "Global Social Platforms 2016: A Country-by-Country Review of Social Network Usage," *eMarketer*, http://www.emarketer.com/Article/Facebook-Remains-Largest-Social-Network-Most-Major-Markets/1013798.

2. See Colleen Dilenschneider, "Real Talk: Why Cultural Organizations Must Engage Better with Millennials," *Know Your Own Bone* (blog), accessed September 28, 2016, http://colleendilen.com/2016/01/13/real-talk-why-cultural-organizations-must-better-engage-millennials-data/.

3. "Study: U.S. Millennials Prefer Instagram to Museums; Purchase and Discover Art Online," Invaluable, http://news.invaluable.com/press-release/art-fine-art-antiques/study-us-millennials-prefer-instagram-museums-purchase-discover-. Survey findings show social media channels, such as Instagram and Pinterest, are the preferred art discovery tool among millennials. Nearly half (44.3 percent) of young millennials ages eighteen to twenty-four and 33.8 percent of older millennials ages twenty-five to thirty-four indicate they discover new art through social media channels, compared to the largest percentage of baby boomers ages sixty-five and older (29.5 percent) who prefer a more traditional discovery path by finding new art through museums.

4. "How Millennials Use and Control Social Media," American Press Institute, March 16, 2015, https://www.americanpressinstitute.org/publications/reports/survey-research/millennials-social-media/.

5. Maeve Duggan, "Mobile Messaging and Social Media 2015, the Demographics of Social Media Users," Pew Research Center, August 19, 2015, http://www.pewinternet.org/2015/08/19/the-demographics-of-social-media-users; Dave Chaffey, "Global Social Media Research Summary 2016," *Smart Insights*, http://www.smartinsights.com/social-media-marketing/social-media-strategy/new-global-social-media-research/.

6. Jacob Poushter, "Smartphone Ownership and Internet Usage Continues to Climb in Emerging Economies," Pew Research Center, February 22, 2016, http://www.pewglobal.org/2016/02/22/smartphone-ownership-and-internet-usage-continues-to-climb-in-emerging-economies/.

7. "Global Social Network Penetration Rate as of January 2016, by Region," *Statista*, https://www.statista.com/statistics/269615/social-network-penetration-by-region/.

8. Dilenschneider, "Real Talk."

9. Palazzo Madama's and CCCB's (Barcelona Center for Contemporary Culture) cases are analyzed at: http://mw2015.museumsandtheweb.com/paper/museums-on-twitter-three-case-studies-of-the-relationship-between-a-museum-and-its-environment-museum-professionals-on-twitter/.

Analytics

Katie Moffat

Digital innovation constantly offers new ways to engage audiences. Whether through a website, established social networks or niche platforms and apps, the Internet has thrown open the doors for all museums, regardless of their size, to connect with national and international visitors. But these opportunities bring their own challenges. How do museum staff know online marketing activity is effective? How can they judge the value of having a Facebook page or Twitter account? Are website visitors interested in online collections? How do staff know about the age, location, likes, and dislikes of online visitors?

It can be easy to fall into the trap of making decisions based on gut instinct or to inadvertently link the success of online activity to output rather than outcomes—that is, you feel good that you've hit your weekly target of posts, tweets, or likes. The danger is that digital activity becomes little more than an exercise in box-ticking. Fortunately, there are myriad tools to help judge the effectiveness, impact, and return on investment of online activities. Asking the right questions and framing the answers in actionable terms will help make meaningful decisions about what to do online.

Good digital analytics data can help us to understand our current audiences: who they are, how they interact with us, what interests them, and what motivates them. It can also identify who audiences aren't and therefore, who they could be. Digital analytics provides insight into what content is appealing and how a website is helping to encourage people to visit the museum, interact with online collections or buy something from the online store.

Insights, Not Numbers

The goal is to turn data into information, and information into insight.
—Carly Fiorina, former CEO, Hewlett-Packard[1]

KEY TERMS

METRICS

Metrics are measurements used to judge performance.

Digital analytics includes the collection, measurement, analysis, visualization, and interpretation of the data that museums collect about their physical and online audiences. That data set might include information collected via in-venue surveys, exhibition ticket sales, or social media activity. Typically these data will come from sources such as Google Analytics or social media platforms.

When using analytics it can be tempting to pull the most easily accessible numbers, organize them into a report, and feel like the analytics "job" has been done. A common mistake is to pluck a number from a platform and use it as an indicator of success with no context. For example, in Google Analytics, an "average session duration" measures the average length of time of each visit to a website. On first consideration, it might sound like a useful metric—the longer the session, the better, right? Well maybe, but also, maybe not. Anything that is an "average" across an entire site is not going to be particularly useful. Different parts of a site should and do perform differently. Someone who is planning a visit might quickly access the website to find out about parking. Once they have what they need, they will exit the site. So it will be a short session, but one that rates high satisfaction with a visitor. In contrast, successful sessions with online collections would likely last longer.

Unearthing useful and meaningful analytics usually takes time, a clear understanding of the questions that need answering, and a willingness to develop familiarity with the tools of analytics. To use analytics effectively, it is necessary to think in terms of "insight" rather than raw numbers. Insight is understanding that enables you to make informed decisions, act upon those decisions, and as a result improve outcomes. Insights also provide stakeholders with understanding of performance that deepens over time.

The focus of this chapter, therefore, is on evolving an approach to analytics that results in deeper insights rather than raw numbers.

Establishing Key Performance Indicators (KPIs)

Insight gained from analytics tools is used to help improve the performance of a website or digital marketing activity, but alongside this, analytics data help measure progress and success. Key performance indicators are specific measures, or **success metrics**, that help stakeholders understand progress toward organizational goals.

Before starting to collect and interpret analytics it is important for a museum to have a clear sense of what they want to find out and why. In chapter 3, Rob Stein explores the importance of "measuring what matters" and gives some tips to ensure that a museum's key performance indicators are linked to your mission and overall organizational objectives. Similarly, in chapter 6, Ngaire Blankenberg explores how to set up explicit success metrics that measure learning, whether tied to a museum's mission or its learning strategy or both.

KPIs should meet the SMART criteria—each one should be Specific, Measureable, Actionable, Relevant, and Time-bound. Running KPIs through the SMART framework means organizations are less likely to mistakenly focus on data that, while interesting, may not actually relate to success.

Note: Much of the data for analytics KPIs will come from a digital analytics tool like Google Analytics, and some will certainly be linked to the goals that have been set up. However, it is usually of value to include data from sources such as social media, email and other digital marketing campaigns.

Tools to Help Gather Data

There are many free and paid digital analytics tools that can help gather data about online audiences. The precise nature of available data varies by tool, and therefore it is not always possible to exactly compare engagement on one platform with visitors on another. At the higher cost end of the spectrum, there are tools, such as Hitwise,[2] that can provide detailed information about online behavior, but for most museums the cost of such tools is usually a barrier. The good news is that many of the free or low-cost tools can provide ample data to help understand the effectiveness of digital activity and learn more about online visitors.

DEFINING SMART KPIs

The SMART framework is frequently used in all sectors to define and manage goals and key performance indicators. Museums should strive for KPIs that are:

- **Specific:** target a specific area for improvement; for example, number of new visits; overall revenue generated via ecommerce; or percentage of visits that result in goal completion such as sign-up to a newsletter.
- **Measurable:** quantify, or at least suggest, an indicator of progress; for example, measuring growth rates, open rates, or **click-through rates**.
- **Actionable and Assignable:** specify who will do it; for example, one staff member may be in charge of website traffic while another may be assigned to track reach-through social media.
- **Realistic:** state what results can realistically be achieved given available resources. This often refers to frequency of reporting.
- **Time-bound:** specify when the result can be achieved.[1] This is important in order to establish clear benchmarks and track trends.

[1] Duncan Haughey, "A Brief History of Smart Goals," *Project Smart* (blog), December 13, 2014, accessed September 22, 2016. https://www.projectsmart.co.uk/brief-history-of-smart-goals.php.

TABLE 5.1 COMMONLY USED ANALYTICS TOOLS

ANALYTICS TOOL	COST
Google Analytics	Free website analytics[1]
Clicky	Paid website analytics
Facebook Insights	Free, Platform specific
Twitter analytics	Free, Platform specific
YouTube analytics	Free, Platform specific
Pinterest analytics	Free, Platform specific—business accounts only
Iconosquare—Instagram	Paid, Platform specific
Hootsuite	Free or paid-for version, multiple social platforms
Sprout Social	Free or paid-for version, multiple social platforms
Mention	Paid monitoring tool, multiple social platforms
SumAll	Paid reporting tool, multiple platforms

[1] Google Analytics is free up to ten million "hits" (a hit is an interaction like a pageview or other type of interaction, e.g., watching a video) per month per account. This means that in reality very few museums will be getting enough web traffic to have to pay for it.

Google Analytics

KEY TERMS

CLICK-THROUGH RATE (CTR)

Percentage of people who clicked on one or more links in an email.

Google Analytics is a free tool that tracks and reports visits to a website and one of the most popular tools used by museums. It can tell you how people arrived at your site; for example, via social media; a search engine or another website; in which country or city they reside; what pages of the website are most popular; and whether visitors are watching videos, buying tickets, or taking other important actions. Although it is widely used, Google Analytics is an incredibly sophisticated tool that can take years of use to become an expert. However, with practice and a small amount of knowledge it is relatively straightforward to extract meaningful insights.

GETTING STARTED

For new users, Google Analytics can be overwhelming. It is not uncommon to look at all the different reports, figures, and options and be unsure about where to start. Starting with questions rather than trying to decipher answers is more useful in order to ensure that Google Analytics work for you. You may want to know:

- Are we growing visits to our website?
- Do we get better results from some marketing channels than others?

- Which channel generates the most donations?
- What are the most popular pages on our website?
- Are different types of audience (age, first-time or returning, UK or international) more or less likely to watch videos?

Your questions will be specific to your organization, but the reasons for wanting answers are usually the same. You want to ensure your website or social media page is performing well or identify opportunities to improve.

GETTING THE MOST OUT OF GOOGLE ANALYTICS

In this section I offer a primer that describes some important features to consider when you are setting up Google Analytics. It is not meant as a comprehensive guide to Google Analytics (for that I recommend a book such as *Advanced Web Metrics with Google Analytics* by Brian Clifton[3]) but rather some tips to ensure your data becomes insight that helps to constantly improve your museum.

Ensure Google Analytics Is Configured Correctly

The code that makes Google Analytics function is usually added by developers when building a website. Once set up, anyone who has been granted **admin privileges** can login and view reports for the site. The standard setup logs visits to a website and then tracks a visitor's journey through the site. However, there are additional configurations (that can either be done through the online Google Analytics Help Center,[4] or added by a developer) that can ensure the data you collect is accurate and useful.

Filter Out Traffic from Staff

The way in which staff use a website will be different from the way customers use it, and for this reason it is a good idea to filter (remove) staff visits from data-gathering

> **KEY TERMS**
>
> **CHANNELS**
>
> A group of traffic sources of the same type. For example, the "social" channel would include Facebook, Twitter, Pinterest, and so on.
>
> **WHAT ARE ADMIN PRIVILEGES, AND WHO SHOULD GET THEM?**
>
> For security reasons it is important that you don't share the login details for your Google Analytics account. If you need other members of staff or people outside of the organization to access the account—for example—consultants or agencies, you should grant them access via the "Admin" tab. There are different levels of access depending on whether you need someone only to look at reports, edit them, or manage the account. In Google Analytics you can give people administration access to the entire Account or to an individual Property or View. Which one you choose is dependent on what their role is in relation to the analytics.

exercises. Within Google Analytics, you can set up a filter to remove any visits that are from staff so that you can be more confident that the data viewing truly reflects customer behavior (in the *Google Analytics Help Center*, search for *Create and manage view filters* under the tab *Manage accounts and users*).[5]

Setup Goals

> *Defining and measuring your website's visitor goals are the building blocks for your KPIs.*
> —Brian Clifton, *Successful Analytics*

In Google Analytics, the term *goal* is used. Goals support achieving your KPIs as they measure anything of value to you that a visitor does on a site. A goal can have a real monetary value, such as buying a ticket, or it can be an indication of engagement or interest; for example, watching a video or subscribing to a newsletter. Within the goal setup, you can give actions that have no actual monetary worth a "value" (see *Create and manage goals* under the *Conversion reports* tab in the *Google Analytics Help Center*).[6] Setting up appropriate goals can help to make the resulting analysis more meaningful to staff and stakeholders.

Once goals are set up you will be able to view them within the context of various Google Analytics reports. For example, you will be able to see if more sessions that come from Facebook result in a goal conversion (the desired action taking place), as compared with sessions from Twitter.

Enable Event Tracking

This is something you will probably need a developer to do, since it requires additional code to be added to your website (the exception to this would be if you are using Google Tag Manager[7] to manage your Google Analytics account). Event tracking is a useful and important feature since it provides information about *in-page interactions*.

By default Google Analytics tracks a visitor's journey through a website as they click from page to page, but it doesn't capture information about interactions with content or other elements *within* the page; for example, whether or not a visitor watches a video, downloads a brochure, or clicks on an external link. Enabling event tracking (under the *Behavior Reports* tab in the *Google Analytics Help Center*) means data is captured on these kinds of actions, or, as Google refers to them, "events."

An additional benefit of having event tracking enabled is that the "bounce rate" figure will be more accurate. A bounce rate is the percentage of visitors that view a single page of a site with no other interaction. Bounced visits automatically record a session time of zero minutes. Generally a high bounce rate is considered bad, since it means visitors are not engaged enough to bother clicking onto another page or otherwise interacting with the site.

Imagine the scenario where someone follows a link from Facebook to your website, clicks to watch an exhibition trailer video, then leaves the site. Ideally, the video piqued his interest so much that he decided to ask his friend if he would like to go to the exhibition this weekend. By most standards, this would count as a successful visit. However, without *Event Tracking* enabled, that visit would count as a bounced visit and would register as zero time on site. With video-enabled event-tracking software, the interaction with the video would be captured, and the visit would no longer be tallied as a bounce.

Switch On Demographic and Interest Reports

Google Analytics automatically provides demographic data about visitors. This includes geographic location, devices they are using to access your site (e.g., desktop or mobile), and whether they are first-time or returning visitors. However, you can also switch on demographic and interest reports to give you information about the age and gender of your visitors and their broad interests, as defined by Google's advertising categories[8] (search for *Enable Demographics and Interests Reports* under the *Audience Reports* tab in the *Google Analytics Help Center*[9]). This can be useful when targeting particular age groups or analyzing whether particular pages or pieces of content are more or less popular with different genders or age groups.

Use Campaign Tagging

Google Analytics' "Acquisitions" report provides information about where people were before they arrived at your site and how they got there; for example, via a search engine, by clicking on an ad, or by following a link on social media. Although this data can be extremely useful, it is inaccurate if Google Analytics is unable to determine a visitor's location. When marketing or programming proactively, it is particularly important to have a clear understanding of which channels and methods are working. For example, if you email a newsletter and someone clicks on it from webmail, that visit may be labeled as a referral from Yahoo! instead of your campaign.

Campaign tagging[10] helps to ensure that the information about site referrals is more accurate (see *Custom Campaigns*, under the *Acquisitions Reports* tab in the *Google Analytics Help Center*). By appending "tags" to a shared URL, Google Analytics is able to accurately record how someone arrived at your site. In the above scenario, a tagged link in the email newsletter would mean the visit was correctly attributed as coming from your campaign.

Additional benefits of using Campaign tagging are that you are able to compare the effectiveness of campaigns against each other and see at a more granular level how much traffic from social networks is general as compared with traffic coming via posts from your page or account. This is a great help when it comes to establishing early baselines and tracking trends, as discussed by Rob Stein in chapter 3. For a comprehensive guide to campaign tagging, read "The Definitive Guide to Campaign Tagging in Google Analytics" by Annie Cushing.[11]

Social Media Analytics

Most museums interact with visitors through multiple online platforms. When used effectively, social media channels are a powerful way to raise awareness about the museum, online collections, particular exhibitions, or events, and they can help build loyalty to encourage repeat visits both offline and online. In chapter 4, Alex Espinós describes how museums can use social media to support audience engagement and development.

Once a museum has established accounts on social media, it is possible to learn more about the people following or engaging with those accounts. Many social networks and apps have built-in analytics, and although the detail they provide varies from platform to platform, the insights can be grouped into two general types: (1) data about individuals—for example, demographic band, location, or interests—and (2) data about interaction with your content—for example, most popular posts, tweets, videos, or images. By monitoring this information you can understand more about what your online audience finds interesting or engaging.

GETTING THE MOST OUT OF SOCIAL MEDIA ANALYTICS

As with Google Analytics, it can be easy to get only superficial information about social media analytics. For example, metrics that measure engagement—that is, retweets or likes—can be seen as the only measures of success. For better insights, however, you should also be looking at the relationship between social media and your website. You may discover, for example, that although you get a higher level of engagement on one platform, another one results in more visits to your website, subscriptions to your newsletter, or purchases from your online shop. That's why, in order to have a true picture of how your social media are performing, you need to ensure that you measure *action* as well as *growth* and *reach*. Growth will measure whether or not your accounts are gaining more followers/fans and reach will measure if the content shared through social channels is being seen or being engaging positively with.

Action measures whether or not people are taking a specific action (conversion) as a result of a particular post. **Conversion rates** are a commonly used key performance indicator.

Reporting: Becoming a Digitally Savvy Organization

For a museum to become user-centric with data at its heart, it is critically important that the reports arising out of analytics and others be communicated clearly, effectively, and to the right people. Although the creation of **dashboards** and reports (see below) may fall to a particular department, these should refer to key performance indicators that are agreed on and shared across the museum.

Depending on the size of the organization, it may be that different reports are reported to different teams. Trustees may receive a top-level overview, while the collections team or the marketing team receives more detailed reports. However, for most museums there will be a general report that is meaningful to all.

> **KEY TERMS**
>
> **CONVERSION RATE**
>
> The percentage of users who take a desired action, for example, visiting your website, buying a ticket, or browsing the online collection.
>
> **DASHBOARD**
>
> A visualization of the data about important KPIs (key performance indicators).

DASHBOARDS AND REPORTS

Many of the analytics tools used to gather data have built-in dashboards and reports.

Google Analytics, for example, has many standard reports that can be easily exported in addition to a dashboard feature[12] that can be used to quickly see a top-level overview of key metrics. Similarly, the Facebook Insights tool provides lots of useful information about how people are engaging with Facebook content. However, while these platform-specific reporting tools are undoubtedly useful, most organizations, particularly when reporting to stakeholders, like to combine data from several sources into one report. There are many options for doing this, whether using a paid tool that automates the process or creating your own display using Excel or a similar tool.

Regardless of which combination of tools is chosen, it is important to present the data in a clear, meaningful way. This usually means including a short narrative with words that helps explain the progress of certain key performance indicators within the context of the organizational objectives.

Data dashboards can also be shared; however, it is important that these are carefully explained, using jargon-free language. In addition, when reporting on analytics, percentages and ratios are more useful than raw numbers, as they show progress more effectively. It's also important to keep data visualizations simple. Stakeholders should be able to understand charts with minimal explanation. Examples of different organizational reports and dashboards can be found on the following page.

Digital metrics report
June 2013

Highlights
(Summary of the results of the digital activity for this month)

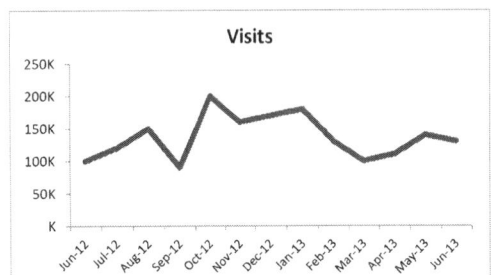

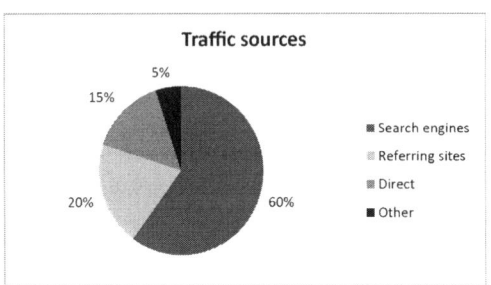

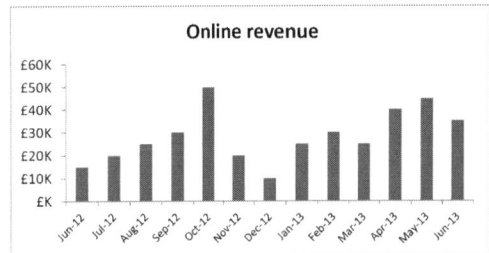

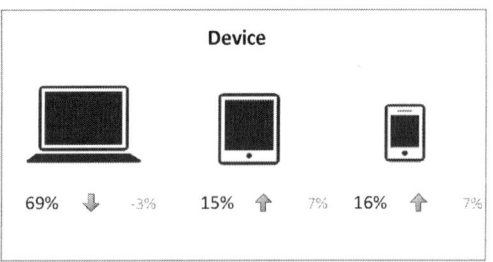

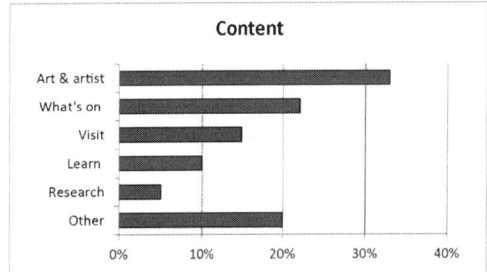

Most viewed artworks		Most viewed artists	
Artwork	Views	Artist	Views
Ophelia	2,000	JMW Turner	4,000
Weeping Woman	1,800	LS Lowry	3,800
Fountain	1,700	Roy Lichtenstein	3,600
Whaam	1,600	David Hockney	3,400
The lady of Shalott	1,500	Mark Rothko	3,200
The snail	1,400	Piet Mondrian	3,000
The passing winter	1,300	Marc Chagall	2,800
A bigger splash	1,200	Francis Bacon	2,600
Marilyn Diptych	1,100	Lucian Freud	2,400
Lopster telephone	1,000	Patrick Caulfield	2,200

Apps			
Downloads	5,000	⬇	-29%
Revenue	£ 130	⬇	-7%

Email subscribers			
Main	220,000	⬆	5%
Members	22,000	⬆	5%

FIGURE 5.1 Digital Metrics Dashboard Template.
Lord Cultural Resources

It may also be useful to look beyond reports to encourage all museum staff to engage with the digital activity and results. Monthly "learning lunches" can be a great way to engage staff. In these meetings, staff can discuss the latest analytics reports, as well as a digital-related topic, for example, new plans for the website or the latest app everyone is talking about.

Conclusion

As the museum learns what does and does not work, it should be continuously revising its KPIs and its reporting, which in turn, will help to improve and refine its programs. Museums may also decide to open their data to museum visitors themselves, for example, as discussed in chapter 6, to support learners in charting their progress or level of mastery related to a specific learning module or skill set. Data trends can also be shared with the wider public as a mode of public engagement.

> **COMBINING ANALYTICS DATA FOR BETTER REPORTING**
>
> Combining data can provide a more holistic and nuanced understanding of how you are meeting your KPIs. There are several options for combining data. The manual approach is to export the raw data from each source and import it into a tool such as Excel. You can then create a report using whatever format you prefer. Alternatively, there are paid tools that will combine data from different sources and automatically create the corresponding reports (for example, SumAll, Cyfe, or Microsoft's Power BI). The decision as to which approach to take will rely on a number of factors including available budget, internal experience (of working with software like Excel), and the audience for the report.

Collecting, analyzing, and sharing KPIs and analytics data can foster shared ownership of the overall digital footprint of the museum. It can support the museum in learning quickly from its success and mistakes and ultimately becoming a more user-centric, vital member of its communities.

A HEAD FOR NUMBERS
Katie Moffat Interviews Mark Pajak, Head of Digital, Bristol Culture

> **KM:** What type of analytics data do you collect at Bristol Culture?
>
> **MP:** We operate through multiple sites and across many teams. We have a standard set of KPIs, which each team collects, and this is broken down by site. We collect information about our audiences, their behavior, and how they interact with our services, including exhibitions, retail, and online and social media. We count the number of people through the doors at our sites and also the numbers attending

workshops and events. Through feedback forms we gather qualitative and quantitative stats on demographics and satisfaction as well as asking key questions about attitudes, reasons for visiting, and the effects of any marketing campaigns we are running. Through our retail and ticket sales we generate a lot of transactional data, and through exporting web analytics we can get an understanding of how visitors are accessing and navigating through our websites. From these primary information sources we are also developing analyses that help us build more complex data such as cost per transaction and conversion rates for digital services.

Regarding social media, we record the number of followers for each of our main accounts in Twitter, Facebook, and Instagram. These are cross-referenced with figures for the previous month to show the percentage increase or decrease over time. While there are lots of other metrics we could collect, such as likes or shares—these are less standard across the different social media platforms, and so we may use them as part of an investigation into the effectiveness of a campaign, but not as a measure of success overall.

KM: How do you use the data?

MP: What we use is an indication of performance by comparing it with previous months or years. We can also compare the data with external factors; for example, our visitor figures are influenced by the citywide arts and festivals program, and we need to qualify the data with this information to get an understanding of how we are doing.

We recently redeveloped our website based on evidence gleaned from Google Analytics, which indicated that "what's on" and "how to find us" were the most visited pages, and so we made sure these were prioritized in the navigation of the new site. We also compared how people navigated through online collections versus blog posts and made improvements to how we display information about objects based on this data. We are also building analytics into new technology. For example, we can use in-device metrics to understand which areas of an audio tour are underused with a view to repositioning the content accordingly.

KM: Do you produce any kind of dashboard that is shared internally?

MP: Yes, we produce a monthly performance dashboard that is available on demand. This gives a quick overview of the current status of visitor numbers, web visits, and other KPIs.

Our main tool for collating and displaying information is Excel, as most staff are familiar with it and different sheets can be linked together to aggregate information across sites. We produce a monthly performance dashboard that gives a quick overview of the current status of visitor numbers, web visits, and other KPIs. For the monthly dashboard we use an Excel template that contains a data sheet and a report sheet. We add the raw data into the Excel file and the graphs on the report adjust automatically. We can then save each month as a PDF to send to staff. We also leave space for some narrative text to explain any trends or anomalies in the report. The report uses infographic-style representations of the data along with arrows to indicate percentage difference comparison with the previous month.

In addition, we have several other dashboards that are used for different purposes. We have a dashboard of website analytics for our main websites to understand any changes in performance of various pages and to understand where our web visitors are arriving from. We have a dashboard that aggregates data from each of our sites to give our service director an understanding of the bigger picture, and we have one that provides real-time information about satisfaction taken directly from web-based in-gallery devices.

KM: What's the biggest challenge when it comes to collecting and using analytics data?

MP: Useful insights only come when using a large standardized data set. For example, when we look at our unique page views for bristolmuseums.gov.uk the figures are quite erratic over short periods; however, when we look at the data for a year, we can see patterns of engagement emerging that roughly correlate with our public programs—the highest spike was during an out-of-hours debate we hosted on assisted dying that sparked some controversy. Knowing whether the pattern of behavior is on an upward curve or tailing off is useful in planning how we market future exhibitions and where to put effort into promoting exhibitions-related online content.

It is challenging when the format and types of data collected change year on year due to organizational change or shifting priorities. Sometimes we find that the information has not been recorded in the correct way in order to answer the questions we need. For example, we had been collecting figures on school bookings for the year in a particular way, allocating each booking to various categories—for example, facilitated versus independent. When it came to do the end-of-year reporting we realized the question we were trying to answer was concerning sessions rather than bookings (one booking can contain several sessions). This meant we had to revisit the source data and manually reenter the data. This is an example of how knowing the data structure is fundamental to performing your analysis—you need to know what you are going to do with the data before you start recording it or you can face problems later.

KM: Turning specifically to Google Analytics, what do you find to be the most useful aspects of it?

MP: We can drill down into the data to ask very specific questions about web performance; for example, we can tell exactly which of our collections are most popular and which keywords people use to find our pages. This information can help us design and build better digital services.

Although Google Analytics as a whole can be tricky to navigate, once we have a particular method we can easily get what we need. We also have had success incorporating information into our own dashboards through the API.

We know more about the behavior of our web visitors than we do about how people navigate physical sites—this information is vital if we are to improve and optimize our online presence.

KM: Have you ever had any "eureka" moments with digital analytics, where it's provided particularly useful (or previously unknown) insights, or is it usually smaller but regular insights?

MP: We have had our assumptions proved wrong by the data: we maintain several legacy websites that are now dated and no longer seem viable. While considering how to decommission a particular website we found that it has a considerable amount of web traffic (more so than our main museum website). This traffic mainly originates from the United States during term time, and so we can infer that the website is used as a teaching resource. Although we don't yet know what this means for the site, it made us reconsider decommissioning it.

The graphs over time can be interesting to look at, as they make it easy to spot patterns where the peaks and troughs are regular. Where the patterns peak on a daily or weekly basis this can inform how we approach particular marketing campaigns.

KM: What advice would you give to a museum that was completely new to analytics and data? Where should they start, and how should they approach building an analytics program? What are the pitfalls to avoid?

MP: I would start by doing an audit of who is currently collecting data, and how. Try to eliminate duplication of effort, and standardize terminology across departments.

If the data is automatically captured in a database, maybe it does not need to be stored elsewhere—look at the reporting functionality or programmability of any digital data sources as you might just be able to link to them; for example, in Excel you can link to external data sources.

Review why some data is collected at all—sometimes the reason for collecting the data is lost in the mists of time, or the data collected does not answer the question, or at worst the data being collected is in breach of data protection laws.

Consider replacing paper-based systems with digital; for example, a tool like SurveyMonkey for feedback forms. Multi-choice questions can quickly turn into useful structured data sets.

Try to record data in a standard way for at least a year—this will allow you to compare on a monthly basis. Excel can be a useful way to aggregate across various data stores, but try not to be too clever—complex Excel documents quickly become unmanageable. Google Sheets (Google Docs) can be useful in those cases where collaboration across teams is needed, as Excel does not like simultaneous access.

If possible, try to keep the raw data separate from the reports. You might want to query the raw data in different ways, and that's hard when the data is hard-coded into a specific report.

KEY TAKEAWAYS: MAKING ANALYTICS WORK FOR YOU

1. In order to gain insights from analytics, it is important to establish Smart Measurable Assignable Realistic Time-bound key performance indicators, which then get reported on and shared throughout the museum.

2. Google Analytics can be set up in such a way to ensure that it tracks and compares data such as progress toward goals, in-page interactions, more nuanced demographics, and more accurate site referrals.

3. Social media analytics can be combined with website analytics for greater insight.

4. Analytics reports should be shared in an accessible, jargon-free way as widely as possible across the museum.

5. Try to record data in a standard way over time to enable comparisons; where possible, convert analog formats to digital formats.

Notes

1. Carly Fiorina, "Information: The Currency of the Digital Age," HP, accessed September 22, 2016. http://www.hp.com/hpinfo/execteam/speeches/fiorina/04openworld.html.

2. "Understand How Your Customers Use the Web," *Connexity*, accessed September 22, 2016. http://connexity.com/gb/hitwise/online-intelligence.

3. Brian Clifton, *Advanced Web Metrics with Google Analytics* (Indianapolis, IN: John Wiley & Sons, 2012).

4. "Analytics Help," Google, accessed September 22, 2016. https://support.google.com/analytics.

5. "Create and Manage View Filters," Google, accessed September 22, 2016. https://support.google.com/analytics/answer/1034823?hl=en.

6. "About Goals: Use Goals to Measure How Often Users Complete Specific Actions," Google, accessed September 22, 2016. https://support.google.com/analytics/answer/1012040?hl=en&ref_topic=6150889.

7. "Google Tag Manager: Overview," Google, accessed September 22, 2016. https://www.google.co.uk/analytics/tag-manager.

8. "About Demographics and Interests," Google, accessed September 22, 2016. https://support.google.com/analytics/answer/2799357?hl=en.

9. "Enable Demographics and Interests Reports," Google, accessed September 22, 2016. https://support.google.com/analytics/answer/2819948?hl=en&ref_topic=2799375.

10. "Custom Campaigns," Google, accessed September 22, 2016. https://support.google.com/analytics/answer/1033863?hl=en.

11. Annie Cushing, "The Definitive Guide to Campaign Tagging in Google Analytics," *Annielytics*, accessed September 22, 2016. https://www.annielytics.com/guides/definitive-guide-campaign-tagging-google-analytics.

12. "About Dashboards," Google, accessed September 22, 2016. https://support.google.com/analytics/answer/1068216?hl=en.

Museum Learning in the Digital Age

Ngaire Blankenberg

Museums are informal learning institutions and therefore most aspects of the visitor experience can be said to support learning. Museum learning is touted as effective and unique because it is informal (you don't pass or fail museums), voluntary and self-directed (most people choose to visit and decide for themselves what to read, see, engage with), contextual (informed by our personal, social, and cultural contexts and experiences[1]), and people centered (designed with the needs of the end users in mind). Given these very positive characteristics, many museums assume that their very existence supports learning regardless of what they do or don't do. This chapter, however, is written to guide museums in embedding learning in their museum by proactively developing a learning strategy and/or policy that is relevant and useful for a range of learners in the Digital Age.

In this chapter, I begin by providing an overview of new pedagogies such as multimodal and new media literacies, learning for change, connected learning, blended learning, and sociotechnical interaction networks, and review how these have shifted the focus of learning from the transmission of information to providing the skills needed for learners to navigate through a networked world mediated by various forms of digital

DEVELOPING A LEARNING STRATEGY

A Museum's learning strategy is a document that makes explicit a museum's approach to learning. It is primarily for internal use but can also be used to support funding applications or positioning and communication material. Typically, sections include

1. The vision and mission of the institution (ideally that includes learning);
2. Approach and strategic goals for learning;
3. Mechanisms and metrics for evaluation;
4. Overview of the learning resources of the museum—including collections, exhibitions, facilities, and digital infrastructure;
5. Learning programs and services—that is, ways of making the museum's resources available, including objectives and description of museum-led learning activities;
6. Staffing, equipment, and budget resources required; and
7. An action plan for implementation, including person responsible, timeline, and budget.

technologies. I explore new ways of measuring learning including evaluation mechanisms supported by technology, such as learning analytics and adaptive learning. We look at ways that museum resources can be used for learning purposes, whether as programs and projects designed and implemented by museum staff or for projects designed by "incomers," teachers, trainers, or individuals. Finally, we explore how "going digital" is creating new networks of teaching—not only altering the organizational structure of the museum and the job descriptions of staff but also how the museum interacts with a range of partners for the design and implementation of learning projects.

New Pedagogies of the Digital Age

A number of educational frameworks help to analyze how new technologies are impacting on how people are learning now and into the future. These pedagogies identify ways to understand and support learners in maneuvering through new relationships and dynamics of the digital age. Each of these pedagogies warrants further exploration; however, some common characteristics listed below provide good guidelines when developing or updating a museum's vision, mission, strategic goals, and approach.

1. THE GOAL OF LEARNING IS TO ENABLE EQUITABLE PARTICIPATION AND ENGAGEMENT.

Given the increasing "complexity, connectivity, and velocity of our new knowledge society,"[2] and growing inequality and social exclusion—many of the new pedagogies speak of social transformation and aim to foster equitable participation in work, family, social and civic realms.

For example, connected learning[3] is an educational approach that aims to address "the gap between in-school and out-of-school learning, intergenerational disconnects, and

MUSEUM LEARNING IN THE DIGITAL AGE

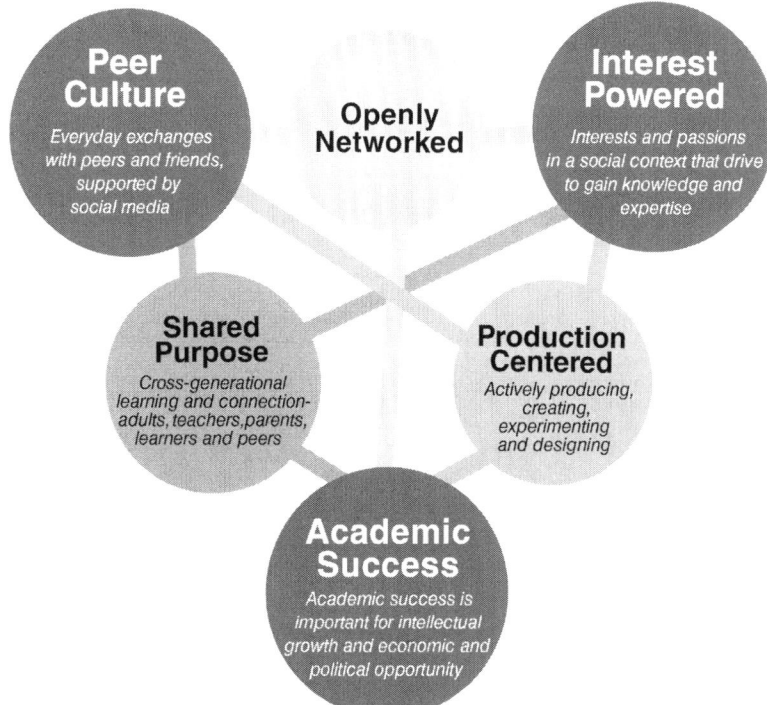

FIGURE 6.1 Connected learning is a model of learning for the digital age that emphasizes three methods of learning (production centered, shared purpose, openly networked) within three integrated spheres of learning (peer culture, interest powered, academic), as demonstrated below.

This diagram is adapted from the Connected Learning Infographic, licensed under a Creative Commons Attribution 3.0 Unported License. http://connectedlearning.tv/infographic.

Lord Cultural Resources

new equity gaps arising from the privatization of learning . . . faced by many countries, especially in the Global North."[4] It is an approach founded on the values of *equity*, where educational opportunity is available and accessible to all young people; *full participation*, all members actively engaging and contributing to learning environments and civic life; and *social connection*, meaningful learning as "part of valued social relationships and shared practice, culture, and identity."[5]

In my chapter "Learning for Change," in the *Manual of Museum Learning*,[6] I devise a model that helps museums support people to respond to the massive ongoing change around us brought about by new technology, urbanization, increased inequality, migration, globalization, climate change, and other factors.

These explicitly transformative, "learning" aspirations can be reflected in a museum's vision, which articulates the desired impact of the museum on visitors and the broader community. Museum strategic goals that embrace an educational mission not only guide program or curriculum design but also how they evaluate their success.

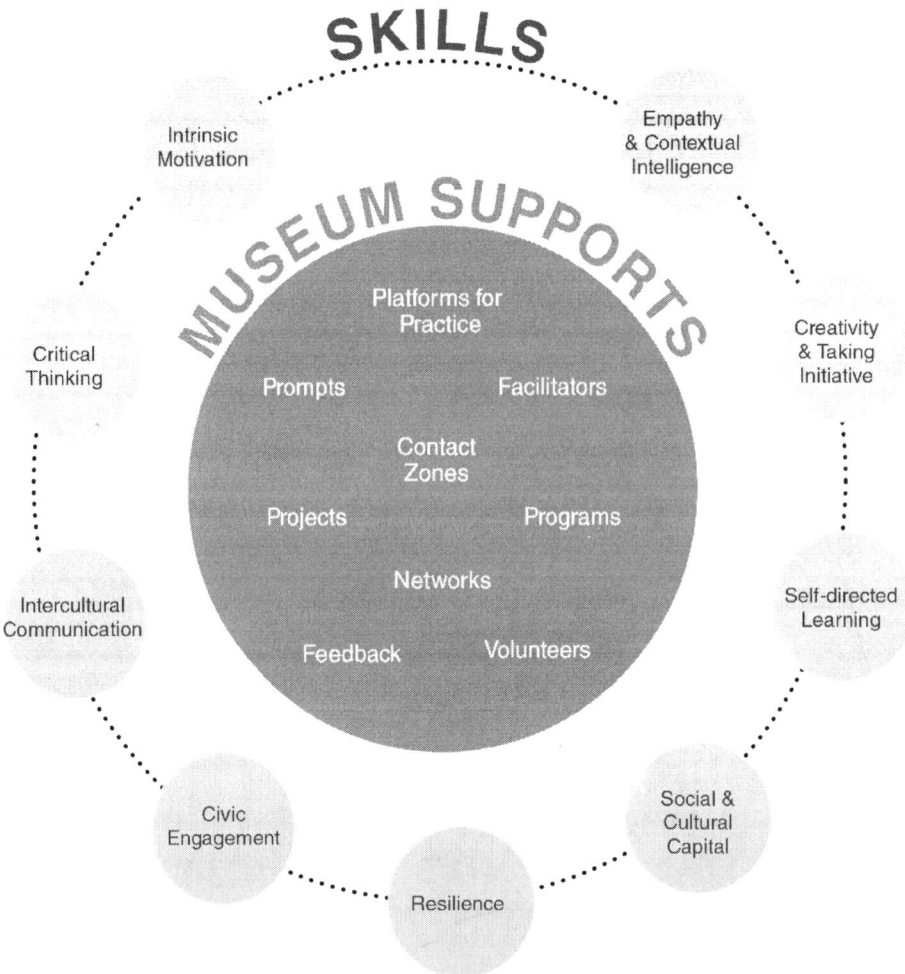

FIGURE 6.2 Learning for change is a framework that encourages museums to use their resources (museum supports) to build critical twenty-first century skills as represented in the diagram below.
Lord Cultural Resources

2. FOCUS ON SKILLS AND LITERACY RATHER THAN KNOWLEDGE TRANSFER.

Information is now broadly accessible through the Internet but navigating a rapidly changing world requires specific skills. Skills regarded as crucial for life and work today may vary depending on the theory and context of use, but there is consensus that learners need to learn *how* to think and do throughout their whole lives rather than *what* to think and do at any given point in time.

Henry Jenkins et al. identify eleven new media literacies—a set of cultural competencies and social skills that young people need in the new media landscape.

Similarly, the New London Group advocates for education that fosters "multiliteracies."[7] Multiliteracies expand the traditional emphasis on literacy that is

TABLE 6.1 NEW MEDIA LITERACIES

SKILL/LITERACY	EXAMPLE IN A MUSEUM CONTEXT
• Play: The capacity to experiment with the surroundings as a form of problem solving.	*Challenges to find out which dinosaur bone is firm.*
• Performance: The ability to adopt alternative identities for the purpose of improvisation and discovery.	*Role-play is a common technique used in history museums. Avatars are a great way to enable people to role-play on a digital platform.*
• Simulation: The ability to interpret and construct dynamic models of real-world processes.	*Simulations in which participants try to adjust different consumption levels to see the impact on climate change and pollution.*
• Appropriation: The ability to meaningfully sample and remix media content.	*Providing visitors with prints from museum art collections, or archive video with which to make their own stories.*
• Multitasking: The ability to scan the environment and shift focus onto salient details.	*Museum exhibits with multiple things to see and do support this.*
• Distributed cognition: The ability to interact meaningfully with tools that expand mental capacities.	*Specially designed digital and analogue games can exercise the brain.*
• Collective intelligence: The ability to pool knowledge and compare notes with others toward a common goal.	*Group activities in which a group is challenged to solve a particular problem while working together.*
• Judgment: The ability to evaluate the reliability and credibility of different information sources.	*Scenarios in which visitors are given different sources and asked, "What would you do?"*
• Trans-media navigation: The ability to follow the flow of stories and information across multiple modalities.	*Like multitasking, different trans-media exhibit forms enable a story to be told as an installation, a digital interactive, on mobile and through a performance.*
• Networking: The ability to search for, synthesize, and disseminate information.	*This skill is supported when museums provide sources.*
• Negotiation: The ability to travel across diverse communities, discerning and respecting multiple perspectives, and grasping and following alternative norms.	*Debates and other forms of public programming.*

solely about deciphering written or spoken language to literacies that include being able to understand and create linguistic, visual, audio, gestural and spatial, and multimodal meanings.

Visiting a museum is an excellent way for people to practice multiple literacies; museums are essentially multimodal—they enable meaning making via diverse communication tools. Visitors decipher linguistic meaning through text panels and interactive media interfaces; visual meaning through art collections, graphic and exhibition design,

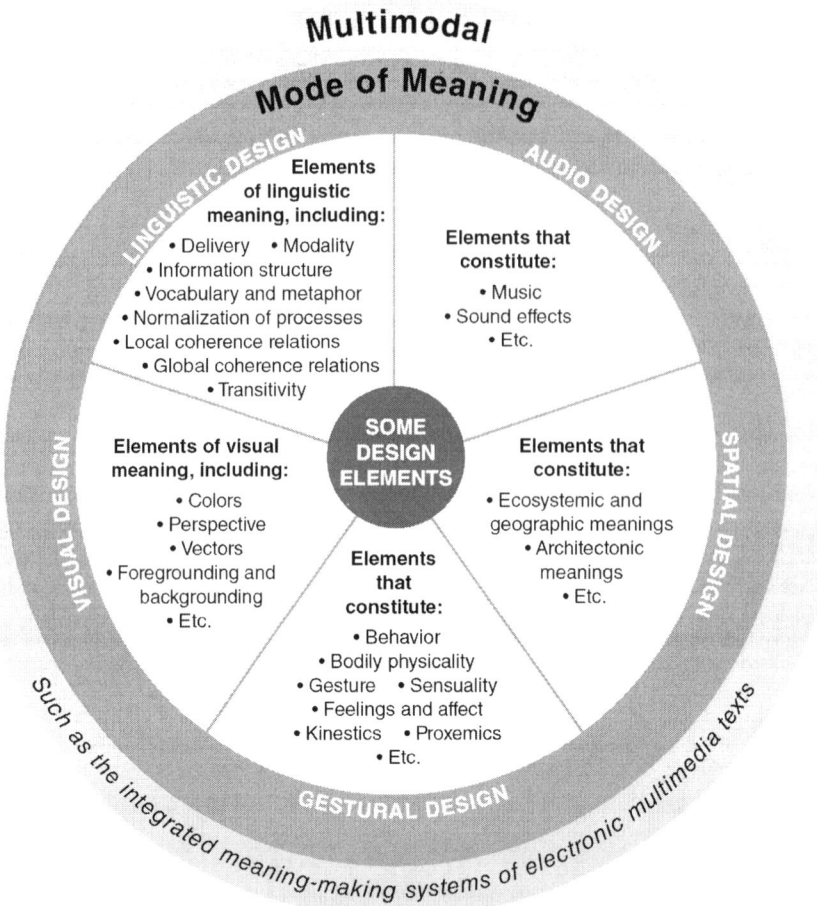

FIGURE 6.3 The New London Group has identified six multiliteracies important to navigating work and life today as depicted in the above diagram. Learners who participate in designing within these literacies also gain greater skills in interpreting meaning delivered in multimodal formats.
The New London Group, A Pedagogy of Multiliteracies: Designing Social Futures, *Harvard Educational Review* 66, no 1. (Spring 1996), p. 83.
Lord Cultural Resources

infographics, visualizations, and video; audio meaning is explored through listening to audio installations or mobile tours. Video, performance, live interpretation, gestural interfaces, and guides support understanding gestural meaning, while architecture and exhibition design support understanding spatial meaning.

Rather than focus on the content they seek to impart, the strategic goals of a museum should identify which skills and literacies their content and programs can support. Evaluation of these programs should be based on outcomes—what skills learners gain or learn through the engagement, rather than the specific content imparted by teachers.

3. PEOPLE LEARN BY FOCUSING, DOING AND REFLECTING.

Psychologist Mihaly Csikszentmihalyi describes the state of flow,[8] in which people are completely immersed in an activity leading to greater energy, happiness, and productivity. Flow tends to happen when somebody is intrinsically motivated to do an activity in which they have a clear set of goals and a sense of progress, there is a balance between opportunity and capacity, and in which they can receive immediate feedback.

Constructivists[9] and the related **constructionist** approach advocate for project-based learning where students discover, design, and create concrete things in order to build knowledge and make sense of the world. Seymour Papert, a pioneer in interaction design for children, believed strongly that technology can provide children with new ways to learn—particularly when they program, code, and design themselves. Similarly, connected learning pedagogy emphasizes projects that are production centered—that is, people actively "create, make, produce, experiment, remix, decode, and design."

Museums are increasingly offering maker spaces, bio-labs and art studios as a key component of their learning programming.[11] *In these spaces (which can also extend online, for example, as with the online Rijks Studio of the Rijksmuseum*[12]*), museum visitors are given tools, space and materials such as wood, metal, electronic, textiles, computers, 3D printing, laser cutting, biomaterial, clay, paint, high resolution, rights-free photographs, and so on to work on projects either guided by the museum or developed independently by participants themselves.*

4. TEACHERS AS FACILITATORS FOR SELF-DIRECTED LEARNING RATHER THAN THE "SAGE ON A STAGE."

In the new pedagogies the role of educators (whether teachers at school or museum educators) is to guide and facilitate rather than to simply impart information. New research in neuroscience has given rise to the AGES model—most often used in training adults in the workplace[13]—in which four key factors are identified as essential for learning:

KEY TERMS

CONSTRUCTIVISM AND CONSTRUCTIONISM

"The word constructionism is a mnemonic for two aspects of the theory of science education underlying this project. From constructivist theories of psychology we take a view of learning as a reconstruction rather than as a transmission of knowledge. Then we extend the idea of manipulative materials to the idea that learning is most effective when part of an activity the learner experiences as constructing a meaningful product."

1. Seymour Papert, "Constuctionism: A New Opportunity for Elementary Science Education," National Science Foundation, http://nsf.gov/awardsearch/showAward?AWD_ID=8751190.

SKILLS FOR TEACHERS

Museum staff or volunteers tasked with "teaching" should have strong skills in the following:

- **Interpersonal Communication:** This includes the ability to dialogue with diverse visitors of different cultures, ages, and interests; strong listening, problem-solving, and negotiation skills; and willingness to create a positive, welcoming environment for learning.

- **Facilitation:** The ability to shape and guide a discussion among groups of people; reinforcement through positive association; supporting people to create and make themselves; creating space for self-reflection and self-discovery.

- **Scaffolding:** The ability to break down learning material into digestible chunks relating to how much people already know.

- **Managing Groups:** Managing power dynamics in a group including controversy and emotional or "hot" moments—that is, topics that provoke emotional reactions among group members.

- **Attention on new material**: People learn better when they focus on something new.

- **Generation**: Learners create their own connections to knowledge they already possess.

- **Emotion**: Positive emotion inspires and motivates people to learn.

- **Spacing**: Having the space and time to reflect—including sleep, which is proven to help people retain new skills.

This means that the skills for museum educators should not only include familiarity with the subject matter and the museum exhibits, but also (and crucially) skills in "teaching" for the twenty-first century. Museum educators should be able to connect and refer people to various museum resources that relate to their interests, as well as to online sources, and other (partner) organizations where visitors may also like to go on their "learning journey." As mentors, museum educators can introduce learners to new pathways and resources, and inspire them to continue learning in and outside of the museum.

5. PEOPLE LEARN WITHIN A NETWORK.

The digital age is an age of connectivity because the Internet allows us to transcend geography, time, and place. In "real life" learning rarely happens only in one place—discovering new ideas, making and reinforcing connections, reflection, and creation happen in multiple places at multiple times, and can be facilitated by new technologies.

The connected learning approach identifies how optimal learning happens when three critical spheres of learning intersect—*academics* (most likely in formal learning environments such as schools and universities), a *learner's interests*, and *inspiring mentors and peers*—the latter two can take place at home, online, through social media, in popular culture, and within informal learning institutions such as museums, science centers, sports and community centers, clubs, and libraries. People learn naturally when they can learn about and participate in something they are interested in in all spheres of their life—not just in one particular space.

The sociotechnical interaction network (STIN)[14] is an approach that recognizes the relationship between people, technology, and practices, and acknowledges that the degree to which technology can facilitate learning is influenced not only by the affordances of the technology or the familiarity of people with that technology but also by local context, social influence, multiple roles and relationships of users, and other critical interactions within many learning networks.

Understanding each of the different and complementary nodes in the learning networks of museum visitors, how they engage with one another, and how they may change, helps museums to identify where they can most make a difference and how to forge meaningful and complementary partnerships with individuals and with other institutions. Museum educators planning a learning program may find it useful to map out the learning networks of potential participants in order to identify how to build on experiences and knowledges of their visitors as well as support learning to continue after the museum visit. This network can also guide the museum in identifying data collection points and methodologies that can be used in evaluation and dynamic assessment of the learning process (see the section on measuring learning below). On the left are nodes in a learning network, on the right are how an educator may identify which nodes are the most relevant for his or her context.

Measuring Learning

> *The learning that matters is the learning that is used. . . . What matters is "know-how"; "know-what" matters only insofar as it is mobilized in practice.*[15]

How to assess learning is an age-old challenge that educators know well. Documentation and assessment tools are continuously being reviewed, rejected, invented, and embraced. In informal learning environments, evaluating "success" when it comes to learning is even harder to do—since the impact of engaging with a museum or group of museums tends to have long-term contextual benefits rather than an instant pay-off, and museum educators often only get to engage with learners during one school visit. Nevertheless having "good enough" evaluation mechanisms in place at the outset has a number of benefits: (1) they help museums know whether their learning strategy is indeed making any kind of impact, especially the kind they intend (increasingly a requirement from funders); (2) they support "teachers" (whether museum educators, school teachers, or event front-of-house staff—see below) to adapt and amend their programs and their behavior to better respond to diverse learners, as the program takes place; and

> **KEY TERMS**
>
> **LEARNING ANALYTICS**
>
> Learning analytics is "an educational application of web analytics aimed at learner profiling, a process of gathering and analyzing details of individual student interactions in online learning activities."[1]
>
> ---
>
> [1] L. Johnson, S. Beck Adams, M. Cummins, V. Estrada, A. Freeman and C. Hall, *NMC Horizon Report: 2016 Higher Education Edition* (Austin, TX: The New Media Consortium, 2016), 38.
>
> **ADAPTIVE LEARNING**
>
> "Adaptive learning is when teachers are able to adapt the presentation of material in response to student performance. It can be embedded into a computer-based and/or online educational system that captures fine-grained data and use learning analytics to enable human tailoring of responses."[1]
>
> ---
>
> [1] "Adaptive Learning," Dreambox Learning, accessed September 23, 2016. http://www.dreambox.com/adaptive-learning.

(3) they can help individual or group learners reflect on their own progress as they move through their learning journeys. Research techniques drawn from ethnography that emphasize immersive rather than intrusive evaluation methods are more adapted to evaluating informal and continuous learning. Software programs that provide nascent **learning analytics** and **educational data mining** can help by enabling collection, analysis, and comparison of quantitative and qualitative data[16] to be used in **adaptive learning**.

In chapter 3, Rob Stein emphasizes the importance of measuring what matters. A museum's strategic goals for learning (or in general) are a good basis for evaluation frameworks and, when it comes to data collection, in identifying key performance indicators. Museum learning aims to support participation and engagement, build skills and literacy, and provide opportunities for doing and making in the context of learners' own lives, and that exists within a network and needs to be evaluated on those terms and not on the ability of students to regurgitate facts based on one visit—although a certain amount of content knowledge should be expected. Ideally learning outcomes in informal learning environments should be based on social, emotional, and developmental outcomes; should recognize group learning as well as individual learning; and should accommodate a range of engagements—an hour visit, several repeat visits, or participation over years.[17] A form of **longitudinal design** can be explored to capture individual and group processes of improvement throughout various activities and pathways during a single visit, repeat visitation, and program participation and so on.

Outcomes need to be accompanied by measures (the assessment tools) and key performance indicators—benchmarks used to assess whether or not an outcome has been achieved.

New outcomes require new measures of assessment. Museums traditionally use surveys, focus groups, and in some cases participant observation to evaluate their learning programs. Often these are done as formative (during the planning stages) or summative (at the end of the project) evaluations, which leave little room for improvement during a program, or for learners themselves to be kept abreast of their own progress. However, as visitors leave a growing digital footprint in museums, through their interaction with multimedia interactive exhibits, mobile apps, websites, digital memberships and social media, museums have a greater ability to collect and analyze a large amount of visitor data. Tracking, video documentation and observation, rapid prototyping, **embedded assessment** in learning games and learning analytics are all ways that museums can find out about the context, skills, motivation, and behavior of learners (learning profiles) while the activity takes place. These forms of "stealth assessment,"[18] where teachers can observe hard-to-measure learning such as perseverance, critical thinking, making connections, and such without making students stop for a test can support the development of a learning profile and provide ongoing data about a learner's progress in order to be able to make adjustments while the activity is going on. Adaptive learning acts on **actionable data**, such as a learner's previous and current learning, time spent reading, self-assessment, and others to create a personalized journey through content. With such data, teachers can recommend where to start new content, when to review old content, how to monitor one's progress and additional resources to support mastery of difficult content.[19]

These forms of research, however, raise many ethical concerns around privacy. Museums need to have clear, accessible policies and codes of conduct regarding data collection, ensuring that visitors give informed consent before such methods are used. It is a best practice to make data collection and analysis anonymous where possible. One way to do so is to make data gathering transparent to the participant by enabling them to review data collected about them at the same time as the museum via a personalized dashboard—where individuals themselves can also see this data visualized. For example, Gooru (www.gooru.org) is a digital learning navigator that brings together assessment and analytics in order to provide real-time data to learners and teachers on their progress toward achieving their goals.

Learning profiles can start with gathering basic data about the individual or group. This is done in the same way as one would collect visitor data, but in addition to certain demographic data (e.g., age, education level, gender) one can also ask individuals to answer questions relating to their preferred ways of engagement, their learning network, interests,

> **KEY TERMS**
>
> **EDUCATIONAL DATA MINING**
>
> "Educational Data Mining is an emerging discipline, concerned with developing methods for exploring the unique and increasingly large-scale data that come from educational settings, and using those methods to better understand students, and the settings which they learn in."[1]
>
> [1] "Educational Data Mining, International Educational Data Mining Society, accessed September 23, 2016. http://www.educationaldatamining.org/.
>
> **LONGITUDINAL DESIGN**
>
> A longitudinal design is a research study involving repeated observations of a group of people over long periods of time. They allow researchers to tell the difference between short- and long-term reactions and actions, and can be used to compare the same people at different ages or life stages.

> **KEY TERMS**
>
> **LEARNING PROFILE**
>
> "A learning profile is the complete picture of [a student's] learning preferences, strengths, and challenges and can be shaped by categories of learning style, intelligence preference, culture, and gender."[1] Learning profiles can be developed through gathering data of students who engage in digital learning.
>
> ---
>
> [1] "What Is the Best Way to Identify and Address All of My Students' Learning Profiles?" *EL Education*, accessed September 23, 2016, http://plp.eleducation.org/learning-profile/.

and perceived strengths and weaknesses.[20] Learning profiles are then further elaborated by collecting and analyzing data resulting from participation in an activity at the museum.

Tracking is enabled when visitors use mobile devices equipped with location-based technology during their museum visit. Through these devices, museums can collect data relating to the length of stay at a particular exhibit, as well as visitor pathways through the museum. When this is accompanied by observation and data from a learner's profile, museum staff can draw conclusions on what areas are more engaging to different learning categories. In addition to spatial tracking, learning games, commonly played in exhibition interactives or on mobile devices, can also be designed with embedded assessment. This can include games in which learners must demonstrate proficiency on one level in order to move to another level, or, in its more high-tech manifestation—programs with intuitive algorithms and machine learning software that adapt automatically to the learner's performance.[21]

Video documentation is an ethnographic qualitative research method in which visitors are videoed doing an activity in a natural setting and their actions and behavior are analyzed and contemplated (often with participants). This can also be used in experience design, explored by Marco Mason in chapter 12.

In chapters 3 and 5, Stein and Moffat explore the use of data analytics in museums. One interesting development in higher education is the use of learning analytics[22]—a form of tailored analytics that draws from data wherever digital technologies are deployed in the learning process.[23] In addition to tracking visitor movement throughout a website or on social media, digital tools may be programmed to collect data related to "learning conversations" and "reflection," as summarized by Shum and Ferguson in figure 6.4.[24] Here one can see how adapting traditional Google analytics into learning analytics requires the collection of data linked to an individual's learning profile within a learning network and providing visualizations and recommendations based on this profile and activities rather than on navigation or ratings.

Museums as a Learning Resource

In addition to being a place of inspiration and a platform to acquire and practice new skills and new relationships, museums are a repository of knowledge in all forms.

Sometimes this knowledge requires a visit and/or a museum learning program to unlock; at other times, it is activated as a learning object that forms part of a school project, for example, or it is digitized and available on the web to be discovered by an online browser or visitor. A learning object is a relatively small, mostly digital "chunk" of content that can be reused and repurposed a number of times in different learning contexts. Learning objects can be stored in a database, and searched for on websites, and they can be described using **metadata**.[25]

Below we describe a range of museum-led learning activities. We also explain how museums can ensure their content is "fit for purpose" as learning objects that are universally accessible.

Museum-Led Activities and Projects

New technologies are continuously enhancing museum-led learning activities and projects. Educators and digital designers are combining their respective insights into pedagogy, teaching, human-computer interaction and technology in order to find new ways for people to connect, remember, and use aspects of their museum visit or series of visits. In chapter 7, "New Frontiers in the Visitor Experience," Lisa Wright describes many of the new technology-led developments in the visitor experience. These are equally appropriate for learning objectives (if designed and evaluated with learning in mind), as they are for all aspects of visitor engagement. Those that are particularly useful as a learning activity tend to fall into seven categories:

1. INTERACTIVE MULTIMEDIA EXHIBITS

Interactive exhibits enable people to choose aspects of multimedia content they want to explore and support **embodied learning**—the idea that bodily actions such as drawing on a screen or larger-scaled physical movements result in longer-lasting memory and better knowledge retention. Simple technologies that enable people to

KEY TERMS

ACTIONABLE DATA

The term *actionable data* is used in program evaluation, business analytics, marketing, and other areas of research. Simply put, actionable data is information that can be viewed, interpreted, and acted upon. This is contrasted with data that is not actionable because of one of many possible reasons, such as it was collected poorly, doesn't answer the question it was set out to answer, or was not used due to lack of stakeholder interest.

METADATA

Metadata is data that gives information about other data. *Descriptive metadata* is information to help discover and identify a resource. *Structural metadata* describes the different parts of a resource (for example, title or abstract). *Administrative metadata* provides the information that helps to manage a resource, such as when and how it was created. There are a variety of metadata schemes and element sets that define what metadata should be included for different types of resources, these vary by discipline and environments.

> **KEY TERMS**
>
> **EMBEDDED ASSESSMENT**
>
> "Embedded assessment is when an assessment of a student's competencies and progress is tracked during the learning process. This kind of assessment gives both teachers and students data in real time, which can be used to gauge and further support learning. These assessments are also so well integrated into the flow of learning that oftentimes students do not even notice they are being assessed. Embedded assessments are different from typical assessments, such as quizzes, tests, and reports, because typical assessments focus mainly on what students know, whereas embedded assessments allow for teachers to gauge what students know and how students use the knowledge in action."[1]
>
> ---
>
> [1] Eliza Spang, "Embedded Assessment at Quest to Learn," Institute of Play, January 23, 2012, accessed September 23, 2016. http://www.instituteofplay.org/2012/01/embedded-assessment-at-quest-to-learn/.

manipulate digital information with their fingers (e.g., rotating shapes on screen, setting objects in motion, curating a digital exhibition) or new developments in wearable technologies, motion-capture, or immersive experiences enable museum visitors to learn and remember through their bodies as well as their minds.

2. CONTENT RESOURCES

Museums provide content as learning resources to be downloaded or viewed by learners. This can include videos, podcasts, digitized collections, and others. Some museums are developing whole curricula for integration into the classroom. For example, the Henry Ford Museum has developed a digital curriculum, *Innovation 101*, to support developing innovation and entrepreneurship skills.

3. TOURS

Tours guide visitors around the physical or virtual museum. Face-to-face contact with a museum guide is often the most powerful form of a museum tour—particularly when tour guides are trained in facilitation and dialogic listening. Effective tours for learning include prompts to encourage self-discovery (for example, *Look closely at the painting. What do you notice about the brush strokes?*), questioning (*What would you do if you were president?*), reflection (*Why did you draw a circle? What do you think that says about you?*) and interactivity via practice and feedback (e.g., *If this woolly mammoth could talk, what would you ask him about the Ice Age? Can you draw a face in the style of this artist?*). Tours given via a mobile device can further support learning by enabling personalization, multiple language options, accessibility provisions for people with disabilities, options for various age or education levels, and so on. Tours enhanced by digital technology include audio tours, multimedia tours, live video tours on social media, virtual reality/augmented reality tours, robot-led tours. Most tours—in the museum, in the physical world or in a virtual

MUSEUM LEARNING IN THE DIGITAL AGE

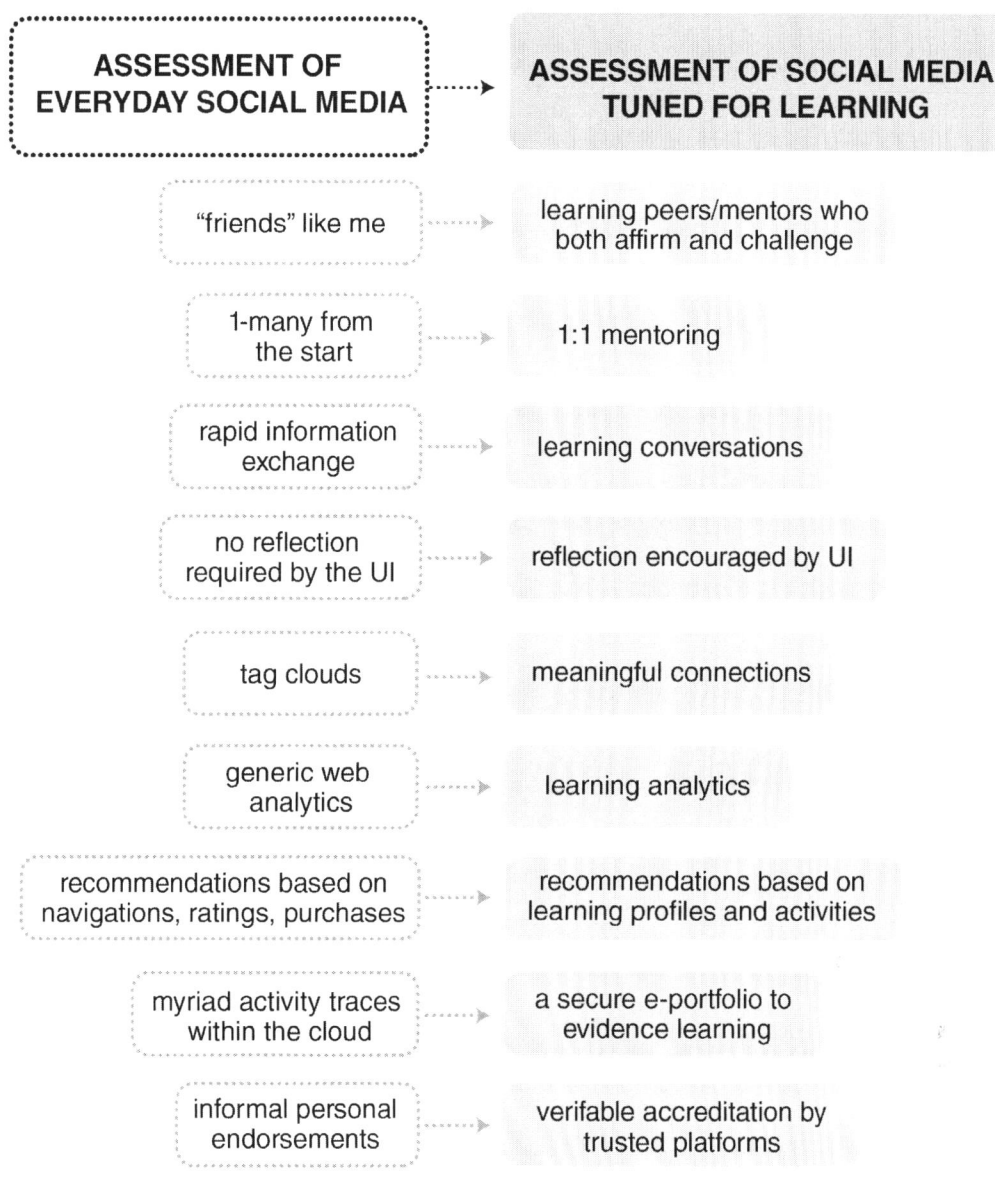

FIGURE 6.4 Evaluating Social Media for Learning.
Lord Cultural Resources

world—support context-based learning in which students can evaluate and practice skills in a real context and compare activities across multiple contexts. It helps students learn from the world around them, see how general principles in science and society relate to everyday lives and appreciate how learning is a continuous, enjoyable adventure.

4. TEACHER/FAMILY/FACILITATOR GUIDES

Downloadable teacher or facilitator guides are a mainstay of museum education. These can be personalized by curriculum, outcome, grade level, discipline and so on. Different technologies can help the facilitator to guide learners at different points in the visit. For example, the Children's Museum of Houston's "More CMH" app provides parents with tools so they can help to engage their children with the museum exhibits.[26] The Franklin Institute provides a downloadable trip planner[27] that gives teachers an overview of exhibits and a recommended itinerary depending on grade level and subject.

5. ACTIVITY WORKSHEETS/TREASURE HUNTS

These continue to be simple and effective ways to encourage groups and individuals to discover the museum. The best worksheets and treasure hunts involve people having to figure out something on their own, with a reward when they do so. Location-based technologies, gaming features such as goals, rewards and rules, and multimedia and interactivity all serve to enhance the traditional paper worksheet. For example, at the Science Museum in London, the InfoAge+ app provides students with four creative challenges to help them find out more about communication technologies during a visit to the Information Age gallery. In the "Newsflash, " you find a news story in the gallery that will please your demanding editor, and create a video report about it. In "My Timeline," you put yourself into a two-hundred-year-plus timeline of incredible stories about information technologies and add your own objects.[28]

6. GAMES

A variety of apps and games are used to create new visitor-centric connections between the museum exhibits, collections and spaces, and visitors. Apps and games can also introduce an element of fun, competition, and/or serendipity into a visit, making it more interesting and engaging. Incidental learning can happen in games that set challenges and offer rewards, as well as provide opportunities for learners to understand rules, reflect on the motives and actions of game characters, and develop strategy.[29] Some, such as citizen science apps, support people collecting data and feeding it into real research projects.

7. PROJECTS

Projects are more in-depth activities, often done over repeat visits or at home or at school, in which visitors design and make something themselves in the museum's maker spaces, labs, or studios. Projects support group learning, and skill development as discussed above. Projects also provide opportunities for dynamic assessment whereby facilitators and learners can track their progress, reflect on it, and adjust their actions accordingly.

8. (E-) COURSES

Museums are increasingly offering specific courses—on-site, online, and in combination of both (blended learning). Online courses can be given by the museum or developed as a module for e-learning on another platform. Massive open online courses (MOOCs) are free, accessible online courses based on learning through peer conversation and social networking.

Incomer-Led Learning

Many studies have shown that people regard museums as an extremely trusted source of content,[30] and curators are lauded for their ability to generate new knowledge out of existing collections or ideas. It stands to reason, therefore, that *all* museum content represents a largely untapped resource that is potentially valuable to educators and learners, not only as part of a museum visit but also independently from it. Constructionist and constructivist learning approaches posit that learners who create learn more effectively. Digital technology can help make museum resources accessible to museum "incomers"—that is, educators who are not part of the museum staff but who wish to make use of museum learning resources in the classroom, to support adult learning courses, in personal projects and so on.

Typically a museum's exhibition is considered its primary resource for learning. In an exhibition, different communication tools—interactives, artifacts, graphics, videos, installations—are brought together to form a specific experience, defined by a curator and an exhibition designer. But that exhibition can also be deconstructed into discrete digital "learning objects" made up of collection images and metadata, archival material, videos, graphics, images, and text to be repurposed for learning according to different objectives in different environments. In chapter 9, Corey Timpson writes about the way in which the Canadian Museum for Human Rights created an enterprise content management system—premised on the separation of content from presentation—in which each digital asset (such as an image, video, piece of text, audio file) of the museum is

> **KEY TERMS**
>
> **SEARCH ENGINE OPTIMIZATION**
>
> Search engine optimization (SEO) is the process through which websites maximize their number of visitors in order to ensure that the site appears high on the list of results returned by a search engine. Title tag and meta description, URL normalization, using canonical link elements, 301 redirects, and cross-linking are all ways that content can be tailored to optimize results from search engines.

stored in the system in standard-compliant formats at as high a quality as possible. These digital assets can be equally seen as learning objects—waiting to be unlocked, repurposed and used by others within and without the museum.

Below are seven ways museums can unlock their content for learning even if other people are in charge of the teaching.

1. DISCOVERY (SEARCH)

Helping people to access the content they seek efficiently and easily through search, digital maps, physical signs, on a mobile device, or on a museum's website is an important functionality for learning. For example, a digital museum plan that is searchable by content areas and themes (or even skills to practice), and not just room names, helps learners to find and go directly to content that interests them—supporting the important self-directed nature of learning and paving the way for a personalized learning experience.[31]

One can assume that a learner searching online is using a search engine such as Google rather than going to the museum website. In this instance, a museum's digital content is competing with thousands of other resources on the Web. **Search engine optimization** (SEO) uses a combination of meta-tagging, **reciprocal links**, and clever naming in order to help content appear in relevant results. If digital content is tagged with a particular *description tag* (155-character-long description embedded within the HTML code of a particular page) and *title tag*, it will help that content show up in a search.

Over the years many museums have explored different forms of **tagging** in an effort to bridge the gap between the words used by museum professionals to identify something versus the terms that people use to search. New developments in semantic web have improved search functions so they draw from all the museum's sources of digital content—collections, exhibitions, publications, programs and activities, articles and blogs and so on in order to provide tailored results to people who engage with the museum. Keywords can include tags with "learning objectives" such as skills or outcomes or grade level to facilitate use as learning objects.

Museums are also joining linked open-data projects[32] in which museums follow certain standards[33] to structure their data in order to make it accessible (often for free) to other websites. This makes it easier for museums to refer people not only to their own assets but also assets in other locations.

2. PERSONALIZATION (PUSH)

Personalization enables a museum to cater to individual learning motivations and preferences as well as connect or refer visitors to other resources and content sources within or outside of the museum. Personalization enables museums to push recommendations to visitors, exposing them to new content and perspectives rather than relying on them to search for it themselves according to their own ideas. Location-based technology is now able to quite accurately assess someone's exact location, using GPS satellites or WiFi hotspots or iBeacons for indoor positioning (where GPS often doesn't work) in order to direct a visitor from where they are to where they want to go. This same technology can also make recommendations to visitors based on preferences they may have entered previously or based on the length of their stay in front of a particular exhibit. However, with the benefits of data-driven personalization come concerns over privacy.

For optimal learning, museums need to support self-directed discovery (through search and push) as well as provide personalized guidance and/or **scaffolding** for visitors. Scaffolding can be done by a skilled facilitator as well as through embedded assessment within interactives (see above).

Personalization for teachers on a museum's website may also include downloadable teacher guides linked to specific curriculum areas and levels, examples for ways to use museum resources in the classroom or teacher tours that are recommended for specific content areas or learning objectives. It may mean tagging online learning objects with levels and subject areas (depending on teacher priorities) so that they can be easily found and adapted. With the advent of the Internet of Things—it may be possible to tag collection items or physical learning objects with similar keywords that can be easily found during a museum visit.

New technologies, such as digital text panels, or text on digital paper[34]—enables text panels and object labels to be

KEY TERMS

RECIPROCAL LINKS

Reciprocal links are mutual links between two objects. Commonly these are links between two websites in order to ensure mutual traffic. Often established using reciprocal link exchange directories this practice can help achieve higher rankings in search engine optimization, and is one type of cross linking used in SEO.

TAGGING

Tagging refers to the practice of assigning nonhierarchical keywords or terms to a piece of information. This kind of metadata helps to describe an item and assists with browsing and searching. Tagging was popularized by websites associated with Web 2.0.

SCAFFOLDING

Scaffolding is a teaching strategy whereby facilitators provide successive level of support that help people reach increasing levels of comprehension and skill. These supports are then removed as students become autonomous.

updated and managed in real time via a special CMS platform—so that information can be updated or adapted to a specific time of year for example or in response to current events.

3. ACCESS

Accessibility is similar to discoverability but also speaks to the way in which people are able to receive museum content. When considering technology, accessibility refers to whether or not digital content is optimized for mobile, that is, whether people can access the same content in the same or similar way, whether they are on a desktop computer, a tablet, or a smartphone. Accessibility considerations include whether a digital experience is available on a visitor's own device or if they have to rent or borrow it from the institution. Other factors include interface design and availability of free WiFi to assure coverage and minimize data charges from cellular networks.

Accessibility also refers to whether or not content is optimized for people with disabilities. Universal design is the term used to make sure that everyone has access to digital content. Individuals may use their own specialized software and hardware, called assistive technology, to operate software products—e.g., a screen reader program with a speech synthesizer for someone who is blind. Museums can ensure that their software and media supports the use of assistive technologies, but also seek to maximize accessibility even without it (See the sidebar on Technologies to Support Universal Access).

4. SHARING

Museum content that can be shared easily through social media platforms and other sites can be put to better use. Sharing includes not only the technical functionality to encourage sharing, but also an invitation to people to share and comment or blog about a particular topic. Blogs and social media are important fora for professional development and continuous learning among museum professionals.

5. RETRIEVABILITY

Learners should be able to discover content and return to it when needed. In order for content to be used independently, it needs to be separable from its museum context; for example, through download, bookmarking, or some other means of retrieval. In a physical museum, this means that people can "take" or "save" museum text or images to be used in another context. People already do this, whether they are allowed or not, through taking photos with their smartphones, however, museums can make this process easier by enabling content to be retrieved and manipulated (see annotation and adaptability below). This action is supported by the use of scanners or markers. Other museums have used QR codes, but uptake on QR codes is uneven. Used widely in Asia, they are less popular in the rest of the world. Online portals such as Google Art Project enable browsers to save images into collections that can be retrieved at a later date.

6. ANNOTATION

Visitors need to be able to adapt content to their own purposes.[35] At the very least, this means teachers should be able to annotate a learning object to guide students, and students should be able to annotate it with their own thoughts, questions, and emphasis during the museum visit or at any point afterward. They should also be able to share annotations with teachers or each other. There are a number of social software tools for screen annotation that can be used in museum media.

7. ADAPTABILITY OR APPROPRIATION

Appropriation is a crucial next step—enabling learners to take museum content and use it for their own purposes. Museums may balk at adaptation and appropriation because of concerns about copyright or attribution, but many museums are choosing to make their content and metadata **open source**, with high-resolution image files, text files, or even audio and video files that can be easily cut and pasted,

TECHNOLOGIES TO SUPPORT UNIVERSAL ACCESS

These are some ways that a museum can ensure its experiences are universally accessible.

a. *Language*: In a multilingual environment, translation options are a basic way to ensure accessibility for all. Easy-to-read language ensures that language is accessible for people with intellectual disabilities.

b. *Size of text*: Options to increase the size of text is helpful for people with visual impairments.

c. *Captioning video*: Text is present on the screen at all times (open captioning) or providing text that can be read with a specific decoder (closed captioning) to support people who are hearing impaired.

d. *Transcriptions*: Word-for-word translation of audio content into a text file—it can also be made available to accompany audio content.

e. *Audio Description (or Visual Description)*: Audio of a specially trained person reading title names and describing visual information is added to a video soundtrack when there are pauses. This can include a talking menu on a website or DVD.

f. *Touch tours*: Providing Braille and three-dimensional representations of museum exhibits enables touch tours for people with visual impairments. These can also be exciting ways of learning for all visitors.

g. *Assistive technology to operate software products*: For example, a screen reader program with a speech synthesizer.

> **KEY TERMS**
>
> **OPEN SOURCE**
>
> A software application whose source code is available for download, review and modification by anyone.

translated, or edited. Digital watermarks now enable attribution to be embedded into digital content.

An extension of the principle of adaptability are maker spaces and projects. Museums increasingly provide resources such as equipment and supplies for people to make and tinker with content.

Teaching with Museums

To teach is to model and demonstrate, to learn is to practice and reflect.[36]

In theory everyone in the museum is focused on maximizing learning. In practice this job falls to the educators on site and sometimes to digital officers online. In chapter 13, we see how the digital age is transforming the organizational structures of museums—creating departments that are increasingly in charge of visitor engagement and whose focus, ideally, is on ensuring visitors have an enriching experience from the museum. The challenge in such a structure is for the essential competencies of both educators and technologists to come together to enhance both the digital and learning outputs of the museum in the most resource-effective way.

Museum teaching is not just for the on-site, online, or off-site visitor. Museums share their learnings internally and with other museum and education professionals locally and internationally through professional networks maintained through conferences, publications, and social media. Given the speed with which new technologies arise and die, this form of ongoing professional learning is an important way for museums to be continuously updating and experimenting with teaching and learning.

Teaching Networks

Just as we can map a learning network for insight into the connections and processes involved in a learner's journey to understanding, we can also map a teaching network to understand how different roles within and outside the museum can work together for more effective teaching. A teaching network can help us identify who needs to work together to support learning, and it can identify key points for evaluation and intervention.

The teaching network could include the following positions and functions with respect to learning:

- **Head of department:** Responsible for learning strategy and planning—and resource allocation.

- **Schools manager:** Manages relationships with schools and teachers and makes links with the school curriculum and calendar.

- **Adult learning:** Provides adult learning opportunities such as courses and seminars.

- **Digital engagement:** Typically in charge of social media, and online programs. May also be in charge of online dissemination of internal learnings of the museum—whether through blogs or tweets.

- **Public programs:** Responsible for engaging people through a range of on-site and online activities.

- **Audience evaluation:** Undertakes ongoing evaluation of museum programs and manages analytics for online programs.

- **Front-of-house staff:** Engage directly with visitors—whether as docents in galleries, security, or selling tickets.

- **Partnerships:** Responsible for identifying and maintaining partnerships, including with schools, departments of education, or other informal learning institutions.

- **Documentation and publications:** Responsible for gathering, filtering, and processing data for publication. Produces newsletters, video, catalogs. Typically in charge of ensuring usage rights for images, which is important for use in appropriation, remixing, and reuse contexts. Also responsible for gathering information supplied by each of the museum's departments to input into connected databases and content management systems.

- **Exhibition designers:** Design exhibitions, sometimes external provider.

- **Curators:** Research content and organize exhibitions.

- **Conservators and/or registrar:** Responsible for taking care of, documenting, digitizing and moving the collection.

- **Partners:** Includes schools, colleges, and universities; community organizations; other museums, libraries, and archives; digital platforms (social media, search engines) and others. Having partners can help to support learning in different spheres of an individual's life.

- **Fundraising:** Connect museum programs and strategy to fund priorities and interests.

- **Marketing:** Promoting the museum through advertising or public engagement.

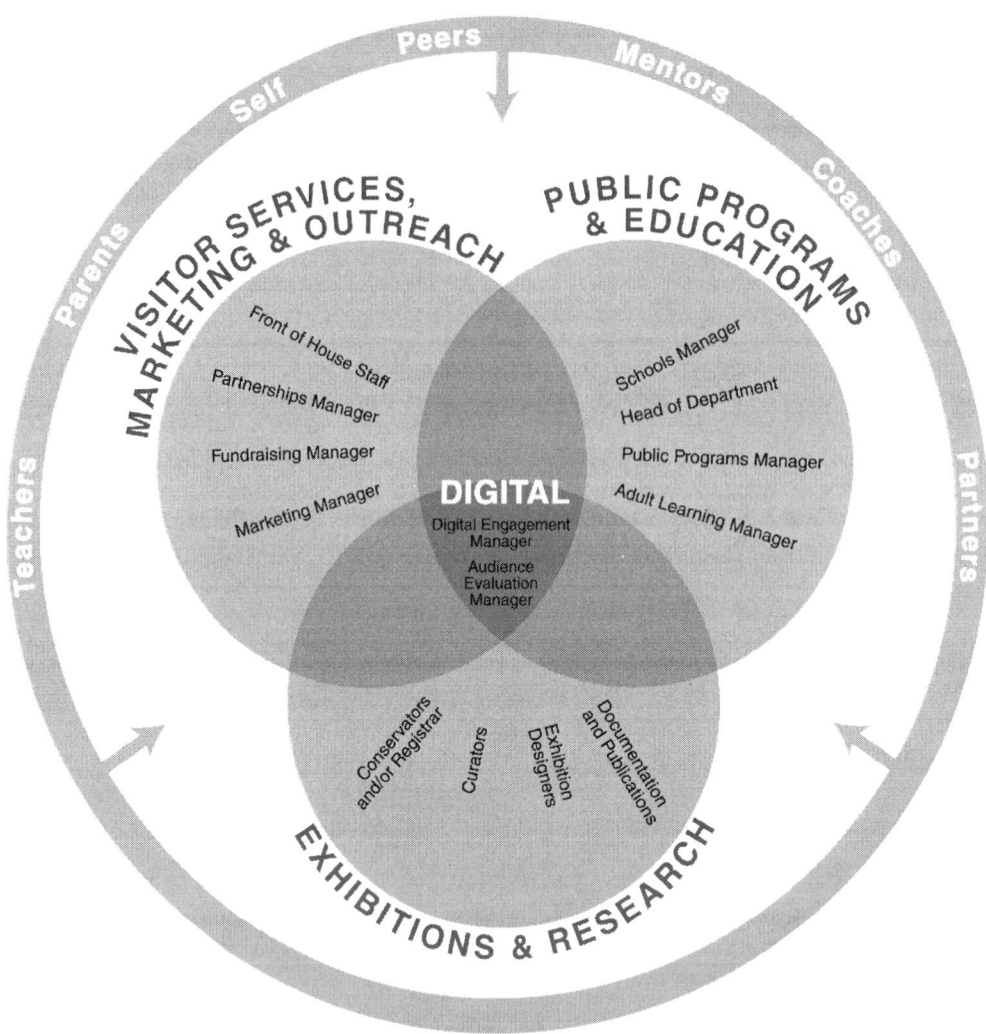

FIGURE 6.5 Teaching Network: A range of people inside the museum or external to the museum can be seen within the museum's teaching networks, and planning should take their roles into account.
Lord Cultural Resources

Once a museum has identified who is in the teaching network, these individuals should work together to plan, design, and implement the institution's learning strategy. Each node in the network has a specific role to play in a particular project, and mapping these nodes in relation to one another helps to make this clear.

Mapping Learning Networks

Museum educators who are planning a learning program may find it useful to map learning networks of potential participants. This network can guide the museum in identifying data collection points and methodologies for evaluation and dynamic assessment of the learning process—as examined in the section "Measuring Learning." Consider the following:

Learner

- Individual, small group (family/peer) or big group (school)?
- Is his/her/their museum experience mediated by teacher/parent/host?
- Does he/she understand the language of exhibits or of the program?
- Does he/she have any disabilities that may prevent him/her from enjoying the full experience?
- Are there other identity considerations (gender, race, newcomer, etc.) that may impact on how he/she experiences the content?
- Does he/she take part in informal activities that may be related to the museum (for example, sports team, club, community center), or is he/she doing a related internship or volunteering?
  - What social networks does he/she use?
  - Other?

Facilitator (This is particularly important if the facilitator in this instance is a volunteer or someone outside of the education department, or a host or teacher external to the museum.)

- Is he/she trained in facilitation?
- Is he/she trained in managing (school) groups?
- Does he/she have subject matter expertise?
- Is he/she familiar with museum learning?
- Does he/she speak the languages of the learner(s) and or museum?
- Other?

Exhibit

- Are there clear key messages and communication objectives?
- What literacies are involved in interpretation/understanding?
- Are there opportunities for interactivity and participation?
  - How accessible is the text? (The rule of thumb is that if all text is written to be comprehensible for a twelve-year-old it will likely be comprehensible for most members of the public.)
  - Can learners retrieve, annotate, and appropriate exhibit content?

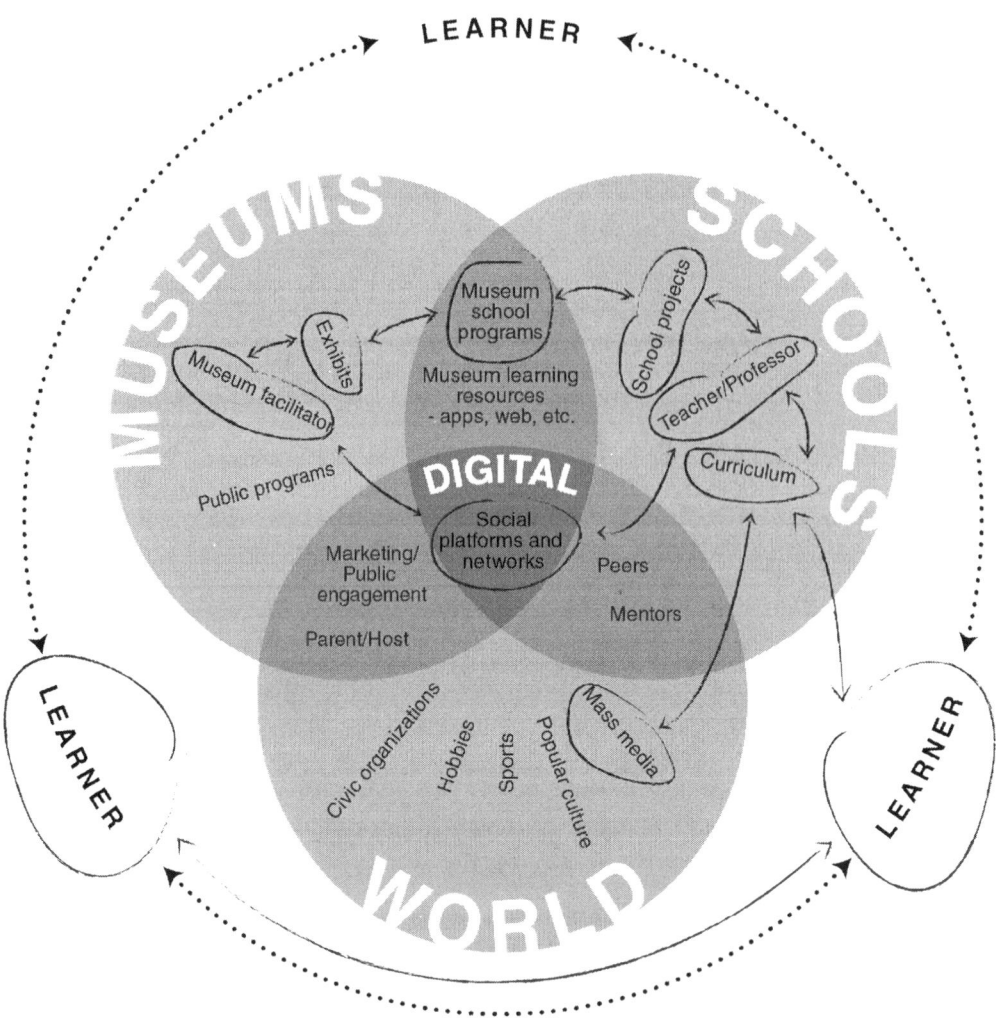

Learning theme/subject	*French Revolution*
Learning outcomes (skills and knowledge)	*Understand roots of democracy* *Skills in critical thinking, collective intelligence and empathy*

FIGURE 6.6 A Learning Network.
Lord Cultural Resources

Public/Schools Program

- Is there an opportunity to create?
- Which skills does it support?
- Repeat or one-off?
- Is it aligned to curriculum or educational approach with specific mechanisms for assessment? If different, how and what are they learning at school? What assessment matters?
- Is the teacher on the visit?
- Are there clear outcomes?

Marketing and Public Engagement

- How did the learner, teacher, or host hear about the museum?
- What messages are communicated about the value of the museum in this material?
- Are there opportunities to rate, follow up on the visit?

Learning Resources

- What learning resources are provided for independent learners in programs (apps, worksheets, reference material, etc.)?
- How do learners/teacher/host access museum learning resources during and after the visit (paper, online etc.)?
- Can learning resources be discovered, downloaded, annotated, remixed?

Mentors and Peers

- Do learners share this experience/interest with peers?
- Do learners have access to mentors such as older siblings, coaches, friends, friends' parents, or teachers?

Access to Computers/Mobile and Online Content

- Do the learners have access to computer, tablet, or smartphone? How often?
- Are there firewalls that may be blocking access/downloads of learning content?
- Are learners familiar with a particular software/interface? (PC, Mac, iPhone, etc.?)
- What are the most common ways learners find content online?
- What search engines do they use?

Conclusion

Developing and implementing a learning strategy for the Digital Age requires both an insight into the processes of learning and an understanding of the museum and community resources that can be made accessible to support that learning. Technologies are evolving that can help make delivering learning easier and more effective. However, these need to be selected carefully. Museums that prioritize learning outcomes at the outset can ensure that the technologies they select provide for the collection of data that measure behavior related to specific learning indicators as outlined above and can feed assessments back into the learning process.

💡 KEY TAKEAWAYS: LEARNING IN THE DIGITAL AGE

1. New pedagogies for the digital age focus on a number of key principles:
   - The goal of learning is to enable equitable participation and engagement.
   - Focus on skills and literacy rather than knowledge transfer.
   - People learn by focusing, doing and reflecting.
   - Teachers as facilitators for self-directed learning rather than the "sage on a stage."
   - People learn within a network.
2. Mapping teaching and learning networks helps museums to plan different tools and mechanisms for learning, where and how evaluation should take place, as well as to recognize the role many different people play within a learning ecosystem.
3. Learning objectives should be part of the key performance indicators of a museum.
4. Learning can be evaluated during the visit through learning analytics, tracking, video documentation and observation, rapid prototyping, and embedded assessment in learning games.
5. Museums are a learning resource for museum educators as well as visitors such as teachers, parents, and others who wish to use museum content for their own purposes.
6. Common museum-led digital activities and projects for learning include:
   - Interactive multimedia exhibits
   - Content resources
   - Tours

- Teacher/family/facilitator guides
- Activity worksheets/treasure hunts
- Games
- Projects

7. Museums can optimize their content for learning through enabling
   - Discovery (Search)
   - Personalization (Push)
   - Access
   - Sharing
   - Retrieval
   - Annotation
   - Adaptability or appropriation

Notes

1. John Falk, *Identity and the Museum Visitor Experience* (Walnut Creek, CA: Left Coast Press, 2009), 34–36.

2. "Connected Learning Principles," Connected Learning, accessed September 9, 2016, http://connectedlearning.tv/connected-learning-principles.

3. Ibid.

4. Bill Penuel et al., *Connected Learning: An Agenda for Research and Design* (Irvine, CA: Digital Media and Learning Research Hub, 2013), p. 4.

5. "Connected Learning Principles."

6. Ngaire Blankenberg, "Learning for Change," in *The Manual of Museum Learning*, ed. Brad King and Barry Lord (Lanham, MD: Rowman & Littlefield, 2016), 29–52.

7. The New London Group, "A Pedagogy of Multiliteracies: Designing Social Futures," *Harvard Educational Review* 66, no. 1 (Spring 1996): 60–93.

8. Mihaly Csikszentmihalyi, *Flow: The Psychology of Optimal Experience* (New York: Harper & Row, 1990).

9. See the work of Jean Piaget and Lev Vygotsky.

10. "Learning Spaces," Tate, accessed September 16, 2016, http://www.tate.org.uk/about/projects/tate-modern-project/learning-spaces. For example, the Tate Modern's new wing includes integrated learning and gallery spaces and a dedicated research and hands-on learning facility. And "Discover Uppland with Biotopia," *Biotopia*, accessed September 16, 2016, http://www.biotopia.nu/besok-oss/in-english/. Biotopia has the biolab, which offers hands-on experiences.

11. "RijksStudio," *Rijksmuseum*, accessed September 20, 2016. https://www.rijksmuseum.nl/en/rijksstudio.

12. Lila Davachi, Tobias Kiefer, David Rock, and Lisa Rock, "Learning That Lasts through AGES," *NeuroLeadership Journal* 3 (2010); Josh Davis, Maite Balda, David Rock, Pail McGinniss, and Lila Davachi, "The Science of Making Learning Stick: An Update to the AGES Model," *NeuroLeadership Journal* 5 (2014).

13. Steve Walker and Linda Creanor, "The STIN in the Tale: A Socio-Technical Interaction Perspective on Networked Learning," *Educational Technology & Society* 12, no. 4 (2009): 307.

14. Jay Lemke, Robert Lecusay, Michael Cole, and Vera Michalchik, *Documenting and Assessing Learning in Informal and Media-Rich Environments* (Cambridge, MA: The MIT Press, 2015), p. 6.

15. Mike Sharples et al., *Innovating Pedagogy 2015: Open University Innovation Report 4* (Milton Keynes, UK: Open University, 2015). https://www.sri.com/sites/default/files/publications/innovating_pedagogy_2015.pdf. A good source of innovations in pedagogy and digital assessment.

16. Jay Lemke, Robert Lecusay, Michael Cole, and Vera Michalchik, *Documenting and Assessing Learning in Informal and Media-Rich Environments* (Cambridge, MA: The MIT Press, 2015), 91.

17. Niall Slater, Alice Peasgood, and Joel Mullan, "Learning Analytics in Higher Education: A Review of UK and International Practice," *Jisc*, April 19, 2016, accessed September 10, 2016. https://www.jisc.ac.uk/reports/learning-analytics-in-higher-education.

18. Mike Sharples et al., *Innovating Pedagogy 2015*. Open University Innovation Report 4.

19. John McCarthy, "Learning Profile Cards," *Opening Paths*, January 15, 2014, accessed September 10, 2016, http://openingpaths.org/blog/2014/01/learning-profile-cards/. Useful activity to develop Learning Profiles.

20. Amanda Opperman, "Embedded Assessment Upgrades Personized Learning for the 21st Century," *Association for Talent Development*, March 27, 2015, accessed September 10, 2016. https://www.td.org/Publications/Blogs/Science-of-Learning-Blog/2015/03/Embedded-Assessment-Upgrades-Personalized-Learning; DreamBox Learning Inc., *Intelligent Adaptive Learning: An Essential Element of 21st Century Teaching and Learning*, 2014. http://www2.dreambox.com/e/14872/lligent-adaptive-learning-21st/bd367/606617662.

21. For a good report on learning analytics in higher education: Niall Sclater, Alice Peasgood, Joel Mullan, *Learning Analytics in Higher Education, A Review of UK and International Practice*, JISC, April 2016, accessed October 4 2016, https://www.jisc.ac.uk/sites/default/files/learning-analytics-in-he-v3.pdf.

22. Data can potentially be captured from those systems to help understand student engagement from the increased use of virtual learning environments—a digital platform in which students view timetables and assessments, access course information and learning materials, interact with others, and submit assignments, combined with data about students—such as their prior qualifications, socioeconomic status, ethnic group, module selections and grades obtained to date, and data gathered from visits to the library.

23. Simon Buckingham Shum and Rebecca Ferguson, "Social Learning Analytics," *Educational Technology & Society* 15, no. 3 (2012).

24. "Learning Object," *EdutTech Wiki*, December 3, 2010, accessed September 19, 2016. http://edutechwiki.unige.ch/en/Learning_object.

25. The Children's Museum of Houston is part of the 21-Tech project, which explores how gallery facilitators can use personal mobile technologies (PMTs) in their work with visitors at primarily science museums. See http://www.21-tech.org/about-xcl/.

26. See https://www.fi.edu/sites/default/files/FieldTripPlanner_TFI_FieldTripPlanner_2016.pdf.

27. InfoAge+ app, accessed September 27, 2016, http://www.sciencemuseum.org.uk/educators/things-to-do/activitysheets-trails-apps/info-age-app.

28. Mike Sharples et al., *Innovating Pedagogy 2015*, Open University Innovation Report 4.

29. For example, "Interconnections: The IMLS National Study on the Use of Libraries, Museums and the Internet. See http://interconnectionsreport.org/.

30. For example, visitors can input key words into the search field of the web-based Victoria and Albert Museum's Digital Explorer Map (http://www.vam.ac.uk/digital/map/) on their mobile devices and be directed to where they can find related museum collections or exhibitions. Because it is linked to the V&A's collections API (applied programming interface, which contains metadata about the digitized collections) and therefore also provides information about the collection items, the experience is useful whether accessed from within the museum or outside the museum online.

31. For an example of Prado Museum: Javier Pantoja, Javier Docampo, Ana Martin, Ricardo Alonso Maturana, Carlos Navalon, "The New Prado Museum Website: A (Semantic) Challenge," *MW2016: Museums and the Web 2016*, January 28, 2016, accessed September 19, 2016, http://mw2016.museumsandtheweb.com/paper/the-new-prado-museum-website-a-semantic-challenge/.

32. "To publish in accordance with Linked Data Web principles, it is necessary to follow certain standards, including HTTP, OWL/RDF, and URIs, which are used not so much to serve as pages read by persons as to edit pages that can automatically interpret systems and thus share information with them." Ibid.

33. Ursa Priozic, "Using Electronic Paper for Museum Labels," *Museum Next*, August 26, 2016, accessed September 20, 2016, http://www.museumnext.com/conference/using-electronic-paper-museum-labels/.

34. According to research from the Smithsonian, educators have special needs when it comes to digital learning objects including that they can be adapted, annotated, saved, and appropriated. See Smithsonian Center for Education and Museum Studies Digital Learning Resources Project, volume 5, Final Report, October 2012, https://smithsonian-digital-learning.wikispaces.com/file/view/DLRP_Volume-5_Final-Report.pdf and the wikispaces from the same project: https://smithsonian-digital-learning.wikispaces.com/.

35. Stephen Downes, "What Connectivism Is," *Half an Hour* (blog), February 3, 2007, accessed September 19, 2016. http://halfanhour.blogspot.com.br/2007/02/what-connectivism-is.html.

New Frontiers in the Visitor Experience

Lisa Wright

The visitor experience in museum exhibitions is undergoing a fundamental shift with the emergence of new technologies and approaches to technology. Rather than separate experiences—that touchscreen, this listening station—new types of media allow for technology to be woven throughout the visitor experience and can continue to connect and inform visitors even after they leave the physical museum. This aligns with how most people use technology in their personal lives—not separate from their real lives but an ongoing and seamless part of it. Technology is inevitable in a museum; so how do museums use this to their advantage rather than resist it?

Museum exhibitions are not a place for visitors to walk through while staring at their phones, oblivious to their surroundings. The best technology-based exhibits facilitate experiences that are interactive, hands-on, and social. New forms of media are better able to facilitate "looking up" at objects and other displays, and "looking sideways"—encouraging families, friends, and strangers to learn together.

Digital experiences cannot be just about the technology. Technology changes so rapidly that museums that invest a lot of time and money in the actual hardware do so at the risk of becoming outdated quickly. Rather, investment in digital experiences needs to be on the content—the narratives that the museum wants to tell about its collection, its place, and its stories. Exhibitions are about storytelling, and today's museums have a wealth of tools at their disposal to help tell these stories and to ask their visitors to share their stories as well.

MOBILE APP EXAMPLES

The Rijksmuseum app lets visitors access additional information on the collection and building, share their perspectives, listen to 3D audio compositions, and play games as a family.

The Canadian Museum for Human Rights has an app that includes an audio tour, online ticketing capability, interactive map, and a visual "mood meter" that lets visitors share their feelings about the experience with the museum and other visitors.

Museums must design experiences to capture the visitor's imagination through creative use of digital media that blends the line between physical and digital without detracting from the experience of being present in the museum.

Exploring New Technologies

There are many exciting new digital technologies that can be incorporated into museum exhibitions today, each with their own set of benefits and challenges.

MOBILE APPLICATIONS

Mobile applications are software programs designed to run on mobile devices such as tablets and smartphones. The majority of visitors who visit exhibitions will carry a mobile device. Particularly if there is contact with ears or other parts of the face, most people express a strong desire to use their own device whenever possible. Consequently, a museum that adopts a BYOD (bring your own device) strategy may only need to have a few units on reserve to loan to visitors who do not.

Mobile apps can allow visitors to personalize their museum experience based on interest, learning preferences, and available time. It can also let them contribute reactions, thoughts, and content through social media and other platforms. Museums can use the app software or physical beacons and sensors in the exhibit to collect information on what visitors are interested in and details of their visit, and also make pre- and post-visit connections. These data can then be analyzed using software such as Google Analytics to inform future visitor-experience projects. Collection of visitor information can, however, have privacy issues, particularly if visitors do not know information is being collected. Another challenge is the amount of data required by mobile apps, especially for tourists who do not have a local data plan. Museums should ideally provide free public WiFi or a way to download the app before arriving. When developing apps the museum also needs to consider if it will be multiplatform (i.e., available on Apple and Android devices), which is ideal but can have higher development costs. The biggest challenge of mobile apps is designing the experience to be complementary to the physical museum exhibition to avoid visitors engaging solely with their devices rather than the objects and other visitors.

NEW FRONTIERS IN THE VISITOR EXPERIENCE

NATURAL USER INTERFACES AND WEARABLE TECHNOLOGY

Natural user interfaces and wearable technology aim to eliminate awareness of the hardware needed to access digital content. For example, instead of pressing buttons or handling a touchscreen in order to watch a video or play a game, a natural user interface could use voice activation, gesture, or eye-tracking technology to control the technology in a more intuitive way. Xbox Kinect, for example, lets players interact with its games through gestures and verbal commands rather than a controller. In a museum exhibition, this type of natural interaction allows visitors to focus on the content rather than the technology and can facilitate interactive and social experiences. Wearable technologies such as watches, glasses, and other accessories use biometric technologies to capture visitors' physical and emotional reactions to exhibits. These technologies have important accessibility potential for visitors with physical and mental disabilities. Challenges surrounding these technologies include security and safety, as well as privacy and ethical concerns.

> **NATURAL USER INTERFACES AND WEARABLE TECHNOLOGY EXAMPLES**
>
> Sculpture Lens in the Cleveland Museum of Art's Gallery One uses face-recognition software to match a photo of a visitor's facial expression with a work of art in the collection.
>
> Another experience challenges visitors to pose like a sculpture on display and then give them feedback on how accurate they were. The Body Metrics exhibit at the Tech Museum of Innovation uses cutting-edge biometric wearable technology to gather details about visitors' heart rate, brainwaves, and muscle tension and provides feedback on their health profile in the actual museum displays.

AUGMENTED AND VIRTUAL REALITY

Augmented and virtual reality are two of the most talked-about digital technologies at this time, particularly with the rapid rise in popularity of Pokémon GO and excitement around new virtual reality headsets. Augmented reality layers digital content onto the real world, and virtual reality transports visitors to a completely different digital world. Both of these technologies have made huge strides in recent years and are becoming more feasible and affordable for use in museum exhibitions.

Augmented reality has particular relevance for museums, since it can provide visitors with more information on what they are seeing in the "real world"—that is, objects from the museum collection, historic buildings, or monuments. Its flexibility allows visitors to make connections to other parts of the exhibition, museum, and their world at large. Virtual reality can allow visitors to experience a completely different time or place that may be the focus of a museum exhibition; for example, Ancient Rome or Antarctica. These technologies can be very engaging for museum visitors, but they also have their challenges. Development of AR and VR experiences is becoming more affordable, but

AUGMENTED AND VIRTUAL REALITY EXAMPLES

The Andy Warhol Museum has an augmented reality app called Warhol Layar that lets people find locations around Pittsburgh and New York City that relate to the life of the famous artist, and to access images, stories, and more about that location.

In the Rosa Parks Experience, visitors use Samsung Gear VR to step into the role of Rosa Parks when she was asked to give up her seat for a white passenger on a bus in Montgomery, Alabama, in 1955.

GAMES AND GAMING EXAMPLES

The V&A in London created a *Games Designer in Residence* program to allow a young person to create digital games based on its collection.

The TIFF Bell Lightbox hosts an annual *digiPlaySpace* in which they invite game designers, artists, and others to create immersive learning experiences using the latest digital technologies, including AR and VR, robots, and more.

quality productions can still be very expensive. They also need to be designed to complement but not detract from or override the exhibition experience—for example, certain AR or VR experiences might prompt some visitors to ask, "Why should I go to the museum if I can have the same virtual reality experience from my home?" There are also the safety and security concerns of distracting people when they are walking in the exhibition.

Games and Gaming

Games and gaming are one of the most popular uses of digital technology in the broader world, and elements can be successfully applied in museum exhibitions. Many people enjoy playing video games on their mobile devices and gaming systems, and museums are tapping into this in order to draw visitors to their institutions. People like games because they are fun, and it is commonly accepted now that adults as well as children learn more when they are having fun. Games can encourage museum visitors to be curious, explore, solve problems, and work together. Customized games can be expensive to develop, although they have the benefit of being tailored to the museum exhibition experience. Some museums have tapped into popular games such as Minecraft and Pokémon GO as a way to draw visitors. Complex games may require too much time or effort in the actual exhibition itself, but could be available through apps or the museum website for continued engagement after the visit.

Internet of Things

Internet of Things is a network of connected objects that link the physical world with the world of information through the Internet. Using this approach, artifacts in the museum can "tell their own stories" by transmitting information directly to visitors using embedded chips, sensors, or tiny processors such as iBeacons, WiFi Aware, and RFID. This technology allows museums to customize the visitor experience and extend it beyond the actual visit. It also lets them collect information on how visitors navigate the exhibition, providing information that can inform future exhibit development. As with any technology that collects information about its visitors, there are ethical considerations surrounding the Internet of Things that museums need to consider.

ROBOTICS TECHNOLOGY

Robotics technology has developed in recent years, meaning that robots are now making their way into museums. Telepresence robots can serve as docents that are remotely operated by experts or community members in other locations. Robots can also visit the museum in the place of people or groups who cannot physically make it to the museum because of distance, cost, mobility issues, or other accessibility concerns. Although there are many implications for overall museum operations (e.g., conservation, security, safety, fabrication), the major advantage of telepresence robots is access.

THE INTERNET OF THINGS EXAMPLES

The Pen at the Cooper Hewitt, Smithsonian Design Museum is an example of the kind of "smart object" that is part of the Internet of Things. At the start of their visit, visitors are given a digital Pen to "collect" objects that they like from the exhibits, which they can use later for their own design inspiration. For more details, see the interview with experience designer Jake Barton about this project.

ROBOTICS EXAMPLES

The Computer History Museum in California offers a *Beam Virtual Tour Program* that allows school classes and other groups to virtually visit the museum using its own telepresence robot named Beam.

The American Museum of Natural History in New York and the Haida Gwaii Museum in British Columbia have partnered on a project to offer a unique visitor experience. Using a telepresence robot named BeamPro SPS, curators at the Haida Gwaii Museum give tours of Haida artifacts in the AMNH's Hall of Northwest Coast Indians.

DIGITAL MULTISENSORY TECHNOLOGIES

Digital multisensory technologies are new technologies that are allowing people to have transformative multisensory experiences. They can let you smell, taste, and touch things digitally. These technological advances are also allowing museums to capture, preserve, and present nonphysical aspects of our culture; for example, smell, sound, touch, and taste in ways never before possible, enhancing and enriching exhibitions. These technologies can also enrich the experience of visitors with sensory impairments.

DIGITAL MULTISENSORY TECHNOLOGIES EXAMPLES

Rain Room is an art installation that has travelled to multiple museums and uses 3D tracking cameras and other technologies to let visitors walk through a rainstorm without getting wet.

The Natural History Museum in London hosted an event called City's Circus for the Senses, where visitors got to smell virtual flower bouquets and taste digital lollipops.

General Principles for Assessment and Planning

Deciding on the kind of digital experience appropriate for a particular museum or exhibit can be a challenge. It is always a mistake to leap into a potentially expensive design process without being sure as to what you really want or need. The following general principles and guidelines can contribute to making the right choice for both the visitor and museum.

EARLY INTEGRATION

Planning for digital experiences should begin at the very start of the exhibition planning process. The design brief or interpretive plan should identify potential digital components at the outset, including preliminary ideas about means of expression (e.g., is it a mobile app, a virtual game, a touchscreen?) and also the content it will communicate. Digital experiences have design, content, schedule, and budget implications that must be planned for from the beginning.

AVOID "TECHNOLOGY FOR TECHNOLOGY'S SAKE"

It can be tempting to fill an exhibition with the latest and greatest technology, but often this is neither feasible nor desirable. During the interpretive planning phase, exhibit planners must decide which experiences will really benefit from being digital and which will not. In some cases, visitors may learn more by doing something physical or by reading a text panel, while in others a digital experience will be valuable. Digital is not always the answer.

LOOK BEFORE YOU LEAP

Once the planning team has decided that an experience will be digital, they should spend some time researching and evaluating the technology before committing to a particular platform or device. Ideally, they should get a hold of several different types of technologies in order to find what works best in their context. Talk to colleagues and read case studies that describe how the technologies have been used elsewhere, including outside museums. Conduct front-end evaluations and find out what technologies visitors would like to see.

THINK ABOUT YOUR AUDIENCE

What types of visitors does the museum currently have? What types does it want to attract? What forms of digital media will appeal to these groups, and what will not? Complex, content-heavy experiences are not typically suited to children's museums, where young visitors have short attention spans and may have difficulty connecting to virtual content. Games may not be appropriate for museums that have a memorial focus; for example, Holocaust or war museums.

CONSIDER YOUR SPACE

Although digital experiences are nonphysical, the space in which visitors experience them matters. Projection technology and screens are often not as effective in well-lit galleries. Exhibits with a lot of audio may suffer from sound bleed. Historic buildings and sites and outdoor exhibits may have limitations in terms of WiFi and the infrastructure needed for A/V hardware. These obstacles can be overcome but need to be considered at the planning and design stage.

DRAW UPON EXISTING ASSETS

Content creation for digital experiences can be very time consuming and expensive. Can this content be drawn from existing resources—that is, from a physical exhibition? Or, can new digital content be reused elsewhere such as on the website or in a catalog? Can information on objects provided through an augmented reality app be drawn directly from the museum's collection database? Planning for content to do "double-duty" can create efficiencies and economies that can make digital projects more realistic.

OFFER PERSONALIZED EXPERIENCES

One of the great advantages of digital technologies is the ability to personalize the visitor experience. Personalization can make an experience more meaningful, memorable, and enjoyable for the visitor. Consider ways to let visitors choose how deep they want to delve into content, create their own tours through the museum, and make connections while exploring.

ENCOURAGE ACTIVE PARTICIPATION

Ensure that digital media allows opportunities for visitors to be active participants in the experience and not just passive consumers. Can visitors contribute their own opinions, content, images, or videos related to the exhibition? Can they share their thoughts with the museum and other visitors via social media? This allows for multiple perspectives and shared authority between the museum and its visitors.

CONSIDER ACCESSIBILITY

New digital technologies offer great opportunities for minimizing physical and intellectual barriers, as long as this is considered in the initial stages of planning and not just an afterthought. Voice activation, captioning, and "read aloud" options, among others, can ensure that visitors with disabilities can access content in the exhibition.

COLLABORATE

Integrating new digital technologies can be daunting for many museums—large and small—and considering strategies for collaborating with other museums, individuals, artists, start-up tech companies, universities or colleges, and others can make projects more feasible. Once a project has been implemented, share your experience with colleagues through conference presentations, blog posts, or other means in order to help others in the field. Be sure to detail failures as well as successes.

How to Plan a Digital Project

Planning a digital project for a museum exhibition involves the same basic steps, regardless of what form that experience will take:

1. Planning
2. Design and Production
3. Installation

These steps are present even if the design and production of the project gets outsourced to an external supplier. In chapter 11, Rachel Walker explores how to manage digital projects—informed by the museum's planning and covering the design and production and installation steps of work. In chapter 12, Marco Mason delves more deeply into the design process for digital projects.

Planning

ASSESSMENT AND GOALS

At the outset of planning for any digital media project, it is the museum's job to identify its goals for the project and do an assessment of what resources it needs to accomplish those goals. The museum may need to consult with external suppliers for support in evaluating the feasibility of the budget, the availability of the technology and the long-term maintenance plan.

Questions to ask at this stage include:

- What type of digital experience do we want to have?
- What are the outcomes that we want to see?
- What is our target audience for this experience?
- Do we have the staff and expertise to do this internally, or do we need external help (i.e., a consultant or external producer)?
- Who will serve on the development team?
- Is the budget adequate? If not, where can funds be acquired?
- Will visitors be charged for this experience?
- Will visitors be required to have their own devices, or will we provide them?
- Is the experience satisfying for people who do want to use devices?
- Is there a plan for dealing with equipment failure?
- What are the long-term costs (i.e., maintenance, updating, etc.)?
- Is the technology available off-the-shelf or do we need a custom product?
- Do we have the content required in-house, or will this need to be sourced elsewhere?
- Are there safety/privacy/copyright/ethical concerns that we need to be conscious of with this type of media?

Consideration of these questions and others is important at the outset to determine the feasibility of the digital project before proceeding into detailed interpretive planning and project planning. Based on the answers to these questions, compromises may need to be made in terms of the types of experiences desired and/or the project's goals. If the museum determines that it does not have the in-house capability to undertake the project, it would be ideal to begin consulting with external digital media specialists at this stage to ensure the project is viable moving forward.

Ultimately, the answers to these questions and others make up the business case (see chapter 11), which then gets handed to the digital project team.

INTERPRETIVE PLANNING

An interpretive plan is an essential tool in planning for any museum exhibition whether digital or non-digital. An interpretive plan should be developed that addresses the entire experience, including the digital media. The final interpretive plan will describe, using words and perhaps reference images or diagrams, what the visitor will see, hear, and do. It will identify learning objectives, visitor-experience goals, themes, and topics of the overall experience. In terms of the specific digital experience, it will answer questions including:

- **Standalone or Integrated?** Will the digital experience be part of a larger exhibit, such as a re-created historic environment, or is it a discrete experience such as a film?

- **Permanent or Temporary?** Is the experience intended to be permanently installed in the museum, or is it part of a temporary or traveling exhibition? This has implications for design, budget, and hardware selection.

- **Single or Multiuser?** Is the experience intended as a solo experience—for example, an audio tour on a mobile app—or is it a group-based experience, such as a multi-player game? The user interface for the experience will vary depending on how many people are intended to use it at a time, and how they interact with the media and other visitors.

- **Level of Participation?** Is this a passive experience for visitors—that is, are they watching a video or listening to an audio clip? Or, are they participating in some way, for example, answering questions or submitting their own interpretation?

- **What are the content resources needed?** What are the stories that will be told? Does the museum have the resources needed to tell those stories? What are they? What resources need to be acquired elsewhere?

- **Design Integration?** Will the digital experience be planned to fit with the design aesthetic for other experiences (e.g., text panels)? This will need to be coordinated with the exhibit designers.

- **Hardware Requirements?** Is the museum expecting visitors to use their own mobile devices? If so, will it have devices that can be borrowed by visitors who do not have their own device?

- **Multiple Platforms?** Will content be available across multiple platforms (i.e., iOS and Android), or just one?

- **Collection of Data?** Does the Museum want to collect data on how visitors have accessed the digital content and who those visitors are?

MULTIMEDIA TREATMENTS

Once the digital media needs have been identified in the interpretive plan, the next step is to further develop the digital experiences. Each experience will require a multimedia treatment that will identify the interpretive goals, target audience, operational requirements, and outcomes that need to be achieved. The multimedia treatment will also begin to identify the content needs for each experience, identifying resources both within the museum and those that need to be created or sourced elsewhere. Preliminary hardware requirements should also be identified at this stage—that is, does the experience require a monitor, audio speakers, projector, etc.? Once the multimedia treatment has been finalized, an initial production and hardware budget can be created. This budget will be further refined during the Design and Production phases.

Design

In chapter 12, Marco Mason describes the experience design approach, which relates to this next phase of work. This level of design may be done in-house by 3D or exhibit designers at museums with this internal capacity, or they may be done by an external media firm in collaboration with the museum. In either case, development should follow the approach outlined in the interpretive plan and multimedia treatments, although adjustments may need to be made in order to achieve goals and an optimal experience while staying in budget. If this level of design and production is done by an external producer, the museum needs to confirm who will own the content and software, and if not the museum (this is strongly advised), how will they be able to make edits in the future?

STEPS OF DESIGN

As outlined by Marco Mason in chapter 12, design and production follow a number of steps, including:

1. Identifying the design requirements for visitor experience, content, functionality, and look and feel.
2. Developing the design using design and visual frameworks such as storyboards, wireframes, and mood boards.
3. Refining the design including interface layout, user-friendly navigation, and appropriate graphics.

    (See chapter 12 for further description of the design phase.)

BUDGET

Budget control becomes very important during this phase of work, as this is when the actual cost of media production mounts. It is important to have a strong project manager who tracks costs and ensures expenditures do not exceed the planned budget. The cost of acquiring and producing content is often underestimated at the planning stage. Costs that can fluctuate widely and must be tracked carefully include:

- Content acquisition costs (e.g., purchasing rights to images, audio, and video clips)
- Content production costs (e.g., new audio or video productions, actors, voiceovers, etc.)
- Software development (e.g., visual effects, editing, animations, etc.)
- Hardware costs (e.g., monitors, speakers, projectors, mobile devices, wiring, racks, control room, etc.)

Budget review should happen at a number of points during this stage of work, with value engineering and cost-cutting as necessary.

A/V HARDWARE AND INTEGRATION

Identification of hardware requirements begins in the planning phase (see chapter 11). In this later stage, it becomes more refined and concrete based on the content, software, and design needs of the experience. The person or team responsible for hardware selection and fabrication needs to conduct research into the best solutions and to test them to ensure they will be suitable, durable, and affordable. Once software is complete, it needs to be integrated with the hardware prior to installation. Additional testing needs to be done at this point to ensure the media programs run properly on the devices. Further changes may need to be made if there are problems with functionality.

Production

SOFTWARE DEVELOPMENT

Software development often occurs concurrently with content development for media experiences, and both teams should work closely to ensure compatibility. The content team will feed the software development team with content as it is ready in order to begin to populate the media programs. The media development team will provide guidance to the content team on the types and amount of content that will work best in the software.

Software development happens in stages, which can include storyboards, mock-ups, and prototyping, depending on the type of media.

Installation

A generous installation schedule allows media experiences to be tested on-site for usability and functionality, and to work out bugs prior to launch. Ideally there have been a series of prototypes prior to installation in order to test out the visitor experience, but the installation period enables the experience to be tested in situ. A "soft-opening" can occur with museum staff or friends and family in order to fix any deficiencies before public launch.

The museum staff who will be responsible for operating, maintaining, and facilitating media experiences for visitors should be involved in the installation and testing. Once installation is complete, a staff training day should be planned in order to walk through the operation and maintenance of each media element. Staff training is essential in order to ensure knowledge transfer. Ideally some staff have been involved in the planning and design process; however, now is an opportunity to do a refresher course or to engage with other staff and volunteers. The suppliers must also provide an operations and maintenance manual for all software and hardware. It should outline operating instructions, maintenance, and troubleshooting for each experience as well as instructions for updating content if applicable.

Wherever possible, museums should obtain at least a one-year warranty and/or an extended support agreement from media and hardware suppliers. If this is not in the museum's budget it is even more essential that museum staff participate in thorough training and receive a comprehensive operations and maintenance manual. Operations and maintenance costs should be budgeted for the anticipated lifespan of the media. These can be substantial, so in-house expertise is invaluable.

DIGITAL PEN AT THE COOPER HEWITT MUSEUM
Lisa Wright Interviews Jake Barton

Jake Barton is principal and founder of Local Projects, a media and physical design firm that creates groundbreaking experiences. Credits include landmark projects like the 9/11 Memorial Museum, the Cooper Hewitt Smithsonian Design Museum, and the Cleveland Museum of Art. His TED talk has nearly a million views, and he is on Fast Company magazine's list of top fifty designers.

Local Projects was hired by the Cooper Hewitt Museum in New York City to plan a number of interactive experiences for their redesign project. In this interview, Barton talks about his firm's experience creating a digital interactive pen that allows visitors to "collect" and "save" objects they like from the galleries.

> **LW:** Can you tell us about the digital Pen project that you did for the Cooper Hewitt Design Museum?
>
> **JB:** We were the experience designers in partnership with Diller Scofidio + Renfro, creating a new experience for the Cooper Hewitt Smithsonian Design Museum in their existing, but expanding, location at the Carnegie Mansion on the Upper East Side of New York City.
>
> The challenge that was presented to us was to help them grow new audiences for the museum, expanding beyond hard-core designers and residents of the Upper East Side, to fans of design, and families with kids—sometimes young kids. So our solution across the board was to pitch the museum on what was a crazy idea, that we wanted to teach design by inviting every visitor to play designer, and we wanted to facilitate that relationship by giving them a pen that would allow them to both gather and self-curate objects from the galleries, and to use those as inspiration to design their own materials inside of the museum. So we had the ability for visitors to gather a range of different materials and unique items that they were inspired by, and then a series of experiences culminated with what is called the Immersion Room, inviting visitors to themselves be designers and to understand design by actualizing their own vision.
>
> **LW:** Have you had any feedback on how the experience has been working since it opened?
>
> **JB:** The statistics that have come back have demonstrated that 99 percent of visitors actually take the Pen, which was one early cause of concern. What happens if people don't want the Pen and they are not interested in it? Turns out it is now so core to the experience that virtually everybody takes the Pen. People are collecting an enormous amount. It really shows the level of agency and connection visitors have, that they are inspired to engage with, is very high. And the most impressive is the percentage of people who return online to retrieve both their saved items and their created designs, and that's close to a third of the visitors as of the first year.
>
> **LW:** What were some of the key aspects of your planning process that helped this project to succeed?

JB: On a practical level, we spent a lot of time trying to get the right balance for this institution, its visitorship, its administration, and board. How much digital should be involved? Where should digital be, and where shouldn't it be? What level of comfort did different aspects of the museum have in delivering digital? And, most importantly, what was the nature of those digital experiences?

Once you get the Pen into people's hands, the first thing it does is it gets the phone out of their hands. Inside the galleries, you have a digital device that is able to collect and gather your point of view and the curatorial materials that you want to take with you. So it really activates you as a visitor in a way that is really exciting. These are essentially very traditional galleries to the extent that they are casework and objects and labels. And yet, because you have this device, for those seeking a larger digital story and interaction, they can gather materials and then they can spill them out on the digital tables as inspiration for designs that they are going to be creating.

Finding the right balance between digital and physical was really an iterative process developed over time together. Here is this Pen, it's going to make visitors active, it's going to reinvent the museum experience and turn audiences into participants, but it won't do it at the expense of the traditional galleries, which will remain artifact-based and without digital technology. All of those priorities and choices were worked out over time. Essentially, we started with the layout of the galleries. We started to think about the early ideas for the technology and engagement and then, as we developed from that plan, we started looking at the designs themselves and felt out what was appropriate and what wasn't about digital technology.

LW: What are some of the key things that you learned in this process?

JB: One is that you definitely need a range of strong teammates to make a project come together. We relied on the in-house digital team at the Cooper-Hewitt to assure the overall museum staff and board that this was a strong direction, that the digital technology would be well employed, and that this was the right approach to accessing and inspiring the audiences that they were going for. By having that diffusion of talent and vision throughout the team we were able to approach the challenge from multiple angles. And we got through the planning process into concept with a very strong and ambitious approach.

The next thing we learned, and this is core to our process, is the importance of what we call "prototype first." Seeing iterative mock-ups of these ideas early on allows the board, the curators, the administration, and the partners to see, touch, and feel a prototype that confirms that our approach is achievable. As we made these different mock-ups and prototypes, we were able to bring them forward for everyone from funders to press and PR people, and it really made this thing a material reality very early on, allowing us to critique and change things. When the museum saw things in full scale they were able to react much more quickly, deeply, and more productively. It helped us to pivot way before the opening on exhibit experiences that didn't work. And it helped convince everyone across the board, us included, that this was not just a great idea, but more importantly, that it would become a great experience.

LW: Is there any other advice that you could share with others who might be planning digital projects for their museums?

JB: We are always trying to find a way to make an emotional connection with visitors steeped in storytelling, in incredible collections, and to make new ideas and age-old truths connect with audiences. But the key for us is that the timelessness of the experiences is what makes them investments that will last. Meaning, yes, we use new technologies; yes, there are all sorts of incredible transformations and new opportunities that are afforded. But the key is what is innovative and meaningful, what creates innovation with a point. And that is typically really strong storytelling and very impactful emotional engagement. Those are the things that are going to age really well. So any time a collaborator or potential partner brings in a new technology, and says "this is amazing, it is the latest and greatest," it's never the reason to use a specific technique or solution. Anything that's new and cutting edge needs to be employed in a meaningful way, where it will age past the novelty of the hardware invention, because that's what will; that emotional engagement, that meaning making is what will age well for tomorrow and into the future.

PLANNING NEW TECHNOLOGIES
Lisa Wright Interviews Jessica Doig

Jessica Doig is vice president and executive producer at NGX Interactive. NGX is an award-winning technology firm that is driven by meaningful, inspirational, and educational exhibits. They create digital interactive storytelling experiences for museums, science centers, and cultural destinations.

LW: What is your number-one tip for museum professionals thinking about embarking on a project involving new technologies?

JD: Don't be rushed by peer pressure to try the latest trend. Where possible, get your hands on the technology and play with it yourself. Determine what you like and dislike about it, and decide how to best apply this in your organization. Take the time to validate ideas against your organization's goals, operational constraints, and target audience. Engage learning, curatorial, digital, and exhibitions teams in this early planning process to ensure ideas are achievable and expectations are managed. Engage the target audience to provide feedback on prototypes of digital exhibits through focus groups and beta testing sessions.

LW: What is the biggest pitfall when it comes to planning media exhibits?

JD: We recommend that museums don't lock in on hardware models and specific solutions until absolutely necessary to procure the equipment. The earlier visioning should be focused on the content and visitor experience, with the technology solution serving those requirements. Additionally, the long-term operational considerations of the technology need to be planned at these early stages, whether those considerations are consumables, replacements, future upgrades, or ongoing cleaning and maintenance.

LW: With digital media, is there ever too much content?

JD: At one time, digital media was seen as the answer to all the overflow content that couldn't fit on the graphic panels or interpretive displays. This approach has now evolved to feature select stories within digital media, rather than copious quantities of text. That being said, there is still value in the technique of progressive disclosure, presenting content in a visually engaging manner and limiting the amount of text on screen at one time. With compelling imagery and effective hooks, the programs can capture the audience's attention. If the visitor's curiosity is not sated, they can delve deeper into the story at will.

LW: What are some recommendations for operational impacts of technology?

JD: Hardware should be commercial grade where possible; for software, be clear on whether there are ongoing fees for licensing third-party solutions. Plan ahead where possible, for consumables, such as projector bulbs, and extra inventory of unique hardware. We recommend minimizing the number of unique brands and models. For example, rather than five or six different touchscreen sizes, choose three variations (small, medium, large) and stick to those variations to make service and replacements easier. Museum exhibits need to be robust and durable for museum visitors, thus "leading edge" is more appropriate than "bleeding edge." The approach needs to balance quality over quantity; the goal should be to create a museum with clever use of technology, rather than one with "so many screens!" The focus of the experience should be technology that encourages visitors to delight in the experience of learning, rather than the latest gadget.

LW: What are some of the ways museums can integrate digital without spending a lot of money to jump on short-term trends?

JD: Just as not everyone should try out the latest fashion trends, not all technology trends will be appropriate for every museum. The aim should be to have the best use of technology, not the museum with the most screens. A few easy suggestions are:

- A mobile compatible website rather than a downloadable app.
- A touchscreen program that focuses on affective learning objectives rather than a deep dive on content.
- A display of user-generated content that is created from predetermined statements, like magnetic poetry, rather than an open-ended keyboard entry that requires moderation.

LW: How can museum professionals and students educate themselves about new technologies?

JD: Tap into communities of interest and practice through four key ways:

1. On an industry scale, become familiar with special interest groups whose focus is museums and technology—in North America, Museums and the web, as well as the Museum Computer Network conferences are at the heart of some of the longest-running and relevant conversations for our sector. Joining these online and in-person conversations with peers is an unparalleled way to understand the unique considerations of the museum/technology space.

2. Look to the broader art/technology community. Whether it is subscribing to a technology and culture publication (online or via mail) such as *Wired* magazine; reading tech blogs like *Mashable*, *TechCrunch*, or *The Verge*; keeping an eye on curators and artists affiliated with art/music/technology festivals such as Eyeo and ISEA through their Instagram and Facebook accounts—the future of technology usually begins in these communities, and it is a great place to understand

and see how others are talking about, using, and envisioning how technologies become part of our everyday lives.

3. Academic research offers myriad resources and material for learning about new technologies for museum professionals. In particular, social scientists and educators who have been grappling with the intricacies of human-computer engagement have a lot to say, and the interdisciplinary and applied nature of much of this research can be found by delving into resources offered by consortiums such as HASTAC (Humanities, Arts, Science, and Technology Alliance and Collaboratory).

4. Getting your hands on gadgets and new technologies is one of the best ways to understand for yourself how they could be applied in the museum space.

LW: What are the top three things that museums can do in order to create successful digital experiences?

JD: First, identify thematic goals, desired visitor experience, and learning objectives, before deciding on the appropriate means of expression—whether it is technology based or not. Second, create cross-disciplinary teams to support the project from the beginning—having team members that champion content, design, and operations, ensures that a balanced set of priorities and needs are represented and understood and will result in a better outcome. And third, be realistic with what engagement with the digital exhibit/experience will be—crafting a visitor experience that is both cognitively and emotionally engaging is often an exercise in restraint; it is tempting to overload the experience with content or complexity simply because the technology can handle it.

💡 KEY TAKEAWAYS: NEW FRONTIERS IN THE VISITOR EXPERIENCE

1. There are a number of new technologies that can enhance the visitor experience, each with their own benefits and challenges. These include

    - Mobile applications
    - Natural user interfaces and wearable technology
    - Augmented and virtual reality
    - Games and gaming
    - The Internet of Things (IOT)
    - Robotics technology
    - Digital multisensory technologies

2. General Principles for Assessment and Planning

    - Early integration
    - Avoid "technology for technology's sake"
    - Look before you leap
    - Think about your audience
    - Consider your space
    - Draw upon existing sssets
    - Offer personalized experiences
    - Encourage active participation
    - Consider accessibility
    - Collaborate

3. Stages of Digital Projects

    - Planning: the museum identifies its goals and resources, and develops an interpretive plan and multimedia treatments
    - Design and production—in-house or outsourced, includes more detailed budgeting, hardware integration, and software development
    - Installation

SECTION 3: TRANSFORMING THE WAY WE WORK

Content for Every Channel

Ali Hossaini

Building an omnichannel museum is a theme that runs throughout this book. Chapter 2 presents omnichannel as a proposition that unites museums and visitors in a common quest for value. It also positions omnichannel as a key facet of strategic planning. This chapter moves from strategy to implementation. Omnichannel is not an all-or-nothing proposition. It can—and most likely should—be implemented gradually. Different avenues can be explored; benefits can be tested; and, most importantly, your organization can adapt to the changes demanded by omnichannel thinking, user-centrism, and other principles of digital society.

Your content strategy is probably closer to being omnichannel than you realize. Most museums maintain a website, and your museum probably has several social media accounts. Like every other public space, museums are adding digital signage, monitors, and ticketing systems throughout their facilities. Collections and catalogs are being transformed into digital assets through image capture; databasing; and embedded tags used for identification, search, and security. Preparing content for omnichannel engagement is a natural step from maintaining the multichannel facilities that already exist.

A parallel evolution is occurring in consumer electronics. Your visitors connect to the world through a universe of devices. Shoes, clothing, and glasses are joining tablets, phones, e-readers, watches, cameras, and pens as the next wave of computing platforms. Whether public or private, large or small, everything is connected and "smart." Smart devices share some common features. They recognize individuals. They are interactive. They are on the Internet. And they are media savvy.

Omnichannel thinking recognizes that smart devices are channels for information, services, and relationships. Each innovation creates new opportunities for content and interaction. For example, consider how social networks and apps have joined websites as important sources of digital content. It is almost impossible to stay current with the hardware, software and acronyms that describe digital media platforms, so it is probably best to think of them collectively as digital channels. (But don't be afraid of using other phrases that are more current.) A digital channel refers to any touchpoint where a visitor encounters your content, and omnichannel means you are committed to serving visitors on the channels they prefer.

Museums have unprecedented opportunities to serve a digital world that is hungry for experience. Exhibitions are the proverbial tip of the iceberg that reveals only a tiny portion of what's available. What emerges from the vast holdings of museums is highly filtered by curators, collections managers, designers, educators, and others. By digitizing research, reports, interpretation, catalogs and ultimately their collections, museums can connect content directly to the global public. Without abandoning standards of excellence, they can adopt sharing, crowdsourcing, and other digital tactics to extend the work of museum staff into communities that could never access their resources previously. Through social networks they can create exciting live events that let people converse directly with curators and other experts. By adopting common standards, they can also link their resources to create a universal knowledge base.

The process of building an omnichannel museum involves five integrated activities:

1. Understanding the people who use the museum
2. Creating digital assets that mirror and extend physical assets
3. Implementing content and collections management systems
4. Engaging the public through open access, interactivity (especially with experts), personalization, and other user-centric principles
5. Ensuring that a robust technology and performance plan keeps the system contemporary and responsive

Understanding Users

A key objective of the omnichannel museum is to seamlessly engage visitors wherever they are. But in order to engage, you need to understand current behavior, expectations, and motivations. Your success is predicated on satisfying your visitors, so your planning should focus on giving visitors a satisfying experience with the content you offer.

Visitor research is an important field of study for tourism, museums, zoos, visitor centers, historic sites, parks, and other informal learning settings. The focus of visitor research is trying to understand why different visitors come to these places, what they expect to get out of the experience, and how to assess the value of the experience both qualitatively and quantitatively. These days visitor research is increasingly focused on how technologies can help to collect, analyze and present information about visitors in order to improve the way in which they are served.

> **KEY TERMS**
>
> **PSYCHOGRAPHIC SEGMENTATION**
>
> Grouping users and potential users by their personality traits, lifestyle, social class, values and attitudes, interests, and others in order to provide more personalized experiences for each segment.

User Segmentation

User segmentation places users in categories in order to be able to make certain generalizations that can guide planners and designers. Although most often focused on members of the public, they should also include people who engage with the museum for professional purposes, for example, visiting researchers, or professionals from other institutions with whom you collaborate. Segmentation affects how visitor research is executed and reported.

Segmentation comes from marketing, and it organizes museum visitors into populations with distinct characteristics. Some museums adopt **psychographic or lifestyle segmentation** used by tourism destination marketers, or they develop their own segmentation based on surveys, interviews, and focus groups.

As with everything else, digital technologies are changing how we understand visitors. By relying on records rather than self-reporting, the analytics methodologies explored in chapters 3 and 5 give objective insight into the nuances of actual behavior. At the same time, as chapter 12 describes, traditional ethnographic methodologies such as field research, observation, and interviews are being used by experience designers to develop empathy for visitors and create more impactful museum experiences. These qualitative research methods complement analytics. They explore the motivations and psychology of visitors, and they represent them as narratives that can inform experience design.

Visitor or learning profiles, or *personas*, are terms used in website and mobile development and e-learning. They refer to a form of segmentation that enables digital designers to build user profiles and use cases of visitors. Visitor profiles start with assumptions made by knowledgeable people within the institution who have experience working with the public. However, they should be constantly updated with new information; for example, focus groups, data analytics, and others that challenge assumptions of how a type of visitor behaves. Although establishing profiles can provide a starting point for research, it is also the result of research. Initial profiles are created through interviews or focus group and demographic information, which then can be verified through cross-checking data from an actual visit. Do youth really use more digital interactives than older visitors? Do

SAMPLE USER PROFILE FOR AN OMNICHANNEL MUSEUM

A person gets an enthusiastic notice of a show on Twitter. Friends have posted images on Instagram, and these link to the show's Facebook page. Visitors receive a 10 percent discount if they post the show to their own news feed. Tickets are purchased, and the visitor chooses to hold them on their smartphone. They check the museum website to plan their visit.

Upon exiting mass transit, they go back to the website on their smartphone. The responsive website formats pages for the visitor's mobile device and foregrounds directions to the museum because it is within visiting hours. The directions link to Google Maps, which guide the visitor directly to the entrance. In the lobby they may take a selfie in front of an iconic installation which they immediately post to their social networks via museum WiFi. They can also choose to post it to the museum's social pages and monitors within the museum.

Upon entering, the visitor scans their mobile ticket, which prompts them to download an electronic guide to the exhibition. In the lobby they can view a large touch screen that previews all exhibitions and events. The visitor can download a map to selected exhibits, arrange to be reminded via email about a lecture, and reserve a table at the museum restaurant for lunch.

As they pass through the exhibit, they can wave their phone over a post to download high-resolution images and extended interpretation.

children respond better to facilitated or self-directed experiences? Do baby boomers really donate more than millennials?

USE CASES

A use case imagines the way in which a visitor engages with a museum by focusing on a particular visitor profile; for example, a forty-seven-year-old single professional or a group of five teenage school learners. Use cases have been traditionally applied to website planning, but in an omnichannel environment it can include many different channels. Planners and designers build a use case by imagining every stage of a person's engagement with the museum. They may start with a social media post, follow an exhibition review, find a way to buy tickets, download a map or address, and end by looking at the menu of a restaurant. The role of use cases in digital development is to understand the touchpoints between visitor and museum.

With a use case one can model the different ways a particular user connects with the museum. Have they seen an ad in the metro? Are they searching on a term, say, "art Saturday morning"? Or maybe they are just passing by, and their attention is captured by a digital sign. To develop a use case, enumerate various paths into your museum, then project how people move step by step (or click by click) according to specific motivations. As you imagine the visitor journey keep asking yourself "what" and "how" to ensure you think through details of the content and channel through which it is received.

Creating Digital Assets

Museums are repositories for all kinds of content. Exhibitions, catalogs, publications, collections,

CONTENT FOR EVERY CHANNEL

and other sources offer an endless stream of information, knowledge, and experiences. In order to capitalize on this content in an omnichannel environment, it needs to be converted into digital assets. Digital assets can be shared and repurposed in a way that analog content cannot, and they can ultimately create efficiencies throughout the museum, as Corey Timpson explains in chapter 9.

The Content Audit

The first step in creating a bank of digital assets for your museum is to assess your existing content resources. This can be done by doing a content audit, which categorizes all the possible sources of content in your museum, evaluates their quality, and considers whether different visitor segments could find it interesting. This is best done as a museum-wide exercise because all departments are potential resources for content.

Types of content include:

- Collections and documentation
- Digital art
- Virtual or augmented reality
- Exhibition media (and its components including text, images, graphics, video, interactives, and display collections)
- Mobile experiences and games
- Learning resources
- Research and publications

The team can consider the quality and uniqueness of their content, whether or not it exists in digital format, and whether or not it will be interesting to a particular audience.

From Content Resource to Digital Assets

The process of converting a museum's content into digital assets differs depending on the format of the original content. Legacy collections and archives require digitization, while contemporary digital content created on aging formats raises questions of preservation, storage, and access. Museum-created content such as learning resources, research and publications, and exhibition media require other considerations largely related to the channels that may carry them. For example, an exhibition video may need to be edited for length on website, and a teacher's guide accessed via mobile in a live exhibition is used differently than a printed pamphlet. The process of converting content resources to

THE BENEFITS OF DIGITIZATION

Think of an item in your collection, such as a vase. The vase may have a digital identity—that is, a unique tag or uniform resource locator (URL). This web address becomes a way for anyone in the world to call up a page—more accurately, a data file—that corresponds to the physical object.

Several layers of data attach to the vase. First there is its name or identification in the museum's catalog, along with its internal identification code. It likely has provenance; year or time period of manufacture; and notes about its material, manufacture, maker(s), owner(s), style, technique, decoration, and uses.

Thanks to the web, each of these data points may link to hundreds or even thousands of references.

Starting from its identification, someone could read about ceramics fabrication, an ancient dynasty, the forced relocation of artisans, and/or international trade routes. They might order a book on vases, buy a reproduction of your vase, or download a 3D scan to print at home. Interest in the vase may lead them to discover the rest of your ceramics collection online. Then they may visit, donate or become a member.

digital assets is done in three steps: digitization, databasing, and distribution. Below we look at some considerations involved in transforming legacy or printed content into digital assets.

COLLECTIONS AND ARCHIVES

Collections management is an obvious place to start for museums that hold items.

Digitizing collections themselves is a mammoth undertaking. The sheer volume of holdings in most museums is daunting, and automation is difficult in many situations. Items come in a variety of forms, and the difficulty of creating digital files from a mounted insect, an oil painting, or a medieval mechanism varies wildly.

Two-dimensional objects are relatively easy to digitize. Paintings, photographs, drawings, the pages of books and manuscripts, and many scientific specimens are flat if not strictly 2D. A variety of instruments can be used for 2D capture, mainly cameras and laser scanners, and the nature of the material makes automation possible in many cases. Scanning offers an advantage for written texts that can be presented independently of their typographic context. **Optical character recognition** (OCR) software is improving every day, and it can be used to convert a scanned image to text that is searchable, translatable, and accessible to people with disabilities.

Your museum may also have film and video collections. There are well-established technologies for digitizing this content, but the safe transfer of legacy materials requires experienced technicians as well as equipment.

Three-dimensional objects are even more complex. Two examples illustrate the extremes of difficulty. Many natural history museums contain large collections of mounted insects. These delicate specimens are usually mounted on pins with descriptions underneath. Digital capture requires dismounting the specimen to create a digital record. This can be done safely, but the arduous process requires time and skill, and feasible techniques are still being explored. The other extreme is a jet airplane, which presents an obvious contrast to its tiny biological counterpart.

Among the challenges of digital capture are questions of resolution, documentation, and dimension, ultimately related to context of use in the present and, even more trickily, the future. A digital photograph of moderate resolution may suffice for collections management. But digital records can be used by a broader audience that ranges from scientists, designers, and scholars to students and the curious public. Designers may need ultra-high resolution to use images in their own work; scientists may require specialized imaging techniques such as X-ray, tomography (commonly known as CT scans), spectroscopy, or electron microscopy.

The technology for capturing 3D objects exists, as does the capacity to present it, but neither exists in a form that is useable at the scale required by museums. Both issues are likely to be solved in the near future as 3D scanning and printing technologies improve. The biggest issue with 3D digitization is preparing objects for cameras, scanners, and other capture devices. Dexterous robots managed by artificial intelligence (AI) are already being put into industrial use, and, as they advance in the marketplace, they may be adapted to the museum environment with a relatively low threshold of investment.

The other question raised by 3D image capture is how to present the results. While it is possible to examine 3D objects through a website, the obvious limitation is that web pages are 2D. Virtual reality offers a robust visual experience in 3D, and both virtual and augmented reality enable objects to be placed in an environment where they make sense. The exciting yet daunting possibilities of these new platforms are discussed below.

Digitization of this nature also raises questions. There are no set criteria for what constitutes a digital record versus a digital replica. If the museum creates an indistinguishable copy, at what point can the digital artifact substitute for the object? At what point should it? In the art world, there are precedents for handling high-quality copies, but what about history museums and science museums? How are **born-digital** collections managed for rights and authenticity?

Real life is overtaking philosophic debates about access, authenticity, and expertise. Google Art Project requires participating museums to offer ultra-high-resolution images of paintings. Now anyone can put a "virtual magnifying glass" on great artworks from their home, classroom or study. Already there are anecdotes about scholars who have made discoveries with this resource. As high-resolution images become the norm, we

KEY TERMS

OPTICAL CHARACTER RECOGNITION

Optical character recognition (OCR) is a software application that detects text within an image and converts it into text that can be edited.

BORN DIGITAL

Born digital refers to objects that are created on a computer or another digital platform such as a digital camera.

can imagine a world where crowd-sourced scholarship—think Wikipedia—merges with the work of dedicated specialists.

The addition of scientific imaging to digitization workflow adds a significant amount of complexity to planning. But it is a question that should be addressed early in the planning process with expert advice from science advisors. The task of handling thousands, or even millions, of delicate objects is enormous, and it should probably be tackled only once.

DIGITAL ART

Although recognized as a valid art form, digital art, like performance art, exists in a kind of limbo. Standards for presentation, preservation, and even contemplation are still evolving, and it is no doubt difficult for curators to exercise judgment about artistic canon when we are barely past the first generation of artists. Still the field is burgeoning, and, as Kevin Cunningham describes with conviction in his interview in chapter 14, the means for exhibiting digital art and closely related forms of performance, installation, and media art have never been more accessible. Digital art is born-digital, yet, like performance art, it can also be ephemeral. The challenge lies not only in how but whether it should be an asset that the museum can make available over more than one channel or whether this compromises its artistic integrity.

Some museums have been closely involved with commissioning digital art, and both the techniques and equipment used by digital artists can be also used for exhibition design. The field is closely aligned with progress in other sectors—much as Renaissance painting supported advances in botanical drawing—and, as artists are doing already, museums can benefit from advances made in advertising, commercial media, and open source software movements that democratize access to production tools.

Like many other aspects of digital culture, digital art requires ongoing support from its makers. Rapid obsolescence looms over much of this book, and it is particularly acute in a field that draws on an ad hoc toolkit. Does the artwork die if its hardware or software no longer operates? What constitutes the artwork? How does one value works that can be easily reproduced? Digital art is similar to software, and artists and museums need to understand how to support its creation, its exhibition, and its distribution in a changing technological environment.

There is no one approach to digital art. Pieces range from a dedicated piece of hardware to generative software that plays on any website. Preserving the work may require expert documentation from software developers, hardware engineers, and other IT-related skill sets.

Fortunately we have ample precedent for establishing standards around digital art. Photography and especially video presented similar issues to the artistic establishment in the twentieth century, but both mediums are now embedded in accepted rules of practice. A dedicated core of artists, curators, and collectors are doing the same for digital art, and there is little doubt they will be resolved in coming years.

VIRTUAL REALITY AND AUGMENTED REALITY

Virtual reality and augmented reality create born digital experiences that equally defy classification. They are created as digital content, but the challenge lies in presentation and distribution for the widest possible user group.

Virtual reality (VR) is the creation of an immersive 3D environment with the use of video goggles, high-resolution audio, and haptic (hand-and-touch-based) interfaces. It provides a high-quality simulation of physical experience, hence the term virtual reality—it is virtually real.

VR offers museums ample opportunities for positive change and disruption. As of this writing, viable VR platforms are on the market, and, with immense resources behind them, they are poised to become mass mediums. At present, museums offer VR experiences as part of an exhibition, but the technology allows for VR to be experienced anywhere by anyone with a headset. As they increase in sophistication and reach, they will likely absorb other media, becoming a universal platform for content and rich, immersive experiences.

VIRTUAL REALITY

Here are some guidelines for introducing VR capacity in your museums.

- Test a number of hardware platforms to judge which works best in your environment.
- Develop a continuous series of small projects with open-ended criteria for success so you develop a learning organization.
- Present projects in a lab environment to encourage risk taking.
- Create consensus by involving as many colleagues and external partners as possible in your projects.
- Attend events from every sector for inspiration.
- Write restrictive licenses that can be rescinded in a reasonable fashion.
- Take care not to allow digital models of your museum to be accessed by the public until legal and technical standards for protecting them emerge.
- Ignore the above advice on licensing if your organization advocates releasing data under open source or Creative Commons rules.

Major steps toward the virtualization of the museum experience have already happened, laying the foundation for virtual reality. Many aspects once thought only accessible physically can now be experienced virtually. As collections become digitized, objects become data, and records become metadata. The opportunity for museums to exploit these digital assets is tremendous.

High-quality digital reproductions already offer superior experiences on some counts, but, more importantly, they offer developers content that can be manipulated in a software environment. The next step is the absorption of the museum environment itself—transforming every aspect of the physical museum into a virtual experience. Virtual reality is an immersive medium, and it lends itself—indeed demands—an architectural presentation. Within VR the building itself becomes content. After an initial phase of translating existing architecture and architectural paradigms into virtual reality environments, it is likely that new architectural plans, which are already digital files, will simply be mapped into VR buildings that are cheap to construct, easy to maintain, and have no limits on capacity.

A key issue for museums is to protect their ownership over their own physicality—a powerful digital asset in the VR environment. There is no doubt that many people want proximity to originals, and physical museums will remain as a relatively luxurious experience for the public and sometimes indispensable material resource for researchers. Yet the lines between original and copy will blur as the quality of digital replicas increases. Thanks to advanced imaging techniques, the amount of information available in a digital file will surpass anything but an intrusive inspection of the original. At the same time, virtual reality will offer far more access to the object. Current VR platforms offer a high-fidelity visual experience that will continue to improve. Within years, haptic gloves and other touch-based interfaces will give people the ability to handle objects with realistic perceptions of texture, weight and flexibility. (These technologies are already being tested for telesurgery, a high stakes endeavor that surpasses the requirements for digital objects.) For now, museums are unique in the physical experience they give of their building, their artifacts, and their people—but for how long? The move to open access and open source is a positive one when it comes to the democratization of knowledge, but can museums afford to do the same when it comes to the knowledge and its physical manifestation?

Augmented reality (AR) is breaking out in a similar way. AR combines the qualities of virtual and physical experience by superimposing digital images on a particular place. Originally conceived for glasses, the technology is most widely used on smartphones and tablets. Both platforms are somewhat awkward, but other solutions including direct retinal stimulation by tiny lasers are in development. When it comes to AR, the current state of flux threatens the relevance of anything written here, but the success of Pokémon Go shows that the right concept can breathe life into a moribund invention. Museums and other organizations have experimented with AR in the past, but it has not caught on with the public. Trends are often self-reinforcing cycles where an extremely successful app triggers acceptance of similar concepts. Given the limited floor space and wall space of museums, and the need to avoid clutter, there are ample opportunities to introduce AR as public habits evolve.

The prospects of VR and AR may seem daunting, risky and expensive but they represent a new kind of digital asset that museums would do well to recognize. Any large-scale bets are dangerous, so the most effective approach is small-scale, experimental, and, most importantly, gradualist. Like any pioneers, the first waves of digital innovators often die in obscurity, while the second make a fortune. Museums should form measured programs to develop, preserve, and distribute these media according to emerging standards and public habits.

LEARNING RESOURCES

In chapter 6, Ngaire Blankenberg discusses how museums have rich content resources that can become digital assets for museum educators and external people by ensuring that it is made discoverable, retrievable, personalizable, annotatable, and shareable. Each of these is done through the application of technology, starting with digitization:

> **KEY TERMS**
>
> **LEARNING OBJECTS (LOs)**
>
> Learning objects is a term originating in e-learning to refer to digital content "chunks" that can be searched through (with descriptive metadata), re-used, and re-purposed for different groups and lessons or courses.

- Discoverability can happen through location-based technologies and search engine optimization.

- Retrievability means that all museum objects are in a digital file that can be accessed by the public inside and outside of the museums.

- Personalization draws on understanding the individual profiles of users that may include information such as grade or education level, learning goals and special needs and ensuring that the right information gets to these users through various channels.

- Annotation has important repercussions related to the form that content is made available in. Text files are annotatable more easily than PDFs, for example, although advances in optical character recognition are making this conversion increasingly easier.

- Shareability requires the technical ability to share on social media, email or others.

In chapter 9, Corey Timpson explains one of the principles that allow the enterprise content management system to function: separation of content from presentation. This means that if, for example, a photograph is displayed in an exhibition interactive—the photograph, the interactive interface, and the data about the photograph are saved as separate digital assets stored in the system in its standard-compliant format, at as high a quality as possible.

In the context of learning, these independent digital assets can be seen as **learning objects**. Documentation about the photograph and the interactive interface can include skills that it promotes, or links to more information. The same photograph previously used only in an exhibition can therefore be used in a myriad of learning contexts—in an activity sheet, a bespoke learning game, a mobile app.

Thus, turning learning resources into digital assets involves the same process of digitization, databasing, and distribution, although the information recorded in the database and the distribution channels may be different.

RESEARCH AND PUBLICATIONS

Museums generate a great deal of knowledge outside of the exhibitions, but it is often only published once in one format, and then saved in the museum archive—if at all. Curators often write journal articles, or blogs, other staff send out newsletters or make presentations. Museum researchers may also be part of larger networked projects involving other museums, universities, and other institutions; for example, the iDigBio (Integrated Digitized Biocollections) based at University of Florida.

It is technically straightforward to liberate this content into the museum's various channels, but this also requires a recognition that this content is valuable and is part of the knowledge resource that museums are uniquely placed to make broadly accessible. Being imaginative about different channels for research and publications may require some editing, but will ultimately enhance the museum's ability to superserve its community. Consider, for example, if exhibition visitors could easily access a journal article related to an artifact on display, or if teachers could encourage learners to read a blog, watch a presentation at a professional conference, and visit an exhibition all on the same subject as a way of introducing them to perspective, sources, and modes of presentation.

EXHIBITION MEDIA

There is little doubt that much of the media your museum produces is created on computers—whether exhibition text, photographs, videos or interactive games or experiences. In theory, this content can be repurposed for every digital channel, but in reality the ability to repurpose digital content rarely happens without planning.

Organizational silos persist in the digital world, and overcoming them requires coordination across departments. In the following chapter, Corey Timpson describes how an enterprise content management system greatly facilitates re-purposing of exhibition content.

Digital Channels

Digital channels are the ways that your users encounter your content. Channels include:

- Website
- Search

- WiFi
- Location awareness
- Social media
- Blogs
- Email
- Digital signage
- Distribution networks
- Exhibitions

Each channel has particular requirements for content, which can be described in a content plan. Some of these requirements are discussed in the following sections. Please note that the discussions are not exhaustive, and also that best practices change monthly. Therefore use these as an introduction, but ensure that you have reviewed the state of the art in the museum sector and beyond before engaging in a planning exercise. In addition, visitor expectations change depending on the channel, and centralized digital management makes it easy to optimize content for a particular context.

Table 8.1 gives an example of how you might begin to summarize existing and current digital channels in your museum. It should be elaborated in a way that makes sense within your current technology and operational audits. From this you can generate a strategic overview that enables you to plan channel integration against the realities of budget and operating procedure.

WEBSITE

What is the boundary between online and physical experiences? This is not a metaphysical question. Virtually all museums have a website, and your website is a natural foundation for building a suite of omnichannel services. Your website can be the platform for content created elsewhere in the museum, but it can also generate content that reaches people through other channels; for example, through social media or smartphones.

Your website is as important for some users as your building is for others. As a key platform for content, you need to ensure that web content is relevant and engaging for online visitors who may never visit your physical exhibitions.

Digital projects have multiple stakeholders that may include curators, marketers, sales directors, and other parties with diverging agendas. Just as all departments are involved in doing your content audit, so should all be involved in planning and prioritizing elements of your website.

TABLE 8.1 SAMPLE LIST OF DIGITAL CHANNELS AND RELEVANT INFORMATION

PLATFORM	STATUS	SIZE	LOCATION	CONTENT
Website	Live	Responsive	User outside	Full
Facebook	Live	800 x 600	User	Image + post
Pinterest	Live	400 x 300	User	Image
Twitter	Live	Text	User	Text
Captive Portal (WiFi)	Planned	Responsive	User in house	What's Happening Now, flash discounts, audio tours
Monitors	Live	42-inch	Lobbies	What's Happening Now, flash discounts
Signage	Live	6-inch ticker	Information Desk	Ticket price, flash discounts, live Twitter feed
Tablet A1	Live	8-inch iPad	Gallery A	Item A-1001
Tablet A2	Live	8-inch iPad	Gallery A	Item A-2002
Projector A1	Live	HD	Gallery A	Exhibition A1
Projector A2	Live	HD	Gallery A	Exhibition A2
Projector B1	Planned	4K	Gallery B	Exhibition B1
Projector B2	Planned	4K	Gallery B	Exhibition B2

Developing a Content Plan for Your Website

Each department should be involved in doing the content plan (either collectively or individually), which describes what they want people to experience on your website. The plan should be comprehensive, and it should contain as much detail as possible in order to avoid expensive and difficult modifications later on. In the online world, the definition of content includes interactivity, and your plan should specify functionality such as registration alongside text, images and video.

You may want to begin your planning process by envisioning your ideal website. Once you know what you want, compare it with your budget and other resources. Make sure you include your operational budget that forecasts incremental costs. If ambition outstrips resources, your plan can adapt your vision to reality. It is always possible to drop options or launch a basic website and add new features in phases.

To start developing a content plan, it is best to work from the general to specifics. First ask the question, *What does the site do for which visitors?* Or it can also be phrased, *What do specific visitors do when they visit the site?* Your colleagues may answer:

1. The website gets visitors excited about current exhibitions at the museum.
2. The website tells visitors how to get to the museum.
3. The website encourages people to buy exhibition tickets online.
4. The website builds interest in membership by showing the range of activities at the museum.
5. The website makes the museum store the first stop for people who want to buy gifts.
6. The website offers educational opportunities for people of all ages.
7. The website shows the positive economic impact of the museum on surrounding communities.

The next question is what kind of content best achieves each of the outcomes framed in your planning exercise. Build a table that details your ambitions and draws from the content audit. It is best to start simply with general categories:

- **Format:** For example, text, image, video, game.
- **Topic** (for media): For example, ancient, medieval, and modern.
- **Purpose** (for interaction): For example, register, share, comment, upload, donate.
- **Update cycle:** For example, daily, weekly, monthly.
- **Outcome:** For example, inspire visits, sell tickets, build membership.

Once you have done your table, add another column that ranks each item according to priority. The priority needs to take into account all the different departments and stakeholders in your museum. This will be important when you brief the web designers.

Your content table informs the phasing of your operational plan. From it you can project the staffing, budget, and resource requirements necessary to maintain the website. You can also judge the effectiveness of content, and the effort required to produce it, by comparing outcomes to costs.

Chapter 11 gives a detailed explanation of how to develop an operations budget. A website requires maintenance, and the departments supporting it will need budget, skills, and management to deliver content.

The next step is to elaborate your framework. Add categories that make sense within your museum. Many of them you can derive from working knowledge of your current website and industry practices. But they should also be derived from your use cases. Let the rubber hit the road with your user profiles. What might a fifteen-year-old gamer who loves dinosaurs want to do? Be prosaic about the must-have features such as "What's on Now," but be creative about new features that might generate interest in specific audience.

Each new item should be assigned a purpose, an update cycle, and the resources required to maintain it on the live website. Categories commonly found on museum websites include:

- Things to do
- Access to collections
- Ecommerce
- Tickets
- Online store
- Directions
- Contact information
- Development
- Fundraising
- Sponsor information
- User-generated content

Finally you should use the planning framework to generate a detailed content plan. This should show how the website appears day to day, even hour to hour, through a season.

Create a budget that includes the human and technical resources necessary to realize the season's schedule. With this in hand, you are in a position to judge the overall cost of maintaining the site with details on how specific items impact outcomes.

Your next step is design, which may be outsourced or done internally. The content plan with its rankings is an important brief for the designers. In chapter 12, Marco Mason describes the user-experience design process. His guidance applies equally to websites as it does to exhibitions, as does the overview of project management given in chapter 11.

SEARCH

Just because you have created an superb website doesn't mean people will visit it. Most visitors go to museum websites for directions or admissions prices not for a remarkable experience or to learn something. This is where marketing enters, similar to physical exhibitions and programs, your virtual exhibitions and programs require an investment of marketing time and resources.

Many of your visitors probably find your website through a search engine. Search engine optimization (SEO) is an important discipline in its own right, and it is critical for you because museums are major content providers. SEO works on metadata. The concept of metadata should be absorbed throughout your organization. Metadata is composed of tags—that is, bits of information that describe either the content or structural characteristics of a data file. Metadata are composed according to standard formats that search engines can interpret, and they enable keyword searches to discover files that have been tagged with a particular word or, increasingly, an associated concept. Even though image recognition is improving, applying metadata to a file is still the most effective way of exposing images and video to search engines.

While Google often sets the pace for SEO standards, there are other significant search engines that should not be ignored; for example, Yahoo and DuckDuckGo. SEO guidelines change rapidly and arbitrarily, so it is necessary to retain expertise to engage in a neverending process of optimization.

WIFI

Though indoor smartphone usage still inspires debate, it is inevitable that museums will respond to demand from visitors. In-house mobile engagement is a critical step toward becoming an omnichannel museum, and people expect to be able to get the exact same (if not more) functionality and information from the smartphone as they do from a website. Museum visitors use smartphones in museums as they do in their daily lives. For the most part, they take photos, share experiences, chat with friends (even the ones beside them), or perform activities unrelated to the museum. Smartphones can be seen as a diversion for your visitors and something to be shunned, or they can be embraced as a way to enhance your visitor's engagement with the museum.

> **KEY TERMS**
>
> **LOCATION AWARENESS**
>
> Location awareness and analytics is the use of digital systems such as beacons or WiFi to identify the location and movements of individuals through buildings or other public spaces. It is combined with analytics to optimize wayfinding, circulation management, security, and visitor engagement.
>
> **RESPONSIVE**
>
> A responsive website recognizes the end user's device and serves content in the appropriate format. It is now industry standard for CMS software because search engines take responsiveness into account when generating a website's rank.

LOCATION AWARENESS

Smartphones enable location awareness, which supports personalization during or outside of the visit.

Your content management system (CMS) should be location aware. It can judge a user's location from an IP address, and, if they are on a mobile phone, it may have access to much more specific information. Your CMS should also be **responsive**. Responsive is a term of art in web development, and a responsive website optimizes its transmissions for the size, resolution, and bandwidth of a user's display. It is particularly valuable for smartphones that may access the Internet under wildly different conditions.

SOCIAL MEDIA

Social media are accessed through the web, but they function through their own standards, imperatives, and cultures. The largest social networks are global communities in their own right, and they offer sophisticated (though ultimately self-interested) tools for posting, sharing, and discovering content. Your museum almost certainly has presence on multiple social networks, and they probably are already major drivers of online and physical visits. Chapter 4 focuses specifically on social media as a channel, a platform, a tool for engagement and marketing.

BLOGS

Blogs are web content that includes writing, photographs, and other multimedia. What distinguishes them from other web content is the informal, serial nature of the content. Blogs generally take a personal view, and the writer uses his or her own voice on topics that matter to them.

EMAIL

Email is still a major channel for many museums that send out e-blasts, newsletters, and other content. An email newsletter functions as an extension of your website—it is essentially a webpage delivered to someone's inbox. But newsletters make it possible to calibrate your messaging. Suppose your team has three different ideas for a marketing campaign. How do you find which is most effective? By testing alternatives in a mass email, you can track which has the most impact—that is, the highest open rate. You can segment your subscribers, and you even develop approaches that target specific demographics. See the discussion on A/B testing at the end of this chapter for more detail on how to calibrate the performance of email campaigns.

DIGITAL SIGNAGE

Numerous systems for digital signage exist. Some use proprietary content formats, and it is best to avoid these. As Kevin Cunningham points out in chapter 14, proprietary systems bind museums to a company's maintenance and upgrade fees, and many companies charge considerably more than the open source software market. Digital signage should be based on open source standards that allow a variety of formats to be selected, and ideally content management should converge on the **HTML5** standard used for the web and other digital channels.

DISTRIBUTION NETWORKS

There are many methods to distribute your digital content beyond the channels you own. Recorded and, increasingly, live video YouTube, Facebook, Vimeo, and more specialized networks are commonly used. They make it easy to keep people on your website by hosting your video on their services and offering embeddable players. WebEx, Periscope, and **MOOC** platforms enable live interaction with audiences. By supporting Q&A formats, these are particularly useful for lectures, workshops, and educational events.

If reach is a necessity, content distribution networks (CDNs) will promote your content for a fee. If you offer open databases of images, the communities that populate noncommercial aggregators such Wikipedia, Europeana, and a host of specialized sites may use your content. You may also find interest from tourist bureaus and tourism partners such as hotels and airlines. When distributing your content, it is important to attach usage rights or licenses to individual items. If you are allowing some degree of free usage, **Creative Commons** licenses allow you to designate which uses are allowed in a globally recognized format.

> **KEY TERMS**
>
> **HTML5**
>
> HTML5 is the globally recognized language for coding websites and web-compliant digital media channels.
>
> **MOOC**
>
> MOOC stands for massive open online course, and it is a software platform that enables thousands of students to participate in an academic course remotely.
>
> **CREATIVE COMMONS**
>
> Creative Commons is a global standard for managing various levels of copyright for publicly available content and intellectual property.

EXHIBITIONS

Exhibitions increasingly use digital technologies, and in many museums management of exhibitions is separate from both digital content departments and IT. But, as Corey Timpson describes in chapter 9, there are considerable advantages to adopting a common digital infrastructure. Chapters 12 and 13 describe how museums can begin to converge their development and management structures around the advantages offered by digital platforms in a gradual process that realizes benefits at every stage.

The Content Management System (CMS)

Digital technology is supposed to create efficiencies, but many organizations experience the opposite. In some cases, staff have more, not less, to do after a promising new installation. For example, consider the case of digital signage.

Digital signs seem better than print signs because they can be updated electronically. However, the updates still need to be written, designed, and transmitted. If the digital sign is not networked, updates have to be inserted manually via a jump drive or some other media. If the signs are on a network, they can be delivered centrally, but they still require some kind of content management system. At this point, the only real saving is in the cost and labor of printing and replacing signs. This saving may be offset by the failure to meet expectations of frequent updates and customized digital designs, both of which are labor intensive when not managed centrally.

As we can see with this example, a major problem with digital upgrades is the lack of operational planning. Unlike the physical objects they replace, digital systems carry a spectrum of invisible costs related to operations and maintenance. With little precedent for reference, these costs are often overlooked when planning, and staff are stretched thin after the system launches. However, this can be fixed through consolidating content management, and ultimately all forms of visitor engagement, into one system. For a strong perspective of centralized data management, and its benefits to museums and visitors, see Cory Timpson's discussion of enterprise content management in chapter 9.

Content management is essential to creating an omnichannel experience. Digital content is managed through a content management system, or CMS, a piece of software that automatically formats text and graphics in a digital presentation (not to be confused with a collections management system, also called a CMS, as described in chapter 10). Selection of a CMS is no simple matter. There are hundreds of CMS applications on the market. Each offers some unique value, and larger, more complex systems have attracted communities of developers who specialize in adapting them for customers. The CMS was originally developed for web publishing, but now they are used for virtually any digital channel. Digital signage and other hardware platforms usually come with their own CMS, and, because these systems work out of the box, they are often used by default.

The enterprise CMS described by Corey Timpson was built from scratch for a new museum, but a completely fresh start is not necessary. Any organization can work toward omnichannel content management in a series of steps. The most important part is to make a strategic decision to do so, then to lay out a clear road map for each stage of integration.

Great efficiencies result from consolidating content management into one system. Imagine you are promoting a blockbuster exhibition. Every promotion requires collateral, and a single reference can contain the official name, logo treatments, colors, images, copy, schedule, maps, and video. Staff responsible for the website, newsletter (electronic and printed), social media accounts, digital signage and lobby monitors, in-house WiFi, memberships, and even exhibitions and the museum shop can each draw the collateral they need with complete consistency.

It gets better. Your organization can also set up templates for the functions listed above. Rather than have someone pull files, the person entering the data could simply tick a box to send live information to a digital channel.

Integration with other systems creates a more seamless experience for your visitors. Your museum may have dozens of databases, but in simplest terms you need to ensure your content management, collections management, and customer relationship management systems share data. Ideally, data are never entered more than once throughout your systems—especially by visitors. To achieve this omnichannel state, it is important to bear the following in mind: Content means any experience available on your digital channels.

It is not necessary to build the ultimate CMS in one round. As Rachel Walker describes in chapter 11, it is necessary to plan the project around the needs of the organization. Some of your digital channels may be managed by separate departments with legacy systems, and you can integrate systems in stages that let operations adapt in a comfortable time frame.

Technology Plan

You have identified your users (and a plan for continuing to get to know them), made a plan for transforming content into digital assets you can manage via a content management system, but you still need to make sure it all works properly. In digital systems, technology failures are as catastrophic as operational ones.

Your technology plan describes the engineering that supports your digital channels. It is a comprehensive, living document, and even though the systems it describes are invisible to most of your organization, it should be diligently maintained. This applies whether the work is outsourced or performed in-house. Technical systems need to be upgraded regularly to maintain security, functionality, and a contemporary user experience. If personnel responsible for your digital channels changes, full documentation will ease the transition. Without it, developers could spend months deciphering the code that powers your digital presence.

The technology plan should include the following:

- Functional requirements
- Software specification
- Hardware specification
- Operations and maintenance procedures

Each of these categories describes a distinct "layer" of your digital publishing systems. But even though they are treated separately, they must be planned together, and they form a functional whole. To understand how the layers interact, please review the discussion of engineering stacks in the omnichannel planning section of chapter 2.

Functional Requirements

The best-designed digital experiences start with usability. There are two types of users, visitors and producers. Visitors are essentially the customers of a system—and user-centric design usually refers to them. But the people maintaining the site should not be overlooked in a plan. When describing a channel's functionality (what it does), profiles of both end users and producers should be considered. The functional requirements are the toolkit used to create experiences.

Generally, functional requirements are gathered into specification. The functional specification is generated by listing types of content, how they are presented to users, and the desired management process. For instance, you may want to serve video. To translate this requirement into a specification, consider how your requirements can be "specified."

- Desired resolution of the video frame
- Length of content and size of data files
- Content hosting platform (e.g., in-house, YouTube or Vimeo)
- Controls offered to users (e.g., fast forward, view later)
- Appearance of the controls
- Are there ads or marketing pre-rolls?
- What happens when video ends (e.g., rolls to another video)?
- Frequency of updates
- Upload and queuing path
- Calendaring tools for site managers
- Analytics tracking tools

The behavior of every piece of content should be considered when developing a functional specification. As a matter of course, websites are now responsive, which means the CMS automatically sends content in a format suitable for the end user's device. This means that format specifications are based on the maximum quality available rather than a detailed list of every possible configuration.

The specification should then describe the processes required to manage the content. A modern CMS has a standard user interface (UI) with a wide range of options, and the functional specification mostly selects from the options. Most CMSs are customized, and your developer may guide you into one or more standard options because developing new features is expensive and requires a commitment to upgrades for the life of the system.

Software Specification

The software that enables digital channels is an engineering stack of its own. In simplified form this usually includes:

- Your customized CMS
- Registration systems
- Any plug-ins, add-ons, or additional software
- The CMS environment
- Media hosting software
- Linked ticketing, customer relationship management system (CRM), and collections databases
- The server operating system (OS)

Hardware

Hardware consists of servers and other computers where the software is installed. These machines physically execute software code, and it is sent over networks to user devices. Hardware and the software it runs may be installed in your museum, outsourced to a service provider, or a combination of both.

Operations

As you can see, it takes an ensemble of technology to maintain digital channels. Your technology plan should fully document the systems listed above, and it should also contain user manuals for maintenance, upgrades, troubleshooting, and disaster recovery. Even smoothly running systems cannot be left to their own devices. Online security is a fast-moving field, and any of the systems above may require an emergency software patch that closes a vulnerability. These need to be installed as soon as they are released. Software and hardware systems are on upgrade cycles. Each manufacturer has its own parameters, and they must be actively monitored so your systems remain current. Please consult the sections on software in chapter 14 for more guidance on maintenance procedures.

The Performance Plan

Fast impressions matter. Visitors expect web pages to load in less than two seconds. If a page takes five seconds to load, an average of 25 percent of visitors go elsewhere. The numbers go up with every second of delay, and they are particularly damaging when visitors are trying to purchase tickets or merchandise. When planning digital channels, you should spend as much time on performance metrics as you do on branding, design, and content. If the digital experience performs poorly, visitors may never experience the elements you worked so hard to create.

Risks associated with poor performance can be assigned to two categories: operational and reputational. Operational risks relate to lost revenue and other material consequences of poor user experience. Someone planning a trip to your museum may lose interest if the site loads slowly. This applies to the home page and everything beyond it, including pages that embed functionality from other sources. It does not matter where your content is sourced; visitors will treat it as part of your site. Ticketing and other purchase paths also need to spring into service quickly to encourage completion.

Perceptions of how your channels operate impact your reputation. Just as design reflects your aesthetic, performance creates an image of competence, and it also creates an impression of how much you care for your visitors. In today's world many more people can experience your collections and your programs online than in your building. Museums embody high standards of excellence, and your online experience should match the standards on offer to physical visitors.

Well-established frameworks can assist planning and help translate goals into design and technical specifications.

Branding, content, stories, sales, and mission-driven experiences each carry their own imperatives, but each of them also impacts performance. Performance boils down to numbers, but achieving high standards of performance requires coordination across your entire development process. It is helpful to set performance metrics as early as possible so the entire team develops concepts that can be realized through coherent, practical design.

Design for Performance

Standards for performance have been relatively consistent since the beginning of the web. In his classic writing on software usability, Jakob Nielson observes that if your software responds in 0.1 second, the user feels in control. After 1 second, the user notices the delay, and at 10 seconds a person's attention wanders.[1] Studies made by Kissmetrics and others note defections from a page starting at less than a second. By 4 seconds, a screen loses 25 percent of its users.[2] Performance requirements are unlikely to become more stringent because people are disturbed when a screen responds too quickly.

Ensuring good performance starts with design. A fundamental concept is page weight. Page weight is determined by UI design, and it is defined as the total amount of data that follows a click. For instance, an image may add 100 KB of data to a data transfer. Large or numerous objects increase page weight, and so does third-party content. Your site may embed content from partners. Examples include images, maps, video, social media, and advertising. It may not be possible to eliminate delays in partner services, but you can compensate for them in your planning and design.

Remember that performance cannot be predicted for individual visits. Slow connections, the amount of people online, and even solar flares can impact performance. Thus it is good practice to achieve your objectives with the fewest objects possible. This is difficult when many stakeholders are making demands, so it is critical that someone is empowered to say no. One approach is to give your project manager a page weight budget that triggers a rethink when pages get too heavy. Rather than build a poor user experience, it is more effective to design a compelling user journey that leads visitors to positive outcomes.

Judging Performance Requirements

At the most fundamental level, a website is a database that resides in one or more computers. Its performance thus directly relates to where the server is, where its users are and how many people are trying to visit at any given time. A CMS that can handle five hundred visitors may falter at five thousand and fall over at fifty thousand. Higher performance systems cost more, not just for the software but for the hardware required to operate them.

An important external constraint on a website is the number of visitors. If you are paying for bandwidth, the total number of visitors has budgetary impact. From a performance standpoint, the important figure is the maximum number of simultaneous users. This may be called expected concurrencies or visitor spikes, and it is used to judge the load put on servers during peak usage.

Historical data on web traffic is invaluable. Usage patterns should be reviewed at several levels, and it is particularly important to look at hourly data during spikes. This will give a baseline figure for developers. It is equally important to forecast your future needs. One figure can be calculated by extrapolating trends from historical data. But it is also important to gauge the ambitions of your organization along with factors that may mitigate past trends. A blockbuster show, clever strategic plan or ambitious individual could amplify your traffic. Conversely, closure of the museum or galleries for renovation could precipitate a decline in site visits.

Ticketing, ecommerce, and registration should be treated with special care. These pathways have deep impact on both operations and reputation, and they are often handled independently of your CMS. Poor performance can lower revenue, and security breaches open your museum to legal and reputational hazards. Financial transactions involve payment card companies, and the increasing use of social login opens your content to the imperatives of outside companies. Both require high levels of security, and you should ensure your developers incorporate the latest standards in your CMS.

The Development Process

It is important to discuss performance when negotiating a website hosting agreement. You should also engage an independent firm that specializes in performance testing to ensure your web host delivers the required metrics. It is possible to run automated or self-designed tests, but, for obvious reasons, whoever manages the tests should have experience. Before contracting a website, everyone involved should agree to a methodology that can determine failure points in your site's performance, and payments to agencies should depend on appropriate fixes to problems that emanate from their domain.

After development, your website will be hosted on a test server. Though it resides on the Internet, its address will be hidden until its public launch. Test servers should be identical to public servers so tests will be valid. To prepare for tests, your organization will need to work closely with the testing firm to develop use cases. Each use case traces a typical user journey through your website. For instance, it may start with the home page, a click to a calendar followed by information on an exhibition, a ticket purchase, and finally a map with directions. Use cases should be varied, and they should also consider scenarios such as password recovery that can generate considerable load on a server.

Performance tests, also called load tests, are translated into scripts that are run on one or more servers. These synthetic users emulate the behavior of real persons accessing the website. Generally they start light then incrementally increase the number of requests. Performance characteristics are recorded for each increase, and these can be matched to the performance metrics you agreed to with your web host.

Any methodology will gauge the site's maximum capacity, its stability when in high demand, and its reaction to jumps in demand. Performance testing firms can also probe the website's vulnerability to bottlenecks, scalability, stability, and ability to recover from disaster. Many of these tests are relevant only to commercial websites whose user base greatly exceeds museum properties, but awareness of what they measure can help planners fully understand online business models.

A good performance testing firm issues a report that describes the magnitude of failures and the points where they occur and gives suggestions for how to mitigate them. Reports can also help calculate return on investment (ROI) on options such as scaling fees or deals with content distribution networks (CDNs) that enhance performance by hosting content closer to visitors. Developing, assessing, and optimizing performance requires orchestration of many parties. A performance testing firm should be treated as a collaborator who needs to understand your organization and its stakeholders, objectives, and budgetary constraints.

Websites are works in progress. Your development agency may or not be on retainer, but in any event you should ensure that you have ownership and access to your website's components. This includes the CMS (which is probably under separate license) and the modifications the agency makes to it. Examples of these modifications include HTML formatting code, CSS (Cascading Style Sheets), Javascript, and the visual design. They should also include tools for SEO, databases and database-stored content, and any documentation such as content guidelines, training manuals, logic manuals, flowcharts and principles of operation.

💡 KEY TAKEAWAYS: PLANNING FOR DIGITAL CONTENT

1. Developing an omnichannel museum involves five integrated activities:

- Understanding the people who use the museum;

- Creating digital assets that mirror and extend physical assets;

- Implementing content and collections management systems;

- Engaging the public through open access, interactivity (especially with experts), personalization, and other user-centric principles

- Ensuring that a robust technology and performance plan keeps the system contemporary and responsive.

2. Museums can better understand their users by segmenting them, undertaking qualitative research, and developing personas and use cases.

3. Creating digital assets begins with a content audit which evaluates all sources of content in your museums. These could include collections and documentation, digital art, virtual and augmented reality, exhibition media, research and publications, and learning resources.

4. The process of converting content resources to digital assets involves digitization, databasing, and distribution.

5. Users encounter content via digital channels such as your website, WiFi, digital signage, social media, and exhibitions.

6. A content management system is an essential software tool to support databasing and distributing digital content to many channels of your museums.

7. Your technology plan describes the engineering that supports your digital channels. The technology plan should include the functional requirements, software specification, hardware specifications and operations, and maintenance procedures.

8. A performance plan ensures that the digital experience performs optimally. It helps to mitigate operational and reputational risks.

Notes

1. Jakob Nielsen. Usability Engineering. Morgan Kaufman. 1993.
2. Kissmetrics. http//www.nngroup.com/articles/how-long-do-users-stay-on-web-pages/.

The Pursuit of Efficient Relevance
An Enterprise Content Management System

Corey Timpson

In 2009, a full five years prior to the Canadian Museum for Human Rights opening its doors to the public, museum staff immersed themselves in the detailed planning of the museum experience. This noble museum project, the first of its kind, was not short on ambition—a museum that would provoke reflection and dialogue, foster empathy, empower individuals and groups, and inspire a generation of change makers. An *ideas museum*, whose subject matter is intangible and conceptual. Its artifacts are not material culture but stories themselves. A new type of museum with a different kind of collection and a new design on the museum experience. Yet for all its ambition and exciting

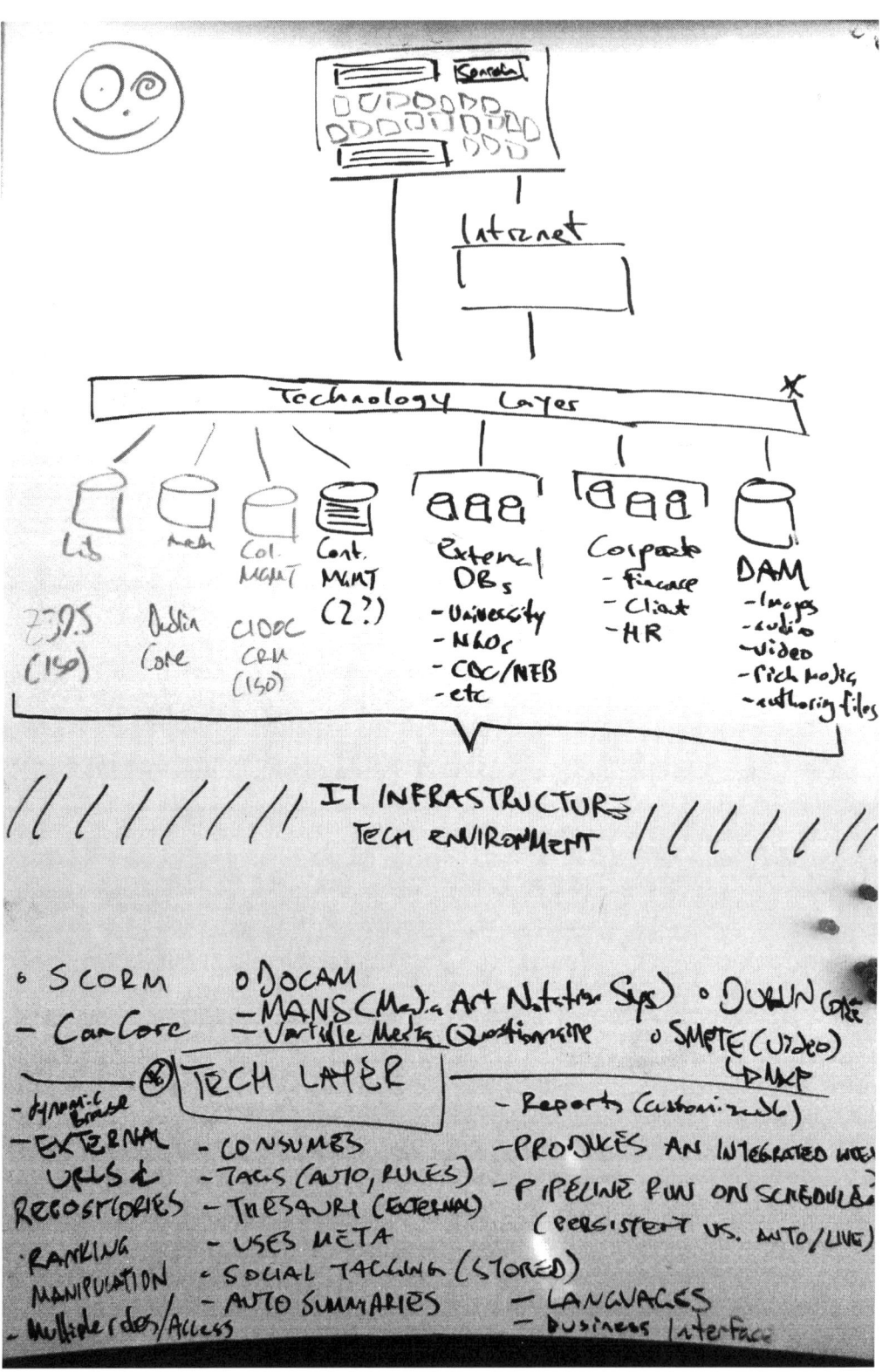

FIGURE 9.1 An early sketch of Canadian Museum of Human Rights' ECMS.
Corey Timpson (author)

programs, such a novel museological concept demanded an equally novel infrastructure of technology and methodology.

The enterprise content management system (ECMS), of the Canadian Museum for Human Rights, was first born as a concept in late 2009 as a sketch on a flipchart (see figure 9.1).

Through careful planning and design, it would grow into a groundbreaking system that today facilitates and ensures standardization in the cataloging, preservation, aggregation, and management of all content, and ensures dynamic distribution of said content to the digital endpoints of the museum where they are experienced by visitors.

A Museum for Human Rights

The Canadian Museum for Human Rights (CMHR) is the first national museum in Canada located outside of the nation's capital of Ottawa. Located at the Forks, a national historic site in Winnipeg, Manitoba, the CMHR's mandate is "to explore the subject of human rights, with special but not exclusive reference to Canada, in order to enhance the public's understanding of human rights, to promote respect for others, and to encourage reflection and dialogue" (Museums Act S.C. 1990, c. 3). The museum's subject matter is not only conceptual but also contemporary. The concept of human rights is a fairly new one, with the phrase itself only being coined in the mid-twentieth century. The cornerstone of the museum's collection is the output of its Oral History Program and first-person storytelling.

This new type of museum was being created just as many museums were recognizing the importance of interactivity in order to ensure an engaged audience. The ECMS was one of

MIXED MEDIA AT CMHR

The Canadian Museum for Human Rights expresses its exhibitions through a variety of mixed media, and much of this media, while of varying shape and presentation, is digital. At its opening in the autumn of 2014, the museum's 4,650 square meters (approx. 50,000 sq. feet) of exhibitions were composed of:

- 8 feature films (4 in English, 4 in French)
- 2 360° films (1 in English, 1 in French)
- 52 small format films
- 1 large-scale, immersive multimedia experience
- 2 soundscapes
- 37 linear media projections
- 1,024 videos
- 18 mixed-media installations
- 2,600 digital images
- 100,000 words
- 300 artifacts/objects and their labels

In addition to the exhibitions the following digital programs were offered:

- 1 mobile app (on 2 platforms—iOS and Android)
- 1 enterprise website
- A social media presence of several channels—Facebook (2), Twitter (2), YouTube (2), Flickr, Instagram, Tumblr
- A digital reference center and library catalog
- Museum-wide digital signage

the first concepts designed and planned at the CMHR. It wasn't an immersive, visitor-facing experience. Rather, it was a piece of technology that no visitor would ever see or directly interact with. Yet its creation would facilitate the spending of valuable, finite resources on those visitor-facing, visitor-engaging aspects of the museum's programs that people think of when they've enjoyed a meaningful cultural experience—and it would serve this purpose during both the design and development of the museum, as well as in perpetuity.

As with any developing subject matter, the ability to adapt and change was a prerequisite of all museum program development at the CMHR. A museum dealing with such a volume of media, in such a variety of forms, with a prerequisite for adaptation, evolution, and change, posed serious implications on the design and development scopes of work.

A content management system (CMS) is not a new concept. However, the notion of applying a CMS across the entirety of a museum enterprise, merging it with a collections management system (see chapter 10), and feeding all content endpoints, no matter the design or mixed-media nature, was extremely ambitious.

Strategically Addressing the Present and the Future

While budget and schedule allowed for the design and creation of all the content required by the Canadian Museum for Human Rights to successfully open to the public, the preoccupation of the design and development team was in dealing with how not to be outdated, either before, right at, or directly following the opening of the museum—in either content or experiential offerings. As such, the ECMS aimed to respond to three strategic design assumptions:

1. *An incessant and continued evolution in audience expectations.* The assumption is that as technology advances so do people's expectations. Imagine entering a public environment and not being granted WiFi. Not meeting an audience's expectations is an immediate barrier to engagement.

2. *Rapid media and technological advancement.* As user expectations increase, it pushes competitive markets to not only respond to, but attempt to exceed, those expectations. As such, the evolution of technology and media, as well as their convergence, grows exponentially. Not being prepared for what comes next, even when what comes next is unknown, represents a future barrier to engagement.

3. *Data ubiquity.* On-demand, ubiquitous information that is aggregated, republished, mashed-up, shared, and re-accessed across both physical and digital landscapes is an increasing reality. Additionally, data (or "content") that is outdated can now be immediately discovered and the content source discredited. Not providing a mechanism to efficiently and effectively meet these realities will create future barriers in experience

design, and it poses risks to the credibility of the museum.

In short, the enterprise content management system was created not only to organize information but also to ensure that the delivery of information, in any form, would be done in a scalable, cost-effective manner in perpetuity. While this was extremely important to the CMHR, given the necessity of change, it is no less important to any cultural institution that is looking to meet the increasingly sophisticated expectations of its audience.

Requirements Definition

The enterprise content management system aimed to be for the benefit of the museum overall, but ultimately it had to be usable by the staff. In the development of the ECMS for the Canadian Museum for Human Rights, an extensive requirements definition phase was done that included the users across all relevant departments of the museum. A broad environmental scan was also completed, product demos were solicited, interviews with various potential providers held, and an elaborate concept design phase was undertaken that included vetting at conferences and symposia and industry professional critique sessions.

> **DEFINING USER REQUIREMENTS**
>
> One of the first phases of any technical project is the requirements definition phase, which includes the participation of clients and users of the intended system, along with technical and system experts.
>
> In the case of the ECMS, this involved the librarian, archivist, collections manager, registrar, data architect, IT director, designers, producers, systems architect, software developers, and more. The multiple perspectives brought together by the multidisciplinary team ensured that the wide-ranging and varying requirements were identified and developed for each client and user type, redundancies were identified and mitigated, and conflicts were reconciled.

ECMS Design Principles

The ECMS is characterized by the following design direction prerequisites:

1. Strict separation of content from presentation
2. A "store content once and reference often" methodology
3. Dynamic delivery of content
4. Must be able to do "anything"
5. System constraints through business rules, not technical limitations
6. Complete modularity and scalability
7. Standards compliance

> **KEY TERMS**
>
> **STANDARDS COMPLIANT FORMAT**
>
> A format that ensures the interoperability of various data and systems.
>
> **INTERFACE DESIGN**
>
> The graphical interface that a user interacts with in order to perform functions on a system or computer.

SEPARATION OF CONTENT FROM PRESENTATION

There are at least two pieces of data for every piece of content you see in an exhibit: the media itself, and the data that describes the media's appearance. *Separation of content from presentation* implies that each digital asset (such as an image, video, piece of text, audio file) is stored in the system in its **standards compliant format**, at as high a quality as possible.

The presentation (how the image, for example, will appear in an exhibit) is also data, and this data, related to the specific installation, is stored as well. The two pieces of data are brought together at the installation—that is, the point of contact between visitors and the media, such as a touch table, video screen, or mobile app. For example, an image is stored in the ECMS—this is the asset data. How the images within an installation will appear (size, resolution, crop area, etc.) is installation data and is also stored. They are brought together via the software of the specific installation.

By separating content from presentation, the museum can now cost-effectively:

- Add more images to the installation without having to perform postproduction on each of them, as the specifications for the presentation are already set up within the installation software;

- Delete images from the installation without having to redesign the installation's presentation (or interface);

- Change the **interface design** without having to reproduce all the images presented in the installation; and

- Reuse the images from one installation in other installations without having to reproduce them all specifically to these new contexts.

STORE ONCE, REFERENCE OFTEN

In the case of the CMHR, the same digital asset can be found in multiple contexts. For example, the same image can be found in a gallery as part of a mixed-media installation providing an environmental experience, in the reference center with associated other data for research purposes, in an image-gallery online via the CMHR website, and on the mobile app as part of a self-guided mobile tour. These are all derivatives of the same asset. The image only exists once. The image was also only licensed and cataloged once, and it appears in all of these contexts, via the ECMS, appearing unique in each context due to the context data that was developed for each installation type.

> **KEY TERMS**
>
> **CACHE**
>
> A space for storing data temporarily so as to improve response time or integrity of the experience should a connection to the system be lost.

DYNAMIC DELIVERY OF CONTENT

Because so much of the content at CMHR is digital, it does not need to actually reside in the installation but can be delivered centrally from the ECMS. If edits or updates are needed to the content, it can be done centrally to feed the various presentation points. One change done at the ECMS can, therefore, update content across multiple presentation points at the same time. Additionally, the CMHR's system was designed to "fail open." This means that each installation, the website, the mobile app, and so on all **cache** content locally, so if there is a service interruption with the CMHR network, the installation doesn't end up void of content. The cache is programmed to fetch, or check, for new content on a set schedule and can also be overridden and have content pushed to it.

MUST BE ABLE TO "DO ANYTHING" AND SYSTEM CONSTRAINTS THROUGH BUSINESS RULES, NOT TECHNICAL LIMITATIONS

These two points are interrelated. *Must be able to do anything* means that in the first instance, the system must be flexible enough to allow users and other systems to do whatever they want. The ECMS was being designed and created concurrently with the design of the museum's exhibitions. The specifics of each museum installation that would eventually require the ECMS were not known at the outset of the ECMS's design, and future-proofing was therefore critical.

System constraints through business rules, not technical limitations means that once the system is constructed to be as open as possible, it then can accommodate constraints placed on it, in terms of business rules. Examples of "business rules constraints" could be information security protocols, user-profile restrictions based on user groups, or limitations to how content can be altered or adapted (such as might be required by copyright). The importance is that it is better to create rules of constraints for business purposes than to have to work around or solve technical constraints in order to achieve various desired use cases.

COMPLETE MODULARITY AND SCALABILITY AND STANDARDS COMPLIANCE

These are also related. The ECMS is a system composed of several different technologies that all work together. In order for integration and **data aggregation** to work, they

> **KEY TERMS**
>
> **DATA AGGREGATION**
>
> The combining of various points of data into a single set in order to facilitate usability.
>
> **COMMON STANDARDS FOR DIGITAL**
>
> One of the first steps in developing the ECMS was to define what types of files the system would accommodate and how. Identifying these technical specifications was key to the development of the system, even though the ambition was to be as flexible as possible.
>
> The most important standards identified and adhered to with the ECMS were the database standards (SQL compliance by all modules was critical) and the metadata standards for each client subject discipline. Archival, library, and museum collection documentation can all use different metadata standards (for example, Z39.5, Dublin Core, Dublin Core Extended, CIDOC CRM, etc.), and the CMHR's ECMS had to be able to identify the standards it would adhere to.

must all be **standards compliant**—especially on the data end. The technology and digital data domains have matured significantly over the past ten years. Sophisticated standards now exist that will help ensure interoperability and scalability into the future. Given that the ECMS is serving both exhibition needs and web needs, managing museum collection data, museum copyright, and more, each of the components of the system also needs to be updatable or even replaceable as those specialized fields demand, without necessitating a re-architecting of the entire system.

ECMS: From A to Z

The enterprise content management system is a system of components that work together in order to allow the museum to strictly manage its content, and in order to allow the museum to be efficient with the human resource spend across the preproduction, production, and postproduction areas of content development.

The ECMS at the Canadian Museum for Human Rights is composed of:

DAM (**digital asset management system**): A system that organizes and manages all digital content within an enterprise (such as images, videos, text, 3D objects, etc.).

ALM (**archives, library, and museum collections management systems**): A system that adheres to professional standards of, and manages the content of, archival collections, library collections, and 3D museum collections).

CMS (**content management system**): A system that manages content, typically at the presentation layer, of a digital endpoint (such as a website).

Enterprise search appliance: A system that aggregates data from a federation of sources and facilitates the findability of information

Thesauri and vocabulary management: Products and services that, when working with an enterprise search appliance, help ensure that redundancies in data are avoided, that specifics of a subject matter are well addressed, and that succinctness and accuracy of both the cataloging and finding of information are improved.

Copyright management module: A function that assists in the tracking and management of copyright across all digital assets.

It's noteworthy that for the purposes of managing all text in the museum, text is considered a digital asset even if the text is only ever printed or added to a built/static exhibit. This ensures that the raw, or original, asset, whether a paragraph of text or a photograph, is always treated the same way, irrespective of medium or asset type.

A series of APIs (**application programming interfaces**) connect the ninety-five different digital installations in the CMHR galleries, the website, the mobile application, and the museum's digital signage with the ECMS. Across the ecosystem of in-gallery installations and remote digital endpoints there is a rich variety of software platforms and programming languages being used. However, via the APIs all systems are integrated with the ECMS.

In the case of the CMHR ECMS, an emphasis was placed on **open source** technologies. Open source technology reflects the museum's ambition to democratize technology and the content and services technology can manage, while also encouraging wide and open standardization. Given that the CMHR had not yet opened and was without any operational experience, proprietary technologies and ongoing licensing agreements were a concern.

> **KEY TERMS**
>
> **APPLICATION PROGRAMMING INTERFACES**
>
> Application programming interfaces (APIs) are protocols and/or tools that facilitate the development and integration of a software application with others. In the case of the CMHR's ECMS, it is through APIs that various digital installations are able to connect with the ECMS and retrieve or accept content.
>
> **OPEN SOURCE**
>
> Open source refers to a software application where the source code is available for download, review, and modification by anyone.

Figure 9.2 is a logical diagram of the system. The components of the system are:

- DAM (Alfresco)
- AtoM (Archival Management System)
- Koha (Library Management System)
- Collective Access (Museum Management System)
- iQvoc (Human Rights Thesaurus)
- Search (Solr)
- CMS (Drupal)

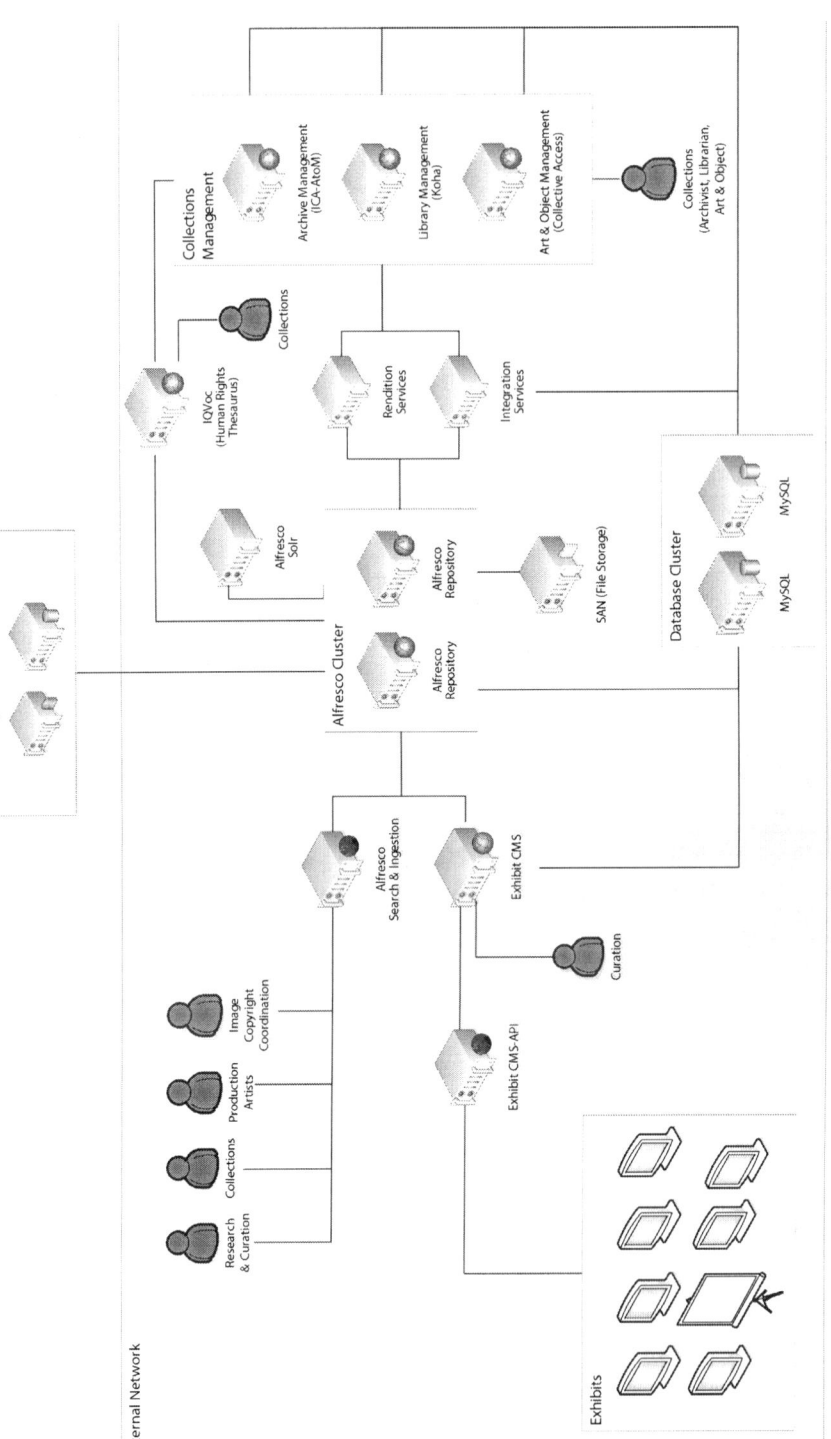

FIGURE 9.2 ECMS diagram.
Corey Timpson (author)

Why an ECMS?

One of the most difficult challenges in designing and developing the enterprise content management system for the CMHR was achieving stakeholder buy-in. It is a difficult concept to describe to nontechnical audiences, and the implications in terms of museological workflow efficiencies is also tough for non-museum professionals working in the field to comprehend.

Imagine the typical workflow for content development such as publishing an image to a digital installation:

Step 1: Research

Step 2: Acquisition of asset (in this case, a photograph)

Step 3: Cataloging of asset

Step 4: Design and layout of the photograph within the installation

Step 5: Production

Step 6: Software development

Step 7: Publish

This is a seven-step process for something as simple as getting an image into a digital interface in a gallery.

When an ECMS exists the process becomes:

Step 1: Research

Step 2: Acquisition of asset

Step 3: Cataloging of asset

Step 4: Publish

This can be illustrated as follows: Imagine a new personal digital device type has been invented and launched by a number of competing companies. It's a wearable, augmented-reality projection device and has quickly become ubiquitous within the museum's audience targets. The museum has excellent stories that would be perfectly presented on such a device, but each of the stories is composed of images and they exist, trapped within the in-gallery installation they are currently presented through. In order to get that existing content onto the new devices, each of the stories' assets must be reproduced to the format needed by the new device. This is a costly scenario, and the museum must either push off other priorities or forego meeting the expectations of their audience. It represents a lost opportunity to engage their audience.

> **KEY TERMS**
>
> **GRAPHICAL USER INTERFACE**
>
> A graphical user interface (GUI) is a video screen that enables people to interact with a computer by manipulating icons and other visual representations of data.

For the museum equipped with an ECMS, all that needs to happen is to define a new API and push the content from the ECMS to the new digital endpoint.

In an institution like the Canadian Museum for Human Rights, one of the greatest advantages of the ECMS is facilitating quick change to existing installations. This can mean either adding or editing stories. For example, in June 2016 the Canadian Truth and Reconciliation Commission submitted its final report on Canada's Residential Schools Program to the Government of Canada. At that point, the story on Canada's Residential Schools program that is presented in the twenty-four-person digital touch table in the CMHR's Breaking the Silence gallery became outdated. The turnaround time to update the story (text and image) was approximately twelve minutes. Curators, having crafted new text in English and French, added it to the ECMS via the system's interface, while the new image was also cataloged and uploaded to the system. The content was published and verified as correct in the digital table.

Next Steps: Unified Interface Designs

The next steps with the enterprise content management system for the Canadian Museum for Human Rights are a unification of the interface designs of the different systems used in the museum. Although the ECMS is functioning and has created enormous efficiencies, the project remains incomplete in that many of the modules within the system presently retain their own native interfaces. This means as a librarian uses the Koha interface and a curator uses the Exhibition Manager (the interface developed to allow curators to manage their own content without the need of a designer or software developer), what they are seeing as interfaces are different from one another. The ideal is to have all **graphical user interfaces** (GUIs) appear as consistent facets of the same suite. This will provide better usability across the institution and learnability of one module of the ECMS with another. As such, someone who is familiar with one user interface would be better able to use another, and eventually, the integration of all interfaces will simply be workflows.

Module customization continues in that there are always better workflows to be created that can better increase efficiencies between teams and task breakdowns. Various task completion scenarios differ somewhat between modules while they could be more consistent. Along with interface integration, customizing workflows will create efficiencies in task completion.

An important lesson, demonstrated by the current status of ECMS at the CMHR, is to realize the illusion of perfection. The GUIs being non-uniform impacts usability on the business user end but in no way prevents the ECMS from providing the extreme efficiencies and scalability to the museum that it does.

Conclusion

The ECMS model produced by the Canadian Museum for Human Rights was a great fit for its needs and was awarded 2015 MUSE Gold by the American Alliance for Museums (AAM) in the Application/API category. It has enabled changeability and evolution of both content and experience, and has created enormous efficiencies in work processes and resource management. While the specifics of the CMHR ECMS might not be ideal for every institution, the concept of the ECMS is a must-have for any museum that would prefer to spend its resources developing rather than redeveloping.

> ### 💡 KEY TAKEAWAYS: AN ENTERPRISE CONTENT MANAGEMENT SYSTEM FOR THE CANADIAN MUSEUM FOR HUMAN RIGHTS
>
> 1. The enterprise content management system (ECMS) is an integrated system that facilitates and ensures standardization in the cataloging, preservation, aggregation, and management of all content, and ensures dynamic distribution of said content to any of the digital endpoints of the museum (present and future) where they can be experienced by visitors.
>   - The ECMS enables the Canadian Museum for Human Rights to:
>   - Strategically address the present and the future;
>   - Respond to an incessant and continued evolution in audience expectations;
>   - Be prepared for rapid media and technological advancement; and
>   - Allow for data ubiquity at all points of the museum.
> 2. The ECMS integrates a
>   - DAM (digital asset management system);
>   - ALM (archives, library, and museum collections management systems);
>   - CMS (content management system);
>   - Enterprise search appliance;
>   - Thesauri and vocabulary management, and
>   - Copyright management module.

3. ECMS design principles are:
    a. Separation of content from presentation;
    b. Store once, reference often;
    c. Dynamic delivery of content;
    d. Must be able to "do anything";
    e. System constraints through business rules, not technical limitations;
    f. Complete modularity and scalability;
    g. Standards compliance.

Acknowledgments

The author wishes to acknowledge his terrific colleagues and collaborators, namely the members of the departments within the Exhibitions, Research, and Design division, and the IT Department at the Canadian Museum for Human Rights, and Justin Funke and the team at Daemon Defense.

Digital Collections Management

Edward Purvis

All museums have different systems to manage their collections, but most conform to certain sector standards to ensure that the data they contain is accurate and of a high quality. This ensures accountability but also that objects are managed for the greatest public benefit, a key mission statement for many museums and cultural organizations around the world. In the digital world, collection management is commonly handled through a software application called a collections management system (CMS). A CMS manages physical collection items as well as items that are born digital.

Society is producing cultural footprints that by their definition are of a throw-away nature. The prolific presence of smartphones and other computer devices have given us the ability to instantly upload media for dissemination and comment. This new ephemeral culture, such as social media—designed to capture a snapshot of emotion at a particular point in time—or artwork made from time-based media such as film, video, or projections, presents museums with certain preservation challenges. Nevertheless, museums must be receptive to culture being created and accessed in this way by embracing new ways of working and more importantly new ways of capturing data for posterity.

Components of a Collections Management System

A CMS for a physical or **born digital** collection is comprised of a database, metadata, a general interface, a graphical user interface, and an application programming interface.

DATABASE

In a heritage context, a database is a group of information about objects. The information may be physical or electronic in form. Physical databases have existed in organizations for many years, typically as card indices giving a basic list of information about an object. This usually includes the object types—for example, book or uniform, who or what is associated with the item, and the item's **provenance**.

With the advent of digital, different electronic databases have been used worldwide. These can be as basic as a word-processed list of data in Excel, primarily designed to replicate card indices, to a full CMS that enables ever-increasing fields and points of user entry.

A CMS includes much of the same information as the physical lists. Core **entry fields** include a unique numbering system to identify the object, how it was acquired, and information about the object's history. However, a CMS also enables more detailed information to be captured, such as which collection items are for display or for conservation or additional research.

METADATA

Metadata is information about other data, or put more usefully, structured sets of information about a resource. In a museum or gallery context, the collection is the resource, and organized or *structured* lists allow the user of the CMS to query (i.e., search for) electronic information about the collection. Metadata must be consistent and accurate

---

KEY TERMS

BORN DIGITAL

Describes items or collections that begin their life in a computer or another digital format; for example, digital photographs or computer art.

PROVENANCE

A record of the chronology of ownership, custody, and location of a work of art or an artifact including how it came into the possession of the museum.

ENTRY FIELDS

The place in a CMS where data can be inputted and reviewed.

COLLECTIONS MANAGEMENT SYSTEM VS. CONTENT MANAGEMENT SYSTEM

The acronym CMS is used for both content management system, a term used in software publishing for a system that publishes data to the web and other online platforms, and collections management system, a tool for storing and managing data. The two applications should not be confused.

so that information can be easily retrieved. For example, a user may do a search for how many jigsaws are in a particular collection. For accurate information retrieval, the jigsaw must be described as such, not, for example, as a board game.

INTERFACE

An interface is how a user physically accesses the database. This could be a touchscreen device in the museum or through a personal computer.

GRAPHICAL USER INTERFACE (GUI)

The graphical user interface is the way in which the user can navigate information in a CMS. It includes entry fields, pull-down menus, checkboxes, and others. The GUI enables inputting, searching, locating, and sorting data as well as exporting reports (e.g., the number of jigsaws in a collection) and research.

APPLICATION PROGRAMMING INTERFACE (API)

Compatibility is one of the challenges of working with databases. If two systems do not speak the same "language" it is difficult to share data or images. Issues of compatibility may also arise when data are migrated to a new system for an update or to increase security and user control. An API enables different databases and software applications to communicate with one another. In practice an API allows users to share data about objects between different systems that are otherwise incompatible. APIs are essential to sharing information about collections around the world. (See the section "Moving Toward Open APIs" below.). All of these components and processes related to digital assets can be managed through two controls. (See the section "Managing a CMS" below.)

Planning for a Collection Management System

Planning a CMS should be based on measured innovation, agility, and forward thinking. Rapid changes in technology may create an impulse to leap toward the latest, most technologically impressive system, but steps should be taken to consider if a particular system is right for your museum or organization. Essentially this involves undertaking research with internal and external stakeholders to determine if the latest technology provides the right level of user access and control of information you require.

There are a number of considerations when planning a collections management system:

1. WHO IS THE DATABASE FOR?

The primary users of the collections management system will most likely be staff assigned to look after the collection. Internal CMS users can be grouped into four categories, each with their own requirements of a CMS as indicated in table 10.1. An audit of user requirement should be done to identify what the specific requirements are for each category within a particular museum.

2. TO WHAT DEGREE WILL THE DATABASE BE ACCESSIBLE TO OTHER INSTITUTIONS AND THE PUBLIC?

A collections management system may have many internal users, but a system must face outward as well. Museums may share access to their collections with other institutions, as well as to the public. Understanding the external accessibility requirements of a CMS means understanding what CMSs other partner organizations use and ensuring that the APIs are compatible and potentially "open."

It means identifying which public bodies would access and use the data (e.g., educators, researchers, academics, designers, entrepreneurs, etc.) and in which way. It also means planning for the internal resource requirements needed to service demands such as digitization, requests for loan, scholarly viewings of collections, and so on.

In addition, public access to a CMS may provide a foundation for crowdsourcing documentation of collections, and care must be taken to ensure such a process can be managed in terms of quality and access. (See section "CMS and Public Engagement" below.)

3. WHAT ASSETS SHOULD THE CMS CONTAIN?

The CMS should naturally focus on the collections, but there may be a need to integrate other data within the organization. For example, the CMS database could support a visitor's journey from making an inquiry to seeing a collection item to buying a replica from the museum shop to making a donation. Integrated systems allow effective cross-pollination between the public and many facets of the collection. Data or knowledge kept within isolated silos can lead to the duplication of work or effort. For example, research into copyright may be dealt with separately within an organization. This must be integrated into the work of the licensing or commercial department, so that income revenue can be increased for items in the collection that have become copyright free. In chapter 9, Corey Timpson describes the experience of

TABLE 10.1 CMS USERS AND THEIR REQUIREMENTS

USERS	REQUIREMENTS
Data inputters create the content that goes into a CMS. Can include • curators, • conservators, • volunteers, • interns.	• Accessibility: How easy is it for this group of users to input data? Are there enough fields? • Automation: Can known fields be pre-populated to speed up input—e.g., associated group names and provenance when documenting a large collection? • Permissions: Who can edit the data put into the system—are there tiered levels of control? • Scalability: What fields will need to be used for complex collections that span multiple disciplines and cataloging standards—e.g., a collection comprising archives and medals? • Version control: e.g., archiving previous conservation work and method to attach files to a data set. • Data enrichment: Ability to add detail to records and how this is monitored
Developers create fields and other associated technical content. They include • Documentation managers or specialists • IT staff • Curators • Public (in the case of crowdsourced documentation, see "Crowdsourcing Collections")	• Editing: How and when data should be checked and edited—monthly, quarterly, etc. • Quality control: How and when is the data reviewed and by whom? Could this be automated through workflows? • External development—If the public are inputting data remotely, how is this checked? • IT maintenance: When and how is the system backed up and plans for IT outages.
Managers also ensure quality control and assigning permissions to access the collections, but they are primarily responsible for the strategic plan and development of the CMS. They tend to be • IT staff, • documentation specialists, and • external IT specialists.	• Review—How and when should CMS be reviewed? • If system should be migrated, how and when should this be done? • What is the system going to look like in ten years?

the Canadian Museum for Human Rights in developing a fully integrated enterprise content management system.

4. WHAT FIELDS SHOULD THE CMS HAVE? WILL MORE FIELDS OR DATA NEED TO BE ADDED IN THE FUTURE?

There are many reasons why a CMS may require new fields and new workflows after its initial setup. These include:

MOVING TOWARD OPEN APIS

While many museums have put their collections online, the use of APIs, and in particular open ones, will allow the public to use collections information in new and meaningful ways. Open APIs allow full access to the data by external parties. However, museums must be confident about both the security and integrity of the data they hold before embarking on this next step.

- **Legal reasons:** Changes in copyright or information on provenance
- **New research:** Additional text, imagery, or links to files held externally
- **Enhance efficiency:** Changes in how data is viewed; hierarchy of text
- **Conservation considerations:** Additional data fields or new information required
- **Enable migration:** Movement of data between different platforms
- **Changes to display:** Items selected for public view may need new information or updates such as measurements, weights, and location
- **Digitization:** Changes in how material is viewed and stored

These changes may require fields to be reordered or the GUI changed, which may require further training of the users. The ability to easily add new fields or data without compromising current data should be an important consideration when choosing a CMS.

5. WILL THE MUSEUM BE MANAGING LOANS?

Collections management systems are best placed as the sole reference point to ensure data about loans are secure, accurate, and current. Records are important to ensure a museum can distinguish between items it owns and those it does not. The museum may wish to use an alternative numbering system to its own items to avoid confusion within the collections management system. Nevertheless, all items within a CMS, whether owned or held temporarily, must be treated with equal care. This includes undertaking the same environmental and security controls; ensuring an accurate location is recorded at all times; and that loan agreements are up-to-date.

6. WHO WILL DEVELOP THE DATABASE?

Databases can be developed, maintained, and upgraded in-house by museum staff or by a third party. An experienced software developer can run a system remotely, but this option usually costs more money than running the system in-house. Whether the database development is led internally or externally, all users must be consulted on the advantages and disadvantages of current systems and workflow. Both approaches should maximize long-term public access to collections, including the flexibility to add unforeseen modes of access in the future. A **steering committee** can monitor the development and maintenance of the CMS.

7. HOW OFTEN WILL THE CMS BE REVIEWED AND/OR UPGRADED?

All collections management databases should be reviewed on a yearly cycle to ensure the right technologies are being used to achieve the organization's aims. The review must take into account the likelihood of the system becoming obsolete. It is important to time upgrades wisely, waiting to see if new technology has been properly tested and as many bugs removed as possible.

8. WILL THE MUSEUM NEED TO MIGRATE DATA?

> **WHO SHOULD BE ON A COLLECTIONS STEERING COMMITTEE?**
>
> The steering committees should be made up of:
>
> 1. Main primary users—the content creators
> 2. IT specialists
> 3. Documentation manager
> 4. Selection of non-primary users from education, marketing, and other departments
> 5. Select members of the public—particularly if collections originate in a particular community such as an indigenous community and there are various cultural factors influencing how it should be handled and made accessible

The museum in time may introduce a completely new system. In such an instance, the new system should be compatible with the structure of current data. It is also important that CMS upgrades be compatible with the life cycle of the hardware it runs on. In practice, this means upgrading the CMS and its operating environment in tandem with servers and current best practices relating to security, user interface and other factors.

9. HOW WILL CHANGES TO THE CMS BE COMMUNICATED TO ITS USERS?

All changes can create uncertainty for the main users of the CMS. Such developments should be carefully communicated to everyone who accesses the system so workflow efficiency is not compromised. Organizations that guide users through change rather than enact it stand a better chance of upgrading smoothly and efficiently.

10. WHERE SHOULD DATA BE HELD?

Data backup and security is strongly linked to the review process. Collections management systems, by their very nature, hold personal data about donors, lenders, and

ENTRY DOCUMENTATION

Object entry forms can be used to record vital information about an object's condition, as well as transferring legal title (ownership) to the museum. The forms can also be used to record items that may enter the museum's premises for a short while and then be returned in cases, for example, of when a donation has been refused and returned to the owner. The entry documentation should include:

a. Name of depositor
b. How the item was acquired
c. Description of object (important when defining its classification at the cataloging stage)
d. The condition of the object—good, fair, poor (an organization must have an agreed definition for what these terms mean)
e. The number of objects
f. Reason for entry—gift, loan, sale, or copying
g. Declaration regarding ownership (if applicable)
h. Signatures from the depositor or authorized person acting on behalf of the depositor/owner
i. Signature from authorized representative of the museum or gallery
j. Space for both parties to sign for confirmation an object has been returned

borrowers, such as telephone numbers and addresses. These should be held securely in line with the requisite country's laws. Security is discussed further in Security of Digital Systems.

Functions of a Collection Management System

A CMS is particularly effective (if not essential) in helping museums manage their collections and their data in the following areas:

Object Entry and Acquisition

Museums must be able to account for all items in their care, whether digital or physical assets. Object entry forms support this requirement by recording who has given or loaned an item to the museum.

The collections management system must be able to adequately reference entry documentation so a museum knows what items are in its care. This is most easily done through a unique numbering system that is different than the main accessioning process. (See "Cataloging" below.)

Ideally the CMS must be able to support the creation of sequential numbers that are unique and easy to reference when retrieving information or creating core fields in the database. It must also have the capacity to be expanded or modified without a full redesign. Unique numeric identifiers can either be automatically generated by the CMS or controlled by a select number of documentation managers using strictly defined protocols. The critical step of assigning numbers should be rigorously enforced to minimize errors and maximize efficiency. Additionally, good systems will have the ability to flag incomplete data to main users or not allow the entry to proceed without completion of critical fields.

DIGITAL COLLECTIONS MANAGEMENT

Cataloging

This is the most important area of the collections management system and ensures core accountability for items.[1]

It is prudent to ensure that the system assigns security levels to ensure legal provisions attached to data are adequately met. Basic security—that is, the correct access permissions—should be in place so data is not compromised or lost. Only users with the relevant skills, training, and authority should be able to modify fields. This is because some fields, unless inaccurate, should never change. Core data about an object, such as where it came from and its unique accession number should be preserved in perpetuity.

FIGURE 10.1A Cataloging Data Fields.
Lord Cultural Resources

Field	Value	Description
Previous ID Numbers:	UNI 001	The temporary number or other identifying system used (if applicable)
File Number of the Correspondence:	GIFT FILE 2	The reference to further information about the object – e.g. acquisition correspondence.
Cataloguer's Name:	JANE SMITH	The individual who entered the item onto the CMS
Copyright Status:	BELONGS TO ORGANIZATION	Some simple classifications: 1. Belongs to organization 2. Doesn't belong to organization 3. Orphan (known but holder can't be contacted) The above categories may have associated permissions or associated agreements.
Associated Names:	COLONEL BROWN	Who used the item
Associated Units:	2ND BATTALION 69TH (SOUTH LINCOLNSHIRE) REGIMENT	The organization or unit linked to the object (if applicable)
Associated Places:	BELGIUM	Where the item was worn
Event Information:	BATTLE OF WATERLOO	If the item was linked to a key moment in history.
Keywords:	BATTLE; UNIFORM	The main words associated with the object; usable for searches and metadata.
Production Details:	UNKNOWN	Who made the item

FIGURE 10.1B Cataloging Data Fields.
Lord Cultural Resources

In this case of new research or where an item has been inaccurately cataloged, previous entries should be archived, as all data, whether inaccurate or not, serves as part of an object's biography. (See section on "Appropriate Access Controls.")

Location and Movement Control

All systems must have the ability to track and retrieve assets to ensure accountability and security of collections. Most collection management systems have fields or structures in place to track items that have changed location either temporarily or permanently.

Items that have moved temporarily are items that may move for several days or even weeks from their permanent **store** location. This might be because objects are required for loan, conservation or outreach work, which necessitates them being removed from their place within a store. Items may be in a store for a short period of time, for example, new acquisitions in quarantine pending transfer to the main store. Items may change their permanent locations when the store or main area where they are housed long term changes.

All location changes, whether temporary or permanent, must have a date logged and the name of the person who moved it to ensure items can be tracked. Only approved users should have the authority to change locations so that data standards and security are not compromised. This should usually be the main users moving or working with the collection, and not all users. To ensure accountability and prevent data theft, third-party users or contractors should not be allowed uncontrolled, full access to the CMS.

All items, whether temporarily or permanently moved, should have physical and, if possible, electronic tags to distinguish them from other objects. To prevent the tags being lost or switched, access to movement should be controlled through both physical access to the stores and database permissions.

> **KEY TERMS**
>
> **STORE**
>
> The physical area where items are located when not on display—this can be for short periods of time (e.g., a transit store), if awaiting imminent display, or permanent areas when not in use (e.g., shelves containing swords).
>
> **DEACCESSION**
>
> Formal removal of an object from the collection. This may be for a number of reasons, such as transfer to another museum or a sale, usually in exceptional circumstances.

Object Exit

Items may leave a museum for a number of reasons such as conservation measures, loans to other museums, public outreach, being reproduced or digitized, for research, or to be sold or disposed of. Collections management databases must be able to show, using the location field, when items have left the premises. In the case of items that have been transferred to another museum, or disposed of for other reasons, these can be marked as "**deaccessioned**" on the system. This shows that the museum no longer holds these items and also must record the date and method of disposal.

Any permanent changes to the CMS, such as these, should be undertaken by authorized individuals and be formally signed off on by the governing body or another delegated power. Paper records, like entry forms above, must be kept to show who moved the item, when and for what reason. Again, items can also be scanned in and out (through electronic tags) to record the location change to the CMS.

Loans

Collections management systems also need to sometimes hold information on items it may not own. Museums hold and manage this data in similar ways to objects it does own; however, as mentioned earlier, the museum may wish to use an alternative numbering system to its own items to avoid confusion within the collections management system. Loan information may be distinct fields or part of a larger collections management structure.

Loans will be of two types: inward loans to a museum for a short, defined period of time—such as for a special exhibition—and outward loans: items that a museum wishes to lend out to other institutions or individuals, again for a defined period of time. In the case of outward loans, it is important that there be adequate records to show what collection items have been loaned to other institutions. When an item is returned from loan, its location must be updated on the CMS.

Table 10.2 indicates what kind of information a CMS should hold for both inward and outward loans.

Some museums may have both long-standing outward and inward loans that for whatever reason have lapsed. This may be because the lender or borrower has died and cannot be traced. This information may also be recorded in the collections management system, and most museums, for ethical reasons, take steps to resolve or appropriately manage these collections.

Retrospective Documentation

Museums may have items in the collection where the original documentation has become separated or disassociated with the object. If this is the case, it is best practice to take steps to audit any affected collections so that museums can regain accountability for all items within its care. An audit may be undertaken for the following reasons:

- To undertake a general collections survey—such as one in every five items—for when it is not feasible to undertake a full check of every item, but an accurate sample is required.
- In order to carry out a conservation survey
- To review security
- To review items for disposal

TABLE 10.2 INWARD LOAN AND OUTWARD LOAN INFORMATION

Inward Loan	Outward Loan
1. Period of loan	1. Period of loan
2. Contact details of the lender	2. Contact details of the borrower
3. Associated information such as photographs or conservation records	3. Associated information such as photographs or conservation records
4. When loan is to be reviewed	4. When loan is to be reviewed

Managing a CMS

Whether assets are physical or born digital, once captured, electronic data and content requires ongoing management. Effective management depends on the centralization of data, consistent naming conventions, appropriate access controls, regular audits and reviews, communication protocols, and staff and volunteer training and security. These dependencies that affect the assets can be controlled through digital asset management (DAM) software, which can also incorporate digital rights management (DRM), too.

CENTRALIZATION OF DATA

Data, whether concerned with a physical item (such as notes about an object's history) or a born-digital object, must be centralized in one area for users and various stakeholders to access and manage. This might be on a central server or access points where users can view the information. Paper files relating to collection items may be in several locations or stores when organizations move or change staff. A member of the organization—usually called a records manager—should be tasked with bringing this information together so that the organization can not only function effectively but know where data is held for security and legal reasons. Whenever possible this should be backed up with knowledge transfer between senior and new colleagues.

DAM VS. DRM

In the context of museums, DAM (digital asset management) refers to the ongoing management of primarily born digital items, but can also relate to physical items once digitized. Broadly speaking, this encompasses all facets of their management: from creation to storage, cataloging, and retrieval of assets.

DAM may be part of a wider API framework or digitization strategy. DRM (digital rights management) refers to the management of rights within objects as a clearly defined workflow. This begins with determining rights (e.g., copyright) in an item before acquisition; documenting and managing the right (e.g., through digitization if a physical item) and then licensing the right (if applicable) to third parties or through commercial ventures.

The rights may need to be protected through additional software or watermarking. Items that are free of copyright restrictions can be automatically put on online collections through workflows.

Centralization supports digitization, as well as integration. Digitization is an important way to ensure that the museum's collections and metadata are more widely accessible and can also ensure its preservation. (See the section on digitization below.) Integration of collections with other digital systems of the museum is explored in chapter 9.

Data must be backed up regularly, and systems should be regularly reviewed so that data can be accessed in years to come. The CMS must also cross-reference where the data is held (e.g., file path for the shared drive) or the relevant material embedded into the actual system itself. For example, an oral history recording may have accompanying photographs when donated. Therefore it is best practice in this situation to have in-built

COMMON PROBLEMS IN A CMS

Every effort should be made to ensure data standards are not compromised. Here are the most common problems in a CMS:

- Data incompatibility: Data are not held or displayed in a sufficient way for it to be migrated.
- Terminology (how items are described) is not of a consistent standard.
- Statistics about the objects (weights and measurements) are not consistent (metric, imperial, etc.).
- Software compatibility: The CMS and associated interfaces do not work with new software.
- Hardware compatibility: Personal computers or servers are not capable of running the new software.

CMS functionality so that both the photographs and recordings can be viewed together. In practice this means having a linking function between the individual records through an associated item field or view tab between the items on the CMS.

Consistent Naming Conventions

Accessibility for all users must be considered when developing naming conventions. For example, a curator may create a document detailing a museum's acquisitions during the month of January 2016. She names the file Acquisitions16.doc and saves it to her personal drive. In this instance, it is not clear from the filename who the author was, when the document was created, and whether the document is a draft or a final version. Good file naming conventions will show at a glance what information the document contains.

Appropriate Access Controls

Access to data that are shared internally must be managed according to an organization's data protection policies. This is not only true for information about objects but also for information that contains personal data. Museums and galleries need to collect names, addresses, and contact information of individuals so collections can be effectively managed. This applies especially to entry forms for gifts and loans.

If personal data are shared outside an organization, it must be in accordance with the country's data protection laws. In general, personal data must not be used for unreasonable purposes—that is, for any reason other than why it was collected. An example is passing a donor's personal information to an outside organization without the donor's consent.

Aside from personal data, some information may be restricted for legal or operational reasons. This includes information relating to emergency planning or material that is not given to the public for security reasons.

Data permissions define which users need access to data and when. These permissions are a set of data controls that manage user access, changes to fields, and the overall

DIGITAL COLLECTIONS MANAGEMENT

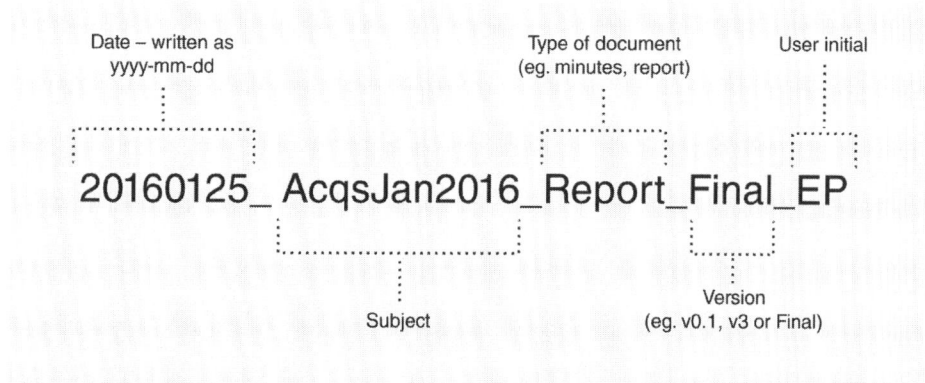

FIGURE 10.2 Guidelines for Naming.
Lord Cultural Resources

structure of the CMS. The permissions can be managed according to the museum's operational structure:

- Data inputters have controlled **write access** to mandatory cataloging fields; they can change location fields.

- Developers and documentation managers periodically edit and review work of inputters.

- Managers control overall development of system and review of workflows, fields, and associated structures.

- The public has **read access** to the material created and contribute to data enrichment.

In managing permissions, consideration must be given to regularly changing passwords and backing up the system, with the ability to revert records if required.

> **KEY TERMS**
>
> **WRITE AND READ ACCESS**
>
> Those who can edit and make changes to a document have write access, and those who can merely read it and can't make changes have read access.

Regular Audit

Like information held within the CMS, information on shared drives must be subject to audit and review. It is prudent to review who uses the system, how often, and whether access should be a short-term or a longer-term one. For example, a volunteer may only need access to information for a research project. In cases where temporary access is needed, registration and password records should be amended immediately when staff, contractors, or volunteers leave.

Managing Workflow

Good workflow can support the efficient and accurate use of a collections management system. Primary and secondary users interact differently with the CMS. Primary users are the staff members who regularly use the collections management system as a core part of their job. This includes curators, conservators, documentation managers or specialists, and IT staff—internal or external. Primary users may also include volunteers and interns.

Figure 10.3 and 10.4 show basic, typical workflow of how data is processed by primary and secondary users.

Any good collections management system will also have a large secondary user base, and this will usually involve staff whose primary role is not to maintain data but to exploit the information in the course of their duties. These staff may include marketing, fundraising, and photography staff, who will need to access the system for a wide range

FIGURE 10.3 Data Processing Workflow for Primary Users.
Lord Cultural Resources

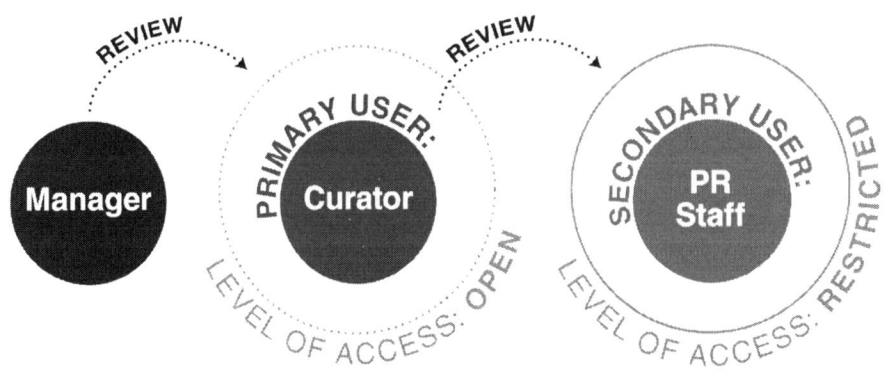

FIGURE 10.4 Workflow Diagram for Secondary Users.
Lord Cultural Resources

of reasons. Marketing staff may need information on the latest acquisitions to communicate to visitors; fundraising teams may need accurate information on what items need conserving or high-resolution images for publicity. Photographers (whether on the staff, freelance, or hired) can be a powerful secondary user of systems: directly inputting images of collection items and being responsible for direct asset creation and how this is managed within the system itself.

> **TYPICAL SEARCHES FOR INTERNAL REPORTING**
>
> Typical searches that a CMS should be able to accommodate could include:
>
> - The number of items loaned out in 2014,
> - The number of items dating from 2014 in the collection,
> - The number of items used for outreach in a particular month,
> - The number of items requested for photography last month.

REPORTING

The CMS must have a sound reporting function so data can be analyzed and captured for senior managers and trustees. The CMS must be able to support these searches and generate reports for the CMS users. For example, a manager might want to know what items have been acquired in April 2015 or loaned out in February 2016. Correct implementation of fields and associated names aids information retrieval and allows metadata to be captured for a range of purposes.

COMMUNICATION

Effective sharing of all data is necessary for effective collections management. This includes data that are not held within the CMS and its associated databases. Material must not be left in personal folders, emails, or drives where access is restricted. A culture of sharing and transfer of knowledge, ideas and experience across an organization ensures maximum cultural benefit is achieved. Staff must be aware of other work of departments so effort is not duplicated during collaboration. For collections management planning this is particularly important. Retired curators, for example, may have built up many years of knowledge that needs to be captured. Collateral or tacit knowledge can be obtained through oral histories or through work-shadowing in the months leading up to departure.

SECURITY OF DIGITAL SYSTEMS

All systems are vulnerable to hacking, slow down, or hardware failure. Security processes should be reviewed constantly, and investments should be made in the software necessary to prevent penetration. As mentioned earlier, museums and galleries hold vast amounts of personal data that must be protected from theft and data loss. Access to data should be monitored regularly and read/write privileges changed according to user need. The CMS should also be regularly backed up to guard against outages or other IT hardware failure.[2]

THE USER MANUAL

All collections management policies should be written down in a manual for staff to consult. The document should cover how policies, procedures and plans work in an organization and explain clearly the steps that must be followed to look after the collection. It is best to have a separate manual covering the use of the CMS, as this will contain more technical processes and procedures such as:

1. **Basic cataloging techniques:** How items should be recorded and managed over time
2. **Data enrichment:** How additional information should be added to existing records to enhance our understanding of them
3. **Version control:** Who has the right to change current records and when
4. **Review procedures:** When they should be reviewed and by whom
5. **Access control** (read/write privileges): Who has the ability to edit documents and who only has authority to view them

In all cases the manual should be approved by a body with sufficient powers to enforce procedures and rules. This is usually a senior management team on behalf of the governing body (trustees) of a museum or gallery.

Benefits and Challenges of Digitization

Digitization in a museum or gallery context usually means laser or optical scanning of objects that are then stored within the collection management system. Digitization can be a time-consuming, resource-intensive process that has benefits and challenges.

Benefits of Digitization

There are clearly many benefits of digitization:

1. *Greater public engagement with the collection and with the Museum.* Digitized items can be displayed as an online collection accessed anywhere anytime or as an exhibition on a screen in-gallery, creating a more meaningful connection between the public and the collections and in some instances increasing traffic to the museum's website to promote exhibitions and other events. In addition, original data sets can be augmented through

crowdsourcing. (See section "CMS and Public Engagement" below.)

2. *More opportunities for commercialization of assets.* Digitized items, subject to copyright checks, can more readily be used for income generation, such as postcards in the museum shop or for publication in books and online. Digital images can be used over and over again without needing to access the original. It is important to capture a range of sizes and resolutions at the point of capture so that they can be used in a range of media.

3. *Preservation of light-sensitive material.* Digitization, particularly of archival material, can preserve the originals for longer as archives are often light sensitive and light damage is accumulative. Digitization allows alternative versions to be viewed, although sometimes at the expense of the emotional impact of seeing an original.

4. *Increased productivity within the organization.* Digitization allows the organization to use the scanned material for a range of uses—not just for commercialization. The new assets can be embedded into new learning programs, downloadable exhibitions, or touring programs where the original material cannot be displayed for conservation or logistical reasons.

DIGITIZATION FOR AN ONLINE COLLECTION

A good online collection is supported by a good CMS. It should have:

- A clear implementation process that checks data before it is uploaded, which can be added as a function within an existing CMS;
- A clear export process from the CMS that uses an API or another tool, APIs being desirable because any developer can write applications for them;
- Search fields with simple keyword and advanced functions;
- Digitized imagery showing the item concerned, together with the accession number and provenance details;
- Opportunities to comment on information (subject to review);
- Embedded links to request viewing, images, or other access to the object;
- A separate area detailing new acquisitions and how the collection will appear on the website (if applicable).

Challenges of Digitization

Despite the benefits, there are many challenges that must be considered when engaging in digitization:

1. *Copyright.* Museums must be confident they own the copyright in any item they are digitizing or, if not, that they have captured the licensing terms under which digital reproductions can be used. For example, it can be released for PR but not for commercial reproduction. Additionally, if the scanning is outsourced to a third party, that copyright will not be withheld or restricted as part of the agreement. This can usually be

overcome by entering into contracts where copyright is assigned to the organization for a specific time period. This can be managed through DRM.

2. *Technological change.* Like items that are born digital, there must be a strong awareness of changing file formats. It is not certain that a digital photograph taken today will be viewable in ten years. New technologies may limit the ability for a museum or gallery to access older digital data. This can be mitigated by ensuring that upgrades to the current system support older file formats. Organizations could also convert older formats to newer ones, although this raises issues of authenticity and preservation.

3. *Conservation.* Some items may not be suitable for certain digitization methods such as flat-bed scanning—for example, if they are cockled or mounted works. Care should be taken to keep scanner glass free of dirt so these are not transferred onto objects. Good handling guidelines should be in place before any scanning commences, and overhead photography is one of the best methods to lessen the possibility of damage. Scanning requires plenty of room; clean surfaces and hands; and, if necessary, the use of gloves for delicate works.

4. *Cost.* The staff or volunteer time required to scan material can be high, and there are incremental data storage and security costs once the material is digitized.

5. *Stakeholder expectation.* Funders and external parties may expect the museum to digitize its collection within unrealistic time frames. In addition, online access tends to create demand for more digital records, which can strain organizational capacity.

Methods of Image Capture

Methods of image capture range in quality and cost. They include taking curatorial snapshots, in-house scanning, photography, or outsourced scanning.

CURATORIAL SNAPSHOTS

Most museums do not have a photographic record of every object in their collection. One way of overcoming this limitation is to embed image capture within retrospective documentation projects or other workflows that require items to be physically audited. Curators, volunteers, or interns can take basic images using smartphones or compact cameras, which can then be uploaded to the CMS. These images are unlikely to have commercial use, but they still provide a useful audit trail.

IN-HOUSE SCANNING OR PHOTOGRAPHY

Aside from using museum photographers, some museums purchase or hire book scanners to input flat archives directly into the CMS. Photogrammetry (3D modeling of objects) can also be used. These all provide high-quality images for a range of uses:

- In classrooms or through downloadable content or lectures;
- Publication on the organization's online collection portal;
- Metadata (building up sets of information to enhance knowledge about specific collections);
- Selling either rights to the film or to use or reproduce the material in any media, including publication; or
- For graphics or in place of light-sensitive items.

> **KEY TERMS**
>
> **OBSOLESCENCE**
>
> In this context, the status of hardware or software that is no longer in use (usually because a more efficient system has replaced it), which impedes a museum's ability to preserve older media.

However, museums must factor in the ongoing cost of maintaining and servicing the machines. Machines may also become **obsolete** and need to be replaced, which may have an impact on the overall digitization program.

In addition, museums must ensure that the staff or volunteers who carry out the often repetitive work of digitization have the right skill set, such as the ability to focus for long periods of time, attention to detail, ability to meet tight deadlines, and good communication skills. The latter is particularly important when organizing for the material to come from storage at the right time and in the right quantity—that is, to make a good "production line."

OUTSOURCED SCANNING

For large-scale projects, particularly when a museum wants to provide paid access to the captured data (e.g., a census or service record), it may be more cost effective to send mass material off site to be processed. A single company that specializes in digitization can manage the whole process, including quality control and data security. This method can be the most expensive of options, but it can provide huge benefits quickly, particularly if the museum has limited staff.

CMS and Public Engagement

While databases have a strong inward-facing organizational remit, CMSs are most powerful when linked to strong public engagement programs, such as online collections and displays. This gives the public unique access to the collections of a museum, especially those that are not on display, and creates the closest bond between a museum, its visitors, and its mission. In a collections management context, collections are held in trust by museums and galleries on behalf of the public, and an outward-facing CMS helps museums deliver on public trust.

TABLE 10.3 PUBLIC ENGAGEMENT WITH COLLECTIONS: CHALLENGES AND SOLUTIONS

CHALLENGES	SOLUTIONS
Different CMSs and collections management processes The lack of a universal collections management worldwide means there are inconsistencies between museums about how culture is recorded.	*Move toward universal collections management standards* Museums can work together in subject-specialist networks or groups toward common standards and practices. A well-designed CMS interacts with other software applications as well as people. It may have an API that allows users to have object data delivered to them through Wikipedia or another museum website. Robust, well-documented APIs are essential to enabling a collections database to distribute information to web browsers and other reading applications.
Competing knowledge and information online Since the rise of the Internet, access to knowledge and information is even easier than before: instantaneous and always available. However information on the Internet is of varying standards and sometimes difficult to verify.	*Work with teachers and schools to package high-quality knowledge and information for learners.* Identify what kind of search terms, formats, and metadata they need.
Different ownership of collections across museums In many museums, collections are legally held in trust for society by different governing bodies. Trustee boards may have differing priorities, agendas and strategies that are difficult to bridge. Collections management may not be at the forefront of a board's strategic plans, and boards may have varying views on how much access is desirable.	*Partnerships and an ethos of sharing and collaboration* Despite collections being owned by different legal entities, museums, galleries and community groups can develop regional partnerships and initiatives to support each other. In loans, new acquisitions and disposal may lead to the reinterpretation of an object or its display for the first time, if it has been in storage all its previous life.

In theory, public engagement is where collections management meets its true zenith, but in practice there are barriers to linking a museum CMS to the wider world. However, these can be overcome. Some of the key challenges and potential solutions are summarized in table 10.3.

Making a Collection Management System Succeed

Caring for collections delivers a potent legacy. Systems, standards, and people come and go, but, whether physical or digital, the object delivers long-standing cultural resonance, which can be amplified through new technologies. Digitization strategies will evolve and improve with time—the needs of the object and associated conservation should always be at the forefront.

Museum professionals should think creatively about collections and understand that processes and systems to manage collections are evolving within new processes for data capture, management, and display. Interpretation has become a fluid concept that is responding to digital immersion and the reorganization of society by crowdsourcing, personalization, and other digitally driven trends. Allied to this is the issue of contemporary collecting of ephemeral objects, either recorded or born digitally or "living objects" such as bio-art. Professionals will need to identify trends and strategies to deal with changing formats and how data is captured.

> **CROWDSOURCING COLLECTIONS**
>
> This involves using large groups of people to obtain new services, ideas, or content. These groups are usually online rather than employees. In a museum context, this usually means asking online users to contribute to collections data or expand on an idea or project. Contributions can be either paid or unpaid, depending on a museum's business model.

Collections are not a means to an end, and the art of collecting is a fluid process that changes according to context. Items were collected in the Victorian period as curiosities, but now items are collected for many reasons, such as their unique value or ability to tell a powerful story or as evidence of historical or scientific events and/or processes. As human culture changes, so will collecting priorities; rationalization of collections should be seen as part of the normal cycle of museum collections—just as items are acquired, museums must be prepared to review their collections to ensure they remain fit to uphold an organization's remit.

As public bodies, museums deliver value through wise investments in the management, preservation, and presentation of historical legacy. Collections are held in trust for society, and, as we have seen in other sectors, digital processes offer a means to increase the return on the resources in meaningful, measurable ways. These processes may reduce the overall human interaction with original objects face-to-face or may enhance them—as with virtual reality, 3D printing and holograms. Digitization is a balancing act between conservation, engagement, and commercialization, and a collection management system can hold the key to that balance.

USING VOLUNTEERS FOR DIGITIZATION PROJECTS
Ed Purvis Interviews Pam Babes

Pam Babes is the Collections Information Manager for National Museums Scotland, where she manages a team of information and photography professionals along with a team of dedicated volunteers from the surrounding community.

EP: How can volunteers contribute to the development of collection management systems?

PB: We have found that volunteers can be extremely useful when it comes to the labor-intensive work of digitizing collections. We use volunteers to add new records and improve existing records through proofreading, checking for errors and omissions, and fielding out information. They can also add value to existing records through carrying out research to fill in gaps, using their own subject knowledge to enhance records, and adding information to records from internal resources. We also find that standardizing terminology is a big issue, and our volunteers help us with that. They can also be useful when it comes to capturing new images of objects and inserting captions and keywords into images to help with searching and retrieval.

EP: What are the advantages of using volunteers to input data and create content?

PN: There are many advantages when we have committed volunteers. They fulfill an important function in information capturing that often can slip down the priority list of paid staff, given what else they are juggling. They can also help to speed up data capture—more "hands on deck" means these tasks get done more quickly and we can get through records more quickly. Volunteers can also have specialist skills and knowledge not available in-house (for example, certain fields of archaeology) so it is wonderful when we can benefit from this. We find that generally volunteers want to be in the museum doing something valuable, so they are committed. For some museums, volunteers are the only way for a museum to build a collections management system.

EP: And the disadvantages?

PB: Well, volunteer time may be limited to one day or few hours a week or a few days a month, and this is challenging. Also, volunteering may be used as a means to an end for some people in achieving experience to gain employment, so you are always facing the question—How long will they stay? "Dipping in and out" of a collections management system can lead to lack of consistency and standards, although this is also true of paid staff. On the whole, maintaining standards and accuracy can be challenges, and their work needs to be monitored. Training and support is also important.

EP: How can the interrelationship between staff and volunteers be adequately managed?

PB: Volunteers should be treated as much as possible the same as paid staff—there should be an induction process and volunteers should be introduced to staff; they should be provided with training and support and they should have clear line management or supervision in place. Volunteers should be invited to participate in meetings, as appropriate, where they should be encouraged to talk about their work and present so that they feel they are valued and their opinion counts. They should also be invited to social events.

EP: What is the long-term sustainability of using volunteers in collections management?

PB: The use of volunteers is becoming more prevalent and will likely increase due to reductions in staff and funding and museums reaching out in new ways to their communities. There is no doubt that the contribution of volunteers is significant and valuable, and it is sustainable if the required support is in place. There is a risk, though, that as we take on more and more volunteers, not only to supplement existing structures and teams and plug/replace the gaps left when paid staff leave, that supporting and managing volunteers becomes the day job for someone. Ultimately you end up with museums that are run wholly by volunteers without any qualified and or experienced staff.

I believe that the use of volunteers in collections management is a good thing as long as there is the time and skills to manage our volunteers properly. They have to have a truly positive experience, and the work they are asked to carry out or contribute has to have value.

💡 KEY TAKEAWAYS: DIGITAL COLLECTIONS MANAGEMENT

1. A collection management system CMS is comprised of a database, metadata, an interface, graphical user interface (GUI) and an application programming interface (API).

2. Planning for a collections management system means answering questions relating to users, assets, fields, loans, workflow, revisions, communication, and central storage as well as considering the CMS of partner organizations and public access to collections.

3. A CMS supports a number of aspects of collections management; namely, object entry and acquisition; cataloging location and movement control; object exit; loans; and retrospective documentation.

4. Managing a CMS includes ensuring centralized data; consistent naming conventions; appropriate access controls; managed workflow; reporting; regular audits; good communication (including a user manual); and security.

5. Digitization comes with benefits and challenges. Benefits include greater public engagement with collections and museums, more opportunities for commercialization of assets; preservation of light-sensitive material; and increased productivity within the organization. Challenges are around issues of copyright, technological change, conservation, cost, and managing stakeholder expectation.

Notes

1. The Embedded Metadata Working Group (EMDaWG) of the Smithsonian Institution suggests that digital assets include: document title, copyright notice, source, creator, date, description, keywords, job identifier, and headline (caption).

2. Ben Sullivan, "Museum Collections at the Core of Learning," *SlideShare*, slide 18, accessed October 5, 2016, http://www.slideshare.net/BenSullivan5/museum-collections-at-the-core-of-learning.

Digital Project Management

Rachel Clements Walker

The topics discussed in this volume are inspiring. They reflect a time when museums are constantly rethinking and renegotiating digital experiences in galleries and online in response to ever-changing technology, user expectations, and behavior. This leads to innovative digital projects being proposed, business cases being drawn up, and presentations being made to museum boards.

The moment when a large digital museum project is approved and a budget is assigned is often the culmination of months of work and planning. Whether an updated museum website, a collections management system, or an in-gallery interactive, project approval marks a high point for the project owner and the start of the daunting task of delivery. It's at this transition point that this chapter kicks off. The following sections will outline why good project management is essential to the success of your digital project, walk through the project stages with guidance on the factors that can impact digital projects in museums, and provide interviews with museum staff and tips on how to ensure that your project meets its aims on time and within budget.

This chapter will provide an introduction for those who are new to project management, or to digital projects, in museums. The concepts discussed can be applied to projects of all sizes, with more complex or in-depth techniques simplified to adapt them for smaller efforts. Examples are included where possible, and draw on personal experiences of digital projects in a variety of organizations over the past ten years.

Introduction to Digital Project Management

A project is a temporary endeavor undertaken to create a unique product, service or result.
—Project Management Institute, *A Guide to the Project Management Body of Knowledge*, chapter 1.2

Project work is different from day-to-day operational work. A project is initiated to create change within an organization rather than maintain the status quo. It is important to acknowledge this difference in order to create the conditions required for a project to succeed. This can be particularly important in the museum environment where resources are tight and expectations on digital project delivery can be very high.

The project manager's role is to use a series of techniques and apply appropriate tools to ensure successful project delivery, with a focus on ensuring the product meets the initial aims of the project; balancing time, scope, and quality; managing people; and keeping communication clear.

Ensuring the Ultimate Product Meets the Initial Aims of the Project

All projects should have a project aim that states the desired outcome(s) of the project and answers the following questions in as clear and specific a way as possible:

- Why is this project needed?
- What will this project achieve?

Articulating the project aim (often as part of a business case), communicating it to all stakeholders, and ensuring understanding and buy-in is part of the project manager's role in the early stages of a project. As the project progresses, the project manager will check back at regular intervals to ensure the project remains on track in meeting its original aim.

An example of the project aim for a museum's digital project is as follows: "The current website platform is eight years old and has not been upgraded in the past two years. Performance and speed are unreliable and the online user experience is not in line with current best practices. This project aims to transition the museum's website to a new web platform, in order to improve the performance, speed, and user experience of the website."

Balancing Time, Scope, Cost, and Quality

Projects are time-bound with a clear start date and end date, and are undertaken with a specific end product as their aim. Since projects are also undertaken outside day-to-day

DIGITAL PROJECT MANAGEMENT

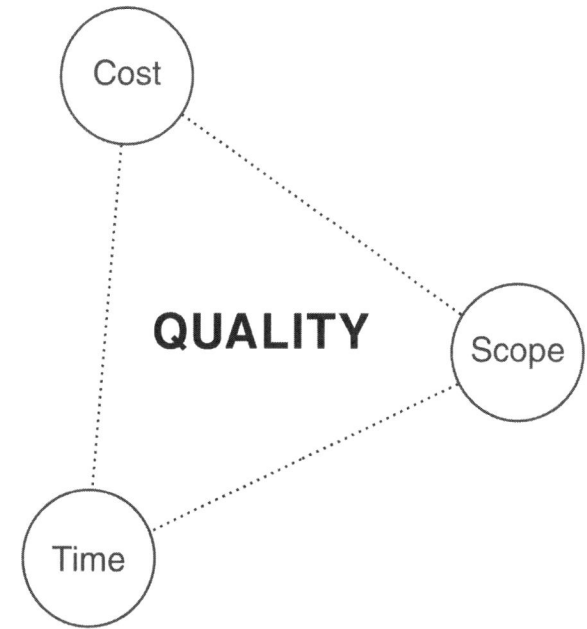

FIGURE 11.1 The Triple Constraint.
Lord Cultural Resources

operations, they usually have a specific budget assigned for the work. Balancing these attributes—time, scope, and cost—in order to meet the project's aim on time and within budget forms the basis of the project management discipline. These attributes are often represented as a triangle (see figure 11.1) to illustrate what is known as the "triple constraint": a change to one of these factors will impact the others. It is the project manager's job to achieve a balance in order to deliver the project within these constraints to the required level of quality.

For museums, and other not-for-profits, project budgets are often fixed with little room for flexibility. (See the section on "Managing Project Delivery" for more on budgets.) Therefore, when a change to the project occurs it is frequently the other constraints that need to be adjusted.

For example: A project team working on the delivery of an internal museum system with a third-party developer discovers a disconnect between the internal expectations of quality and those delivered by the developer: the deliverables do not meet the project requirements. (See the section on "Managing Project Delivery" for more on managing quality.) The budget for the project cannot be exceeded, so the decision is taken to both cut back on the initial scope and also to extend the launch timetable by several weeks. This change to the time frame is acceptable because a review confirms that it does not have a significant impact on operations. This additional time and decreased scope enables the developer to rework the deliverables to an acceptable quality. (Note that if a change to the time frame had not been possible, either quality or scope would need to be sacrificed more significantly in order to make the original dates.)

Managing People and Keeping Communications Clear

Project teams are frequently made up of individuals from different departments who may not work together on a day-to-day basis. The performance of the project team is a key factor in the project's success, and project managers have a vital role to play in facilitating communications and motivating and directing the energy of the team. This can be especially important during periods of high-intensity work prior to a deadline, and for projects where team members are based in different locations or time zones.

Project management tools and techniques help to ensure that communications among the project team, and with other stakeholders, remain clear. These include:

Project documentation

- Creating and updating project documents
- Sharing updated versions
- Managing version control

Schedules

- Creating, monitoring and updating schedules
- Alerting team members about upcoming deadlines
- Warning stakeholders when timelines are at risk

Project meetings

- Scheduling meetings and managing attendees
- Setting meeting agendas
- Circulating documentation prior to meetings
- Documenting meeting notes and action points

Digital Project Management Methodologies

A range of methodologies are available for planning digital projects, and almost all are suitable for use in the museum environment. The selection of a particular method depends on the complexity of the project, standards or skillsets within the organization, software development approach (see section on "Different Approaches to Digital Development"), and the methods used by any third parties. Most can be adapted and scaled to meet the needs of your organization, and your project.

Some of the most commonly used methodologies are as follows (note that this is far from exhaustive):

- PRINCE2 (Projects in Controlled Environments).[1] Used by the UK government and recognized internationally, PRINCE2 focuses on breaking down project work into distinct and manageable stages. It can be adapted for use with both **agile** and **waterfall** development approaches (see section on "Different Approaches to Digital Development") and is a robust method for large digital projects, especially when multiple teams are involved. However, it is a document- and process-heavy methodology and can be unwieldy for smaller projects and teams. Adapting the level of process to fit the needs of the project and organization is important.

- PMBOK (Project Management Body of Knowledge).[2] Managed and overseen by the Project Management Institute (PMI), and widely used internationally, PMBOK is not strictly a methodology but an accepted series of standards and best practices. PMI oversees a range of certifications in project management, the most widely known of which is Project Management Professional (PMP), and also offers a certification specifically designed for agile project management.

- Scrum.[3] One of the most popular methodologies for agile projects, scrum structures project work around two-week cycles of development (Sprints). Scrum is light on documentation and highly collaborative, with end users involved throughout. It aims for quick, iterative development and testing, and is particularly suited to focused project work and small teams. It can be applied successfully on larger projects with multiple teams and strands, but this can require wider organizational commitment to agile techniques and a level of experience in agile projects. (See section on "Different Approaches to Digital Development" for more on agile projects in museums.)

Planning for Project Kickoff

All parties must be clear on what the project is intended to achieve, why it is needed, how the outcome is to be achieved and what their responsibilities are, so that there can be genuine commitment to the project.[4]

Selecting and assigning a project manager should happen as soon as possible after project approval, so that they can begin the work to prepare for project kickoff. The project manager will focus initially on creating the documentation to formally start the project and on setting up the project team and communication structure. The latter is done by scheduling a series of kickoff meetings, defining roles and responsibilities, assembling the project team, and engaging stakeholders. This stage is essential to laying the foundations for successful project delivery, and sufficient time should be allotted to ensure it is not rushed. Each of these activities will be discussed in some detail below.

Kickoff Documentation

Project documentation is important to aid planning, management and communication. The type of documentation and level of detail required will vary depending on the complexity of the project and its methodology, however, the following key documents are commonly used in all digital projects. These documents can be helpful for communicating plans to museum stakeholders and securing support and funding even with agile or other document-light approaches.

Templates can be found online, or your organization might use a standard format. If you are using a lighter documentation method then components could be adapted to slides for a presentation, and/or uploaded to an online project team tool for increased collaboration (see section on "Managing Project Delivery").

BUSINESS CASE

This answers the question, "Why should we do this project?" Ideally, a business case document already exists for a project that has reached the kickoff stage, as it is generally used to gain organizational sign off and budgetary approval. However, in not-for-profit environments this is not always the case, and if the business case has not been documented during the project approval process, then it should be done now.

This document should articulate the project aim and scope, summarize project costs, and detail the expected benefits to the organization of doing this work—ideally expressed as a monetary return over several years. The business case document should be reviewed and approved at the senior level before the project is formally initiated. This ensures that senior management understands why the project is being undertaken at this time and what it aims to achieve, and that there is consensus that project returns are worth the estimated investment of time and resources. A project should not proceed if no business case exists, or if the case is not sufficiently strong.

The audience for this document is the senior management team and any other stakeholders across the organization whose buy-in is required in order for the project to be a success. As part of the business case, it's therefore important to state clearly which teams across the organization will need to support this effort, and to estimate at a high level the involvement required from each.

Business case templates vary, and the level of detail and rigor required will depend on the organization, the size of the project, and whether funding and resources have already been committed. The following sections are frequently included:

- **Project Background**: A brief outline of the factors that underline the need for the project.

- **Project Aim**: This should express clearly, in the form of a problem, the organizational need that this project will help to solve. See the introduction of this chapter for guidance on stating the project aim.

- **Options Identification**: There is frequently more than one possible solution for addressing the project aim. If so, these options should be outlined and the reason(s) for choosing the preferred solution identified.

- **Project Objectives**: The project objectives are more specific than the project aim. They state what will be done in order to meet the aim and address the organizational need. Project objectives frequently use the language, "This project will . . ." For example, "This project will review and select a new platform provider, capable of supporting the museum's website and delivering speed and performance over the next five years in line with the success metrics and growth projections outlined below. This project will also implement a new front-end UX for the website, which will include responsive templates to deliver a best-in-class online user experience on mobile and tablet devices."

- **Project Scope**: State what elements of work are *in* scope for this project, but also state explicitly what is *out of* scope, in order to set stakeholders' expectations. For example: "The front-end UX will be completely reviewed as part of this project. However, a review of the branding and visual design elements is out of scope—the new UX will be implemented using the existing design style guide."

- **Benefits**: List all known benefits of the project being undertaken. Examples of potential benefits include:

    o Increased audience engagement among target demographics;

    o Increased revenue generation;

    o Decreased ongoing costs;

    o Improved compliance with regulatory requirements;

    o Improved user experience; and

    o Increased efficiency.

- **Risks**: Any known risks should be outlined at a high level here. Depending on the project, these might relate to undertaking the project itself and/or to *not* undertaking the project. For example: "If this website platform is not upgraded or replaced this financial year, we will be unsupported by the provider and the risk of a sustained website outage will be increased."

- **Financial Assessment**: Include all anticipated project costs: both direct costs and internal resource commitments. For products that are anticipated to have more than just a one-off use (for example, an internal operational system, rather than an exhibition-specific interactive), include five years of ongoing operating costs (license fees, hosting fees, etc.), plus any enhancements or maintenance that will be required, to give you a total cost of ownership over five years. Also remember to offset project costs with the anticipated benefits. This is much easier for projects involving a transactional element, such as ecommerce websites, or projects that have been undertaken with the aim of longer-term cost savings. For projects that can less easily be linked to revenue driving or cost saving, consider whether the benefits of factors such as increased website sessions, email acquisition, and such can be articulated as a financial benefit. If this is not possible, ensure that these are clearly quantified under the benefits section. See the section on managing project delivery for more information on project budgets. It is also advisable to request help from your finance department in articulating business costs and benefits and preparing the financial assessment.

- **Assumptions and Dependencies**: Ensure that any high-level assumptions and dependencies are stated clearly, especially if these might have an impact on other teams across the organization. A dependency is any factor outside of the project's immediate control that will impact on the project's success in the short or long term. Common factors to consider include:

    o Bandwidth, network or infrastructure upgrades necessary in order for the live product to function efficiently.

    o Other projects underway within the organization at the same time that might compete for resources.

    o Resourcing for ongoing system maintenance and support.

    o Ownership of content creation and updating once the product is live.

    o Support required from other teams—for example, marketing or IT.

- **High-level Timeline**: For the purposes of the business case, this can simply indicate the anticipated start date and delivery date. See below for more on schedules.

- **Measures of Success**: Be clear on what constitutes success for this project, and how it will be measured. Relevant measures will usually relate back to the project objective and benefits outlined above. Set three to five success criteria that will be tracked once the project is live. Depending on whether the project replaces an existing digital product or is a completely new launch, these could be expressed as a specific target for the first few years, or an anticipated lift above current levels. Examples include:

- Number of users;
- Speed of website;
- Level of user interaction (measured in number of comments or average time spent using the product);
- Number of repeat visitors;
- Revenue generated;
- Costs saved; and
- Average transaction time.

- **Sustainability**: Consider the project's sustainability over the longer term and include an estimate of the level of resources that will be required post-launch to maintain and support the product (for example, hosting fees, staffing costs, etc.). Budget for upgrades and enhancements to be completed post-live that will keep the product relevant over the longer term.

PROJECT CHARTER AND PROJECT INITIATION DOCUMENT

This document is more detailed and practical than the business case. It answers the underlying question, "how will we do this project?" by outlining

- What will be done,
- Who will do it,
- When it will deliver.

Setting expectations at the outset with stakeholders across the organization as to how the project will be approached, how decisions will be made, and the anticipated schedule for delivery is essential to avoid misunderstandings. The work undertaken to create this document, and to share and discuss it, helps to ensure that all stakeholders understand the approach and that any questions are raised at the appropriate time.

The audience for this document is the project board, who will approve the document, plus project team members, who should be involved in the production of the document. Ensure that you get agreement and sign off on the points covered in this document from key project stakeholders—any concerns, queries or disagreements should be discussed and resolved before proceeding.

A project charter is higher level than a project initiation document (PID), but they contain many of the same elements, so they are dealt with here together. These documents are also sometimes referred to as a project kickoff document. The decision on what type of document to use and how much detail it should contain again will depend on the methodology used and the project's complexity. At a minimum, the document should include the following sections, some of which can reference other documents such as the business case:

- **Project Aim, Scope, and Objectives**: Restate these from the business case, as they will provide important reference points at later stages in the project; for example, during change control.

- **Schedule and Key Milestones**: In this document, the project manager should identify high-level project milestones, and their anticipated date of delivery. The detailed project schedule should be referenced (see schedules below).

- **Deliverables**: List clearly, and in as much detail as possible, what the high-level deliverables for each phase of the work will be. For example: "Design phase: content map; navigational hierarchy; process flow and UX wireframes for all key functionality; design comps and layered PSD files for all major templates."

- **Assumptions and Dependencies**: Restate these from the business case.

- **Project Governance and Decision Making**: Outline how change requests and issues will be handled as the project progresses, and where decisions will be made.

- **Budget and Other Constraints**: Detail the budget that was agreed via the business case. Also outline any other known constraints or interdependencies (for example, timing constraints related to the start of a major exhibition, or periods of peak visitor attendance).

- **Roles and Responsibilities**: Name the project team and key stakeholders. Define the role of those named, and their responsibilities during the project (see defining roles below). Balancing the intensity of project activity against the operational needs of the organization can be challenging in all environments, and particularly for not-for-profits where resources may already be tight. Thinking through the project staffing and resource needs and how these will be met alongside the demands of everyday work is one of the most important tasks in preparation for the start of a project. Approaching managers early in the process to ensure support, and their team member's time, will help to set up the right conditions for project success.

- **Risks**: This section should be more detailed than in the business case, and should outline risks specific to the project itself. All identified high-level risks should be stated, along with the proposed approach to address them (see risk management below).

Setting Up the Project Team and Communication Structure

ASSEMBLING THE PROJECT TEAM

A project team can consist of individuals from different areas of the organization, short-term contractors brought in specifically for the project, and third-party agencies who have won a contract for elements of the project's delivery. When deciding on the makeup of the project team, consider the availability, skill sets, knowledge, and expertise of team members.

Having the right team in place from the beginning is essential to ensure the project is set up for success. If concerns are raised by the project manager about the availability or skillsets of in-house individuals, then these need to be discussed with the senior team as early as possible. Within the not-for-profit environment there can be a tendency, due to budgetary concerns, to underestimate the expertise and effort it will take to deliver a digital project. It is therefore important to set realistic expectations about what can be achieved with in-house resources, and where additional support or training is required. Project responsibilities and anticipated workload, should be discussed with team members during the production of the project schedule to ensure that they and their line managers understand the expectations and are committed to meeting them. In particular, the project manager must be aware of any other commitments that might compete for the project team's time, both work-related (such as other projects or busy times in the operational calendar) and personal (such as planned vacations or holiday periods).

DEFINING ROLES AND DECISION-MAKING PROCESSES

The project manager must outline the responsibilities of each team member clearly and indicate who will be involved in decision making, so that all team members are clear about their role and that of others. Failure to communicate this can lead to delay and misunderstandings when changes or issues arise. Project roles and decision-making criteria will vary depending on the organization and the nature and size of the project, but table 11.1 provides some guidelines to consider.

In particular, empowering the project team to make decisions at appropriate points rather than waiting for senior approval is important if the project is to meet its target dates. For larger museums, where there are many levels of hierarchy, this can be a challenge, and it is therefore helpful to discuss decision-making expectations with senior management early in the process.

TABLE 11.1 PROJECT ROLES AND DECISION MAKING

ROLE	DETAILS	DECISION-MAKING RESPONSIBILITIES	NOTES
Project board / steering committee	Should contain senior representatives of the following: the business / organizational executive; the product end-user(s); the team(s) responsible for delivering and supporting the product	The ultimate point of responsibility for project success, and the point of escalation for any issues that cannot be solved by the project team; responsible for signing off the business case and project charter	Defining the level at which decisions need to be escalated to the board is important. Ideally, post-kickoff the board should only be involved in decision making if changes to project scope, time frame, budget, or deliverables are required.
Project manager	Appointed to run the project and to ensure that it is delivered on time and within budget	Must both make decisions that relate to the control of the project, and facilitate wider decision making within the project team to ensure that these are made in a timely manner and that milestones are met	If the project manager is junior, or if the project is part of a wider program, then they might work with the project sponsor, a more senior project manager, or a program manager for approval on larger project decisions.
Project team	Group of specialists who will deliver the project	Day-to-day decision-making responsibilities in relation to their area of expertise	The project team needs to be empowered to make decisions quickly, without the need for escalation. However, decisions that impact project scope, time frame, budgets, or deliverables will usually be raised with the project board for final approval.
Project sponsor / champion	Advocates for both the project and the project team at a senior level and clears hurdles which might be beyond the project team's immediate control	Provides senior support for the project manager; might be involved in difficult decision making and decide whether matters need escalation to the board	This role is often not clearly defined in museum digital projects, but it is highly recommended to help facilitate a smooth delivery by supporting the project team and providing a sign-off point for larger decisions without the need for escalation to the board.
Product owner / customer	Represents the business and/or end-user interests in the end product	Makes decisions about the product scope and prioritizes business needs and user stories / requirements	The product owner / customer must be empowered to make decisions about the priority of business requirements without the need to escalate these decisions to senior management.

MANAGING STAKEHOLDERS

It is important to engage stakeholders across the organization early in the project. In particular, those who might be difficult to work with or have strong opinions about the project should be brought on board with plans from the outset.

Setting clear expectations early on is key to ensuring good communication with stakeholders as the project progresses. One of the most important points to address is the project scope, since the appearance of a dedicated project budget tends to raise hopes that the project will fix all known user or business issues in a particular area. If this is not possible (and generally speaking, it is not), then it is important to be clear on this from the outset. Be realistic about what is possible with the budget and time frame allotted and communicate clearly to stakeholders what the project end state looks like: if some existing issues will not be fixed, or if some known problems cannot be tackled within the project scope, then say so clearly.

It is advisable to create a stakeholder communication plan, considering the following:

- **Who will be included in stakeholder updates?** The project manager will identify potential stakeholders with the help of the project team and sponsor. To keep all interested parties abreast of progress, while keeping the stakeholder group size manageable, individuals should be selected who can represent the interests of end users of the product or service, teams involved in the project delivery, and teams responsible for ongoing support and maintenance. Members of the stakeholder group should also be able to relay updates to wider teams or departments as required.

- **What information will be shared with stakeholders?** Project information and documentation needs to be shared with stakeholders at the right point: at a stage where plans and objectives can be stated clearly but are not fully set, allowing discussion to take place and feedback to be taken on board.

- **How frequently will stakeholder meetings be scheduled?** Ideally stakeholder meetings throughout the project life cycle should be scheduled as part of kickoff. This provides an efficient way to keep project communications transparent with a cross-organizational group, while making the most effective use of the project manager's time. Depending on the length of the overall project, meeting with stakeholders every six to eight weeks is generally sufficient.

- **What level of stakeholder feedback and engagement is expected, and how will feedback be incorporated?** It is important that discussions are open, and that a forum exists for stakeholders to raise questions and concerns, but that the project team and the product owner are empowered to make final decisions in relation to the project.

PROJECT KICKOFF MEETING

All projects should start with a kickoff meeting with the project team and key stakeholders. This is important to signal that the project has formally begun, to ensure that all those involved have a good understanding of the project fundamentals—the aim, scope, time frame and their roles within it—and to ensure that any questions can be discussed and answered openly. The kickoff meeting is the point at which the documents discussed above are reviewed with the project team and stakeholders. Depending on the size of the project team and stakeholder group, and the complexity of the project, it might be appropriate to hold one kickoff meeting with both groups or separate meetings with each.

A clear agenda helps to set out what the meeting needs to achieve (see figure 11.2 for a sample agenda outline). Ensure that any documents are circulated in advance so that meeting participants have a chance to review and raise any questions or concerns. It's also important to schedule enough time with the group to cover the full agenda, and allow time for discussion and questions.

Summary

Creating the documentation, and undertaking the associated kickoff activities outlined above, will lay the foundations for a well-managed project. The handling of the next

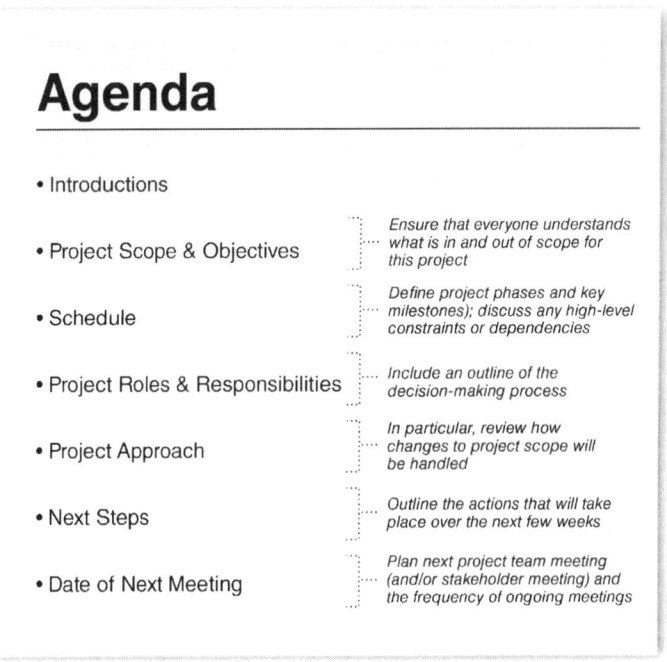

FIGURE 11.2 Sample Agenda.
Lord Cultural Resources

stages of the project will be shaped by both the type of project and the digital development methodology that is being used. The next section provides an overview of some of the different approaches to digital development. The process of project delivery is then discussed in the subsequent section.

Different Approaches to Digital Development: Waterfall and Agile

The most common digital development approaches are waterfall and agile. Both are suitable for use in museum environments, and the selection of a particular approach will depend largely on the preferences of the development team doing the work, the size and scope of the project, and the museum's internal culture and governance processes. Some of their characteristics and distinctions are summarized in table 11.2.

There is a large volume of information about agile and waterfall techniques available online that can help a team trying to make a decision about which approach is most suitable for their project or organization. It's also possible for a hybrid approach to be adopted, although this needs to be carefully thought through with an experienced development team, as the differences between the two mean that cherry-picking elements can result in an approach that doesn't really leverage the full benefits of either. Regardless of what is decided, the approach followed must be clearly agreed upfront with the project manager, so that the schedule and project phases can be set up appropriately.

Managing Project Delivery

Once the project is underway, the role of the project manager is to keep communications clear, monitor progress against the project schedule, manage the budget, motivate the project team and generally steer the project toward successful delivery. To do this, the project manager will utilize a range of tools and techniques that are covered in the following sections.

Communication

Keeping communication among the project team effective and open is one of the most important aspects of project management. When communication becomes strained or when there is misunderstanding among team members it can impact both the quality of the work and the time frame of the project.

The use of the documents and techniques discussed in the sections above helps to ensure that information is shared quickly, clearly, and efficiently. There are also certain

TABLE 11.2 COMPARING WATERFALL AND AGILE DEVELOPMENT METHODS

WATERFALL	ADVANTAGES	DISADVANTAGES
Often referred to as the "traditional" approach. The development process is managed as a linear sequence, with all requirements scoped at the outset.	Since requirements are scoped up front, work and costs can be clearly agreed with third parties at the outset. This level of predictability can be desirable to higher-level museum management, and can be helpful in managing stakeholder expectations.	• Scoping all requirements at the outset puts a heavy weight on those requirements being correct, and can be a strain on the team(s) involved in requirements gathering. • Delivery of a finished product late in the process can make it difficult to accommodate changes and raises the risk of creating an end product that is not optimal. Building contingency into the plan is recommended.
AGILE	**ADVANTAGES**	**DISADVANTAGES**
Increasingly popular for digital projects, Agile is an iterative approach in which working products are released frequently, and the end user is closely involved in the development and review process.	• The process is at its core adaptable and iterative. Changes to requirements and scope are easily dealt with. • A high level of involvement from end users is expected—lots of collaboration and interaction can keep stakeholders highly engaged and result in better end products. • Frequent code releases and early testing can help to identify early whether a project is on the wrong track and allow it to adapt accordingly. • Can be very effective for smaller projects and efficient for delivering in tight time frames.	• Less focus on documentation and process can lead to challenges when dealing with large projects involving multiple stakeholders. Communication and expectations must be carefully managed. • If dealing with third-party developers, agreements need to clearly state the maximum development time and cost in order to set expectations. • For successful use of agile techniques, the project team and product owner must be empowered to make decisions quickly. This can be challenging in larger organizations with hierarchical management structures. • Agile requires regular, frequent communication (ideally in person and onsite) which may be difficult for some organizations or for international teams.

habits that project managers adopt to help to ensure that information is shared effectively. These include:

- Creating some brief notes and a list of agreed action points at the end of every project meeting;
- Sending out a weekly recap for the group, outlining agreed priorities and any other important points to note for the next week's work; and
- Creating a shared location for project documentation that the whole team can access.

In addition to information sharing, the project manager also needs to play a role in managing the relationships among the various groups involved in the project. Project work is intense, and the project manager needs to ensure that sufficient time is spent on: keeping stakeholders informed and managing their expectations, especially if changes occur and compromises need to be made; keeping the project team motivated and on track; and managing third-party providers to keep relationships good. This last point can be especially important if and when the project hits a challenging period, since there can be a tendency for the internal team to blame the third party and vice versa. The project manager needs to act as a facilitator and negotiator in these circumstances to keep the project moving forward.

Project Documentation, Online Tools, and Version Control

The use of online project management and teamwork tools can result in project documentation shifting online and being handled in a more collaborative way. Some of the most popular and effective tools currently in use include JIRA, Smartsheet, Basecamp, Teamwork, and Google Drive.[5] Each of these tools contains a slightly different suite of functions that can help with various aspects of project management. These tools can be highly effective; however, it's important not to become overly concerned about which software to use; good project management on a small digital project can be effectively achieved with nothing more than a set of spreadsheets, so long as there are good processes in place and clear communication.

Regardless of the tools used, one point that must be managed carefully is document version control, as failure to address this can result in unnecessary confusion. The project manager is the owner of all project tools and documentation and has responsibility for tracking changes and ensuring that all stakeholders are always referencing the most recent version. If managing a suite of documents offline, the project manager will need to create a shared location for storing documents, implement clear numbering or version control, and archive older versions. If using an online collaborative tool, and if the project team is able to edit documentation, then a clear procedure for tracking changes is required and the project manager must always control which changes are accepted.

Managing Schedules and Keeping Things on Track

Setting a baseline project schedule, sharing this with the project team and other stakeholders, and then managing project progress against the schedule is one of the fundamental tasks of project management.

For many digital projects, the high-level schedule can be expressed simplistically as sequential phases as shown in figure 11.3.

This flow is typical of waterfall development models, but for the majority of current digital projects these phases rarely run entirely sequentially. The use of more agile techniques means that there is frequently a level of iteration between different phases and that the sequential flow is better expressed as a continuous cycle. However, when communicating project schedules with stakeholders, especially with senior management and those who are less familiar with digital project work, the use of a simple, sequential schedule to communicate project phases and key milestones can be helpful.

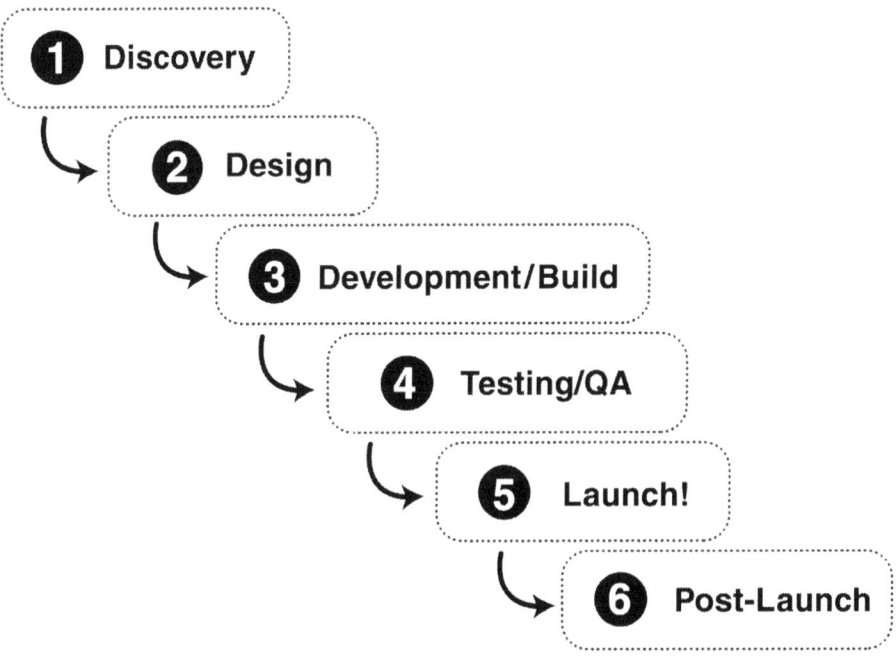

FIGURE 11.3 Outline Project Schedule: Waterfall Development.
Lord Cultural Resources

TABLE 11.3 TYPICAL ACTIVITIES AND DELIVERABLES DURING EACH PROJECT PHASE

PROJECT PHASE	ACTIVITIES	DELIVERABLES
Discovery / requirements gathering	Researching and documenting the business needs, user requirements, and the environment / infrastructure	Business requirements document, use cases / user stories, technical specifications
Design	Prototyping solutions	Wireframes, design mockups, prototypes
Development / build	Coding and product development	Interim or end product (depending on whether working on an Agile release or a more traditional approach)
Testing / user acceptance testing (UAT) / quality assurance (QA)	Testing the solution against user scenarios; fixes applied to identified issues / bugs	Issue / bug log, agreed list of fixes for a viable release
Launch	Preparing environment and operations for go-live	Live release
Post-launch	Addressing issues raised during testing that did not make the first release; developing functionality that was not in the MVP (see below)	Patch of additional fixes that didn't make the initial release, enhanced version of product—version 1.1

The activities undertaken, and deliverables from, each project phase will vary depending on the nature of the project and the methodology used, but some examples of typical activities and deliverables are listed in table 11.3.

GANTT CHARTS

A Gantt chart shows a list of the tasks that are required to complete the project, plotted against time. This is used throughout the project cycle to track progress and manage resources. Used correctly, it should help to ensure that any scheduling assumptions made by the project manager are clearly stated, and that project progress is actively tracked with any changes reported back and proactively addressed. It is also an effective tool for mapping project dependencies—highlighting where one task or series of tasks cannot begin until another task is completed.

The project team must be involved in the preparation of the project plan—especially when it comes to estimating the amount of work required to achieve each task. Estimating is a skill, and asking those who will be doing the work to feed into this process is key.

The chart should be updated by the project manager and consulted by the project team weekly, if not more frequently.

One of the most popular and comprehensive tools for managing Gantt charts is Microsoft Project, which has inbuilt functionality to update time frames according to stated dependencies, resource allocations, and so on. If this is too complex for your project's needs, there are lots of other packages on the market that have functionality for building and updating simple Gantt charts as part of shared teamwork and collaboration tools (see below), or there are templates that allow simple Gantt charts to be built using basic spreadsheet software.

Starting to build a Gantt chart can be a daunting task, especially for complex projects with many moving parts. Here are some tips on how to get started:

1. Outline the high-level schedule, identifying the major project milestones and the stages that they relate to.
2. List all of the tasks required in order to complete each stage of work. List as many tasks as possible initially, and then continue to review and refine until everything is captured.
3. Consider the order in which the tasks need to occur, moving things around as needed. Identify any points at which sign-off is required before the team can move to the next task.

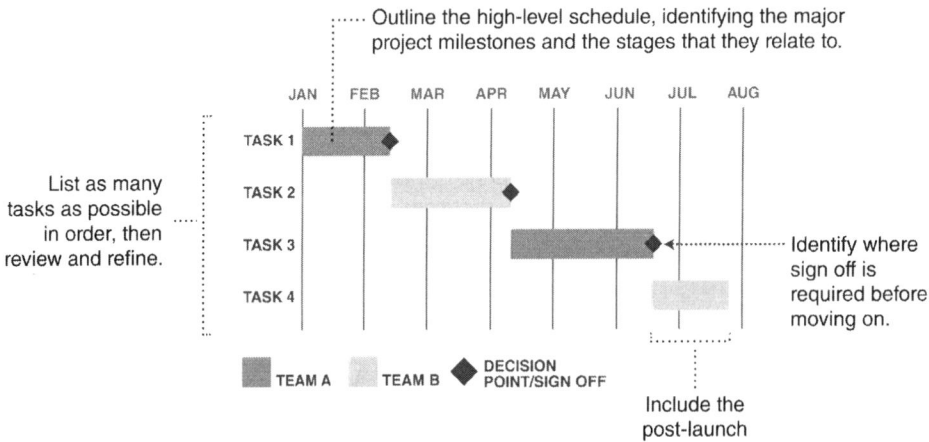

FIGURE 11.4 Tips for Building a Gantt Chart.
Lord Cultural Resources

220 | RACHEL CLEMENTS WALKER

4. Identify the resources assigned to each task, estimate the timeline taken to complete each task, and highlight any dependencies between tasks. If using a specialist Gantt tool, these changes will automatically adjust the schedule, whereas if using a simple spreadsheet these adjustments will need to be made manually. Either way, work iteratively to refine the timeline so that deadlines can be met while accounting for resourcing constraints.

5. Pay attention to periods when multiple tasks are in progress and make sure that team members are not overcommitted to ensure the workload is reasonable. Account for commitments outside of the project and the impact that they have on the time frame. For example: public holidays, project team vacation dates, periods of heavy operational commitments, other projects that the team is also supporting.

6. Be prepared for the plan to change and build in contingency to allow for unanticipated delays.

7. Ensure that you include the post-launch period in the plan.

Note that there can be a tendency, especially for those new to project management, to focus overly on the planning and control aspects of these tools and to forget their role as communication aids. A detailed Gantt chart will not, in itself, ensure that project timelines are met. The only way that these documents can lead to successful project delivery is through active engagement in the documentation by all stakeholders, including frequent discussion and feedback.

MINIMAL VIABLE PRODUCT (MVP)

The concept of minimum viable product (MVP) comes from product development and defines a product that has just enough functionality to warrant a feasible and usable release. In digital projects, MVP can be a helpful concept to incorporate for a few reasons: it forces the project team to prioritize, to clearly define which features are core for launch, and to allocate efforts accordingly; it can facilitate an earlier launch date for the first release, since not all functionality needs to be included; and it provides the opportunity to gather feedback from users post-launch and incorporate this into future releases, resulting in a better, more functional product in the longer term. However, for this to be successful, the post-launch period must be carefully planned as part of the project cycle, with resources and budget allocated to cover future releases.

Museums can find the concept of MVP challenging; they are organizations that through the nature of their work and mission strive for excellence and perfection, so the tolerance for releasing a product to the public which is not fully complete can be low. It is therefore important to explain the benefits of MVP clearly to stakeholders, to set expectations about the planned approach, and to have open discussions about the level of user experience that is acceptable for the MVP if this route is taken.

Project Budgets and Managing Costs

The project budget will summarize all anticipated costs of the project and is used as a management tool throughout the project life cycle. Preparing the budget at the start of the project, tracking project spending, and checking back against the budget regularly to ensure it is on track is an important part of the project manager's role.

Different versions of the project budget will be used with different audiences. The high-level summary will be presented to senior management as part of the business plan. The detailed budget will be used by the project manager and the finance department to track project spend and ensure that costs are controlled effectively. Attention should be paid to the formatting of the budget to ensure that the information presented is clear, readable, and easily understood by the intended audience; templates for digital project budgets can be downloaded for free online and can provide a good starting point.

When estimating, any cost figures that are used should be conservative and should project for the highest anticipated cost for any materials or service. Review estimates with other departments in the organization and seek advice on costs with which you are unfamiliar. For example, if budgeting for hardware, ensure that you involve your IT and procurement departments to advise on current cost and preferred providers. If using a third party for some project deliverables, request that their project costs are itemized and review these in detail. Question thoroughly the assumptions that have been made for each stage of the project and ensure that there is a clear mutual understanding of what services and deliverables are included in the quote and what will be covered by the internal team.

The cost categories included in the project budget will depend on the type of project. Some common cost categories to consider are listed below:

PROJECT COSTS

Software Development

Whether customizing an existing software platform, or building a new solution from scratch, consider the need to bring in external consultants plus any costs charged by third-party suppliers. Ensure any custom work is scoped and customization costs are agreed upon upfront, as this is an area where costs can easily overrun.

Hardware and Infrastructure

Involve the IT department in scoping any hardware and infrastructure requirements for the new product, including upgrades. Consider network bandwidth, WiFi coverage, storage capacity, server rack space, power/connectivity access points, and so on. For products that will be used physically within the museum, ensure that all possible usage locations are considered.

Integration

If the product needs to interface with other museum systems, there will be costs associated with this integration. This is an area that frequently overruns—both in costs and time. Ensure that all required integrations have been identified prior to starting the project, and involve back-end developers early in estimating the level of complexity and cost.

Data Migration

If moving from an existing system to a new platform, consider whether data from the old platform needs to be migrated to the new and, if so, how this will be handled. Support to reformat data and/or check it post upload might be required. Note also that the old system provider may charge a fee for providing this data in a usable format.

Design and UX

Products that are public facing tend to have stronger design and UX (user experience) requirements than those that are internally facing. Depending on the nature of the project and its ambitions, it might be appropriate to bring in a specialist digital design agency.

Content

Depending on the volume of content, support might be required for content creation and checking. Consider what type of images will be required in the new system; do new images or photography need to be created, or do existing images need to be reformatted? Depending on the type of project, there might also be the need for help with copy, including new copy creation, proofreading and keywording.

Testing

Consider whether user testing will be undertaken and, if so, how many rounds of this will take place. Freelance QA support can be required on larger projects and those with strict quality requirements; for example, transaction-based systems or those processing financial data. Load testing may be required to test the robustness of the system under heavy use.

Reporting and Analytics

Consider the reporting needs of the new system—how will performance be tracked and success be measured? Are custom reports required? Setting up reports, or configuring an analytics package, are often not covered under standard setup costs.

Training

Depending on the software, the provider might charge extra for training. The amount of support and whether sessions are handled remotely or on site needs to be negotiated.

Marketing

Will the new product be announced to the public and, if so, what type of campaign is required to raise awareness? The Marketing department might wish to run a series of digital ads, blog posts, press articles, and such, and if so, a budget should be assigned.

Freelance Support/Consultants

Some of the freelance roles you might consider bringing on for a digital project include: project manager, business analyst, front- and back-end developer(s), designer(s), integration architect, and QA support.

Contingency

Include contingency on top of the total cost assumptions for the project. A contingency of anything from 8 percent to 15 percent is common, depending on how confident you are in the estimates. The contingency budget could also be used as the budget to handle unexpected changes (see change management below). If that is the case, the conditions for using this budget need to be agreed with the project board.

ANNUAL OPERATING COSTS

In addition to the project costs, the new project will have implications on the annual operating budget as follows:

Software Licenses

Depending on the product, multiple licenses may be required. For example, a website could require not only the platform license but also additional services, such as content delivery network (if managing large amounts of content) or payment services provider and tax software (if taking transactions). Note that for some software, license fees might be due from the point the team has access to the platform, in which case a portion will need to be covered in the project costs, as well as in ongoing costs.

Storage

Depending on the nature of the project, future storage needs might need to be negotiated based on the anticipated volume of content or data.

Hosting and Maintenance

Involve the IT department in discussions of ongoing maintenance. Consider: hosting fees (for web project or cloud solutions), domain registration, spam monitoring and content moderation (for blogs and user-generated content), SSL certificates, vulnerability scanning, backup processes and uptime monitoring. Also estimate the cost of code upgrades or other maintenance.

Risk Management

Project risk is defined by the Project Management Institute as "an uncertain event or condition that, if it occurs, has a positive or negative effect on a project's objectives."[6] In order to ensure that a project meets its aims on time and within budget, potential risks must be identified and mitigation put in place.

The project manager will lead efforts to identify any potentially negative events or uncertainty, and will take steps to try to either avoid the negative event or remove the uncertainty. If this is not possible, plans will be put in place to try to reduce the impact of the event or uncertainty.

Involving the project team in this process, and encouraging them to speak openly about their concerns regarding what *could* go wrong, is important so that these can be proactively addressed. In an article for the *Harvard Business Review*, Gary Klein referred to this as a "project premortem" and advocated the importance of this process in order to strengthen the overall project plan and set projects up for success.[7]

A risk register, or risk log, is used to aid the project manager in this task (see figure 11.5). This document is usually created as a spreadsheet and lists identified risks, their likelihood of occurring, and their anticipated level of impact, plus proposed mitigation steps. The risk register should be updated weekly, with risks added or closed as appropriate, and reviewed with the project board regularly.

Change Management

All projects will experience changes to the plan during the project life cycle. Preparing for this, and managing changes to control their impact, is essential for keeping a project on track. The project manager must carefully interrogate the need for any changes that arise, pushing back when required in order to protect the project timeline and resources. They must also lead the project team in thinking creatively about how unavoidable changes can be tackled effectively in order to minimize their impact on the schedule and budget.

Types of changes that can occur during a project include:

- Changes to project scope—for example, missed requirements or new functionality requested by stakeholders
- Changes to the environment—for example, a change to the schedule of another project on which this project has a dependency

#	Identified Risk	Probability 1 (low) - 3 (high)	Impact 1 (low) - 3 (high)	Severity*	Mitigation Plan
1	Curators do not approve the final content on time	2	3	5	- Review timeframe for sign off with curators - discuss whether better to batch content or deliver in bulk. - Review draft content plans with curators to identify any concerns early on.

* *Severity* is a combination of probability and impact. Risks can be ranked by severity to prioritize them.

FIGURE 11.5 Example of a Risk Log Entry for an Exhibition-Related Product.
Lord Cultural Resources

- An identified but unavoidable risk occurring—for example, staffing changes within the project team
- An unanticipated problem occurring during development—for example, hidden complexity when addressing a key use case

> **KEY TERMS**
>
> **GO-LIVE**
>
> "Go-live" for a computer system is to literally "become operational." At go-live, the system is launched into the live systems environment and will be available for use by end users (either the public or internal staff) with live data. The term launch could refer to the go-live date or could be a public/press launch, which might happen after the actual go-live for some systems.

The project manager will monitor changes, document them when they occur, and evaluate their potential impact on the project. The following actions must then be taken:

First, evaluate whether the change is required. In the case of an unavoidable risk occurring, there may be no option but to accept the change. However, in the case of scope changes an evaluation must be made of whether the change is necessary to meet the project's aim to the required level of quality. The impact on budget and time frame must also be considered. Depending on the size and impact of the change, the project manager might make this decision, or it might need to be escalated to the project board.

Once the change is approved, the team must decide how to manage it. The project manager should be prepared to present a number of potential options. The following, or a combination of these, are usually considered in order to facilitate a change (note how these align with the triple-constraint model (figure 11.1) discussed earlier in this chapter):

- **Adjust scope**: Can the overall scope of the end product be reduced in some areas while still meeting the project goals?
- **Adjust quality**: Are there elements of the end product that could be delivered to a lesser degree of quality, at least for the initial launch?
- **Adjust schedule**: Can certain elements of the project be delivered after the **go-live** date, or can this date be adjusted?
- **Adjust cost**: Can additional budget be used to pay for the change? There may be savings in other areas which can be used to fund the change, or a contingency or change fund could be used (if available). This might require sign-off from the project board.

Managing Quality

Quality management is a discipline for ensuring that outputs . . . meet stakeholder requirements and are fit for purpose.

—Association for Project Management, 2016

> **KEY TERMS**
>
> **SPRINT**
>
> Sprints are a unit of development used in the scrum method of agile software development to refer to a regular, repeatable work cycle that iterates the product.

It is important to specify what quality means in the context of a particular project as part of the scope. Expectations about the quality that the product will meet, and the mechanisms and measures by which the quality of the end product will be assessed, need to be clearly defined and agreed with the project team and stakeholders early in the process.

Examples that could apply to different types of projects are as follows:

- The end-product will meet all high-priority user requirements, as outlined in the user requirements document.
- Coding must comply with W3C standards for website accessibility.
- Design must precisely confirm to guidelines provided in the organization's style guide.
- Average page load time in the live environment must be no more than X secs.
- X number of records must be processed in no more than Y secs in the live environment.
- X number of emails must be deployed in under Y secs in the live environment.

Quality-control activities determine "that the deliverables conform to specification, are fit for purpose and meet stakeholder expectations."[8] For digital projects, quality control occurs during the testing phase, often referred to as user acceptance testing (UAT) or quality assurance (QA). The amount of work required to complete thorough testing is often underestimated by museums, but the importance of planning for this stage, and allowing adequate time and resources to undertake it, cannot be overstated. It is far more straightforward to identify and resolve issues while a product is in a controlled test environment than when that product is live and has multiple users performing actions at the same time. This is especially important for projects such as ecommerce websites that involve user transactions or financial data, where the potential risks for the organization may be high if quality standards are not met.

DEVELOPING A TEST PLAN

The preparation of the test plan for UAT is usually undertaken by the representative(s) of the end user(s) on the project team. When working with an agile development process, there should be a test plan for each **sprint**; however, when working with a traditional development process the test plan will be for the full product. For particularly complex projects, it is worth considering specialist assistance with this process if there are no internal resources who have experience managing testing.

TABLE 11.4 SAMPLE TEST PLAN FOR ECOMMERCE WEBSITE

Front-end functionality. End users to test the following scenarios:	• User navigates from home page to product page using top navigation • User searches for a product • User adds product to bag • User creates an account • User checks out
Front-end content	• Design team to check each template to ensure that it corresponds to wireframes and to the design style guide. • Copyeditor to check copy on all information pages listed in the requirements document.
Integrations. End users and developers to test the following integrations:	• Payment authorization and settlement sent to PSP (payment services provider) • Orders sent to WMS (warehouse management system) • Customer data sent to CRM (customer relationship management system) • Shipment confirmation returned from WMS • Sales information sent to financial accounting system

To develop the test plan, first begin a high-level outline by listing all of the different areas of the product's functionality. This should be based on the project specifications, requirements documentation, or use cases. Then also list nonfunctional areas that require quality checking; for example, on a copy-heavy website, a proofreader might need to review content. Table 11.4 illustrates how the outline of a high-level test plan might be started for a simple ecommerce website.

This high-level plan is then developed into a test script where the actions involved in each functional area are listed, and the possible variations in user journeys are outlined. Figure 11.6 shows how a simple test script could be developed for a customer registration form on a website.

First, the desired user action (registration) is isolated, and then the variations around the valid data that a user could enter are specified. In this example the user could have an address from different countries, the United States or Canada. Then, once all valid variations have been listed, the next step is to consider invalid options, in this case missing data or incorrectly formatted data. It is advisable to start with the most basic scenario, where a user moves through the product in the most expected way. Once that has been identified, consider the other possible user journeys, and begin to build in additional complexity.

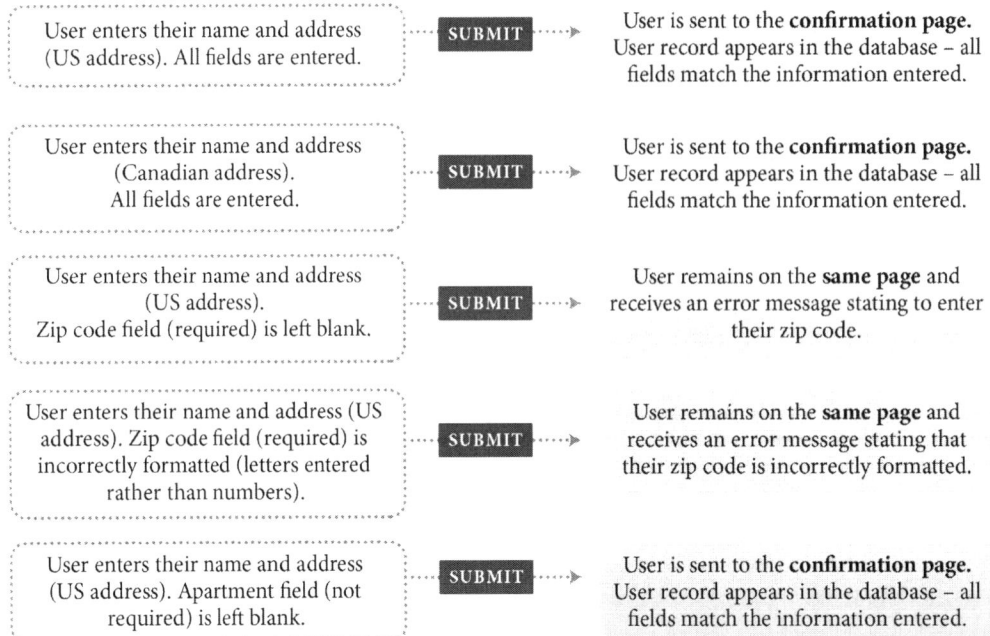

FIGURE 11.6 Example of How to Start Building a Test Script.
Lord Cultural Resources

TEST ENVIRONMENTS

The other important element of the test plan is whether there will be a dedicated test environment for the product and, if integrations with other systems will be tested, whether these other systems also have test environments. It is best practice to maintain a dedicated test environment for all systems once live, as this enables upgrades and changes to be checked without impacting the live environment or live data. However, for smaller projects and for one-off products, this is not always possible. If a test environment will not be used, the test plan must take steps to ensure that test data is isolated from live data and can be cleaned up once testing is completed; for example by carefully tracking and logging all test data or content and then deleting after use.

MANAGING TESTING

The testing process needs to be managed to ensure it is run efficiently and that all areas of functionality are thoroughly tested. Hold a meeting a week or so before testing begins to run through the process and the time frame. Ensure that all testers understand what is required of them and that they have dedicated sufficient time to testing. If possible, have the test team work together in one location with a developer on hand to investigate issues as they arise. This can speed up the process and aid communication for complex issues. If this is not possible, then there should be a daily call between the project manager, the lead developer, and the lead tester to review open issues and discuss any complex fixes.

The test script that was created during the planning phase should be turned into a test log. Once run, each test should be logged as pass/fail with the date and time of the test and the tester's initials. This can aid developers when they need to follow up on a particular scenario, and helps to identify areas that need to be retested following fixes. Testers need to complete all test scripts; however, it is also helpful to encourage them to go off script and to think as an end user would. Actions such as, "I wonder what happens if I click this button here," can often be the most helpful in unearthing issues that might otherwise have gone unnoticed.

Ensure that all testers know how to log any issue they encounter with sufficient details for the developers to investigate. Issues that are logged should include:

- A record of the date and time the issue occurred;

- A description of the environment being used (e.g., browser version and operating system in the case of a web project);

- The user account being used, if appropriate;

- Clear steps to reproduce the issue (STRs), which outline all steps a user took prior to experiencing the error; and

- A screenshot (or set of screenshots) showing the issue if appropriate.

For each element of functionality that is being tested, it is important to consider what factors could cause the product to fail and make sure these are specifically tested. If the product has been built well, then when it fails it should do so elegantly, with the user either unaware that there was a problem, or with an error message displayed that helps the user to correct the issue. If the product exists in a complex environment involving many integrations with other systems, ensure that once each element is confirmed as working well in isolation, the full flow is tested in an "end-to-end" manner that simulates the live environment as closely as possible.

For larger or more complex projects, consider the use of an online issue-logging tool such as JIRA.[9] This ensures that issues are tracked in one place with all required details, which aids visibility into what issues are being worked on. Set up a clear process flow: testers log issues in the tool; the project manager reviews issues to ensure they are clearly described and do not duplicate another issue; the project manager assigns issues to the development team for review; and once a fix is in place, the issue is reassigned to the tester to retest.

Depending on the nature of the project, you might also need to consider whether volume or load tests should be run to check how the product responds under heavy use. This could be done by arranging for a group of users to all try to perform an action simultaneously, or by an automated script being used to simulate high user volumes. If the product requires uploading files, data, or images regularly, large batches should be tested to ensure that these can be run successfully.

USER ACCEPTANCE TESTING (UAT) SIGN-OFF

The testing phase is considered complete when the list of outstanding issues has been reviewed by the project team, all critical issues for launch have been resolved, and a plan has been agreed with the development team to address any noncritical issues during the post-live period. Once this has taken place, the project manager can sign off on the project for launch and the project team will prepare for go-live. This forms the focus of the next section.

Launch and Beyond

As the end of a large project comes into sight, and the go-live date is approaching, it's important to maintain the energy and focus of the project team through the launch date and beyond. This is the time when both the project manager and the project team can be tired and distracted by all of the last-minute development and QA tasks needed to get the product to the launch date itself. It's essential at this point that time is set aside to enable careful thought and planning to be put into preparation for go-live, and the post-live period.

Preparation for Launch

There are a number of activities relating to the launch of a new product that need to be considered early in the project, resourced accordingly, included as part of the project plan, and addressed during the period before launch. These are covered below, before discussing the go-live process itself.

DATA MIGRATION

An early consideration in the prelaunch planning is whether data needs to be migrated from any legacy systems and, if so, how that process should be managed. Due to the volume and size of the records that might be involved in a data migration process, and the need to ensure the accuracy of data transfer, it is necessary to ensure that sufficient time is set aside for the following tasks:

- Mapping data from the legacy system to the new system,
- Cleansing legacy data if needed (for example, removing duplicate records),
- Testing the data import process and validating results,
- Undertaking a trial run of the full data import to monitor timing of the process at volume, and
- Undertaking the full data import and validating results.

Managing the timing of the live data import and the cutover for changes from one system to another can be particularly challenging. For content that is generated internally, for example, museum website content, it might be possible to instigate a change-freeze in the legacy system prior to the data migration. However, in the case of data that is in constant use and is regularly changing, for example, live customer email records in an email service provider, the schedule for the live import will need to be carefully planned to ensure that all changes are captured and moved across to the new system with minimal disruption to live operations and to current users.

TRAINING AND USER PERMISSIONS

One of the most essential prelaunch tasks is to set aside time and resources for user training and for the setup of end user accounts and permission levels. Depending on the type of project, and the number of internal users who will have access to the product, it might be possible to train all users together, or it might be necessary to cascade the training. In the latter situation, super-users will need to be selected throughout the organization to manage the training for other users in their departments or teams. Either way, it is essential that by the time the product goes live all users who will need to use the product on day one have been trained and have had sufficient time to familiarize themselves with the product. An effective way to manage this, while also assisting with QA, can be to loop as many end users as possible into the final stages of the testing process.

When setting up new users on the system, thought also needs to be given to the different levels of access necessary to ensure that users are set up with appropriate permissions to do their job effectively, while preventing unnecessary access to sensitive data. If the product includes customer or staff personal information, or credit card data, then access levels should be discussed with the IT and finance departments.

POST-LIVE MAINTENANCE AND SUPPORT

Attention also needs to be given during the prelaunch stage to questions about how the new product will be maintained once it is live. Some aspects to consider include:

- **Content Updates**: How frequently will content be updated, and who will be responsible for managing this? This is particularly important for web platforms or other products where users will expect content to be regularly refreshed.

- **Data Standards**: Do naming conventions or other standards need to be defined for data entry and followed by users? If so, have these been documented and have users been trained accordingly? Who will maintain those standards and update them once the system is live?

- **Support**: Who will support the product and ensure it is live and operational during business hours? If this responsibility is passing to a different team, have they been briefed on the plans for go-live and have they had sufficient time for training and familiarization with the product?

- **Performance Monitoring**: How will the team ensure that the live product is (a) functioning correctly and (b) meeting its goals? Do alerts, monitoring or reports need to be set up? If so, this is the time to do this.

PROMOTION

Once the product is live and stable, promoting that product to its end users is important to ensure that the product is both properly understood and well used. Managing this correctly and owning the "story" surrounding the product can be an important factor in ensuring the longer-term success and longevity of the product.

For an end product that is public facing, engage the marketing team at an early stage in the project to get their ideas on how to promote the product to current or new user bases. Promotion via social media, the organization's website and email lists, influential blogs, and other media can help to raise the number of users and get the public engaged. If an MVP approach is being taken, then setting user expectations accordingly and encouraging user feedback is particularly important. One point to manage carefully, however, is the timing of press and promotion. If the end product is highly visible, for example, a change to the organization's website, then communication and promotion must be timed carefully so that end users are aware of the coming changes while ensuring that any traffic spikes are timed at a point when the team is confident of the product's stability. Any launch dates communicated publically must be ones that the team is completely confident can be met.

For an end product that is internally facing, promotion can still be an important aspect to consider. An internal marketing effort can be helpful in ensuring that staff throughout the organization are aware of the product, understand its aims, and are enthusiastic about using it. This helps to ensure a strong uptake of the end product. Some ways of accomplishing this include presenting the product at staff meetings, offering informal drop-in sessions with the project team where staff can learn more about the product, and adding information to the intranet or other internal communication channels. The project sponsor/champion is often well placed to lead these efforts for the project team.

Going Live

TIMING

Selecting a date for go-live is often beyond the immediate control of the project manager; for example, if the project is part of a broader program such as the opening of an exhibition. However, there are some best practices that need to be considered when choosing a launch date, and the project manager should push strongly to ensure these are met. A new product, or a change to an existing product, should never be launched on a Friday, since post-live issues may take time to manifest and support teams may not be available during the weekend to mitigate them. Preferred days to launch new products are Tuesday or Wednesday, as this ensures a few days of post-live support with the full team in the office. For similar reasons, go-live processes are generally scheduled for early in the morning so that the project team has the majority of the day to handle any issues with the maximum support available. If the go-live process will impact live users, then a time of least impact, outside of business hours, is generally selected.

CREATING A GO-LIVE PLAN

The go-live process usually involves the full project team, and can be one of the most intensive periods of the project, requiring good cooperation and communication between all parties. Creating a detailed launch plan and a clear communications strategy can help to make this a success.

The go-live plan should include the following:

- List of any prerequisites that must be completed in order for go-live to take place. For example: "data migration and validation must be signed off."

- Confirmed time for a go or no-go decision on whether to proceed with go-live, and a list of team members who will be involved in making that decision.

- Timetable of the activities to be undertaken in the day(s) prior to go-live, the date of go-live itself, and the day(s) following. This should specify the required order of tasks,

> **KEY TERMS**
>
> **POSTMORTEM**
>
> A process, usually at the conclusion of a project, whereby the team evaluates the successes and unsuccessful parts of the project.

highlight any dependencies between tasks, note points at which a sign-off decision is required before proceeding, and assign an owner for each task.

- Contact details for everyone involved in the launch, including mobile phone numbers.

- Details of the circumstances under which a rollback will be considered if issues are experienced, and a detailed plan for how a rollback would be managed.

Once the go-live plan has been created, a meeting should be scheduled to review the plan with the project team to ensure that the all parties fully understand what is expected of them. It is important to encourage the team to raise any concerns and to discuss stages where things could go wrong. Go-live processes rarely proceed exactly as planned, and unexpected issues may well arise. Talking frankly as a team about some of the challenges that might be experienced can help the project manager to mitigate potential problems before they happen and prepare the team mentally for the steps they will take if issues are encountered.

The Post-Live Period

Once the project has been launched successfully and is stable in the live environment, the first priority for the project team is to celebrate a job well done and take some time to relax after the pressures of the launch. But the project does not end here, and as soon as possible, the project manager's focus must shift to the post-live period.

PROJECT POSTMORTEM AND ARCHIVING DOCUMENTATION

Within a few weeks of the launch, it is good practice to conduct a project **postmortem** with the team. This session should capture feedback on what aspects of the project were handled well, what mistakes were made, and what lessons were learned in the process. This is a helpful exercise for the project manager, the team, and the organization to identify whether anything should be done differently on the next project. This meeting can also provide a natural point for the project manager to regroup with the project team and focus attention on any cleanup tasks from the launch that have yet to be completed.

POST-LIVE CLEANUP AND USER FEEDBACK

The product will not remain static during the post-live period. Most projects involve a period of post-live cleanup, where issues that were identified during testing but were not of a severity to prevent launch are fixed and released to the live version. It is also good practice to schedule some sessions at agreed intervals post-live to solicit feedback from end users on whether the product meets their needs and expectations. If a minimum viable product approach was taken, then this feedback is essential to drive plans for the next release. For other projects, the team should review feedback and agree as to whether updates, tweaks to the setup, or other changes can and should be made. It is important this process takes place reasonably soon after launch, but once users have had time to thoroughly use the product, one and three months post-launch are often good points to approach users for feedback.

MEASURING SUCCESS

Mechanisms should be set up to measure the performance of the live product against the project aims and success criteria defined in the business case. Typically, it is helpful to measure at a range of intervals, since the immediate post-live period can be misleading for projecting longer-term performance. One, three, and six months post go-live are common points to measure success. Results should be reported to the project board and compared against the original aims and success measures in the business case. If the product is not meeting its targets, then deeper analysis by the business owner might be needed to determine the cause and whether some optimization or adjustment will improve performance.

HANDOVER TO OPERATIONS

In order to transition the product into everyday operations, it is important to define clear roles and responsibilities within the organization for managing and maintaining the product for years to come. A business owner must be identified who will be responsible for the day-to-day operation of the product, own the user journey, and define any future modifications or enhancements. A support owner will tackle any issues identified in the live product, and will ensure that product performance in the live environment is maintained according to the guidelines for quality agreed during the project.

The project manager must archive a copy of all project documentation to ensure everything is saved in one place, and is clearly organized so as to be usable for anyone in the organization who needs to access this in the future. If user documentation and support guides haven't been created, then this should be done now and the information shared with all relevant stakeholders.

NEXT STEPS

Once the transition to operations has been completed, planning can take place to determine when the first upgrade or update should take place. For products with planned lifespans of two years or more, this is important to ensure the sustainability of the solution. It is generally more cost effective in the long term to ensure regular upgrades are maintained and that the product's functionality is periodically enhanced than to wait several years before completing a major product overhaul. If the project involves the use of a Software as a Service (SaaS) platform, then upgrades and enhancements will be handled by the provider as part of the service contract; however, these updates will still require thorough testing and involvement from the in-house team.

In this way, digital projects are rarely ever "done," and it is important that resources are committed to the product through to the post-live period. When museums plan for the long-term sustainability of the product in this way it helps to ensure that a successful digital project transitions into a successful digital product that enhances the mission of the organization over its entire lifespan.

DIGITAL PROJECTS IN MUSEUMS
Rachel Clements Walker Interviews Eileen Willis

Eileen Willis is the editorial director at Lincoln Center for the Performing Arts. Eileen has substantial experience in developing digital content and managing digital projects in not-for-profit organizations.

> **RCW:** What do you think are the main challenges faced when planning and executing a successful digital project in a museum environment?
>
> **EW:** I think that the challenges can be broken into three main areas: (1) setting realistic goals given the time, budget, and audience; (2) communicating clearly with stakeholders; and (3) managing relationships. The first part—setting realistic goals—can be hard if stakeholders don't understand the level of difficulty of a project, or are mentally trying to compete with for-profit tech companies that have more resources and bigger teams dedicated to digital projects. Within the realistic goals, the audience part is key in terms of establishing how the project's success will eventually be measured. What are the goals for the finished project, and how will you know if and when they've been achieved? What does success look like for a *museum* project, knowing that the museum audience is not as large as the audience for a general digital project?
>
> **RCW:** Can you tell me a little more about the aspects of communication that you think are particularly important?
>
> **EW:** There are so many stages throughout the project where communication is key. For example: securing internal buy-in from stakeholders; managing expectations throughout the project and keeping stakeholders and senior staff on track

throughout the project to avoid scope creep; and keeping the internal team motivated for the duration of the project, especially as compromises need to be made.

RCW: And how about relationship management?

EW: It's important to maintain good relationships with difficult stakeholders so that once the project is complete, the working relationship can still be productive and positive. This can mean knowing when to push back and when to give in to stakeholders' sometimes unreasonable demands.

RCW: If you were to give advice to a colleague managing a digital project for the first time, what would it be?

EW: The success of the project depends so much on how the communication is handled. Define the project clearly from the outset and be firm in terms of scope, even as stakeholders try to add more and more things to the project. Make sure that you have your boss's unwavering support and that you and your boss are on the same page in terms of how the project gets "socialized" inside the institution. Create a communication plan at the beginning to bring in stakeholders—especially the ones that are the most difficult—to make sure they don't (passive aggressively) sabotage the project. Finally, make sure the project plan doesn't end with the launch. The launch date is really the beginning of an entire second phase of the project. I would have the project plan extend past launch for the same length of time that preceded the launch (for example, if it's a ten-month project to launch, the project plan should be for twenty months).

AGILE PROJECTS AT THE METROPOLITAN MUSEUM OF ART
Rachel Clements Walker Interviews Adam Padron

Adam Padron is the senior manager of application and data services in the IT department of the Metropolitan Museum of Art, New York. Adam's team introduced agile techniques to the museum and have now been using agile development processes for several years.

RCW: When did you start using agile within the museum?

AP: Around 2010 we started a tablet project for the Membership department. At that time, memberships were sold on index cards filled out by hand, and this project was to develop a sales tablet that would allow them to sell at the membership desk and to do mobile sales. It was about a quarter of the way through that project when we really started to implement agile.

> **KEY TERMS**
>
> **SCRUM MASTER**
>
> The scrum master is one of the key core roles in the scrum framework for agile projects. The scrum master acts as a facilitator and lead within the development team, and is responsible for removing roadblocks that might delay the team's progress, keeping the team focused, and ensuring that the scrum framework is followed.

I had a team member at the time who had served as a **scrum master**. He had an understanding from some of his previous work of some of the potential benefits and acted as an internal evangelist, and we started to pull the process together. It took a long time, and I would say actually that the initial scrum master wasn't successful in pushing it through—not of his own fault but just because of the sheer amount of cultural movement that needs to occur to adopt the core tenets of what makes agile successful.

RCW: What do you see as the key changes culturally in working agile as opposed to a more traditional way of working?

AP: People who follow agile are kind of allergic to the word "governance," but I think there's this governance piece that has to feed into the whole process. In a place like the Metropolitan Museum of Art, responsibilities can be very diffuse across processes and workflows and systems and you end up with a network of product owners, all with different interests, and that can be very challenging.

RCW: So it's important to have very clear roles and responsibilities within the process?

AP: Yes. The project team, the scrum master and the product owner are really the only people who are supposed to matter in an agile project. The product owner has some defined amount of resources of the team available to them, and has to leverage this to reach the goals that are achievable. So that product owner has to be in a position to be making critical decisions on a very regular basis—that's the agile piece. You need the product owner to be able to say, "I'm going to cut scope from *that* milestone, so I can dedicate resources to *this* milestone. And I know that the executives and the management trust me to be making these balanced choices for the good of the overall project, because in the end we have a certain amount of money, we have a certain amount of resources and we have a certain amount of time." Navigating that, and getting management to respect it, is probably the single most important part of making agile work.

RCW: What do you think are the big advantages of working in an agile way?

AP: The ability for the product owner to make informed tactical decisions about where resources are being utilized. It puts them in such a powerful position to make good decisions and to make them rapidly, which is a challenge in a large organization like the Met. And also the impact on the team—the control that the team begins to feel about their work product, and the pride of ownership. In an agile project, it wasn't someone in a corner office who decided the project scope—we sat around a table and agreed based upon a common understanding of complexity. So when the team has to go into a period of crunch time it's their pride on the line, and their ability to deliver, and their credibility. It creates a very virtuous cycle.

RCW: What advice would you have for those undertaking an agile project for the first time?

AP: A good and strong scrum master is critical—knowing how and when to say no is so important. Every time your scrum master says no they are protecting you from yourself, and you have to learn to trust that. It's so important because if we're going to take on a scope change that means we have to make some hard decisions.

RCW: One of the advantages of an agile process is getting product out to users early, and showing tangible results that can be tested. Have you had any challenges with that in the museum environment?

AP: Yes, the bar for a minimum viable product is too high at a place like the Met. In the last two or three months of the membership tablet project we were able to go live with a sub-version-one functionality, with the idea of testing that out. We would have liked to do that much earlier, but there are some realities from an operational standpoint—such as training and financial reconciliation of processes across multiple channels. But I think it's still a debate that we have. The museum is a certain kind of institution, and what are we comfortable with getting out in front of the public? Where can the edges be rough and where can they not be? I would say that it's challenging; however, it has been getting better with every single phase we take on for our products.

💡 KEY TAKEAWAYS: DIGITAL PROJECT MANAGEMENT

1. A project manager's role is to
   - Ensure that the ultimate product meets the initial aims of the project,
   - Balance time, scope, cost, and quality, and
   - Manage people and keep communications clear.

2. There are a number of digital project management methodologies that can be used for planning digital projects, and almost all are suitable for use in the museum environment. Three of the most commonly used are PRINCE2 (Projects in Controlled Environments); PMBOK (Project Management Body of Knowledge); and Scrum.

3. The most common digital development approaches are waterfall and agile. Each has advantages and disadvantages. The selection of a particular method will influence the shape of the project, and how it is managed.

4. Project management tasks across different stages of the project can be summarized as follows:
   - Preparation and kickoff. This involves:
     - Creating kickoff documentation (e.g., business case and project charter),
     - Setting up the project team and communication structures, and
     - Running a kickoff meeting (or meetings).
   - Managing project delivery. This involves:
     - Managing communications and project documentation,
     - Creating and managing the project schedule,
     - Keeping track of the project budget,
     - Risk management,
     - Change management, and
     - Managing quality, including the planning and management of test phases.
   - Preparing for launch. This includes
     - Data migration,
     - Training and user permissions, and
     - Setting up post-live maintenance and support.

- Going live and the post-live period. This includes:
    - Running a project post mortem,
    - Archiving documentation,
    - Gathering user feedback,
    - Measuring success, and
    - Handing over to operations.

Notes

1. For more information on PRINCE2 methodology and certification, visit: www.axelos.com/best-practice-solutions/prince2.

2. For more information about the PMI, PMBOK, and PMP certification, visit: www.pmi.org.

3. For more information on Scrum, and Professional Scrum MasterTM training, visit: www.scrum.org.

4. Office of Government Commerce, *Managing Successful Projects with PRINCE2* (London: TSO, 2005).

5. Note that the landscape is constantly changing, with new tools becoming available every year. For more information on those mentioned here, visit the following websites: JIRA, www.atlassian.com/software/jira

Smartsheet, www.smartsheet.com

Basecamp, https://basecamp.com

Teamwork, www.teamwork.com

Google Drive, www.google.com/drive.

6. Project Management Institute, *A Guide to the Project Management Body of Knowledge*, 5th edition *(PMBOK® Guide)* (Newtown Square, PA: Project Management Institute, Inc., 2013) [Kindle version].

7. Gary Klein, "Performing a Project Premortem," *Harvard Business Review*, September 2007.

8. Association for Project Management, "Quality Management," *APM Body of Knowledge*, accessed July 31, 2016, http://knowledge.apm.org.uk/bok/quality-management.

9. JIRA is one of the most commonly used online issue tracking tools and can be utilized at various stages in the project. For more information, visit www.atlassian.com/software/jira.

12

Visitor Experience Design

Marco Mason

Technologies migrate as they mature. In early childhood, their very existence is a marvel, even as people wonder what can be made of it. In early adolescence, they become more and more able to perform useful functions for us, and for a while, they are judged primarily on their ability to do more and more, better and better. Finally, in maturity, it is the quality of the experience provided by these technologies that matter.

—Designer and theorist Donald Norman

Designing digital media for museums is no longer about the technology or functionality alone but also about the experiences it delivers to diverse visitors. In chapter 7, Lisa Wright describes some of the ways in which museums are using digital technologies to enhance people's connection with collections, with each other, or with research, ideas, and stories. Those include mobile applications, augmented and virtual reality experience, digital multisensory technologies, and more basic digital interactives (also called "interactives")—such as a touch table or a video game.

Many of these experiences are developed through a process called visitor experience design (VX design) in which design is not just about the form of an object or system, but instead a dynamic method of thinking that places the visitor at the center of the design process. VX design is premised on the idea that a successful experience is the result of understanding and responding to visitor needs, behavior, and expectations. In this

> **KEY TERMS**
>
> **EMPATHY**
>
> Empathy is the "effort to see the world through the eyes of others," "understand the world through their experiences," and "feel the world through their emotions."[1]
>
> ---
>
> [1] Tim Brown, *Change by Design: How Design Thinking Transforms Organizations and Inspires Innovation* (New York: Harper Business, 2009), 50.

aspect, VX design is not specifically for a digital experience, but can also be applied to any aspect of exhibition design. Rather than focusing on a specific technology and what it can do, VX design aims to facilitate or enhance an interaction: the design of the interaction determines the quality of the visitor experience.

This chapter focuses specifically on the VX design approach, which guides the discovery, creation, and development phases of a digital project. I begin by describing certain principles that characterize VX design. I then explore the levels of design that need to be considered in a digital project—working from visitor experience toward the concrete visual design of the interface. Finally, I provide a step-by-step guide to the VX design process, including sample design techniques.

VX Design Principles

Visitor experience design is based on a number of principles that determine a particular way of working.

1. APPROACH DESIGN AS A VISITOR-CENTERED PRACTICE

In chapter 3, Rob Stein explores how museums are learning how to use data in order to become more user-centric in their practice and approach. Putting visitors first also requires that the designer has **empathy** for the visitor—particularly when it comes to understanding why the visitor engages with the experience, what they expect from their engagement, what barriers may stand in the way from them having a full or satisfying experience, and other factors. While data give a good idea of behavior, empathy is built through qualitative visitor research. Ethnographic methods such as interviews, observations, and immersion in the field can provide a more nuanced understanding of motivation, behavior, and expectations than an analysis based only on statistical data (discussed later in "Step 1: Research").

2. EMBRACE DIVERSITY

Museum visitors are diverse. Attempts to empathize with visitors should acknowledge the different types of visitors—teachers, learners, children, teens, artists, scientists, community workers—and attempt to develop a nuanced understanding of each one.

3. COLLABORATION IS KEY

Museum staff have different forms of expertise. Design activities such as creative brainstorming sections, **design charrettes**, and design workshops should include museum professionals from different departments in order to ensure that a wide range of perspectives—from curatorial concerns to technical features—are incorporated into the design process. These charrettes should also ideally include the end users as well.

4. USE VISUALIZATIONS

In a group comprised of people from various backgrounds and areas of expertise, using a range of visual techniques—from deliverables to prototypes—offers a common language that increases communication and, in turn, enhances teamwork collaboration, encourages participation, and boosts creativity, hence fostering innovation. Visual tools effectively support communication because they are effective "tools for thinking."

5. ASSUME CHANGE, BE AGILE

Agile development is a term and practice borrowed from the software industry that foregrounds customer collaboration, enables quick response to change, and emphasizes continuous development. Agile methodologies embrace an iterative process to advance design through cyclical design iterations. A portion of the whole problem may be developed and tested among end users, which is then adjusted based on this feedback.

6. ADOPT PROTOTYPING

Prototyping plays a fundamental role in agile development, as it allows for the evaluation of a possible solution and then the use of the feedback to create a new prototype, advancing the design toward the best solution. Low-fidelity prototypes—which can be as technically simple as a paper mock-up, are particularly useful, especially in the early stages of design.

KEY TERMS

DESIGN CHARRETTE

A design charrette is an intensive planning session where citizens, designers, and others collaborate on a vision for development.[1]

---

[1] "What Is a Charrette?" The Town Paper, accessed October 5, 2016, http://www.tndtownpaper.com/what_is_charrette.htm.

AGILE DEVELOPMENT

Agile is a form of project management, traditionally used in software development that helps teams respond to unpredictability through incremental, iterative work cadences and empirical feedback.[1]

---

[1] "The Agile Movement," Agile Methodology, accessed October 5, 2016, http://agilemethodology.org/.

Creating low-fidelity prototypes does not require specific skills, which enables professionals with different backgrounds, such as curators, conservators, and educators, to play a meaningful role in the design process. In addition, prototyping at any level of design offers the possibility of experimenting and failing early, which encourages early development of many possible options. (See "Prototypes at Every Step.")

The "culture of prototyping" is at the basis of advanced design practice as it relates to the "continuous learning" that takes place during the entire collaborative design process. During the iterative process, team members go through a learning process as they gather knowledge by experimenting; designers and non-designers employ different types of prototypes together in order to explore possible solutions and their suitability, according to the particular problems faced during the three levels of design.

Levels of Design

Visitor experience design treats aesthetic, experiential, and technological issues simultaneously through multiple iterations instead of as a linear process where one hands off to another in a fixed sequence. A good VX design addresses equally the overarching visitor experience; the concrete structure that arranges content, interactions, and functionality; and the final details of the graphic interface (see figure 12.1). This applies to projects at any scale—from complex information systems (for example, a network of multiple devices) to simple interactive designs such as a mobile app. VX design considers the following:

- **The Level of Experience**: This refers to how the experience makes the visitor feel or what the experience will make the visitor do. The "experience" can be understood through a narrative, which outlines the environment, context, needs, and motivations of visitors. This level of design is often informed by audience research—using ethnographic research methodologies such as focus groups or observation.

- **The Level of Interaction**: Levels of interaction refers to the ways visitor experience is structured. These structures are defined by using storyboards, wireframes, and verbal descriptions to represent the way a visitor moves through content. Other techniques such as visual style guides and mood boards can also be used to define the high-level "look and feel" of the interface.

- **The Level of the Interface**: At this level, the designers give form to the structure and functionality of the experience. They address the following questions: What are the graphic components that constitute the interface? What shapes do they take? Where should we place them on the screen? How should visitors move between one graphic element and another?

FIGURE 12.1 Visitor Experience Design.
Lord Cultural Resources

The VX Design Process

The VX design process happens at three different levels. It involves empathy and collaboration with end users, multidisciplinary design teams, and an agile methodology—using prototypes to iterate until a final design solution is achieved. The following is a step-by-step guide to the VX design process, which is summarized in figure 12.2.

Step 1—Research

There are four types of research that inform VX design:

- Visitor research
- Organizational research
- Technical research
- Interpretive plan

Research is done during the planning stages of the project and/or may take place once the design process has begun. Here we will assume that the design process starts with

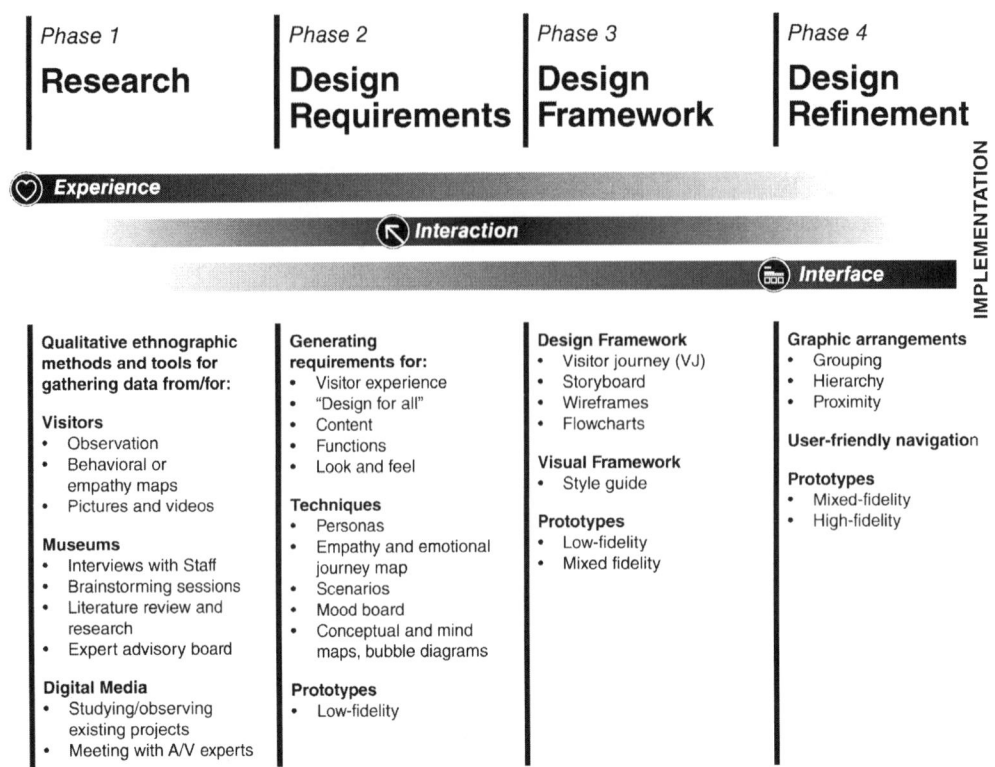

FIGURE 12.2 The Visitor Experience Design Process.
Lord Cultural Resources

understanding potential visitors and their journeys as well as the goals of the institution. The former furnishes a deeper understanding of how the experience can satisfy visitor needs, desires, and expectations, while the latter provides context for the experience, including, for example, organizational goals and exhibition objectives and the physical environment.

VISITOR RESEARCH

In order to understand the potential user or visitor of a digital experience, team members, which usually consist of museum practitioners and/or designers, need to collect data using various forms of research methodologies. These include **ethnographic research methodologies**, which can support the development of empathy; quantitative research to determine audience segments (for example, learners have specific requirements [see chapter 6]), as may families, professionals, and others); and data analytics (see chapters 3 and 5), which can give insight into past interactions. This research then will be analyzed in the subsequent "Design Requirements" phase, where various outcomes are visualized as models.

ORGANIZATIONAL RESEARCH

Data from key members of the organization and project stakeholders should be collected in parallel with visitor studies. This is done in order to collect maximum information about the museum's vision and interpretative goals regarding, for example, how the interactive(s) and information systems should conform to the museum's (digital) strategies and impact its overall mission. Economic issues (e.g., investment of resources, the business model, etc.) and project feasibility are other important aspects of project preparation. Beyond interview sessions with stakeholders, other activities that foster the exchange of knowledge and information should be undertaken though meetings, the exchange of documents, literature reviews, and joint brainstorming sessions.

TECHNICAL RESEARCH

No project is without technical problems: knowing them in advance allows the design team to develop solutions. The experts to interview are those responsible for implementing and maintaining the solution, such as IT/web and new media developers. Valuable data may also come to light from investigations into other mobile projects through direct observation and a review of specialist publications and research reports.

ETHNOGRAPHIC RESEARCH METHODOLOGIES

Ethnographic research methods are aimed at developing insights about the emotions and motivations that drive human behavior. Design ethnography[1] is an approach that can offer a number of user research methods to gather qualitative data by observing visitors performing their activities in their own context using pictures, video and audio records, field notes, and interviews. It includes

- **Fly-on-the-wall**[2] observation of people within their "natural" context;
- **Behavioral mapping** using annotated maps[3] to observe visitors' activities in a specific place by annotating their behaviors (e.g., actions, movements, time spent on each location) on a map;
- **Picture and video recording**[4] accompanied by detailed field notes;
- **Empathy probes**[5] in which the participants are asked to record specific events, feelings or interactions in a notebook during the visit. As the data comes directly from the visitor, this technique provides an insight into visitor behaviors;
- **Camera journals**,[6] which are similar to the empathy probe but the record is made with a camera.

Observations should be conducted together with subject interactions such as contextual open-question interviews.[7]

---

[1] Andrew Crabtree, Mark Rouncefield, and Peter Tolmie, "Design Ethnography in a Nutshell," in *Doing Design Ethnography* (London: Springer, 2012), 183–205.
[2] Dan Saffer, *Designing for Interaction: Creating Innovative Applications and Devices* (Berkeley, CA: New Riders, 2010), 86; Bruce Hanington and Bella Martin, *Universal Methods of Design: 100 Ways to Research Complex Problems, Develop Innovative Ideas, and Design Effective Solutions* (Beverly, MA: Rockport Publishers, 2012), 90.
[3] Robert Curedale, *Design Thinking: Process and Methods Manual* (Topanga, CA: Design Community College, 2013), 205; Hanington and Martin, *Universal Methods of Design*, 18, 90.
[4] Hanington and Martin, *Universal Methods of Design*, 120.
[5] Curedale, *Design Thinking*, 152, 225, 226.
[6] Ibid., 215; Hanington and Martin, *Universal Methods of Design*, 134.
[7] Steiner Kvale, *Doing Interviews* (London: Sage, 2007).

INTERPRETIVE PLAN

The interpretative plan describes in words the visitor journey including the communication objectives of the experience, key messages it seeks to convey and how content should be communicated via the experience. The interpretive plan may make use of diagrammatic sketches such as mind-maps, affinity diagrams, and bubble and Venn diagrams to help gather themes and organize them into groupings based on relationships between arguments. The interpretive plan is typically informed by a basic understanding of the theme and content of the exhibit (based on a curator's briefing and interaction with other content experts), and aims to translate "raw content" into a story that is compelling and relevant to the visitor. It is then assembled into multimedia treatments to guide the development of specific digital experiences.

Multimedia treatments are a narrative description of the digital experience, which can also be depicted visually through a storyboard, as described in more detail in the section "The Design Framework: Storyboards and Wireframes." Also, see chapter 7 for more on interpretive planning and media treatments.

Step 2—Design Requirements

Overabundant data can be confusing and therefore unusable if it is not analyzed, interpreted, and presented in a way that supports the design process. Design requirements bridge the gap between research and design; the visitor experience, which has initially been defined on a more abstract level (see "Levels of Design"), is now translated into more tangible interactions. They are neither features nor interface functions nor technical specifications; rather, they are statements that provide insights into the design as a whole, define what the interactive objects should do, represent and consolidate visitor and stakeholder demands, and set design parameters without being specific about how they will be met.

Clear design requirements constitute a key underlying aspect of the overall project because in their absence each team member might work from a different idea. Clearly articulating what you are designing enables everyone to know the project's goals and when they've been reached. Design requirements can include, but are not limited to, the following:

- Visitor experience requirements
- Content requirements
- Functional requirements
- Look and feel requirements

VISITOR EXPERIENCE DESIGN

FIGURE 12.3 Examples of Personas.
Dr. Marco Mason

VISITOR EXPERIENCE REQUIREMENTS

The first step in generating visitor experience requirements is to define visitor motivations. Without a clear idea of a visitor's reasons for engaging, it is difficult to create a compelling visitor experience. Creating narratives is an effective method for imagining ideal visitor experiences and high-level interactions. Experiences created around a story are more engaging, as digital systems are designed to provoke in the visitor a series of behaviors that take place over time.

One effective narrative technique to analyze the data gathered from visitor research is the *persona*, which is a sketch of an archetypical character—around a page in length—that describes an individual with a name, a picture, and a story that describes their motivations, goals, emotions, and behaviors.

The persona is a great exercise in empathy. During the entire creative process team members constantly refer to it whenever a question or concern arises about how aspects of the digital interactive should be designed to satisfy visitor needs. Other effective techniques include empathy maps, emotional journey maps, and user experience maps.

Once the persona has been created, the team can place him or her into a series of **design scenarios**, thus creating visual narratives of possible end results. These scenarios

> **KEY TERMS**
>
> **SCENARIO (DESIGN OR USER)**
>
> A scenario is a short story about a persona that imagines his or her goals and the actions he or she will take to meet them.

MAPPING VISITOR MOTIVATIONS

Empathy maps help the team to gain a deeper insight into the personas they are designing for. The map can be drawn on a large piece of paper or whiteboard. Team members should research the following questions:

- What would the visitor be thinking and feeling?
- What would the visitors see while using the interactive object in their environment?
- What might the user be saying and/or doing while interacting?
- What are the user's pain points or fears when interacting with the system?
- What would the user hear in these scenarios? What are their worries and aspirations?

Emotional journey maps: These illustrate a visitor's emotional experience throughout an interaction. For example, a visitor using a mobile app experiences emotions as they move between galleries. By modeling visitor movements and identifying emotional responses, the team members can create a story that facilitates a particular visitor journey.

User experience maps: These visualize the experiences and responses that visitors might have while using the interactive (e.g., individual actions, feelings, and perceptions).

can include engaging with the experience but also social interaction with peers or a museum guide during the process. The team thinks about the story visitors might experience, and from this, common elements emerge to help figure out how to satisfy needs and goals. A scenario helps a team to think through how interactive objects can support the personas (i.e., the visitors or users) to achieve their goals—and, in turn, to satisfy their experiential goals by establishing the primary touch points the visitor has with the system. By focusing on high-level actions from the perspective of the visitor, the team members extract design requirements.

CONTENT REQUIREMENTS

Content requirements describe what kind of information needs to be presented to a visitor, and in what form and structure. They are guided by the interpretive plan that identifies how the content should be structured.

Content requirements for digital media experiences will vary depending on the type of experience. Generally, digital content will be text, images, audio, or video. Content for a mobile app audio tour would be descriptions of each stop on the tour; a digital game would need text scripting out the challenges and questions for visitors; an augmented reality experience will need images or video and text to layer onto views in the museum. The assigned content team must work with the experience designers during this stage to ensure that the planned content will work within the digital experience—that is, how much text, how many images, how long of an audio or video clip?

Content requirements might have software implications that are related to the functional requirements. For example, the museum team might decide to handle content

VISITOR EXPERIENCE DESIGN

FIGURE 12.4 Example of a Visual Scenario: This scenario was used in the design of the Tenement Museum's *Shop Life* project in New York City, USA. Frames extracted from the video prototype.
Potion Design Studio and Tenement Museum

through a content management system (CMS) which will enable centralized control and more efficient updating. (See chapters 9 and 10.) This technical requirement has to be decided at the early stage, as it will affect the next design phase and the final software development.

The content and its structure are crucial to define the digital interactive structure and lay out the interface functionality. Without appropriate logical organization of themes and subthemes, the effectiveness of the final digital product will likely be compromised.

FUNCTIONAL REQUIREMENTS

Functional and technology features are factors that, concomitantly with visitor experience requirements and content requirements, influence visitor experience. The functional requirements determine what the product should do—that is, the main (general) actions that visitors will perform (e.g., the system should: visualize statistic data, explore different levels of content, share content through social networks, locate the visitor position, and so on). Functional requirements include considering the languages of the experience, the height (whether it is reachable by children or people with disabilities), access to WiFi and so on.

> **GUIDELINES FOR CONTENT FOR DIGITAL EXPERIENCE**
>
> - **More is not always better**
>   Just because digital media can include a large amount of content, that does not mean that it should. Visitors can get overwhelmed by content-heavy media.
>
> - **Plan for layers of content**
>   Aim to layer information so visitors who want to learn more can without overwhelming those who want only a small amount of information.
>
> - **Offer accessible options**
>   Include captioning for visitors with hearing impairments and audio alternatives for visitors with vision impairments.
>
> - **Text in media experiences**
>   Should typically be written at a grade seven or eight comprehension level, as with graphic text panels.
>
> - **Include visuals where possible**
>   Images and video capture attention more than text.

A technical requirement that might be included in this stage is the form of the experience. For example, a multi-touch table provokes different interactions compared to a large multitouch wall. Another technical requirement might come from technological constraints such as inability to install a WiFi system in the entire building or the limitation of using a particular screen in an open place where the sunlight would prevent a clear visualization of the interface.

Particular kinds of functional requirement are dictated by necessary attention being paid to visitors with disabilities. A universal design approach ensures that digital media is as accessible as possible to everyone. Guidelines for universal design are provided by a number of regulatory documents, such as the USA's Americans with Disabilities Act of 1990 (ADA)—which provides guidelines about, for instance, dimensions of a screen or interactive device or size of text. They may also be addressed in the museum's policies. For example, the Smithsonian's policy is that "all exhibition interactives, audio-only programs (e.g., music with lyrics and texts of speeches), and audiovisuals with soundtracks produced by the Smithsonian must be either open or closed captioned."

LOOK AND FEEL REQUIREMENTS

The look of digital experiences and the physical components around them should create a seamless experience that is welcoming and evokes the exhibition's themes. This is not just important in terms of aesthetic value (as Don Norman says, "attractive things work better"), but also for their meaningfulness. For example, by first looking at all the objects of the collection for which the interactive media has to be designed, it is possible to extract a sense of color or particular geometric shapes that, in turn, can offer insights for visual design. An effective visual technique for defining look and feel is the mood board, which is a visual collage consisting of images with explanatory text. By gathering colors, textures, and patterns the mood board provides a visual definition of the interface's aesthetic.

The design of a digital experience may also touch on the issue of the brand and visual identity of the museum. Because digital interactives are increasingly integrated into the museum's visual identity system, they have to be consistent with all factors—such as color, typography and image style—which govern the visitor's verbal, visual, and behavioral interaction with the museum's branding. It is likely that many museums will have their own brand guidelines, and these should be integrated into the design process from the beginning.

Step 3—Developing the Design: Design and Visual Frameworks

After listening to visitors, understanding the context, and gathering other data from different stakeholders with the aim of defining requirements, the team starts developing the design. As we saw above, the requirements do not specify how design elements should be formed, nor do they define how they work together as a cohesive whole. Working out "the how" takes place in the design development phase when the design framework and visual framework for the interactive are defined.

In this phase we shift from design activities performed for the conceptualization of the visitor experience to ones that define a comprehensive interactive structure (design framework), including high-level visual aspects (visual framework). Even if it is more concrete than previous work, this phase is still performed at a high level of abstraction, as team members are concerned with the overall structure of the visitor experience. Hence, activities do not focus on the granular form of interface components such as buttons or graphical elements, as these aspects will be the focus of the following design refinement phase.

THE DESIGN FRAMEWORK: STORYBOARDS AND WIREFRAMES

The design framework aims to make the visitor journey more tangible. One of the most effective techniques is the storyboard. Storyboards are visual illustrations that represent the sequence of activities that a visitor does to achieve goals (figure 12.5). The storyboard helps to develop the exhibition's visitor journey by defining the actions visitors perform within the exhibition environment through interaction with the digital system.

Wire frames are another useful technique for laying out content and functionality (figures 12.6A and B). The wireframe is the blueprint for the experience. Wireframes can be simple pencil drawings, or realized in editing software. Wireframes are developed considering questions such as:

- What choices can the user make (e.g., start, home, back, forward, language, etc.)?
- What content is presented at each step?
- How does the content relate across steps? Are there layers of stories? Is the content linear or can visitors choose their own path?
- How does the user interact with the content? For example, reading, listening, watching, clicking or gesturing?

Wireframes also identify how each of these choices is presented to visitors, and the results of those choices. Wireframes typically require several revisions before finalization. Once finalized, the wireframe will have identified:

- Interactive platforms that will be used;
- User interface, experience, and journey;
- Content creation guidelines;
- Technology approach and framework.

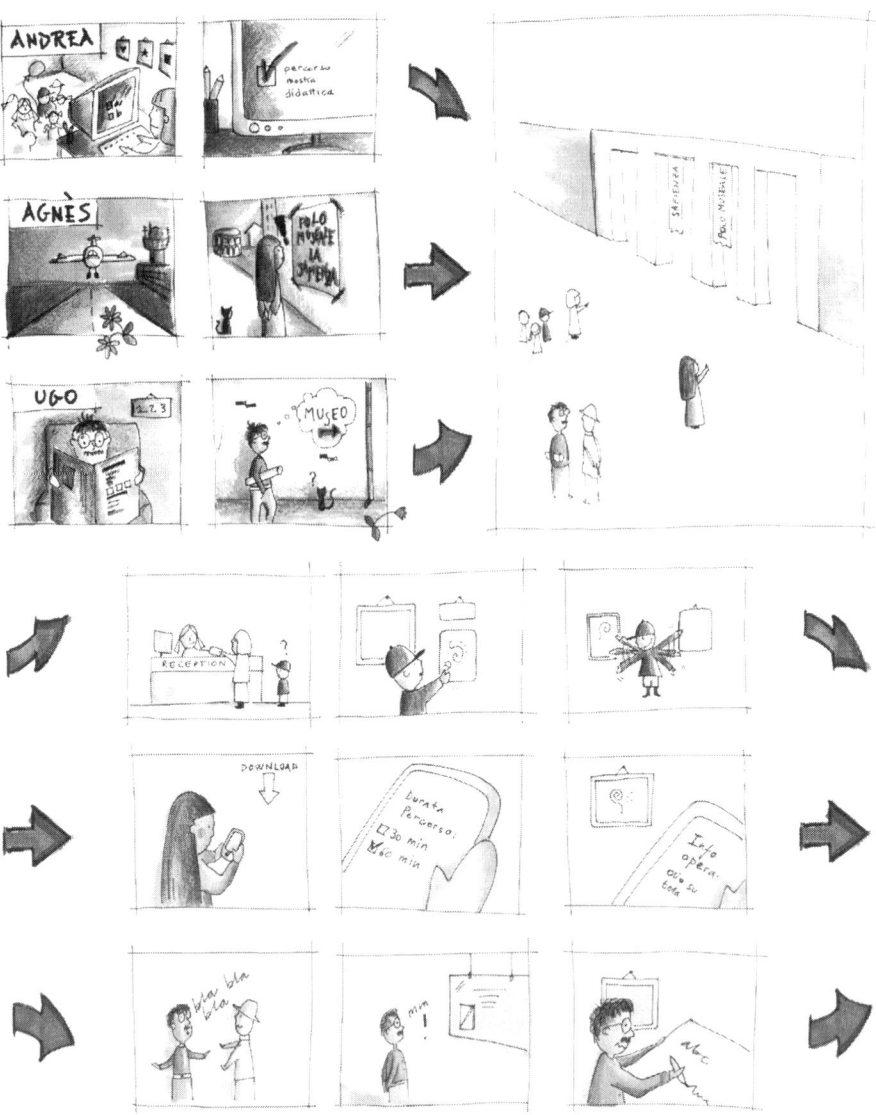

FIGURE 12.5 Sample Storyboard.
Dr. Marco Mason

Wireframes typically do not describe typographic style, color, or graphic details, since the aim is to design functionality and content architecture.

Relationships between different interfaces can be defined using a *flowchart*: a diagram that clearly illustrates the overall structure of the digital experience, showing its key components and presenting its primary workflows as visitors should perceive them (figure 12.7).

Content plays a fundamental role in defining the design framework. This is one of the reasons why the ongoing involvement of curators and educators is critical to designing for visitor experience, even after the development of an interpretive plan. The

VISITOR EXPERIENCE DESIGN

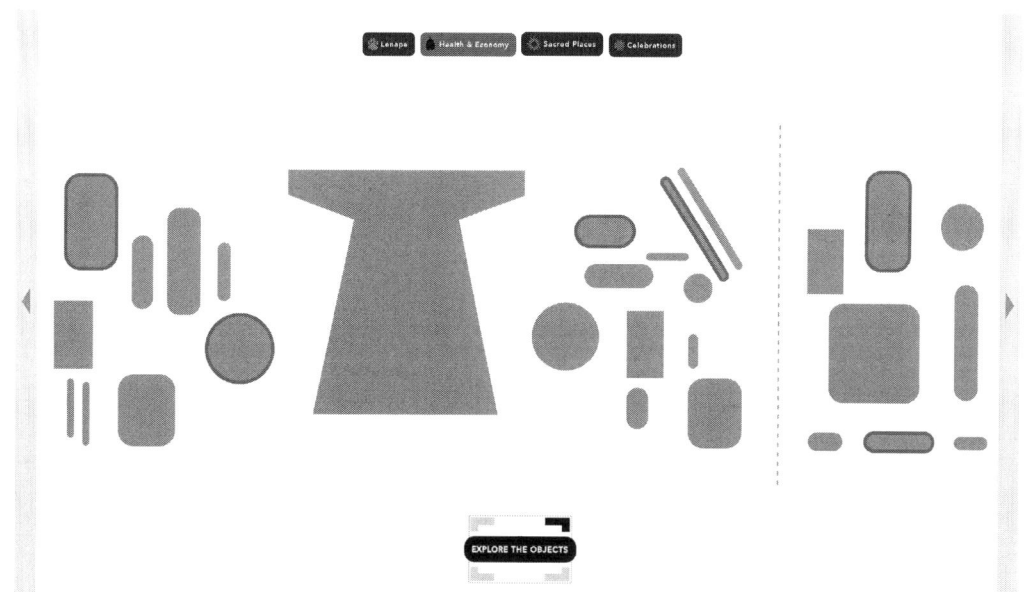

FIGURE 12.6A Wireframe Example.
Dr. Marco Mason

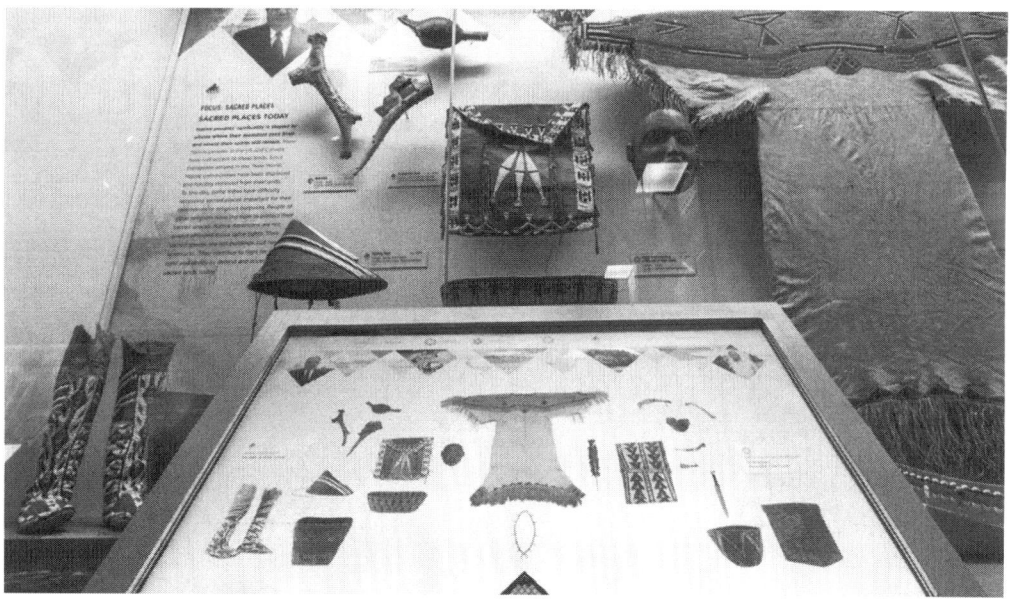

FIGURE 12.6B Final Results.
Dr. Marco Mason

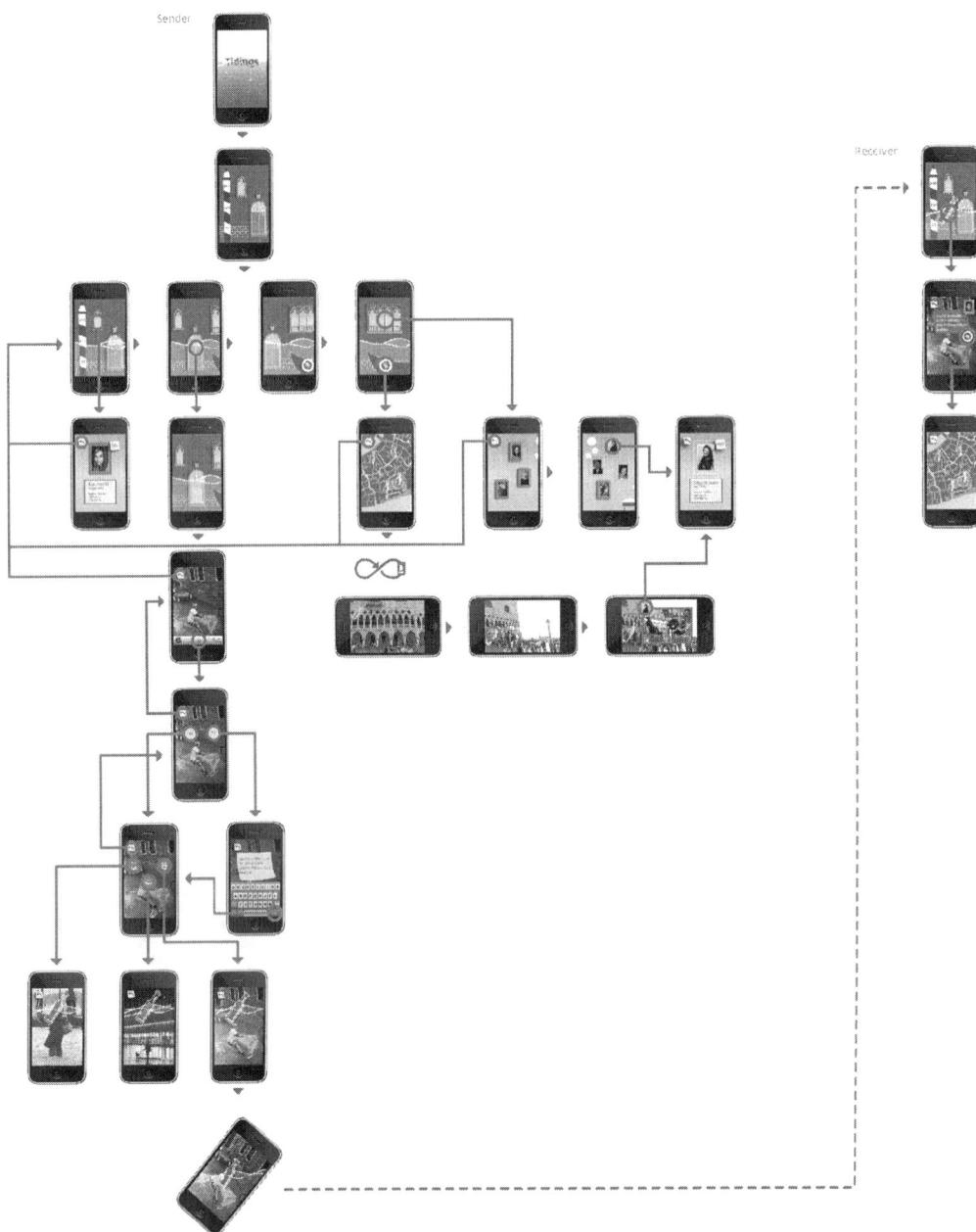

FIGURE 12.7 Flowchart Example.
Dr. Marco Mason

organization, grouping, ordering, and presentation of content is crucial to determining the overall structure of interactions.

VISUAL FRAMEWORK: THE STYLE GUIDE

The visual design framework sets the visual language of the digital experience and is usually integrated with the exhibition graphics. A fundamental technique for defining the visual framework is the visual style guide. It describes the way the interface is intended to look by defining the graphics of key elements. This makes the interface consistent throughout the experience. The main elements defined by the style guide document are

- Guidelines for adequate use of typography by showing samples of the fonts, text styles, and their hierarchy;
- A color palette that depicts the set of colors that must be adopted in the interface picture and video formats;
- The sizes, composition, and style of pages; and
- Key icons and infographics.

Step 4—The Design Refinement Phase

The design refinement phase gives final form to the overriding structure and functionality designed in the previous phases through the design of the interface. In this phase, the team asks questions like: What are the graphic components that constitute the interface? Where should they be placed on the screen? What form should the digital content take? As with other phases, prototypes are used here to test the design.

Good interface design happens when the graphic components are organized to enable effective, user-friendly interaction and user-friendly navigation.

INTERFACE LAYOUT

The interface layout is a crucial aspect of the design because it determines how the visitor comprehends what is on the screen. This structure determines the quality of visual flow, which should allow the visitor to easily recognize elements (or groups of elements) and understand the relationships between different pieces of content. The three general principles of creating a cohesive visual structure are: grouping, hierarchy, and alignment and grid.

Grouping can be achieved by using visual properties such as form, dimension, and proximity. Diverse components can be drawn into relation through the rubric of a common visual form and dimensional parameters. Through proximity we can associate items according to the distance separating them. Placing objects close together within a layout creates a focal point toward which the eye will gravitate.

Hierarchy establishes a sequential order of the components, such as which buttons, icons, images, or videos visitors need to see at first glance, which are secondary, and which only need to be consulted occasionally. The on-screen position of components affects how one element will emerge with respect to another. For instance, icons positioned at the center of the screen may be especially prominent. Another factor for determining visual hierarchy is scale. This is meant not only in the dimensional sense (e.g., a bigger button is more important than a smaller one) but also as it pertains to other parameters. For instance, by adjusting colors and transparency, bright elements can be given greater emphasis than dark ones.

Alignment and grid allow screen components to be systematically ordered and related. Alignment is a fundamental graphic design principle for lining up graphic elements, for example, along their edges or on their centers, according to a grid. These allow

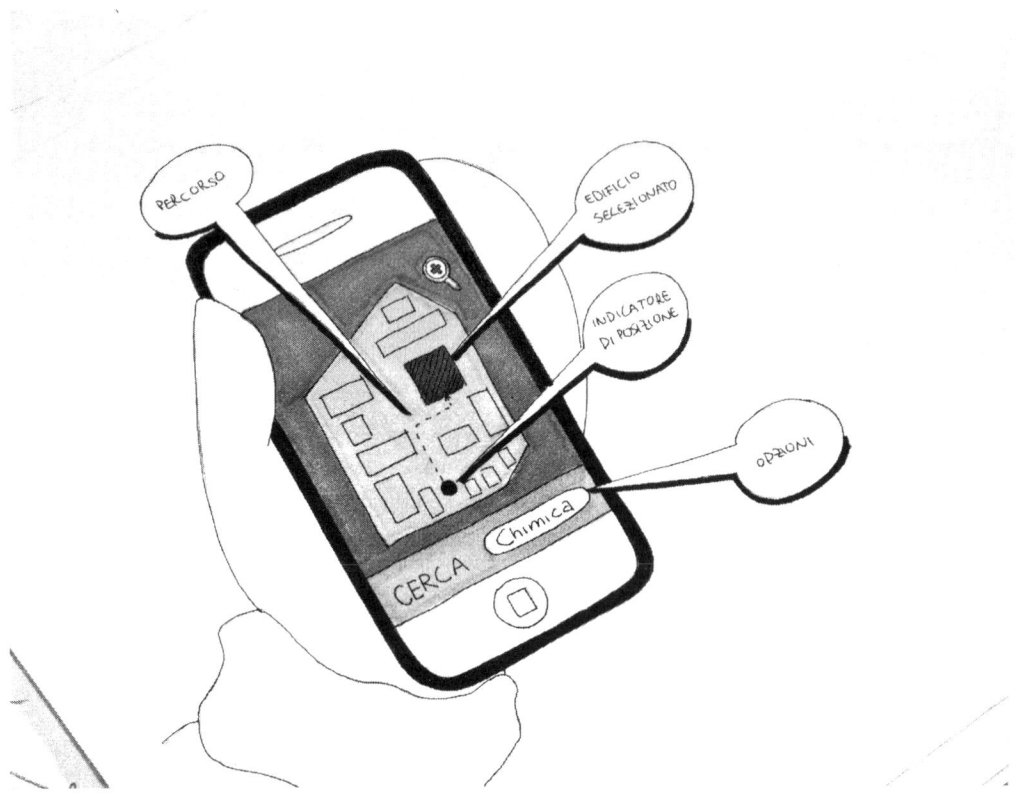

FIGURE 12.8 Low-Fidelity Prototype: Sketches for an iPhone app concept.
Dr. Marco Mason

VISITOR EXPERIENCE DESIGN

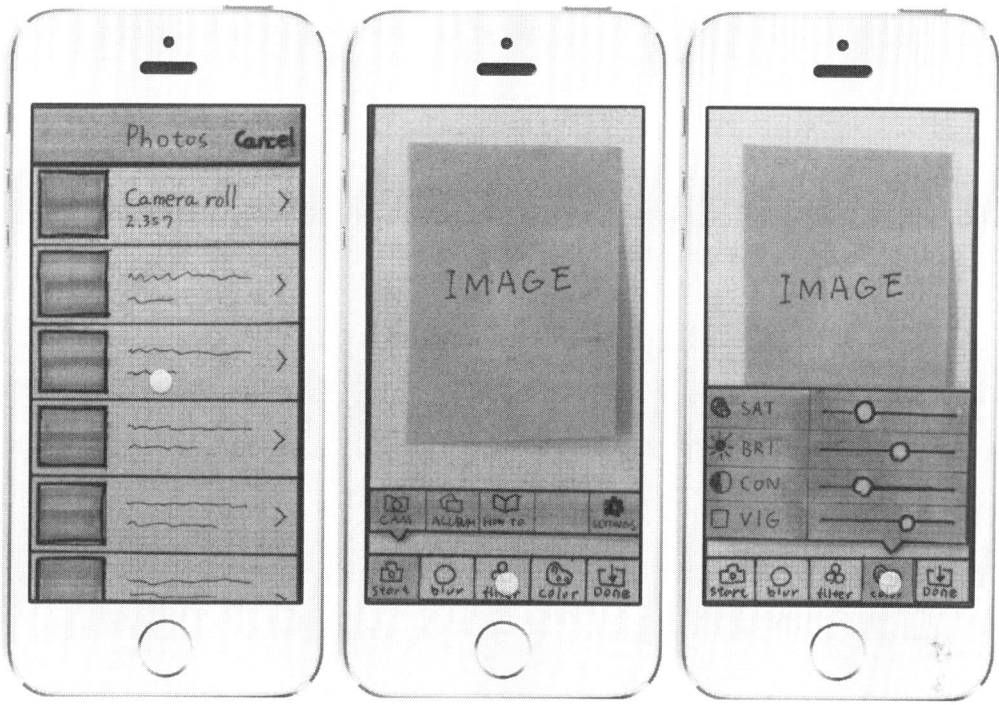

FIGURE 12.9 Low-Fidelity Interactions Created with the POP App.
Dr. Marco Mason

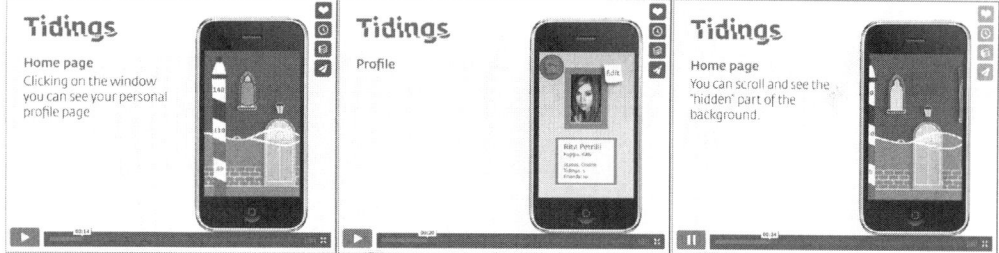

FIGURE 12.10 Frames Extracted from a Video Step-Through.
Dr. Marco Mason

a relationship among components to be suggested and, at the same time reduces the visitor's cognitive fatigue. They also posit a relationship among items and establish recognizable patterns and a sense of continuity, which ultimately lead to a clear, consistent visual structure and layout.

CREATING USER-FRIENDLY NAVIGATION

The interface of a digital interactive is not an assemblage of static components but a dynamic program of events. This means that the interaction itself has to be designed.

263

Hence, the position, shape, and dimension of each interface component influences the way the visitor interaction and orients him or her within the experience. Good navigation is intuitive, easy to understand, and easy to do. A successful navigation design focuses on identifying and tracing the logical connections that support effective movement between pages and contents. In terms of design this means drawing logical connections between each graphic component on the screen in order to show visitors how they are interrelated and suggest possible interactions.

GRAPHICS

Together with interface layout and navigation, graphics play an important role in the visitor experience. Graphics involve the design of key visual features such as visual patterns, icons and imagery, text, and color. Graphics include what seems aesthetically pleasing as well as how the visual elements affect the interface functionality and meaning. A polished design should please the senses while satisfying the criteria of usability and accessibility. For example, we design icons not only for decoration but also to provide meaning and a stronger sense of orientation; color and graphic shapes can (and should) incorporate the meaning of the exhibition into the interface. A compelling graphic contributes visual consistency to the whole interface; for example by differentiating groups of elements and drawing relationships between pieces of information.

Prototypes at Every Step

Prototypes can be used at every step of the design process.

- Low-fidelity prototypes are simple, inexpensive devices used in the conceptual and design development phases. Examples of low-fidelity prototypes might be sketches (hand drawn or created with the support of specific software) or a paper mock-up of screen layouts, which can be used to study the position of the interface elements and even test the interaction with visitors (figure 12.8). They can quickly test concepts, ideas or interaction flows among visitors or be used to communicate with stakeholders.

  POP is software that can turn hand-drawn wireframes into an interactive low-fidelity prototype (see figure 12.9). The designer sketches the app layout on paper, uploads a photo of it to POP, and adds links between the mock-ups. Other software such as Balsamiq and Axure offer more advanced and specialized tools for creating graphical user interface mock-ups.

- During the design requirements and framework stages, designers might use mixed fidelity prototyping approaches, which combine a mix of low- and high-fidelity techniques. For example, a mixed fidelity prototype can show a sequence of non-interactive interfaces (low fidelity) with high-fidelity graphical definition that looks like a final product.

A "step-through" video is a prototype that might simulate navigation between non-interactive interfaces. It is visually defined and looks like a final product.

Mixed fidelity prototypes are particularly useful for exploring a specific aspect of a design (i.e., interaction or graphics) without isolating this element from the overall design context. In this way, a team can tackle a particular problem first, leaving other aspects at low fidelity and undertaking them when resources are available.

- In the design refinement phases, a high-fidelity protoype is used. This appears similar to the final product.
- A high-fidelity prototype is a functional digital product. It provides working examples of interactions, aesthetics, and user interface. Software developers are usually involved in its creation.

Conclusion

Designing digital experiences should focus on empathy as well as aesthetics and technology. Interactive design is a dynamic method of development that places the visitor at the center of the process.

The methods of visitor experience design considers the visitor's perceptions and feelings; the concrete structure that arranges content, interactions, and functionality; and the granular details of the graphic interface. It advocates a collaborative and iterative approach to work that incorporates diverse stakeholders, including many who have traditionally been peripheral to design.

💡 KEY TAKEAWAYS: VISITOR EXPERIENCE DESIGN

1. Visitor experience (VX) design principles are:
   - Approach design as a visitor-centered practice.
   - Embrace diversity.
   - Require collaboration.
   - Use visualizations
   - Be agile.
   - Adopt prototyping.
2. VX design happens on three levels: experience, interaction, and interface.
3. The VX design process happens in four steps:
   - **Research:** involving visitor, organizational, and technical research, and the development of an interpretive plan;
   - **Design Requirements:** establishing requirements for the visitor experience, content, functionality, and look and feel;
   - **Design and Visual Frameworks:** developing storyboards, wireframes, and a visual style guide;
   - **Design Refinement:** finalizing interface layout, user-friendly navigation, and graphics.

SECTION 4: RESILIENCE AND SUSTAINABILITY

Museum Organization for the Future

Ngaire Blankenberg

Digital technologies are bringing fundamental change in the way museums relate to their knowledge resources and to their communities. These changes are resulting in wider organizational changes in order to create decision-making and departmental structures that are more relevant, more networked, and more efficient. Museums in the planning stages are creating new organograms at the outset, while more established museums are either restructuring completely or gradually introducing new positions, new skills, or new lines of accountability. In addition to their internal staff, museums often rely on contractors to deliver essential components of the visitor experience as well as to maintain hardware infrastructure and update software.

Although new museums can plan differently, the majority of museums are not organized for the digital age. Departments tend to be siloed, and hierarchies entrenched. Although in rare cases someone in a leadership position may set about implementing widespread transformation to make an established museum more user-centric, collaborative, data-driven, and iterative, in most instances, these changes happen in incremental steps rather than as a major reset.

In this chapter (and the book as a whole) we assume that gradual change is possible and more realistic than radical restructuring. It involves staff from all departments committing to a new approach or set of principles and then developing new skills and processes to support these. It also may involve hiring new positions that a museum may not have previously had or learning to commission and manage outside suppliers. Below we discuss three new things involved in gradually transforming museums into twenty-first-century centers for omnichannel experiences and education: new ways of working, new skills, and new roles and responsibilities.

Museum Departments for the Digital Age: A New Way of Working

Traditionally museums have been organized into departments that each reflects a unique role within the museum. Curatorial staff responsible for the collections and research are in one department, those who interact with the members of the public are in another, visitor services such as retail and the shop are in yet another, and so on, as reflected in the organogram in figure 13.1. "Serving the visitor," "technology," and "content" tend to be jobs assigned to specific people, while others are more or less exempt from all or any of these.

However, as Ali Hossaini writes in chapter 2, a visitor-centric, networked omnichannel museum operates differently and is therefore organized differently. In this form of museum, all departments are visitor facing, all produce digital and shareable content,

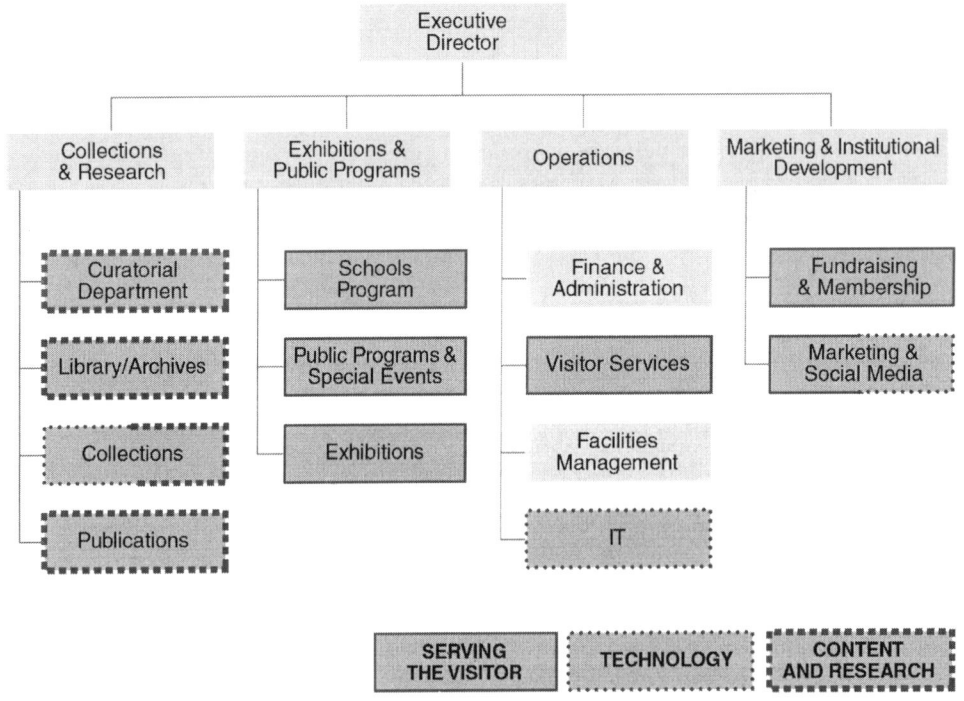

FIGURE 13.1 Traditional Organogram.
Lord Cultural Resources

MUSEUM ORGANIZATION FOR THE FUTURE

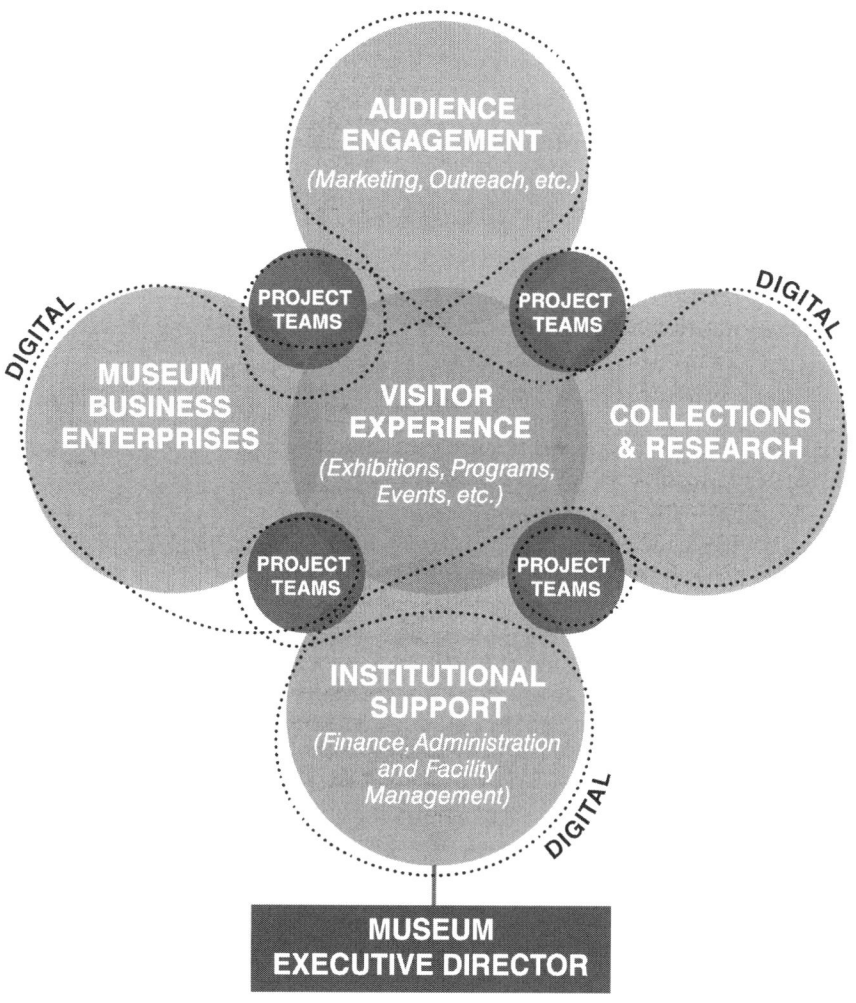

FIGURE 13.2 Visitor-Centered Organogram.
Lord Cultural Resources

and all are technologically connected, resulting in organograms that more resemble the one in figure 13.2.

In this diagram, technology is a thread that runs through the entirety, and all departments are responsible for engaging with the visitors. And with that engagement, there is a greater possibility of collecting visitor data that can then be fed back into all departments (see chapters 10 and 11). Collections and research departments, for example, may be responsible for researching and documenting the collection, but they are also responsible for making that collection accessible online and tracking by whom and why this content are accessed. Those in charge of the museum as a business enterprise may still primarily be focused on revenue generation, but they need to do this by more clever forms of engagement such as using crowdsourcing or ecommerce.

273

> **KEY TERMS**
>
> **MINIMUM VIABLE PRODUCT**
>
> A version of a new product that allows a team to test various aspects of it among users and stakeholders.
>
> **CROWDSOURCING**
>
> Crowdsourcing is a process whereby something is accomplished through outsourcing to a crowd of people. Crowdsourcing is typically supported by technology (web and social media), and can be used to expand knowledge, develop a product, or raise money—called crowdfunding.

New museums may set out to organize themselves as above, or variations thereof from their inception. This is relatively easy, as with a new museum there is no established culture, no staff, and no precedents when it comes to systems and processes. Sometimes staff are brought in from different fields altogether, for example, marketing or not-for-profits or education, allowing for even greater innovation.

For more established museums, organizational change is more complex and necessarily more incremental.

Managing Change

Like many organizations, museums are challenged to face the entwined issues of digital disruption, rapid obsolescence, and audience expectation. Cycles of planning, development, and resource allocation are difficult to align in the long term. As with digital projects, museums themselves need to become more agile. Museum leaders and staff need to be able to perceive change and adapt to it continuously; be responsive, not reactive or defensive; make decisions quickly; and make resources available on "risk."

Responsiveness is a cultural shift, and managing it requires understanding the psychology of change. Any changes, particularly if they come from unfamiliar quarters, are threatening, and digital obsolescence has already had a huge impact on jobs. Leaving aside threats to livelihood, digital processes such as the **minimal viable product** and **crowdsourcing** fly in the face of the professional standards cultivated by museums. People are naturally invested in their training, career path, and professional skills. It is not unreasonable that professionals accustomed to releasing only the most meticulously prepared content to the public or their colleagues may be reluctant to go with "good enough."

The good news is that change can—and should—happen through a gradual process of consensus building. Staff can reorient to a different set of values. Smaller-scale incentives can raise interest, including self-interest, while reducing the perception of threat. Every museum needs to develop an approach that works for its own staff and culture, but the following steps offer suggestions on a gradualist approach to organizational transformation.

STRATEGY

When it comes to digital technologies and processes, it is often the most junior members of an organization that are the early adopters. However, although they may influence some aspects of the organization, most museums are **hierarchical** rather than **flat** or **matrix-driven** institutions, and sustainable organizational change is led from the top.

This does not mean just hiring a chief digital officer and expecting change to filter down. Rather, for a new orientation to take root, it should be reflected in revised foundation statements (if required) adopted by boards, trustees, and the most senior executives in the museum. Visitors, learning, technology, partnerships, and networks can all be mentioned or alluded to in strategic goals with measurable outcomes. This can happen through a strategic planning process.[1]

Revised foundation statements should involve all staff, and once adopted, should be communicated to all staff as values that govern short-term as well as long-term activities. However, bear in mind that although few staff will likely object to introducing a focus on the visitor into the foundation statements (if they are not there already), this does not mean they are necessarily prepared to integrate such change into their own work practice.

PROJECTS

Projects are initiatives that have a clear goal, a timeline, and measurable outcomes. Projects can include developing a new learning experience, or launching a crowdfunding campaign. Projects are an excellent opportunity to practice new ways of working within the organization and to start to internalize new values. Project teams that pull from multiple departments can bring together people who may not be used to collaborating to work together toward a common goal. If the project has reflection built in to it, it is an opportunity to learn and grow, even if there are challenges.

Much of this book advocates an open, experimental attitude based on agile development. (See chapters 11 and 12.) **Agile development** eschews planning for an iterative process composed of short trials. What works moves forward; what does not work is left behind. Though originally created for projects, agile methodology can be applied on a larger scale, and it almost inevitably has organizational consequences because it

ORGANIZATIONAL STRUCTURE

Three common structures for museums are as below:

Hierarchy: In a hierarchical structure, there are a number of supervisory or managerial roles between staff and the executive. There tend to be clear roles and responsibilities and reporting structure is in layers, as shown in figure 13.1, Traditional Organogram.

Matrix: In a matrix structure, employees may be grouped by function and product; for example, they may be in one team as digital content producers but be in another team based on whether they are in visitor services, marketing, or exhibitions. Employees may be accountable to a project leader for some things and to a line manager for others—both of whom share power equally.

Flat: In a flat structure, there are no middle managers. Staff have a direct reporting line to the executive, a fair degree of autonomy, and the power to make decisions themselves. This is a common structure for smaller museums with fewer staff who must multitask.

> **KEY TERMS**
>
> **AGILE DEVELOPMENT**
>
> Agile is a form of project management traditionally used in software development that helps teams respond to unpredictability through incremental, iterative work cadences and empirical feedback.[1]
>
> ---
>
> [1] "The Agile Movement," Agile Methodology, accessed October 5, 2016, http://agilemethodology.org/.
>
> **CHANGE MANAGEMENT**
>
> Change management is a methodology for implementing organizational transition that improves the likelihood of success.

requires teams of equals working in a nonlinear fashion. An agile project erodes hierarchy and traditional boundaries of authority by demanding new professional relationships that can be highly effective. The combination of low-threshold success and low-risk failure makes agile organization compelling.

Museum leaders can decide on small-scale projects to begin to implement change on a wider scale throughout the organization. In this instance, it is important to recognize that the project itself is an experiment, as important to managing organizational change as it is to realizing the product of its focus.

As cycles of planning and implementation repeat, accrued knowledge will eventually have strategic value. With repetition, organizational strengths will emerge along with insights about what works for the museum's public. An agile approach also supports **change management** by reducing the number of variables in given decision. Directors can assess the strategic value of an investment with less time and financial risk.

Staff who feel threatened or sidelined or who simply disagree with digital initiatives have time to adjust. Equally important, everyone will have the chance to contribute to this long-term, cyclical, nonlinear process. Critics may be happy to get involved in evaluations that strengthen the next project. Everyone wants credit for success, and the gradualist approach gives individuals and the organization time to find their own depth in the digital world.

SUPPORTING INNOVATION

Museums tend to be risk-averse, and so they should be as custodians of our collections over decades and centuries. But they are also future looking. Stewardship of collections means anticipating future obsolescence and disaster. It also means anticipating the needs and expectations of future audiences within the context of anticipated technological disruption. Innovation and creativity therefore need to become a greater part of museum culture. A project approach supports this and helps to embed agility and experimentation. But museums can go further. They can allocate resources (money or time) to following experimental pursuits, either for teams or individuals, and they can call out experimentation and creativity when it happens, no matter what the scale.

REFLECTION AND COMMUNICATION

As other authors in this volume emphasize, agile development is an iterative learning process. Failures are just as important as successes, and evaluations should be used to improve the next project plan.

Projects can be stressful, and because they tend to have timelines, they are often rushed. When they involve people with varying skill sets, and sometimes external contractors, they can feel frustrating for some. However, it is important that opportunities for communication and reflection (often integrated) are built into the process. Sharing is deeply engrained in digital culture, and formal and informal networks to trade tips, answer questions, and troubleshoot problems are available for every possible topic.

In chapter 11, Rachel Walker describes three key tools of the project manager: project documentation, schedules, and meetings. If institutional change is a secondary focus of a project, if not its explicit focus, than opportunities for communication and reflection can be built into each of these. Project documentation can include self-assessments of each of the team members; schedules and meetings can include times for postmortems and team discussion specifically devoted to talking about lessons learned. In addition, the business case, measures of success, and assessment of risk can also include change management factors such as skills acquisition, attitude toward new ways of working, teamwork, and collaboration.

As the name implies, gradualism means organizational change happens in increments. While it is clear that many museums require executive leadership, meaningful leadership can emanate from anywhere in the museum, and the reality is that many junior positions may already have digital capacity. It is vital to build teams of people who can actually execute digital projects, and a series of agile projects will reveal both the gaps and hidden potential in your capabilities. You can then hire, train, or revise current job descriptions to create new career paths for the next generation of leaders. In parallel, agile projects will help create fluidity in your organizational culture. Under the pressure of delivery, participants will step out of roles, and they will gradually reorient themselves around structures that deliver success.

WORKING CONDITIONS

An omnichannel museum is a 24/7 affair, but a working day is much shorter. One of the biggest challenges museums face within the digital environment is managing expectations of anywhere and anytime and engaging with communities that may be out of the time zone of the museum staff. This may require staggered working hours as well as arrangements where certain staff can work from home or outside the museum, which may prove challenging if working conditions are fixed by a wider entity such as government (in the case of government line department museums) or unions. As much as possible, working hours should be negotiated that are equitable but that also enable visitors to feel the museum's responsiveness as much as possible.

The balance between permanent and contract staff is also changing. Insecure or temporary employment is becoming the norm in the cultural sector. In many ways, a freelance culture suits the digital age, but in others, it perpetuates inequities, privileging those who may have other household income or fewer financial responsibilities. Museums can be as innovative in their approach to working conditions as other sectors, adopting ways to ensure their employees are valued and incentivized. In a visitor-centric museum, it is the staff who make the most powerful connection with the public, and they need to be cared for. Technology facilitates that connection, but it is doubtful that it will ever replace it.

New Skills

As museum staff participate in projects, new skill requirements and strengths will become evident. Most museums assume their employees have basic computer literacy—they can use a computer and email, do presentations, and use scheduling software or spreadsheets. It is also assumed that most have access to a smartphone or at the very least a personal computer at home that enables information sharing and working after hours. In addition, the following skills will be increasingly important among all museum workers and may be a focus of a museum-wide training plan.

COMMUNICATION—VERBAL AND WRITTEN

As traditionally back-of-house positions become more visitor facing, many staff will need to have strong communication skills, both verbal and written. Many will also be working with diverse stakeholders—for example, other museums or organizations—or directly with colleagues in other departments, particularly if the museum has adopted a project-based approach. Different staff people may also be asked to contribute to the vociferous social media content machine. Staff may also need to communicate the ins and outs of their jobs to the curious public. New partners and ever-diversifying publics mean language and cross-cultural skills will also be increasingly valued. This applies equally to online and physical environments, as inequities at the physical museum building tend to be perpetuated online and the digital divide can contribute to an even starker picture.

Communication also includes visual communication, and staff should be visually literate and able to produce strong pieces of visual communication using basic publishing software such as Adobe InDesign or presentation software such as Keynote or PowerPoint. Using and taking photographs and video (particularly for social media) is also part of this skill set.

COLLABORATION

Projects require collaboration. This may be with colleagues, community members, or professionals (potentially both one and the same) outside of the museum. It may also include online collaboration working with team members who may be located elsewhere. Staff will need to learn how to use teleconference software and groupware collaboration tools to collaborate with geographically dispersed colleagues in their daily work.

AGILITY AND EXPERIMENTATION

People working within an agile process need to be able to let go of a product for early release, listen to feedback from testers, and receive criticism in order to rapidly improve their work. All of these things may be challenging to museum professionals used to only producing a perfect product for public consumption. However, with practice and a positive experience, this will likely become easier.

Agile projects are experimental projects. They come with a certain level of risk and a certain expectation of failure, or at least not 100 percent success. The project team may encounter unexpected obstacles requiring creative responses. Team members may need to look for inspiration outside the sector. This and general problem solving leads to a workplace culture of greater innovation, which should also be supported by management and reflected in individual staff assessments.

CLOSING THE DIGITAL DIVIDE

Many people do not visit or engage with museums because of barriers such as cost, distance, perception that it is not for them, intimidation, racism, and other issues. While accessing museums online may address barriers related to cost or distance, they do not necessarily address the cultural barriers arising out of the perception of museums as elitist places. Although the web holds the promise of equal access, as the barrier to entry is relatively low, engagement with museums on the web tends to reflect visitation demographics.

There is also huge inequity in the digital world created by unequal access to bandwidth, devices, and data. Some people have greater access to WiFi than others, some have smartphones and tablets and others do not, and some communities have access to data about their own behavior and others do not.

Museums can address this inequality by ensuring free WiFi, making sure their digital material is created to be as accessible as possible, and ensuring staff relate and engage with audiences—by themselves reflecting the demographics of their surrounding community, for example, and by ensuring consistent sustained evaluation through data, interviews, focus groups, and other sources in order to gather a deep understanding of what the museum's community needs and wants.

KNOWLEDGE SHARING

Knowledge sharing and communication go hand in hand. Social media has not only enhanced community engagement, it has also enabled the development and maintenance of professional networks among museum employees, contractors, and volunteers. Museum blogs, twitter conferences, and webinars are all ways for museum staff to share their knowledge among their peers. Those familiar with social media as well as software development and agile processes tend to be more adept at reflecting on lessons learned and communicating these quickly. Encouraging all staff, to publish digitally, and pairing less experienced with more experienced staff can support this.

New Roles and Responsibilities

In addition, to these more general skills, new technologies have introduced new jobs in museums. Some of these are done by in-house staff, while others are performed by contractors with specialist competencies or the ability to be more efficient (for example, in the case of digitization). In some instances, museums have had to recruit outside the sector, a practice that sometimes creates challenges with respect to salary expectations or workplace culture.

New developments in technology will also likely mean changes in staff positions. For example, as Ali Hossaini discusses in chapter 14, trends in virtualization and cloud services may mean that more and more IT functions will be off-site, resulting in the disappearance of related positions among museum staff.

Nevertheless, the most common jobs required for digital activities at this time are outlined below. First are two positions that are commonly held in senior management. Following them are descriptions of other roles that add digital capacity to a museum. Positions attached to these roles range from director to manager, coordinator, assistant, and intern. They are described generically as managers because seniority depends on the size, budget, and needs of individual museums. Depending on the size of your organization, people in these roles may perform work directly, oversee the work of others, or be responsible for training and advocacy throughout your organization.

These roles are not assigned to particular departments because there is also a large amount of variety in where they fall. There is no one way to organize around the user, and every museum should feel free to build capacity in the way that makes them most effective.

SENIOR MANAGEMENT JOB DESCRIPTIONS

Chief Digital Officer

The chief digital officer is probably the most senior new job within the museum structure. At senior manager level, this person is typically responsible for supporting all of the museum's departments in taking advantage of efficiencies and pushing out visitor-facing content. This person may have his or her own digital media department that is responsible for the website, mobile platforms, social media sites, digital signage, in-gallery media, and other products. Oftentimes these responsibilities will be cross-departmental.

> **KEY TERMS**
>
> **KEY PERFORMANCE INDICATORS**
>
> Key performance indicators are a set of pre-determined metrics by which a project will be judged at various stages and/or completion.

Head of Technology / Head of IT / Chief Information Officer

This position is responsible for the planning, staffing, and operations of a museum's IT infrastructure, including the LAN, datacom centers, individual systems, and outsourced services. (See chapter 14 for a detailed discussion.) He or she oversees the purchase and maintenance of hardware and software for enterprise and individual use, and ensures appropriate policies and procedures are in place for operations, upgrades, and security. This officer assesses, reports, and responds to risks and failures. Duties include long-range strategic planning to ensure optimal use of technology by all the departments and functions of the museum, long-range technology and infrastructure planning that supports the strategic application plan, operational and capital budgeting, and project management.

GENERIC DIGITAL AND IT JOB DESCRIPTIONS

Digital Content Manager

This person is responsible for developing, maintaining, and promoting information architecture for digital content throughout the museum and should understand principles of knowledge management, taxonomy, tagging, and database design to ensure any system used for digital content is compatible with other systems used within the museum; by museum partners; and, to the greatest degree possible, the sector as a whole. He or she should stay aware of current and emerging standards and best practices for information management and should work with colleagues to implement them through digitization, databasing, and API development. This person should ensure internal and external digital channels are aware of content by publishing summaries of internal resources and methods of access.

Analytics and Evaluation Manager

This position's role is to provide objective information to a variety of staff and the board to evaluate the ability of the strategy and individual projects to meet **key performance indicators** (KPIs).

He or she identifies the best ways to collect information (quantitative or qualitative), supports the design of evaluation, and ensures that data is gathered as much as possible from every touchpoint in keeping with confidentiality regulations. This data is then integrated into reports for use by marketing, sales, outreach, education, development, and other departments. This person should be familiar with qualitative and quantitative research methods, possess the ability to analyze the performance of advertising and social media, set benchmarks, and develop surveys and audience segmentation.

Database Manager

The database manager is responsible for managing servers and applications so as to ensure system availability and integrity. He or she manages databases and software upgrades, liaising with vendors to install and troubleshoot applications, servers, and software. He or she also creates policies and procedures for database system use and maintenance, and administers quality control by monitoring data entry. This person develops, implements, and produces export file and report requests and can establish and oversee the report and mailing list production schedule, including distribution of production files and reports. He or she identifies and recommends improved procedures in data capture, processing, and mapping to streamline operations and improve data quality.

Network Manager

The network manager is responsible for providing operational and project-based support of the organization's LAN and IT infrastructure. The position is responsible for installing, configuring, and supporting all routers, switches, wireless access points, and other parts of the network infrastructure. He or she identifies and troubleshoots issues and provides regular reports on network performance.

Digital Project Manager

A digital project manager is responsible for gathering requirements, creating schedules, ensuring work is performed on time and on budget. Rachel Walker discusses the tasks of digital project managers in depth in chapter 11.

Bookings Manager

The bookings manager is responsible for the scheduling of room and outdoor events, managing tour groups (including schools groups) and ticket sales. He or she is responsible for planning and maintaining events management software and ensuring that data from programs and events is communicated to the relevant people.

Membership and Development Manager

This manager is responsible for developing growing membership; managing member relations with CRM (customer relationship management) software; and using data on member preferences to create new incentives for engagement through education, events, and other channels. He or she supports development efforts to solicit large donations with software profiling and scheduling tools, reviews membership and visitor analytics to identify prospective donors, and produces segmentation reports to facilitate strategic decisions on membership.

Email Marketing Manager

This manager is responsible for strategy, implementation and tracking of direct mail and digital marketing campaigns. Oftentimes this job includes responsibilities for social media.

Social Media Manager

The social media manager is responsible for overseeing the museum's conversation with visitors on any and all social networks that may be relevant to your museum. As of this writing, Facebook, Twitter, Instagram, and Pinterest are important places for visual and written content. The social media manager needs writing skills to write short, attention-grabbing copy, and must be able to create, acquire, and edit photographs to give visitors media they can share with their own friends and followers. This person should be able to track and respond to trends instantly to maximize presence in the digital public sphere.

Collection Information Manager

A technical specialist for administering, expanding, and integrating collection information systems to meet the museum's digital strategy goals, the collection information manager is responsible for support, strategy, management, dissemination, and delivery of collection information, metadata, and digital assets to public-facing technologies. He or she may need to create systems to manage and deliver collection information to the next generation of mobile, responsive, and touch-capable platforms and in-gallery technologies, as well as to establish interoperability with related content, collection, and digital asset management systems.

Digital Archivist

The digital archivist takes responsibility for the process of digitizing written, visual, and physical content held by the museum. This includes records and publications as well as collections, and it increasingly includes content that was created on digital platforms. Qualifications for the job may include knowledge of digital capture including photography and various kinds of scanning, standards of databasing and metadata, data integrity, digital preservation, and knowledge management.

Photographer

The photographer will need to create high-resolution direct digital images (2D and 3D) to digitize and catalog the museum's collection. Image files must be suitable for the highest levels of offset reproduction, and electronic publishing and photographs must be in accordance with museum and international archival imaging standards, including those for color management and metadata. He or she should be proficient with all relevant Photoshop software tools and ensure the welfare of artwork throughout the imaging procedure.

Digital Learning Programs Manager

A digital learning programs manager would have specific expertise in museum learning, curriculum development, and learning technology. He or she would develop and implement programs using technology for primary, secondary, and tertiary schools; teachers; independent learners; adult learners; and others. Skills in managing digital projects, an understanding of hardware and software for learning, and the ability to develop and evaluate KPIs in relation to learning are all important for this position.

Public Participation Officer (PPO)

This person may take responsibility for visitor engagement on multiple platforms—events, marketing campaigns, social media, and programming. He or she should have a strong understanding of the museum's community and should ensure this understanding is supported by data. The PPO is responsible for the management and delivery of the museum's activity and events programs online and face-to-face, ensuring accessibility in order to meet a range of needs and expectations.

Digital Content Producer

A digital content or media producer plans and produces multimedia projects, commissioning media content and working collaboratively with external and internal staff, with an understanding of visitor needs. He or she is skilled in multimedia authoring—that is, the ability to produce multimedia applications such as interactive online exhibits, tutorials, brochures, videos, walk-through demonstrations, or business presentations using authoring tools such as Adobe Flash and Adobe Fireworks.

Media Writer

A media writer develops multimedia content for exhibitions, learning materials, social media, audio tours, or web experiences. This person may work closely with a media producer to adapt content for different media platforms and digital channels.

Graphic Designer

The graphic designer develops all communication material for the museum, including marketing material, schools material, membership communication, and so on. He or she executes UI (user interface) design on public-facing digital products such as websites, apps, digital signage, browser-based applications and WiFi pages. The graphic designer is able to work with templates or custom elements and usually operates from a style guide that dictates the presentation of logos, colors, fonts, and other branding elements.

Web and Digital Media Developer

This person's responsibilities include websites and browser-based utilities that are developed within a museum. This position requires strong working knowledge of coding for websites, digital media, and digital channels, and facility with some or all of the following languages: HTML, CSS, PHP, JavaScript, Java, AJAX, XML, and SQL. He or she should understand information architecture as it relates to digital media; project management; and the hosting, configuration, and maintenance of web and other digital properties. This person should be grounded in the CMS development frameworks that are used or recommended for your museum and should also be able to work with database specialists to integrate APIs into websites or browser-based applications.

Rights and Reproductions Coordinator

The rights and reproductions coordinator oversees all policies, procedures, and activities involving intellectual property rights for the museum's permanent collection, loans of art for temporary exhibitions, publications, and other assets and programs. This job entails managing and coordinating the acquisition of reproduction rights and permissions, as well as licensing fees, for images in all media for use in the museum's exhibitions, public programs, publications, advertising, and promotions. He or she supports, where applicable, licensing museum-generated materials to third parties for all media, including images, text, film, and other audiovisual work.

Ecommerce Manager

The ecommerce manager manages the budgeting and planning process in support of ecommerce and drives new initiatives to increase revenue, with a clear focus on customer experience and onsite optimization. He or she works closely with creative, merchandising, marketing, and finance teams, defining and driving new initiatives, including major site releases, omnichannel efforts, and operational improvements, to improve key performance indicators (KPIs) and customer experience. The position includes site-testing programs and collaborating with merchandising and marketing areas to plan the marketing calendar. If applicable, this person manages the museum's call center and plans, strategizes, and drives business in online marketplaces, creating ongoing and ad hoc reporting as needed.

Conclusion

Curators have traditionally been at the top of the museum hierachy. Most directors came through the curatorial ranks, and the knowledge and concerns of curators, primarily driven by the collection, dictated the direction of the museum. Now directors are likely to have skills in fundraising, development, or arts management, and certain jobs are working their way up the museum hierarchy or, conversely, causing the hierarchy itself to break down.

Some museums have hired or promoted digital officers as change agents whose goal is to introduce digital practices in designated areas or throughout the organization. Others are creating new roles at the director and/or manager level to introduce digital practices more organically. Virtually every museum now needs staff who can manage IT, websites, social media, and digital production. As digital becomes the norm, it is likely that specific digital jobs will fade away, and technical skills and literacy—as described throughout this manual—will be expected for everyone. What will likely remain, however, is the skills required in the digital age—those of communication, collaboration, agility, and innovation. These are the skills that will become increasingly valued, and people who possess these in addition to subject matter expertise or competencies within their work area will become the leaders of tomorrow.

💡 KEY TAKEAWAYS: DIGITAL AND MUSEUM ORGANIZATION

1. Values and practices such as visitor-centricity, networks, and omnichannel are resulting in change in all facets of the museum organization—new organograms, new jobs, new skills, and new ways of working.

2. A gradualist approach recognizes that change is challenging but can become embedded within an institution if embraced by all staff through incremental actions rather than a complete revolution.

3. A gradualist approach includes adopting a long-term strategy for change; introducing a project-based, agile way of working; supporting innovation, reflection, and communication as daily practice; and being fair and flexible when it comes to working conditions.

4. New skills in the digital age for all museum workers include communication and visual literacy, collaboration, agility and experimentation, and knowledge sharing.

5. There are new roles and responsibilities associated with digital. These are present throughout the organization. The chapter provides a list and summary of some of these.

Note

1. See Gail Dexter Lord and Kate Markert, *Manual of Strategic Planning for Cultural Organizations: A Guide for Museums, Science Centers, Gardens, Zoos, Heritage Sites, Libraries, and Performing Art Centers* (Lanham, MD: Rowman & Littlefield, 2017).

Planning for IT Infrastructure

Ali Hossaini

Information technology (IT) is essential to the functioning of a twenty-first-century museum. Like electricity, telephones, and water, it is managed through building infrastructure that connects to outside providers, and it is governed by legal, regulatory, and professional codes. Your IT infrastructure should be planned with the same attention as other vital operations, but it is not an end in itself. Its structure and scale depends on the educational, business, aesthetic and social activities of the museum, and the resources allocated to it should be judged according to the efficiencies and opportunities they create in other departments.

Planning for IT happens in one of two scenarios: developing a new facility or upgrading existing facilities. The last is more common, and it is also more complicated, but the same principles govern both. Upgrades often require new systems design, either because of emerging standards or because current systems were assembled ad hoc and now require strategic planning. Either decision requires a basic understanding among senior museum staff of the way in which IT functions in museums.

This chapter aims to make the planning process comprehensible for museums that are either developing a new facility or planning to upgrade an existing facility. I start by discussing a major consideration for museums—outsourcing and its implications for the present and future. I then introduce the concept of network architecture—a fundamental concept that underpins all of IT. The subsequent sections examine the three interdependent layers of IT infrastructure: physical, logical, and operational and how requirements from one influence the others. The final section closes on the all-important question of sustainability—a subject on which museums have the opportunity (and responsibility) to show leadership. Throughout and particularly in the section on operational infrastructure, I emphasize the importance of documentation, which is often overlooked under the pressure of tight deadlines and tighter budgets, but should not.

This chapter is intended to be read by museum administrators rather than IT professionals. Planning a network requires training and, ideally, experience in a variety of settings far beyond the scope of this book. It is expected that professional support for IT planning is available either in-house or from an outside firm. However, administrators are often expected to manage IT professionals, define expectations for IT departments, or make decisions about IT systems. The following sections therefore aim to give managers sufficient background to understand the scope if not the actual operation of IT infrastructure.

To Outsource or Not

Deciding whether to outsource is one of the most important issues facing IT administrators in museums. Two technologies are determining the future impact of outsourcing: virtualization and wireless connectivity.

Virtualization

As the name implies, virtualization happens when software emulates hardware. As the section on logical infrastructure explains, this may already be happening in your museum. Prior to virtualization, key functions of a server were handled by dedicated physical circuits. Additional functionality required more circuits and thus more servers. While it is still convenient to manage individual servers from an operational standpoint, many servers are now "virtual machines" that run within a single, powerful machine. These systems are now logical rather than physical systems.

Virtualization lies behind the growth of cloud-based services. Virtual machines can be located anywhere that has a broadband connection. "The cloud" is a misnomer, as cloud service vendors use warehouses of servers that draw immense amounts of electricity. For the museum, the cloud offers amorphous and seemingly limitless computing resources without the expense and uncertainty associated with hardware investments. Instead, the museum can subscribe to the level of service needed at the moment, and they can quickly scale their subscription according to circumstances. In business terms, the growth of cloud-based services is leading to the commoditization of IT. Functions that once required specialized, in-house staff and customized equipment can now be purchased in standard packages delivered over the Internet. Outsourcing has become the preferred model in many industries, and the trend is accelerating with improvements to hardware, software, and networks.

The impact of virtualization is spreading beyond IT. As discussed later in this chapter, virtual tickets are replacing printed tickets, and, as discussed elsewhere in this book, virtual reality is providing surrogate, software-driven experiences.

Evolution of Wireless

The evolution of wireless services is bringing similar transformations to networks. Indoor wireless has already achieved rates of 10 megabits per second (Mbps), and by 2020 cellular providers will leapfrog other forms of connectivity when they introduce fifth-generation, or 5G, services. Cellular networks operate more like a real cloud, as data are transmitted via radio, but their use is limited to mobile devices. Current 4G LTE cellular networks are not robust enough to support the connectivity needs of a museum, but 5G will offer data rates of 1 gigabit per second (Gbps) or more with enterprise-grade reliability. Performance enhancements within 5G could eliminate or reduce the need for physically wired networks within buildings. They will also open up new opportunities for commercial partnerships in the form of radio mast placement, WiFi handoffs to cellular networks, and enhanced services to visitors.

Pros and Cons of Outsourcing

Many museums are choosing to outsource IT services for the following reasons:

- Reduced stress on planning—you purchase only what you need within a contracted time period, so adding or reducing levels of service can be achieved quickly
- You don't pay for unused capacity
- You can experiment with high bandwidth and data-intensive processes without committing a large investment
- Lowered capital requirements of failed initiatives
- Enables rapid scaling that may be expensive or technically impossible in the face of runaway success
- Lower levels of staffing
- 24/7 operational support
- Access to higher levels of expertise

> **KEY TERMS**
>
> **LAN**
>
> Local area network (LAN) refers to the collection of data communications cables and equipment that maintains digital connectivity in your building or campus.
>
> **NETWORKED DEVICE**
>
> Any device that relies on data communications through LAN connections. Aside from computers, the term includes fixed and handheld ticket scanners, cash registers, digital signage, tablets, monitors, projectors, and smartphones.

Cons of the Cloud:

- Cloud services will be interrupted if Internet connectivity is lost or diminished.

- Providers may limit customization that a skilled local administrator could implement.

- While servers could hypothetically be in-sourced, in practice an organization can become overly dependent on its cloud provider.

Fortunately, taking advantage of cloud services is not an all-or-nothing proposition. While calculating the risk and benefits of outsourcing, it is possible to migrate selected services to a cloud provider. This can be done where the advantages are clearest or as a way of testing a proposition.

Network Architecture

Your building contains a digital network called a **LAN** (local area network). It connects the computers and other **networked devices** in your facilities with each other and with the Internet. Every network has several basic components. Anyone with financial or management responsibility for network operations should have a conceptual understanding of how a LAN operates. A primary concept is *addressing*, a function that enables machines to communicate over a network.

No matter how complex, every network uses a combination of local and global addresses. Your LAN uses local addresses that only work in your building. There is a direct analogy with the physical world. In New York a message can find its way to 100 Broadway with no other information. To send a message from New York to 100 Broadway in London, the address needs additional routing information, such as country and post code. Local addresses are reused across local networks, but Internet addresses use globally unique codes that enable message to be sent across networks.

Data communications standards grew from engineering necessity. They now enable network administrators to create flexible systems that serve local needs while facilitating global communication. More detail on standards and their role in IT management is found in the sidebar.

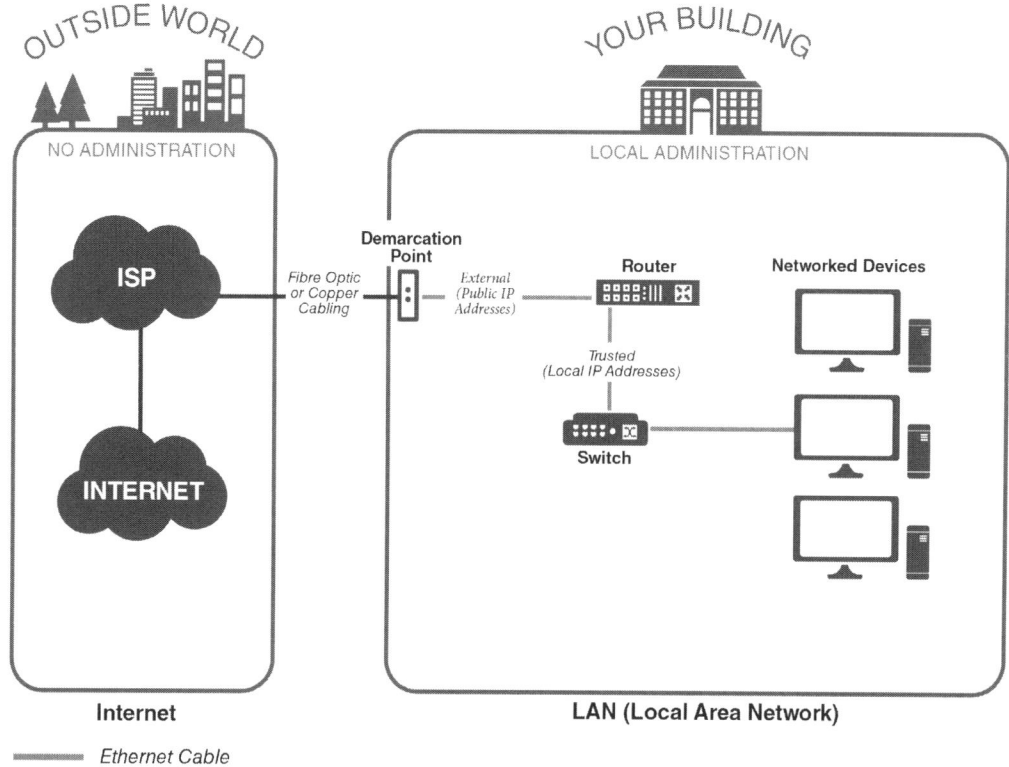

FIGURE 14.1 Basic Network Architecture.
Ali Hossaini and Lord Cultural Resources *With thanks to Labyrinth IT.*

Physical Infrastructure

As the name implies, physical infrastructure is the hardware within your building. It includes wires, radio transmitters, personal and enterprise-level computers, and a variety of specialized networking devices. The most visible parts of physical infrastructure are the information appliances connected to your network: the PCs, scanners, phones, and other devices used by your colleagues. But there is far more to IT management than meets the eye. Most of your physical infrastructure is safely tucked into walls, recesses, and locked equipment closets, and nothing would work without this silent support behind the scenes.

For simplicity many of the physical devices that operate in an IT environment are described

DATACOM STANDARDS

Most of the standards you encounter in IT relate to the communication of data or "datacom." A standard is simply a complete method that can be adopted by anyone. Standards share some common features. Each machine has a unique identifier called an address. Addresses are used to route data. A standard also contains a method for encoding information, and it often contains a method for verifying that it arrived without corruption. Thus the standard is the basis for a collection of machines to become a network. In the hands of human operators, standards are a powerful tool for messaging, sharing information, and coordinating activity.

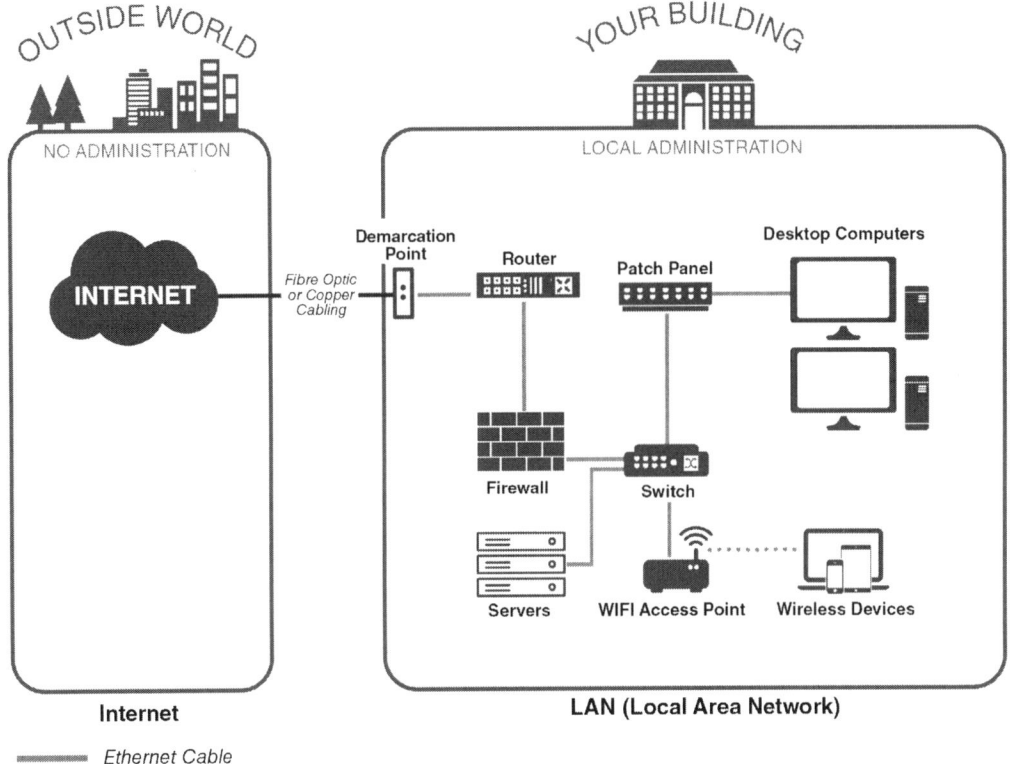

FIGURE 14.2 Physical topology depicts the machines in your facility.
Ali Hossaini and Lord Cultural Resources *with thanks to Labyrinth IT.*

KEY TERMS

ISP

An Internet Service Provider leases equipment that transmits data from Internet-connected servers to customers. An ISP maintains a WAN, or wide area network, that connects to other WANs. ISPs have reciprocity agreements with each other that facilitate global traffic in data, and the sum total of connected networks, including your own, is the Internet.

in the section on logical infrastructure. This is because the logical configuration of a system supersedes its physical configuration in modern facilities. This is another outcome of virtualization, a trend to define functions in software rather than hardware systems. These concepts may seem obscure to some readers. However, they are critical factors in the innovation that drives digital revolutions, and they will clarify as the reader considers their application in their museum and society at large.

Most network administrators use visualization software to design and manage their systems. These network diagrams are invaluable in understanding what and where network components are. A diagram of physical components and their relations is called the "physical topology" of a network. Figure 14.2 shows a highly simplified version of a physical topology, which contrasts with the logical topology that is introduced later.

Connectivity Basics

Connectivity to museums is provided by a company referred to as an **Internet Service Provider** (ISP). All Internet connections use a standard called **TCP/IP** to transmit data from one point to another.

ISPs most commonly include telcos (telephone and telecommunications companies), cable television providers, and municipally owned corporations. The field is broadening to include companies like Google and Facebook, which are offering Internet access to support other products. Internet provision is most commonly provided via cable, but this, too, is changing as disruptive players develop aerial platforms that offer Internet access via microwave towers, balloons, or drones.

Locations vary widely in their choice of ISP. Cities may have several competitive options while rural areas may have just one provider. However, urban locations do not necessarily have superior provision; in many older cities, broadband access is still an issue due to legacy infrastructure or prevailing market conditions. In these cases, it may take months or years to acquire the highest global standards for connectivity.

Broadband connectivity is the baseline requirement for digital infrastructure, and ISPs are chosen mainly based on the speed of the connections they offer. The amount of **bandwidth** anyone needs is a moving target. As of this writing, a broadband connection of at least 100 Mbps is considered a baseline for many organizations, but this is likely to increase to 1 Gbps for facilities that have extensive video, film, or virtual reality (VR) productions.

Ensuring the bandwidth needs of your organization are met is one of the most important aspects that will impact on your choice of an ISP. Contracting for inadequate service can lead to stunted ambitions or expensive upgrades. However, it is a reality that most organizations err in the other direction. ISPs count on their customers paying for more bandwidth than they need. As much as 80 percent of a customer's bandwidth goes unused, and much of this goes into an ISP's profit margin as they oversubscribe capacity and lock customers into fixed contracts. However, until ISPs offer dynamic pricing plans based on actual usage, this situation will likely continue.

HOW MUCH BANDWIDTH DO YOU NEED?

Despite these factors, it is possible to achieve a level of clarity about the bandwidth your organization needs. The first step is to review records of usage for the past year. Ideally

> **KEY TERMS**
>
> **BANDWIDTH**
> Bandwidth is a quantitative measurement of the amount of data that can be transmitted in a measure of time. Measurements are usually given in bits, the fundamental unit of information, and seconds.
>
> **TCP/IP**
> Transmission Control Protocol/Internet Protocol is the standard used to define unique global addresses based on numbers but translatable into words.

this is through a usage report where it is possible to view daily or even hourly traffic. At a minimum, the report should identify how much data is transmitted daily along with spikes that identify peak usage. You need sufficient capacity to handle your maximum demand, particularly if you sell tickets.

You should then combine these data with the number of users in your organization to get an average figure. Confirm this is generated by staff and not some other source. It is important to summarize data usage within your network, especially if your museum offers public WiFi. Congestion on your circuits can impact ticketing, payment card clearance, sharing of files from your collections database, and other vital activities.

After assessing current usage, the next step is to assess demand for bandwidth within your organization. Bandwidth constraints may be deterring staff from performing certain operations—for example, producing or distributing video, VR, or other rich-media initiatives. Management may be planning to expand staff or facilities. Internal surveys are a good way of determining future demand. Questions for staff include:

- Are there activities that are constrained by current levels of service?
- Are there plans to implement bandwidth-intensive activities?
- Are there plans to expand staff, buildings, or services to the public?
- Are staff using services like Dropbox, Microsoft OneDrive, or Google Drive on an informal basis?

Surveys should cover horizontal and vertical cross-sections of your organization. Departments like marketing and exhibitions are generally heavy users of connectivity, and junior staff may have a better sense of bandwidth constraints than managers.

Another factor affecting bandwidth requirements is whether your organization uses or plans to use cloud services. If applications and working files are hosted locally, a substantial amount of traffic will stay on your LAN and you will require less Internet bandwidth. If your organization migrates to cloud services such as Office 365, Google Apps, or Dropbox, then your bandwidth needs will increase. Given current trends, it is best to account for the eventuality of cloud services in your planning.

QUALITY OF SERVICE

QoS or quality of service is a specific engineering term that relates to the ability to assign network resources to a specific activity such as voice or video transmissions. However, many ISPs and network providers are using data management tools to prioritize certain categories of traffic such as video, and it is worthwhile considering whether QoS connectivity or a data management service would be useful. Surveys should gather details on type, scope, and timing of bandwidth-intensive activities. Examples of activities that may benefit from active management include:

- Uploading large images or video on a regular basis
- VoIP (Voice over Internet Protocol) for primary telephony
- Videoconferencing for business or public exhibitions
- Downloading films for theaters or IMAX
- Serving web content or ticketing from local databases
- Joining a content-sharing network
- Plans to launch or expand public WiFi

Selecting Your ISP

Before making any decisions, discuss your requirements with prospective ISPs. Ideally you can contract a service that meets your current needs but also scales with minimal penalty. The topics that should be covered with a prospective ISP make a large, evolving list, but you should certainly discuss the topics outlined below.

> **KEY TERMS**
>
> **NETWORK TERMINATION DEVICE**
>
> A variety of terms are used to describe "network termination device." Your ISP may call it a NID (network interface device), NOD (network optical device), ONT (optical network terminal), or NTE (network termination equipment). Bear in mind that terminology is not consistent. There are other terms for the same device, and the same term may refer to different devices.

SYMMETRY OF THROUGHPUT

Symmetry refers to the balance of upload and download rates within your subscription. Does the proposed service offer equal upload and download rates? Oftentimes download rates are higher by default, but your museum may need to upload large amounts of data. For instance, your collections database may be shared publicly, or your marketing department may regularly create large video files to promote events.

REDUNDANCY OF SERVICE

Redundancy refers to the system's capacity to survive an accident. It is possible for ISPs to install multiple lines, generally at some distance from one another, in case a street accident or other physical breach occurs. However, superior survivability generally involves contracting with two competing ISPs, as each line backs up failure at any point in the other's service.

CONNECTING YOUR BUILDING

Your ISP will install **network termination devices** to connect your building to its WAN (wide area network), which in turn connects to the Internet. From an architectural standpoint, Internet connectivity is a trivial matter. Usually it arrives on a thin

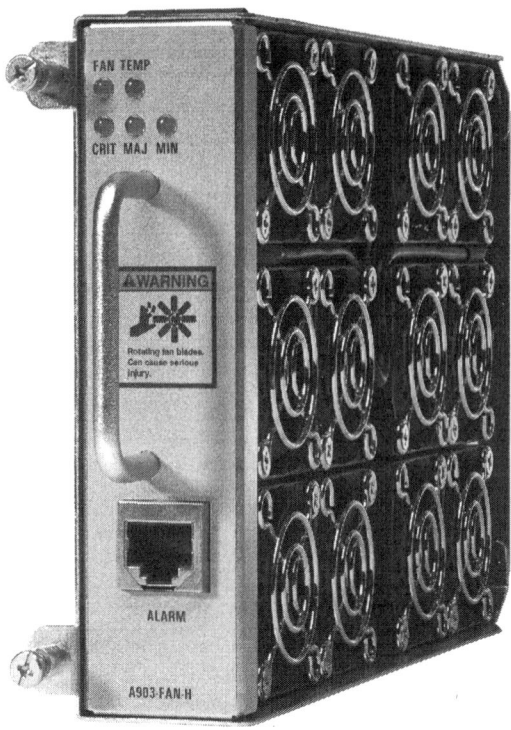

FIGURE 14.3 Network termination devices come in a variety of models.
Courtesy of Cisco Systems, Inc. Unauthorized use not permitted.

underground cable, but it may come from above-ground cable or a radio device. That cable may be fiber for FTTP (fiber to the premises), or it may be copper cables that connect to a nearby fiber cabinet. Whether fiber or copper, streetside cable will likely be pulled through existing ducts for power and telephone, but aerial services require an exterior antenna with line-of-site view to the transmitter. Pulling cable from the antenna to your termination box may require physical entry through a window or exterior wall.

Your network connection has a modest appearance relative to its importance. It is no more than a small socket that accommodates either twisted copper wire or glass cable in a plastic sheath. The connection leads to the network termination device, which is typically the size of a paperback book. This is where your ISP connects their WAN (Wide Area Network) to the LAN that distributes connectivity throughout your building (see figure 14.1).

The network termination device is the formal demarcation between the service areas of your ISP and your network administrator. Technically and contractually, your ISP can test whether their network is working up to the network termination device. Any issues beyond the network determination device are considered your facility, and they must be handled by your museum or its contractors.

> **KEY TERMS**
>
> **DEMARCATION POINT**
>
> The point at which operational control changes from your Internet provider to your network administrators.

Datacom Center

Your network termination device and your **demarcation point** usually resides in a datacom center. Also known as an equipment closet or server room, this facility probably houses some or all of the mission-critical systems that power your LAN. This includes servers, switches, and routers. Your datacom center may also house telecom, for example, a telephone demarcation box, and control boxes for other electrical utilities. Depending on the size and requirements of your organization, you may possess more than one datacom center. Very small organizations may simply have a temperature-controlled cabinet that resides within an office.

The size, location, and number of datacom centers should be decided by network administrators and cablers in tandem with architects and the director of building operations. Datacom equipment is easily disturbed, and it may contain sensitive data such as credit card information. Therefore the datacom center should be a high security room. It should be windowless and possess secure doors that always open from the inside. Access should be limited to IT staff.

Networking equipment is mounted on a rack that allows access to the front and back of devices. Smaller machines such as a network termination device may be mounted directly onto the wall near their physical port or socket. Patch panels are a prominent

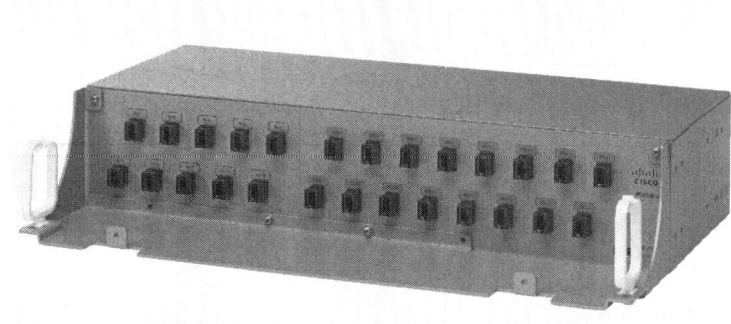

FIGURE 14.4 Patch Panel.
Courtesy of Cisco Systems, Inc. Unauthorized use not permitted.

SERVER RACK STANDARDS

The standard server rack specified by the EIA (Electronic Industries Alliance) encloses a 19-inch-wide equipment bay with mount rails that are 17.75 inches (450.85 mm) apart. Rack height is measured in 1.75-inch (44.45 mm) unit increments. The most common full-size rack is 42U (units) with an internal height dimension of 73.5 inches (1.8669 m). However, external dimensions vary according to manufacturer, and, given the limited space of most server rooms, it is necessary to ensure that any racks you order will fit. Suppliers offer charts that compare the detailed specifications of different racks.

feature on the rack. Also called patch bays, these utilities have rows of jacks (sockets) that enable different devices to be easily connected with a given type of cable. Racks, patch panels and IT devices are built to common standards that make it possible to predict the amount of equipment a given space will accommodate.

Growing demand for rack space is seemingly inevitable, and, even if your organization is migrating to the cloud, it is good practice to have at least ten units (10 U) of empty space to accommodate growth.

Datacom centers have stringent requirements for power and environment. Power must be protected against surges, and it should be uninterruptable if continuous service is required. The latter can be achieved through a UPS (uninterruptable power supply) that uses batteries or a

FIGURE 14.5 Server Rack.
Open source

backup generator. Furthermore, virtually every device requires an individual AC power source, and supplying sufficient outlets rapidly becomes a messy affair. Ideally power strips are built into the server racks to avoid multi-outlet adaptors and trailing cables. A qualified electrician should calculate electrical load and ensure the building can safely supply the room.

> **HEAT AND HUMIDITY STANDARDS**
>
> The American Society of Heating, Refrigerating and Air Conditioning Engineers recommends 18°C (64.4°F) and 27°C (80.6°F) as low and high set points. Recommended humidity is 5.5°C DP to 60 percent RH and 15°C DP within a range of 20–80 percent RH.

IT equipment generates a considerable amount of heat, and it will malfunction if the room is too hot. Humidity can also damage equipment.

Cooling options range from passive ventilation to dedicated heating, ventilation, and air conditioning (HVAC) systems. The amount of cooling required can be calculated from manufacturer guidelines, but facility plans should accommodate expansion.

A properly cooled room may not prevent overheating. Equipment is stacked tightly in racks, and the rack itself must be properly ventilated. This can be through passive convection or forced air. There are also principles that govern how different configurations are stacked. When planning an equipment room, it is important to follow manufacturer guidelines and best practices to ensure stable, efficient operations.

There are hazards associated with heat-generating electrical devices. Local building codes dictate the standards you need to meet, and these are available from the appropriate authorities. The NFPA (National Fire Protection Association) offers a comprehensive library of fire-related codes and standards for the USA and an increasing number of countries.

Of special concern are wall-mounted devices such as network termination devices and power supplies. Under heavy operation 24/7, they generate considerable heat. Many jurisdictions require these to be mounted on fire-retardant backboard to prevent ignition of walls. Generally this is specially treated plywood with a stamp indicating it meets the relevant code. Whether required by code or not, it is a good practice to use certified mounting board for all wall installations. Make sure the relevant stamps are on the front of the panel so it does not have to be removed for inspections.

Fire extinguishers and extinguisher systems should be built according to local codes and prevailing standards for datacom/telecom facilities.

The LAN

A local area network (LAN) carries most of the data traffic within your facility. It consists of the wires and switches that move data between computers, and it also routes data to the Internet through your network termination device. It is analogous to the local roads in a city that connect to intercity highways. In contrast to your Internet connection, which is maintained by your ISP, the design, maintenance, and operation of your LAN rests within your organization.

When designing a LAN, it is best to work from building plans. Since much of the equipment will be difficult to access, it is especially important to document installation and revise documents whenever changes are implemented.

An enormous number of options exist for LAN administrators. As noted earlier, many of these options are becoming virtualized in cloud-based services. However, many facilities will continue using local servers, routers, and switches, though often in conjunction with cloud functionality for specialized services such as web hosting, for example, and most ticketing, ecommerce, marketing, and CRM (customer relationship management) applications. Wireless technology continues to advance for LAN access over WiFi so that local administrators can choose to connect staff computers over WiFi access points. However, this does not obviate the need for cabling. Any mission-critical devices should still have wired connections, but the trend to connect staff via wireless access points continues to grow.

The one exception is cellular data connections, which use a more powerful radio to bypass your LAN. Cellular data connections are available on all phones, many tablets, and some computers through a USB dongle.

ETHERNET

Ethernet is how data is transmitted over wires within a LAN. Although most people associate Ethernet with the ubiquitous twisted wire cables and RJ-45 connectors that physically connect computers to a network, Ethernet is actually a system of engineering rules that make up a global standard for local data transmission.

Although Ethernet also runs via fiber optics, you will most likely use either Cat5e or Cat6 cable in your facility. Cat5e can handle transmission speeds up to 1,000 Mbps (1 Gbps), and Cat6 operates up to 10 Gbps. With the steady increase in demand for data transmission, it is best to use Cat6 for new installations if budget allows.

Ethernet traverses a building through horizontal and vertical channels called runs. Channels can be either conduit, which is preferred in North America, or cable trays, which are favored in the rest of the world. Each approach offers specific benefits, but both offer high standards of safety and usability.

Channels used for Ethernet and other forms of data transmission should be carefully mapped within your building. Many devices generate electromagnetic fields that interfere with data transmissions, and, if they do so intermittently, they may create problems

FIGURE 14.6 An Ethernet cable and RJ-45 plug.
Open source

that are difficult and expensive to identify. Avoid running Ethernet cable close to lighting fixtures and large electrical appliances, and use shielded cable wherever a potential problem is identified. Precise measurements of cable runs are critical because performance drops with distance. Commonly used cables are limited to 100 m, and longer runs of cable need to be augmented by repeaters.

Ensure that cable trays or conduits are adequate by judging the number of cables needed for each run. The conduit size is determined by fill factor, which is a figure that determines the maximum amount of space cables should occupy. (Usually about 40 percent.) It can be calculated by applying a formula or consulting a fill guide. Fill guides also specify the radius of bends in a run.

Reliability is an important factor when installing cable. Bad cable can lead to total or intermittent failure, and the source of failure can be difficult to identify. Certified cable can be purchased at higher cost, but even this cable should be tested before installation is finalized. Common tests include Network Channel Certification, Patch Cord Certification and Continuity Testing. The most comprehensive is Permanent Link Testing. It verifies integrity by testing factors related to cable lengths, termination, internal wiring crosses, and other structural faults. Your cable installers can discuss the ramifications of these tests with you.

WiFi Access Points

WiFi is a two-way radio that opens an Internet session with enabled devices such as mobile phones, tablets, and computers. WiFi devices, called access points, are about the

DATA PROTOCOLS

The Institute of Electronics and Electrical Engineers (IEEE) is an organization of professionals that creates standards for computers and communications networks. The operations described in this chapter are largely defined by IEEE standards, which form the basis of the machinery and training used for network administration.

Anyone who downloads a standard from the IEEE will find highly technical documents of several hundred pages. Few people have the time and training to understand the engineering behind a standard. However, in the context of museum administration, being able to recognize important standards can be sufficient for managing the trained professionals who work with them.

Standards that begin with IEEE 802 govern much of the machinery in a LAN (local area network). This is an area of primary concern for museums because, as the name implies, a LAN operates within a building. Standards that may come to attention are the IEEE 802.2 series; for instance, IEEE 802.3 (Ethernet) and IEEE 802.3U (Fast Ethernet), and or the series that starts with IEEE 802.11 which governs WiFi.

size of a paperback book, and they are governed by IEEE standards that specify speed, range, and capacity of different devices. As of this writing, the most robust specifications are 802.11n and 802.11ac because they offer the best options in terms of speed, range, and capacity. Access points operating on these standards are complementary because they respectively transmit in the 2.4 Ghz and 5 Ghz frequency bands, and they are often used together within high-density environments.

Indoor WiFi typically has a range from 20 m (66 ft) to 60 m (200 ft). Several factors determine range, including the **data protocol** used by the device, power, type, and direction of antenna. Access points require line-of-sight transmission—that is, an unobstructed view of the antenna. Walls limit the range of WiFi. Signals generally will not penetrate metal or concrete, which means that each room may need its own devices. Other factors that passively affect coverage include metal studs; concrete fiberboard; foil-backed insulation, pipes, and electrical wiring; furniture; display cabinets; and other elements commonly found in exhibitions. When changing exhibitions, it is necessary to consider the placement of WiFi access points, and it may be advisable to test them if the installation obstructs the line-of-sight views. A variety of specialized products called boosters or amplifiers will extend the range—but not capacity—of WiFi access points.

Some appliances may also interfere with WiFi. Microwave ovens generate noise in the 2.4 Ghz frequency band, and wireless telephones, security cameras, and Bluetooth devices may degrade service. When installing WiFi it is best to audit all electrical devices in the service area to identify potential conflicts.

Wireless access points must themselves be connected by Ethernet to an internal network. Ethernet standard RJ-45 plugs connect to LAN switches just like other Ethernet devices. Provision must be made for powering an access point. This can be done through standard AC power or PoE (Power over Ethernet), which delivers electrical power over the same cables used for data.

PLANNING FOR IT INFRASTRUCTURE

FIGURE 14.7 WiFi access points come in a variety of models.
Courtesy of Cisco Systems, Inc. Unauthorized use not permitted.

Network Access

Every museum has many places where people connect to your LAN. Examples include offices, ticket counters, kiosks, exhibits, theatres and public WiFi. Planning involves deciding the type, quantity, and quality of network access that will be given to users at each site. Every decision has cost implications.

Although it may be tempting to design your LAN according to the physical characteristics of a room or a generic description of its use, this approach may produce poor results. Design of a LAN should be guided by the needs of the individuals who use it. **Use cases** based on interviews and other research about work processes will assist in identifying current needs and future ambitions. IT upgrades typically happen in three to five year cycles, so it is important to project your museum's needs against your upgrade horizon.

A LAN contains several categories of device as well as wires and wireless access points. The list of devices includes servers, router, and switches. While these devices are clearly physical objects, they also have a functional, or in technical terms, logical, structure. For simplicity, they are defined in the following section which describes how they operate.

Although use cases should determine specifications for your museum, the following are some typical spaces that have their own functional requirements.

FIGURE 14.8 WiFi Access Point.
Open source

BENEFITS OF POWER OVER ETHERNET

- PoE can be supplied from devices connected to a UPS (uninterruptable power supply) so they can continue to operate in the event of general power failure.
- PoE capacity can be added incrementally to the switches that direct data within a LAN through inexpensive devices like injectors, splitters, hubs, and adaptors that add power to the data circuit.
- PoE can also be used for IP telephony. Even if your organization is still using a traditional PBCX (private branch exchange) system, PoE will lower the cost of a telephony migration in the future.

CORE NETWORK

As we saw above in the section describing the LAN, Ethernet is how devices connect within your datacom center. If you have a larger facility with multiple datacom centers, then you will likely use robust Cat6 or optical cable to connect them. These cables will also connect equipment closets, distribution points that house network switches, and wireless access points. Cables should be selected depending on the projected capacity of the network. Given the expense of rewiring a facility, it is best to overprovision cable, as demand for data grows constantly.

OFFICES AND WORKSPACES

Any job that requires reliable high bandwidth connections should connect via Ethernet. This includes staff working from fixed desktop computers or in studios or workstations dedicated to media production. However, if staff are only using their computers to send email, access office databases, and browse the Internet, network administrators may choose to connect new facilities or new workstations solely over WiFi.

WiFi will also likely be used if organizations are implementing flexible workspaces that may include hot desks and open floor plans, or wish to support connectivity for staff wherever they are; for example, in meeting rooms or reception areas where it may be unfeasible to offer Ethernet connections. Visitors generally require wireless connectivity, especially in meeting rooms, as do volunteers and temporary workers who may bring their own computers.

> **KEY TERMS**
>
> **USE CASE**
>
> A detailed profile of a person who actually uses the system in question. (This person is also known as an "end user.") Use cases ensure that system behavior matches the needs of its users. Usually several are developed to cover different classes of user.

FRONT-OF-HOUSE STAFF

Demands for network access are growing throughout the contemporary museum, especially among staff who work at information desks or roam the floors offering mobile assistance. Apple pioneered roaming support to reduce waiting times and serve customers wherever they are. Equipping staff with handheld devices that wirelessly connect to resources could create a superior visitor experience in crowded museums.

TICKETING

Any ticketing system that is built today will be fully digital. Sales are conducted online, on the telephone and at an onsite ticket counter, and they are managed through any number of enterprise ticketing applications. Digital ticketing is in rapid flux, and, as in so many other areas, the trend is toward virtualization. A digital ticket can be printed with a bar code that is read by a scanner. The same bar code can appear on a mobile phone. Increasingly the phone or a smart card will transmit the code wirelessly so ticket holders can enter events with little or no friction.

Digital ticketing systems offer great advantages for museums and visitors. Ticket scanners are much faster than the human eye, and they can be placed anywhere. When properly designed, they reduce waiting time for entry. They can also be combined with membership and CRM initiatives to personalize service and increase engagement in both directions.

SALES

All sales processes can now be handled through an EPOS (**electronic point of sale**) system. As with digital ticketing, an EPOS system combined with proper IT support offers ultimate flexibility in the location of commerce. Pop-up stores can be set up anywhere, and the security of financial transactions can be maintained by setting up a

> **KEY TERMS**
>
> **EPOS**
>
> An electronic point of sale system is used to sell tickets, merchandise and refreshments.

dedicated VLAN for the temporary commerce site. (VLAN is explained the section on "Logical Infrastructure" below.)

DIGITAL SIGNAGE

Monitors and other displays are replacing printed media in public spaces and galleries for information, promotions, wayfinding, and interpretation. While it is possible to load content from individual hard drives, it is far more efficient to connect displays to a network either through Ethernet or WiFi depending on the location, cost of provisioning, and capabilities of the display.

CINEMAS, GALLERIES, AND LECTURE HALLS

Motion pictures use more data than any other format. Films are now being delivered online in the form of DCP (digital cinema protocol) files that run from 500 GB for standard 2K displays to several terabytes for the IMAX films often shown in museums. Video in galleries and lecture halls may use more compressed formats, but the files can still be substantial, and any spaces that might use video should be provisioned with high bandwidth connections.

EXHIBITS

While many museum exhibits do not require connectivity, it is a good idea to anticipate the requirement by installing ducts, Ethernet, or mounts that could provide either wired or wireless service. Fixed tablets or computers may need updates, and new technology-mediated experiences described in chapter 6 may require significant bandwidth.

TOURS

Museums increasingly offer guided tours that visitors access via their own smartphones, as well as the more traditional audio guide on the museum's devices. Both of these may run from apps or web pages that require connectivity that does not, as in the case of personal smartphones, incur cellular data charges. Future innovations such as digital docents will also likely require wireless connectivity.

STUDY CENTERS

Study centers may include fixed-place computers or tablets. Content on these devices may be served from local drives, but they will be far easier to manage if the devices are connected to your LAN.

PLANNING FOR IT INFRASTRUCTURE

PUBLIC WIFI AND CHARGING STATIONS

Providing WiFi access, usually for free, is virtually a requirement of every public space, whether for sharing, communication, or learning. Demand for robust WiFi is coupled with demand for charging stations for visitors who are using smartphones and other wireless devices. It is best to anticipate both when planning for mobile engagement.

When planning charging stations, it is necessary to survey current best practices in this rapidly evolving landscape. Possible locations for charging stations include standing kiosks, tableside outlets in cafes, or lockers that resemble vending machines.

INTERNET OF THINGS

Generally known as IoT, Internet of Things is a concept that describes how everything will be connected to the Internet. For example, with the development of IoT, every item in the collection could be tagged for location awareness or in order to broadcast descriptions, links, and other relevant data. Rapid advances in sensing technology along with creative applications of connectivity make IoT an emerging reality, and its potential uses in a museum are manifold.

Connected devices can also be used to analyze and optimize circulation within the museum through dedicated sensors, or WiFi access points that have been positioned to detect the location of visitors. Both approaches require proper placement of devices, and a good practice is to anticipate the possibility of rigging particular walls and ceilings with devices.

Density of Service

It is safe to say that your organization would grind to a halt without network services. Demand for data transmission is growing, and it is important to plan for the right density—that is, the number of users who access data within a given unit of space. On average, infrastructure plans should project three to five years of service. Having to replace equipment too soon results in higher costs, while a longer time frame may not accommodate progress in capacity, capability, and efficiency.

Judging the number of Ethernet connections that a facility requires is a straightforward matter of accounting for connected devices. WiFi is a different matter, as the capabilities of access points vary widely, and improvements in one area involve trade-offs in others. Numerous variables affect WiFi performance, and not all are predictable. Therefore you should be prepared to test and, if needed, revise plans. It is advisable to reserve budget for upgrading the system after launch.

Despite the limitations, one can make a basic estimation of demands on a WiFi system by multiplying the number of people a place can accommodate by the average amount of data they are likely to transmit. The total flow of data can be controlled by limiting individual usage or disallowing formats—for example, streaming video—that demand excessive bandwidth. For areas that attract large numbers of visitors, or require large data throughput, high-density systems developed for stadiums will be more than adequate within a museum.

Logical Infrastructure

There are many ways to configure a LAN physically, but a diagram of the physical relationship of its components, called physical topology, does not capture the functional relationships among those components. This is determined by the logical topology that is designed by network administrators. Logical topology offers more options than your physical hardware, because one machine can be configured to operate as several. It is usually presented in a diagram that presents how data is transmitted through the network through virtual machines and connections. Note that there is a great deal of overlap between the terminology and functionality of the physical and logical infrastructure. See figure 14.9 for a highly simplified overview of logical topology.

A detailed understanding of network topology requires considerable training. This does not mean that the concepts of networking should be ignored. Digital networks are the primary medium for critical operations like financial transactions, public engagement, and collections management. A security breach can facilitate the theft of valuable objects, or, as in the case of credit card theft, publicly discredit the museum. Cybercriminals operate at a comfortable distance from their victims, and breaches will likely be in the logical, not the physical, infrastructure.

Planners, managers and executives should be familiar with the devices and working concepts of networks so they can understand the stakes involved in decisions. When evaluating proposals, managers should attempt to independently verify the benefits of an IT investment and also judge—or know when to question—assessments offered by network administrators. The following sections offer the basics of the logical topology of a LAN configuration.

Router and Firewall

Opening your LAN to the Internet is a complicated, risky affair. It is complicated because of addressing and traffic management, and it is risky because connecting to the Internet opens pathways to sensitive files such as financial records, collection

PLANNING FOR IT INFRASTRUCTURE

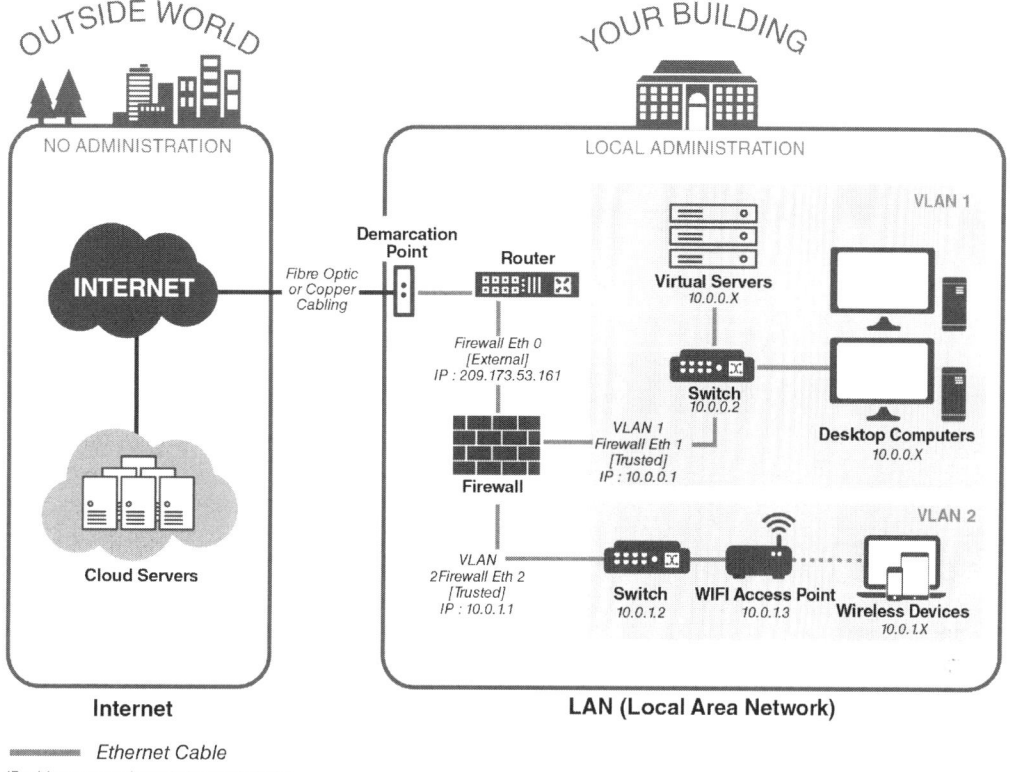

FIGURE 14.9 Logical topology diagrams the virtual machines in your facility.
Ali Hossaini and Lord Cultural Resources *With thanks to Labyrinth IT.*

databases, passwords, and credit card numbers. Access to your LAN is managed by a **router** that handles traffic between your LAN and the Internet. Your facility works behind a **firewall**, which is a software application that acts as gatekeeper between your LAN (a "trusted network") and untrusted networks on the Internet. The network access device is a wide-open door, and the firewall is a security guard that distinguishes friend from foe. Firewalls are essential to maintaining internal security because criminals are constantly searching for victims. For a sense of the threat, consider the following. Within milliseconds of appearing, an IP address on the Internet is probed for vulnerabilities. Once inside your network, cybercriminals can steal data or even hold your files hostage by encrypting them and demanding a ransom for their release.

It is worthwhile to invest in a highly rated firewall from a reputable supplier that offers frequent updates and 24/7 support. It is possible to reduce costs by reducing levels of service in many aspects of infrastructure, but security is *not* the area to seek savings. You should plan to acquire a highly rated firewall with frequent updates and 24/7 support.

Prices for routers vary by capability, and the functionality you select has important ramifications for your operation. One factor is the number of programmable and non-programmable ports on the unit. These impact your ability to segregate traffic, impose

FIGURE 14.10 Router.
Courtesy of Cisco Systems, Inc. Unauthorized use not permitted.

> **KEY TERMS**
>
> **ROUTER**
>
> A router enables computers on your LAN to communicate by issuing local IP addresses.

security, and build flexibility into your system. For instance, your current system may route staff activities, public WiFi, and ecommerce through the same circuit. A more advanced system could respond to changes in the regulatory or security environment by routing sensitive categories of traffic through dedicated ports. Alternatively you may want to ensure that heavy usage of public WiFi does not impact critical business operations or impose varying levels of firewall.

Bandwidth is another factor to consider when selecting your router. You can contract for lower levels of service than the unit can handle. Upfront costs are higher, but this tactic allows you to expand bandwidth and functionality without the expense of replacing equipment. For instance, you could contract for 100 Mbps of bandwidth but acquire a device with 1 Gbps capacity. While it is prudent to plan for expansion, one should also bear in mind that equipment becomes obsolete. If your planning horizon is more than three years, replacing equipment later may be the better option.

Switches

A **switch** is a rack-mounted device that contains rows of Ethernet ports. Every device (or node) on your LAN terminates in a switch, and, along with the router, it is the switch that transforms your facility into a network.

PLANNING FOR IT INFRASTRUCTURE

The purpose of networks is to facilitate communication among its nodes. Data on networks is packaged into units called frames. Like a postal service, a package of data reaches its intended destination through a system of addresses. Every network-ready device has a unique identifier called a MAC or media access control address. Switches are aware of which MAC is connected to each port, and they direct data according to the destination address contained in its frame.

MAC addresses are used for local networking only. For a machine to communicate via the Internet, its MAC address must be translated into an IP address by the router. A useful analogy is the mail. For anyone old enough to remember, the MAC address is the equivalent of interoffice mail. It only works within your facility. An IP address is the equivalent of a postal address. It enables a message to be sent anywhere in the world. Your router has a capability called NAT (network address translation) to direct messages in both directions. NAT is performed by the router or the firewall at the network edge, which is the term used for the boundary between the Internet and a managed network like your LAN. NAT enables network administrators to connect a large number of internal users via one or a small number of external IP addresses.

KEY TERMS

FIREWALL

A firewall is either a software application that resides on your router or a separate piece of hardware/software. It protects your facility by automatically deterring criminal intrusion, viruses, and digital vandalism. Firewalls require constant updates to stay current.

SWITCH

Switches create a LAN by transmitting messages among devices using local address protocols called media access controls (MACs).

FIGURE 14.11 Switch.
Courtesy of Cisco Systems, Inc. Unauthorized use not permitted.

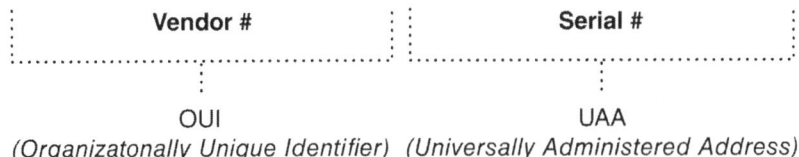

FIGURE 14.12 MAC Address.
Ali Hossaini and Lord Cultural Resources

Servers

Servers are computers that provide resources over a network. Rack servers are the most common, and they reside in the datacom center where they take one to four units of vertical space on a standard rack.

Servers are usually paired for resilience. One server is live, while the other mirrors it by copying all its data at regular intervals. Should the live server fail, the backup takes over with little or no interruption of service.

A server contains the same components as a personal computer, including CPU, RAM, and hard drives, but it is built for high performance and constant operation. There are many types of servers, but they operate similarly in order to

- Provide network storage (fileserving);
- Host email;
- Manage traffic to printers;
- Host applications that are used by multiple parties; and
- Host databases for collections, content, ticketing, and CRM.

While individual PCs can handle many of these tasks, assigning them to a central resource has many benefits. Storage is much less expensive to add on a server, and it can be reassigned to different users or workgroups with a few keystrokes. In the event of failure, it is easier to work with servers than individual PCs. The same applies to email

PLANNING FOR IT INFRASTRUCTURE

FIGURE 14.13 Rack server.
Courtesy of Cisco Systems, Inc. Unauthorized use not permitted.

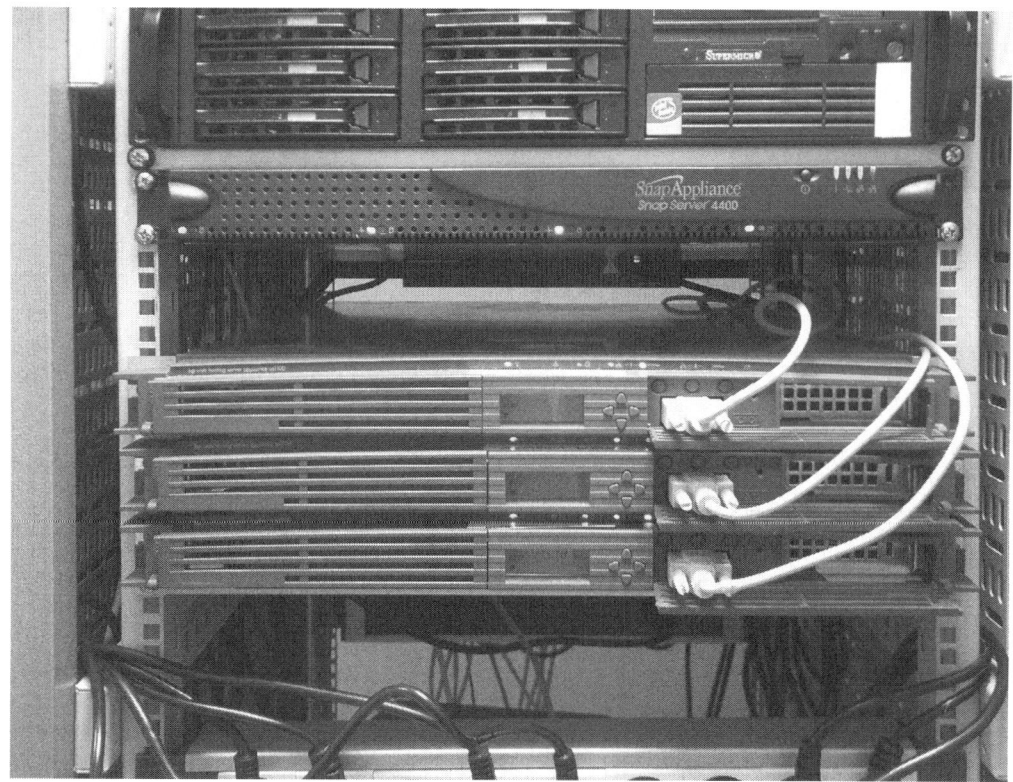

FIGURE 14.14 Rack Server *in situ*.
Open source

archives. In the case of database-driven applications, it would be difficult or impossible to synchronize databases that were dispersed among different PCs.

Servers are selected according to the work demanded of them. Factors that influence the choice of servers include:

- How many users must the server support?
- How much disk storage capacity is needed?
- How many applications will the server be running?
- What are the number and size of databases?

It is good practice to purchase an extended warranty that covers the expected life of the device. If the server runs mission-critical applications, it is worth considering a warranty that offers hardware replacement in as little as four hours.

Like all computers, servers require software to operate. This is usually purchased separately from hardware, although manufacturers will ship devices with a preinstalled OS (**operating system**). There are a wide variety of options for the server OS; the most popular are based in Microsoft and Linux. Network administrators select the OS according to budget, user requirements, operating environment, and, ultimately, their own expertise.

Servers do not work out of the box. Once safely in a rack, the server OS must be configured, and software must be installed for each function. After installation or upgrades, there is generally a period of testing, troubleshooting, and optimization. Servers can be configured as integral units, or they can be virtualized so that one physical server functions as several servers from an operational standpoint.

Virtualization goes a step further with cloud services. The work of a physical server can also be purchased from cloud providers such as Rackspace and Amazon Web Services.

VLAN

Virtual local area networks (VLANs) are a group of devices on one or more LANs that are configured to communicate as if they were attached to the same switch, even though they are located on a number of different LAN segments. It can also do the opposite. Devices on the same network segment can be managed on separate virtual networks—an important feature for maintaining security in a mixed-use environment. VLAN is where the logical and physical topologies of a network separate. Creation of virtual LANs is a fundamental tool for network administrators.

VLANs are used to preserve network resources for bandwidth and latency-sensitive applications, or to simplify administrative tasks by confining changes to specific workgroups. They may also be created to simplify administrative tasks by confining changes to specific workgroups.

A physical diagram of your network shows the position, location, and wiring of devices in terms of your building's layout (see figure 14.2). Thus the PCs in a particular workspace appear next to each other, and they are likely connected to the same switch through wires that share the same tray or conduit. If you have multiple devices and switches, then they are probably clustered in terms that make architectural sense.

However, from the standpoint of workflow, it may make sense to have different devices on different virtual networks. For instance, a **VoIP** telephone may sit next to a PC, but for better performance it should be on a separate network. Rather than build a physically separate LAN, administrators are able to create a logically separate VLAN that shares the same physical infrastructure but prioritizes telephone conversations over content like email that is less time sensitive. From a security standpoint, VLANs are an essential part of the network administrator's toolkit. Payment card clearing and other sensitive transactions must be on a secure network that is segregated from public traffic. VLANs meet the rules for digital security compliance, which are discussed below, and they save the enormous expense of building parallel physical infrastructure for financial systems.

> **KEY TERMS**
>
> **OPERATING SYSTEM**
>
> An operating system (OS) is a software environment that enables software applications to function on a given piece of hardware. Windows, Mac OS, and Linux are all operating systems, and Microsoft Word and Adobe Photoshop are applications.
>
> **VoIP**
>
> VoIP (Voice over Internet Protocol) replaces analog telephone with inexpensive Internet-based voice transmission services.

VLANs offer many benefits, but they do introduce a new level of complexity to network administration. Devices can no longer depend on the switch to communicate, and thus the LAN requires a router to enable communication among devices on various VLANs. Operating VLANs requires a higher level of expertise than a simple switched network, but larger facilities that require flexibility will find the investment worthwhile.

Connected Devices

User devices such as computers, tablets, smartphones, cash registers, mobile payment card readers, and ticket scanners, are the most visible parts of your LAN. In logical terms, each of these connected devices is a node identified by its MAC address. MAC addresses are assigned to machines by their manufacturer, and they are usually printed

> **KEY TERMS**
>
> **DATABASE**
>
> A digital filing system that enables data to be stored, related, manipulated, and retrieved.

on its chassis and embedded in its operating system. They contain alphanumeric characters unique to the manufacturer, plus a set of characters that identify the specific unit.

There are also some connected devices that are not attached to a user. Virtually all security systems, thermostats, and other maintenance systems use IP networks, as do many of the beacons that broadcast content about location or exhibits. As noted above, IoT will greatly expand the population of connected objects, and this will transform management of LANs in unforeseen ways.

Applications and Databases

Applications are software programs that run on servers and PCs. Examples include office software such as word processors, spreadsheets, and design suites. Although office services can be run from the cloud, these applications probably run as stand-alone programs on individual computers. Files may be run from the local drive or from a server. When folders on a server are mapped to a PC, they appear as folders in file manager windows, desktops, and other access windows.

Some applications use **databases**, particularly those devoted to accounting, HR, commerce, ticketing, CRM, and donor development. Databases are maintained on servers because more than one person needs to access them over a network. They may require higher-performance computers, and database management requires a skilled DBA (database administrator).

Your organization may also support applications on tablets, smartphones and specialized devices used to scan entry fobs or cards, collection IDs, barcodes on tickets, payment cards, and other items. Applications of this type require connectivity to a database, and they may also connect to external services that validate payment card transactions or other sensitive data over encrypted connections.

The interplay of hardware, software, and devices on a LAN can be thought of as a local ecosystem. Minor occurrences can impact the entire system, and the broader global environment of the Internet affects the LAN directly and indirectly. Maintaining the compatibility of a LAN's components occupies much of a network administrator's time. Even a simple network has dozens of elements, and each of these has specific operating requirements. To understand the complexity of network administration, and its profound impact on business, it is worth discussing some examples.

Every software program requires an operating system (OS) to work. When an OS is upgraded, a program may lose some or all of its functionality. Thus the program, too, may need to be upgraded. Software developers generally respond to

OS upgrades with revisions of their own, but there may be a lag in release dates. Upgrades may be issued for free, or they may require additional fees. Hardware is not immune to this issue. Manufacturers are constantly inventing more powerful features, and these possibilities enable new versions of software in a positive feedback loop. Customers benefit from better, faster, and cheaper systems. Over time the ability of perfectly functional computers to support emerging standards diminishes, and hardware must be replaced.

The same situation applies to the standards that govern web browsers. Harmonizing content management systems with browser standards is a web-related issue that increasingly impacts in-house administration due to the trend toward cloud services. Cloud services may replace back-office applications, but they are often managed via web browsers. However, browsers are much easier to upgrade than hardware, and this is one more argument for adoption of cloud services.

> **KEY TERMS**
>
> **VPN**
>
> A virtual private network (VPN) is a network that behaves like a LAN over the Internet. The key concepts are security and global. A LAN is secure but local, and the Internet is insecure but global. A VPN is both secure and global, but it involves tradeoffs in other areas.

Remote Access

Your organization may employ staff who work from home or a remote location. Yet they may also need to access LAN resources such as email archives, network files, and shared databases. An inexpensive option for granting remote access while maintaining security is the VPN (**virtual private network**). This virtualizes the LAN so that computers anywhere on the planet can function as if they were in-house. To set up a VPN, network administrators use encryption to create a secure connection between the staff member's PC and the in-house LAN. VPNs can also be used to connect LANs in separate facilities, which is useful in a campus or when a museum has multiple branches.

Operational Infrastructure

There are many different ways to organize IT operations within a museum. Larger museums may have a staff of dedicated IT professionals, but for certain tasks, they still may require outside support. Smaller museums may have a handful of IT staff, or even just one person who may also have responsibilities in other departments. The smallest organizations may assign IT management to a person who is merely well-disposed toward computers.

In today's environment, it is dangerous for an organization to underspend on IT expertise. Savings in wages are easily lost through inefficiency and bad decisions. Outsourcing is an option, but outside parties may be risk-averse. In the best-case scenario, the museum will have someone on staff who can make informed judgments about the business objectives of IT projects. If hiring is not an option, another approach is to recruit a board member with IT skills who is willing to donate time. In chapter 13, Ngaire Blankenberg reviews evolving jobs and job descriptions for the IT and digital departments.

Regardless of its size, every museum should have an IT service management (ITSM) plan that details how it will maintain the integrity, reliability, and compatibility of IT systems. An ITSM plan should address the following topics:

- Management of IT assets
- Problem management
- Change management
- Regulatory compliance
- Security
- Disaster recovery

Whoever directs IT should bear the following in mind. The IT department should respond to the needs of the organization, and it should manage change to accommodate, not disrupt, the workflow of museum staff. The goal of IT should be to give everyone the tools they need to work effectively and comfortably.

Network Topology

While your physical topology has numerous constraints, your logical topology can be optimized according to end user requirements. Much of this can be done by deploying VLANs to manage specific types of data or users. Demanding applications such as VoIP or streaming video can be isolated, and people in the same workgroup can be gathered even if they are dispersed throughout your facilities. Assigning LAN resources is similar to calculating Internet bandwidth. Much of the calculation depends on estimating the performance requirements of the network, and this can be accomplished by understanding how people actually use the resource.

Network Administrators

Network administrators directly manage a LAN and connected devices. They may also have responsibility for specifying equipment and software, generating purchase orders, developing budgets, making business cases and calculating return on investment.

Depending on the size of the facility, network administration can be handled by one person or a team, or it can be outsourced to an agency. If it is outsourced, it is advisable to have the relationship managed by someone with the appropriate expertise. IT systems are prone to slowdowns and failure, and, without strong internal judgment, your organization could be a pushover, a bad client, or both. The following tasks are among a network administrator's duties:

- Performing hardware and software installation
- Adding and deleting user accounts
- Ensuring data are backed up
- Writing network procedures and policy guides
- Network troubleshooting
- Performance analysis and optimization
- Templates for reports from sales and development initiatives
- Disaster recovery planning and implementation
- Managing network security
- Staying abreast of best practices

> **KEY TERMS**
>
> **HELP DESK**
>
> A help desk is a one-stop service bureau operated by IT departments. Anyone with an IT problem can email or call for assistance.

Network administrators should regularly scan systems for problems. Standard practice is to offer a **help desk** service that can be contacted over telephone and email by staff who have issues. Depending on the needs of your organization, the help desk may be available 24/7 or for extended business hours.

All service calls should be issued a ticket that identifies the caller, the issue and location. This is done through software that has been developed for IT services. When a service call has been opened, tickets are sent via email to the caller, a logging system, and other designated parties; for example, a ranking IT manager. When an issue is resolved, notice is sent stating the ticket has been closed.

Oftentimes IT staff operate outside the museum. In such a case they will use remote access software that enables them to take control of computers from any location.

Another important duty is software maintenance. Software uses a variety of file formats and communication protocols. Aside from upgrades, which can be managed in cycles, software is updated frequently through "patches," often in response to security threats. Compatibility issues can create serious problems, so it is necessary to monitor the operating environment, software applications, and current state of software at all times, and especially when implementing change.

Models of your network can be built in a spreadsheet or diagramming software such as Visio. Each system should be inventoried as a functional unit. For example, if there are a hundred staff using PCs, details of each PC should be noted. This includes

- Operating System (OS)
- Office software (version and update status)
- Professional software, for example, design or multimedia
- In-house systems, such as mailing lists or ticketing applications
- Peripherals such as credit/debit card devices

By comparing the version of each application, and charting them against proposed upgrades, compatibility issues can be forecast. The case is especially acute with peripheral devices where manufacturers may not keep pace with OS upgrades.

Documentation

Documentation is critical to the long-term success of a facility. It provides continuity across time, vendors, and personnel, and it is also essential for efficient upgrades and troubleshooting. Every stage of technical development should be documented and accessible in clearly organized files. Printed copies should be available in case of complete failure. Examples of materials that should be documented are:

- Equipment specifications
- Functional specifications
- Warranties
- Network diagrams
- User manuals
- Revision histories

Documentation is particularly important for custom software projects such as collections and content management systems because no other resources are available. Please see chapters 9–12 for more detail about best practices in this arena.

Policies and Procedures

It is equally important to develop a manual of policies and procedures. Policies provide clarity on important issues like security, resource management, and emergencies, and procedures detail what to do in a given situation. In their absence, even a well-designed system will develop inefficient, confusing processes.

The content of a policy and procedures manual is determined by the needs of your organization. These derive from conditions in the marketplace. The topics outlined below are likely to be relevant, but your network managers should maintain a manual that is contemporary and comprehensive.

ADMINISTRATIVE LEVELS

Every computer has different levels of access. Access is often called permission. The highest level of access is called administrator. Administrators can perform any operation on a computer, including actions that will damage the computer and anything connected to it. Administrator access should be given only to qualified technicians who are in a legal relationship with your organization. It is important that administrative passwords are held to the highest security standards.

Regular users should be given a personal profile that gives them access to the software they need, their individual folders on the server (or network drive), and any applications or databases that are hosted on the network. Ideally users should have limited or no permission to install software on their computer as this is a common path to intrusion. This ideal often collides with the reality of museum staff who rely on groupware, file sharing services, and social networks to perform their jobs. As a service department, IT needs to strike a balance between ease of administration—with the very real risks to security—and a world where instant connectivity across a multitude of platforms is a professional, social, and cultural necessity.

DATA ARCHIVES

Virtually every piece of data on a network can be archived. In the present context, archive refers only to business archives, that is, copies of email and working documents that are backed up to a network drive. Decisions on what is archived, as opposed to merely saved for future use, should be made according to the business, regulatory, and historical requirements of your institution. It is not a given that everything should be archived, particularly since the costs and management overhead can become substantial over time. Some organizations delete email past a certain date, though others may be mandated to retain it for legal purposes.

ACCOUNT MANAGEMENT

Everyone who accesses the network should be assigned an account. This includes temporary staff and volunteers who may be given a generic account. Account holders are assigned a user name and password that gives them access to computers and online services. If an account is set up properly, then a user can log into any computer in the facility and find their software and files. This creates efficiencies and simplifies management, as staff can shift locations or computers with little IT overhead.

Account management should be governed by a strict process. New accounts should only be created by formal request from HR or departmental directors. These can be created for employees, as generic inboxes, or for projects. When an employee leaves or a project terminates, accounts should be closed immediately. In some cases, an employee account may be managed for a period of time, but this should be strictly limited. Content should be deleted or archived as a matter of policy.

A list of accounts should be maintained, and it should be regularly reviewed against active employees. Smaller organizations will, of course, have a compressed version of these procedures.

ERROR LOGS

Network administrators and help desk staff should keep logs of every error that occurs on IT systems. These logs should be reviewed regularly to identify chronic problems that should be approached through systemic changes.

STANDARDIZATION

It is best to standardize equipment on a few different types of device. Do not vary your choice of servers, switches, PCs, and peripherals without good reason. Standardization simplifies installation, maintenance, and troubleshooting. It allows machines to be swapped during failures, and makes it easier to manage upgrade cycles from an operational and budgetary perspective.

If your facility does require different devices; for example, more powerful computers for multimedia and assigning standard specifications to different classes. For instance, basic office PCs may be Class A, web multimedia machines may be Class B, and machines for professional media production may be Class C. These classes could be attached to departments or individual job roles to create clarity when projecting support and budgetary allocations.

REDUNDANCY

When planning network infrastructure, it is important to calculate the value of network uptime to your organization. Losing connectivity or vital business functions has a cost attached to it, and this cost can be used to develop policies around redundancy. Equipment failures are inevitable, and the only way to eliminate disruption is to build backup systems. Already we have discussed the possibility of contracting multiple lines for Internet connectivity. It is also possible to incorporate redundancy into your LAN. Backup or cloned servers, duel uplinks from your network termination device to switches, and duel CPU cards in switches are ways to build resilience into your systems.

STORAGE OF DATA

Computers issued to individuals possess storage capacity, but it is not a good practice to encourage its use. Instead each user should be issued a network drive that opens on their computer when they log in. This policy has many benefits. Any individual can use any computer, and upgrades can happen in minutes. More importantly, it is difficult to back up or recover data from local computers as opposed to servers. A practical data policy depends on the use of network storage rather than local drives.

DATA BACKUPS

Loss of data causes considerable harm, and it can happen from equipment failure, human error, criminal intrusion, and many other reasons. As a minimal policy, data should be backed up on-site to hard drives for quick recovery and to tape for longer-term storage. Ideally data is backed up to a cloud storage device or already served from redundant systems in the cloud.

ANTIVIRUS

Targeted and untargeted attacks by viruses and other malware are an unfortunate fact of life. The main line of defense is the firewall, but this is easily breached by the proliferation of portable media. Some experts claim that virtually every USB stick is infected. Smartphones are another source of intrusive software. It is essential to scan connected devices regularly with up-to-date antivirus software.

SECURITY

It is a best practice and, increasingly, a contractual or legal requirement on the part of financial clearing companies to maintain an Information Security Policy. Security is discussed in more depth later.

DISASTER RECOVERY

Even the best designed systems fall prey to disaster. Fire, intrusion, power failures, and a host of other causes can lead to catastrophic loss of systems, and a disaster recovery plan is essential to protecting the integrity of your collections, your operations, and perhaps your facilities if security or other systems rely on digital infrastructure.

A disaster recovery plan incorporates many other aspect of planning including network administration, data backups, and security. It should include the following elements:

1. A clear chain of responsibility with internal and external staff with contact information
2. A manifest of assets that can be used to replace and recover lost functionality, settings, and data
3. Access to insurance policies and budgetary authority to implement recovery procedures

USER PRACTICES

Everyone who uses the network should receive guidance on policies that affect them and procedures they should follow. Your specific environment will dictate the guidelines, but here are some examples.

Nightly shutdown: Not everyone turns off their computer at the end of their shift. Everyone should be mandated to shut down unless their computer is running a process overnight. They should be informed of the reasons, including energy use, security, and system updates. As an alternative, systems can be set to shut down automatically.

Network drives: Users should be mandated to use network drives for the reasons stated earlier. Understanding the potential consequences of using local drives, namely irretrievable loss of their work, should be explained.

Security: Staff awareness is a critical element in security. Emphasis should be placed on procedures relating to security, and staff should have a clear understanding of why these procedures have been implemented.

Location Analytics

Digital technologies are increasingly used to manage circulation, wayfinding, and visitor services. Visitor management is becoming a science that resembles the techniques used to analyze traffic on a website, as described in chapter 5 on analytics. With the use of sensors, individual movements can be tracked to create a heat map that reveals visitor engagement in slices of time. This can be used to identify bottlenecks, improve wayfinding, and test the effectiveness of promotions. Sensor-based systems even deliver real-time information to visitors by triggering content that is delivered over WiFi. As an alternative to sensors, WiFi vendors are delivering systems that can identify individual positions through access points. These systems have built-in analytics features, and they can be linked to publishing and CRM applications.

Location analytics can be used to improve visitor experience in manifold ways, and it can also provide performance metrics for the museum at any scale. Delivering analytics requires collaboration between IT staff and departments responsible for operations, marketing, and visitor engagement. As more public venues use location analytics to provide a better visitor experience, there will be pressure on museums to achieve a similar standard.

> **KEY TERMS**
>
> **LOCATION ANALYTICS**
>
> Location analytics create a real time heat map of people in a given area. It is a circulation management tool that can be used to increase the capacity of a building.

Network Security

Crime may be the biggest risk facing network administrators. The Internet was designed as an open system based on trust, and engineers have been forced to build security features on a foundation that anticipated free exchange of data. It is impossible to detail online security issues. Cybercrime evolves rapidly. New forms emerge daily, and administrators should review best practices regularly. They should strive to create security-aware organizations, as virtually every point of contact with the outside world constitutes an attack surface for criminals.

Many of these practices detailed in these pages have ramifications for security as well as sound management. These include the guidelines outlined below.

CONTROLLED ACCESS

Strict rules for administrative access, terminating access when employees leave, and ensuring that passwords are complex and changed regularly. Network administrators need to change default passwords on equipment—this is still a major source of problems—and they need to install security patches as soon as they are released. Antivirus software should be run at the firewall, and individual devices including smartphones should be scanned regularly with updated definitions. Security breaches should be reported as soon as they happen.

STAFF AWARENESS

It is not sufficient to leave these policies in the hands of IT staff. Whoever is responsible for managing the museum needs to confirm that security policies are in place, and they should not shrink from reviewing a security checklist on a regular basis. Human error is the cause of many security breaches, and management should proactively support IT in avoiding it.

Many intrusions begin with social hacking, for instance, when a criminal poses as a vendor to garner information about systems. Staff should be drilled on administrative processes, and they should greet unknown or unanticipated contact via telephone, email, or even in person with skepticism. Phishing and other email scams are still effective, and publishing stories about recent crimes, especially if they fall close to home, is an effective way to keep colleagues alert.

DATA BACKUPS

Malicious software may simply destroy data. Criminals may hold data for ransom by blocking access. Backing up data regularly to tape or cloud service providers can help counter intrusions, though the backup may also contain the alien code.

PRIVACY AND REGULATION

It is no secret that trust is a major issue for people who go online. Personalization is a double-edged sword because it gives organizations access to private information. Membership and development programs amplify the dangers of a data breach. The best organizations build trust with visitors and members by being completely transparent about how they gather and use data. Security issues evolve rapidly, and your organization should publish its digital security policy to anyone whose data is affected. It is essential that someone in your organization includes digital security as part of their portfolio. The following points give a framework for developing digital security policy, but it is necessary to update your policy regularly with best practices.

- Put all ticketing and EPOS systems on a dedicated VLAN.
- Ensure ports anywhere in the building can be configured for the VLAN.
- Implement laws and regulations pertaining to visitor information.
- Utilize legally compliant systems for financial transactions.
- Post your security and privacy policy in your terms of service.
- Detail to visitors what information you gather and why.
- Make regular reports so the public can see their data at work.
- Regularly review the effectiveness of your policy and consider having a regular audit by an outside agency.

Your museum probably sells ticket and other merchandise. The data generated by financial transactions are a lucrative target for criminals. Thieves may use payment card information directly, or they may sell it in underground marketplaces. Rich spoils feed the growing sophistication of cybercriminals, and the payment card industry has responded with strict rules for how credit and debit cards are handled. This is through the PCI DSS (Payment Card Industry Data Security Standard) issued by a consortium that includes MasterCard, Visa, American Express, and Discover. When new standards are issued, organizations must upgrade any system that takes payment cards, and punishments for neglect are draconian.

> **KEY TERMS**
>
> **ENCRYPTION**
>
> Encryption is a way of mathematically scrambling messages so that only the sender and receiver can read them.

The 2016 PCI DSS release states that financial transactions must be handled by end-to-end **encryption**. Noncompliant organizations can still process payments, but they pay much higher penalties for theft than compliant organizations. It is not unusual for hardware and software vendors to lag well behind regulatory standards, so you need to pay careful attention to the compliance status of your systems. Laggard vendors need to hear from customers.

The PCI DSS offers a comprehensive approach to safeguarding sensitive data for all card brands. It consists of twelve basic requirements, categorized in table 14.1.

Building Security

Building security is now deeply related to information security. Any system governing building access, surveillance, and the integrity of collections should be planned with the expectation that it will be tested. Infrastructure used for building security should be separated from other uses. For instance, it could run on a parallel LAN with its own Ethernet, switches, and routers. If a physical LAN is unaffordable, then a logical VLAN is necessary.

Any network connection can be exploited by criminals, and digital intrusion can be used as a creative accomplice to physical intruders. They may enter the museum with security cards or fobs they have cloned by accessing your internal systems. When they enter restricted areas, they could override live cameras with a recording. Motion detectors could be disabled or set to false alarms that confuse security guards. Finally they may alter records in the collections database to simulate a loan, restoration, or other excuse for an item's absence. Much of the crime could be accomplished remotely from any computer in the world.

When valuables are at stake, regularly consider where systems might be vulnerable and take steps to mitigate the possibility of intrusion.

Sustainability

Sustainability is a crucial issue on every level of society. For museums it lies at the intersection of fiscal and social responsibility. Reducing energy usage and technological waste

TABLE 14.1 PCI DSS GUIDELINES

Build and Maintain a Secure Network	1. Install and maintain a firewall configuration to protect data.
	2. Do not use vendor-supplied defaults for system passwords and other security parameters.
Protect Cardholder Data	3. Protect stored data.
	4. Encrypt transmission of cardholder data and sensitive information across public networks.
Maintain a Vulnerability Management Program	5. Use and regularly update antivirus software.
	6. Develop and maintain secure systems and applications.
Implement Strong Access Control Measures	7. Restrict access to data by business need-to-know.
	8. Assign a unique ID to each person with computer access.
	9. Restrict physical access to cardholder data.
Regularly Monitor and Test Networks	10. Track and monitor all access to network resources and cardholder data.
	11. Regularly test security systems and processes.
Maintain an Information Security Policy	12. Maintain a policy that addresses information security.

lowers operating costs, and it also reduces the environmental budget humanity is spending against the future. Museums exert leadership across the social spectrum, and internal practices must be impeccable for them to maintain their moral authority.

For now many facets of IT are a necessary evil. Much of it is based on mining of metals and rare earths that produces considerable amounts of waste. Mining firms often ignore remedial measures while supporting despotic governments. Once embedded in machinery, these substances are highly polluting. The plastics that form chassis and circuit boards are little better. Manufacturing processes discard large amounts of toxic solvents, and machinery is delivered in sheaths of plastic, foam and cardboard that immediately enters the waste stream. Once installed, IT equipment draws large amounts of electricity, and it generates so much waste heat that equal amounts of energy are required to cool it. The efficiencies introduced by IT often lead to reductions in coveted jobs.

Changes in business practice often begin with customers, and museums are uniquely positioned to lead change. Unlike other large organizations, museums are expected to embody noncommercial values, and thus they can vocalize issues that may not be appropriate for a shareholder-driven company. Museums also have mechanisms for collegially developing best practices that can be translated into commercial demand for sustainable products.

It is important to consider the dilemma facing manufacturers. They are developing systems that use less power and generate less heat. At the same time, demands for higher performance push those indicators back up. Most computers and monitors are given Energy Star ratings, and these can help purchase decisions. Topics to consider when purchasing IT systems include:

- Power requirements
- Use of solvents
- Disassembly rating
- Manufacturer recycling

Bear in mind that manufacturers need customers who demand ecological sustainability to bring improved products to market.

Many of the practices detailed in this chapter have implications for sustainability. Ensure that all systems, even servers, are either switched off or enter low-power modes when possible. The temperature range of datacom centers has crept upward. While it is important to keep your equipment at the proper temperature, make sure you are not overcooling.

Upgrading computer systems is unavoidable, and newer systems are often more efficient than the models they replace. There are companies that specialize in the safest disposal possible, but it will be impossible to dispose of computers safely before manufacturing processes change radically. No process exists for complete recycling of computers and other electronic devices. Consider whether anyone in your staff or community, particularly disadvantaged sectors, could use outdated devices. Preparing computers for public distribution will cost more than discarding them, but it is the only way to keep them out of the waste stream. By offering free computers with training, probably in partnership with other organizations, you can also counter job losses due to automation.

Planning digital infrastructure offers many opportunities for building sustainability into your organization. It is important to keep one thing in mind. The best practices of today fall short of what is needed to avoid catastrophe. You are in a position to bring leadership, creativity and passion to critically important challenges.

DEVELOPING FLEXIBLE INFRASTRUCTURE FOR THE TWENTY-FIRST-CENTURY MUSEUM
Ali Hossaini Interviews Kevin Cunningham

Kevin Cunningham is the founder and Executive Artistic Director of 3-Legged Dog Media and Theater Group and 3LD Art & Technology Center in New York City.

AH: Could you please describe the sort of work 3LD does in museums?

KC: There is a desire among many museums to leverage digital communications, media, and interactive technology to update and expand their capacity, the depth and range of their offerings and their connection to the public. The A/V and so-called systems integration industry often relies on and promotes difficult-to-use, expensive, and unreliable systems to propagate a business model we call the Broken Box model. In this model software and hardware systems are locked out with proprietary technology that the museum doesn't have access to for maintenance and repair or the system uses a proprietary software base that the client cannot control or maintain. The business goal of the Broken Boxers is to create the necessity for long-term maintenance and content contracts with large institutions and to keep those institutions from developing internal capacity.

3-Legged Dog creates designs and technology solutions in the context of immersive experiences and interactive displays for museums that are built to allow the user to control and maintain their own complex multimedia displays if they so choose. 3LD uses common affordable, easily maintained, replaced, and upgraded hardware and affordable open SDK software (that we train the client to use). We also push the limits of artistic expression leveraging immersive, interactive, holographic, theatrical and cinematic techniques and modes to update, deepen, and expand museum displays and environments.

One of the things we bring to our designs is an interdisciplinary framework based in theatrical and cinematic practice. This gives our exhibitions a flow and arc that is unusual in museum displays. The same applies to our events, where we often bring in timing and flow from operatic, theatrical, or cinematic dramaturgical practice. This has had the effect, for example, of bringing the audience to tears at a brand launch.

AH: What are the biggest mistakes museums make when planning digital infrastructure?

KC: When we planned our 21st Century Art & Technology Center in Manhattan we interviewed thirty-two architects. We had a trick question for them: "How should we wire our 21st Century Art & Technology Center?" We got a plethora of answers, most apparently driven by experience with or relationships with the "professional" A/V industry. Each answer was more inappropriate and expensive than the next. The correct answer of course was "You shouldn't 'wire' your 21st Century Art & Technology Center because the wires are going to change or disappear in two years." I've seen many new museums build out and then have to have a capital campaign for a "technology upgrade" immediately after the main capital campaign was over because by the time construction was complete the so-called digital infrastructure was obsolete. We often use a tour specification for our "permanent" installations—that is, everything on wheels, open wire troughs instead of conduit, etc.

The second mistake we see is the creation of "permanent" infrastructure. This is based on a fallacy propagated by the A/V and construction industry that beefy and hardwired is "reliable." Sometimes hardwired "baked" systems are more reliable but they are also usually inflexible, unnecessarily expensive and often require long-term maintenance contracts or expensive proprietary programming or content production to remain fresh. When it comes time to upgrade to a higher standard, the system often must be completely replaced to accommodate basic updating, and because everything is "hardwired" we are now talking about a major demolition and renovation project. If your organization uses capital projects to generate additional cash flow this might be okay, but it is not necessary for a high-end flexible system.

AH: So you reject proprietary systems and hardwiring?

KC: When we see the word "proprietary" we see two things: (1) loss of control over our ability to adapt the technology (loss of flexibility) and (2) money flying out the window. Proprietary locked systems are innately inflexible and require specific proprietary digital standards that often require an unnecessary programming or content creator certified on the system (read expensive) and maintenance. Cloud-based storage systems or web-authorized software systems like the Adobe Suite or Vectorworks create similar difficulties. In some cases there are now no alternatives but to put your organization at the mercy of an abusive license agreement if you want to be able to keep up. Further, the pervasive use of proprietary systems drives up operating budgets and creates barriers to local, personal, or corporate control of media, technology, and content.

One of the biggest mistakes museums make is in thinking in terms of "digital infrastructure" as if the digital aspects of the museum were somehow separate from the other program and functional aspects of the museum. One of the main benefits of digital technology is its ability to work as an integrative connective tissue between physical structure and imagination and to integrate modes and pathways of communication.

We think of digital code as a sort of universal translator between systems and modes of expression. The museum building is a platform, stage or armature upon which the museum experience is built. Recent media techniques like video mapping and large-scale holographic projection can even make solid walls seem to be penetrable or transparent. So one of the big conceptual blockages is the long-held idea of the museum building itself as sacrosanct (this is especially true of historic sites and museums of memory). The new reality is that even heavily landmarked surfaces can be radically altered without any damage to the actual structure by using modern imaging technology, opening up new heretofore unheard-of possibilities for museum display.

AH: What is the alternative? How do you plan media-driven exhibitions?

KC: It helps to have guidelines that are followed from the design phase through to exhibition. When we specify a museum installation we follow certain principles:

1. The system should be moveable and reconfigurable with replaceable, upgradeable units so it can serve multiple exhibitions. (We generally use tour spec equipment and building platforms for museum installations—not "permanent" techniques.)

2. The system should be built on a software platform that can be configured for easy use by a novice or an everyday person. (Proprietary platforms for the most part are innately difficult to use—the "the broken box" business model mentioned above.)

3. The system should be easy to maintain and update by museum personnel with minimal training. (If you have to sign a maintenance contract, you should look twice at the system.)

4. The system should be expandable and reuseable for other exhibitions.

5. The core of the system should be a software engine that aids in the integration of multiple systems (i.e., lighting, sound, media, machine, and device control).

6. The content, digital hardware, and control standards should be common standards that are easy and inexpensive to produce and revise—preferably in-house.

7. Media should be designed for cross-platform deployment. This can be done by creating a workflow and formatting-standards protocol for content creation.

AH: What about the design and production of the media?

KH: The main thing is to use media and architecture to create a deep emotional connection rather than go for a more superficial "wow." Eliciting an emotional response to an exhibit does not have to be a distraction. In fact the wow factor and impressive digital effects should be integrated into the curatorial and dramaturgical structure of an exhibit so as to enhance the intellectual depth and pedagogic effectiveness of an exhibit. Other advice we give to artists and exhibit designers include:

- Hit the corners—design to the architecture for an immersive experience integrated into the existing architecture.
- Avoid "interactive experiences" that only allow one user at a time.
- The user should be seduced, not driven, through the experience.
- The "wow factor" is not just about high end, bright, and loud.
- Museum exhibitions are innately theatrical experiences; dramaturgy and direction are required for an emotional arc.

AH: How can museums create optimal conditions for digital/media installations?

KC: Most of the major innovation in museum exhibits in recent years has centered around the use of video, audio, and interactive technologies to enhance the experience and bring the experience out of the museum and into the world via media production, web-based or otherwise. Many facilities have a great opportunity for digital augmentation if they plan carefully—for example:

- Physical barriers to light need to be minimized or co-opted.
- Exterior light should be controllable via blinds or other methods.
- Avoid or adapt to steel framing or underground structures that block wireless signals.
- Electrical infrastructure should be flexible and have the capacity to accommodate things like bright projectors and theatrical and film lighting systems.
- The existing building structure should be able to easily accommodate rigging of heavy objects. This is a very common failing in new museums.
- Where possible, penetration and anchoring in all surfaces—floor, walls, and ceiling—should be permissible.

AH: How do institutions manage the costs associated with these projects?

KC: It is important for institutions to have an ongoing capital allocation for equipment and software. It is often more cost effective to purchase equipment than to rent it. The cost can be attached to capital budgets, sits positively on your balance sheet, and can be amortized. However, technology changes fast and resolution is addictive—people will notice if you are not up to date. The right equipment purchases can be leveraged over multiple exhibitions. The same projectors that created six displays for a large interior exhibit, for example, with the right software might also be used for an exterior mapping project on the façade for the gala exhibition.

Also museums can consider using smaller, more flexible contractors for development of content and exhibition design. They can be more cost effective and are often more advanced and innovative than larger, well-established contractors.

AH: What should museums look for in a production and exhibition agency?

KC: Make sure the agency has the skill sets you need. One recent extremely high-profile exhibit was an international publicity disaster because the museum hired innovative "LED artists" and tried to use them as immersive video designers. The result: They basically tried to cram Times Square into a museum gallery, blinding the audience and creating content that was improperly formatted for the video display surfaces. The images were warped and distorted, and the resulting exhibit was a major embarrassment to this very important institution.

Also, think twice about using an architect to design your exhibition. Architects can create interesting exhibitions but they are often used to a budget scale and building methods that are unnecessarily expensive as opposed to, for example, production designers for film or theater who are used to creating minor miracles on a budget and have an innately more appropriately interdisciplinary practice than most architects. There are of course several notable exceptions to this.

In summary I would say go with a company that

- has both artistic/aesthetic and technology expertise and a habit of innovating,
- is smallish but able to staff up for big projects,
- is determinedly interdisciplinary,
- demonstrates innovative thinking,
- is focused on useability rather than billability.

AH: What are some of the operational challenges you have come across that hamper the ability of cultural institutions to develop an immersive media project such as the ones you describe?

KC: There are several factors that prevent museums from leveraging new technologies to improve their reach and impact while controlling costs:

The number one impediment to innovation in museums is the outdated and byzantine administrative structure that builds up around larger institutions. This is true of major museums, libraries, and university-based facilities. In the same way that newspapers used to separate advertising and editorial, museums need to allow program staff to work with innovators in digital display and communications technology to push museum display into the twenty-first century. Administrators answerable to boards and the public are often risk averse. It is important to insulate program decisions from this kind of risk aversion if you want true innovation.

This relates to making decisions around staffing structure. A traditional projectionist or boardroom or conference center A/V tech is probably not going to be able to help your museum innovate in leveraging digital technology for more effective exhibitions. Practitioners from the art world and luxury marketing and advertising are constantly innovating, however, and can produce candidates for digital staffing that will be able to help the museum keep up and push the digital advantage. A modern digital creative staff can leverage digital technology in a way that increases the public profile of a museum; creates exhibitions that are richer, deeper, and more buzzworthy; and reduces the physical exhibition budget.

Related to this is the penchant for institutions to stick to outmoded ways of doing things because "this is the way we've always done it" or to use methods that avoid accountability. The CYA method. We worked on an extremely large exhibit for one of the leading institutions in the world and for the entire duration of the eight-month-long project we did not have a basic shared production schedule. We were told that no exhibit in that institution had ever had one.

AH: In your opinion, what makes a show impressive?

KC: Almost all of our exhibits utilize state-of-the-art, large-scale, high-resolution moving-image techniques that can be very impressive, but the old stage adage "If you can't hear it you can't see it and vice versa" also means that all of our exhibition teams also include a qualified sound designer who is also an acoustic engineer. Not only do many museums have appalling acoustics that need to be addressed, but sound gives dimension and flow to moving images and can create whole new layers of meaning beyond just voiceover or a guide track. In addition, shaped sound can be a very effective tool in controlling attention from the viewer and timing of audience flow-through. Making sure that the exhibit is acoustically viable is a very important aspect of exhibition design that is completely ignored in far too many cases.

Our exhibition design usually requires the client to hire us to design all aspects of the exhibit so that the design is truly integrated. To really move the audience, all elements must work together.

Once an integrated design is ensured, we bring in dramaturgy and a director with film or theatrical experience to help us create an arc for the exhibit. In one instance we created one of the largest, highest video projection surfaces ever built. Fifteen thousand square feet of projection with a pixel ratio five times the resolution of IMAX. This was impressive, but what made the audience weep, overwhelmed with beauty, was the pacing of the show overseen by a professional opera director.

KEY TAKEAWAYS: DIGITAL INFRASTRUCTURE

1. Fast, reliable Internet connections make it possible to outsource many IT functions into "the (Internet) cloud." Pros for IT outsourcing include reduced stress on planning, a lower price as you don't pay for unused capacity, less risk associated with experimentation, and the ability to scale rapidly. Cons include vulnerability to loss of Internet connectivity, limits to customization, and dependence on outside providers. It is, however, possible to do partial outsourcing.

2. IT infrastructure consists of:

    - An Internet Service Provider that provides connectivity to other networks.
    - Physical infrastructure that includes: servers, switches, routers, and firewalls; Ethernet cable for a local area network (LAN); WiFi; and network access points (e.g. workspaces, electronic points of sale, exhibits, public WiFi, etc.).
    - Logical infrastructure that includes software, address and communication protocols, databases and virtual servers, virtual switches, and virtual LANs (VLANs).
    - Operational infrastructure that encompasses organization, staff, processes, and procedures.

3. Network security is an ever growing issue that requires full funding and continuous attention. Every organization should maintain a security policy that is regularly reviewed (no less than twice a year) by a person or committee with direct responsibility for implementation. Vital information regarding collections and personal data (staff, visitors, and members) and retail information like payment card numbers must be secured according to the latest standards available through national regulations and industry groups such as PCI DSS.

4. When developing exhibition infrastructure for digital interaction and immersive video, it is best to avoid proprietary systems that lock your museum

into a single vendor. Software should be based on open source standards for content management and systems control. Hardware should be based on units that can be easily replaced, upgraded, and reused in different contexts and with different makes and models.

5. An organization can improve sustainability of their IT infrastructure by considering the power requirements of their equipment, whether or not the equipment uses solvents in their manufacturing, the equipment's disassembly rating, and the opportunities for manufacturer recycling.

Planning for Digital Revenues

Ngaire Blankenberg and Ali Hossaini

Museums are increasingly looking to digital technology as a way to enhance their revenue generation efforts and transform their business models. Taken individually and in the short term, museum websites, digitization programs, apps, public monitors, WiFi, social marketing and other digital initiatives can seem like cost centers. However, when taken as a whole and with a more long-term view, digital technologies become investments with business as well as social returns. After an initial set-up period, investments in digital platforms should be judged by the same standards as investments in buildings, exhibitions, and retail. Returns on investment should be clear and measurable and demonstrably lead to the museum fulfilling its mission. In this chapter, we look at how digital technologies can increase a museum's earned income, as well as support relationship management—an essential aspect of cultivating and maintaining donors. Digital technologies can also be used to support a museum's reporting efforts to its funders—an increasingly stringent requirement of public and private funders alike.

Better Business Models

Museums around the world are looking at new business models to support their growth and ensure their long-term sustainability in the face of uncertain funding. Although new technology-supported innovations such as crowdfunding and content syndication are providing new forms of revenue, there are few changes in the overall business model of the museum sector. In chapter 2, Ali Hossaini describes the omnichannel approach as the beginning of a shift that may in time see radical transformation in museums in much the same way as YouTube has transformed television or Airbnb has transformed the hotel industry. But for the foreseeable future, technology's main role in museums is to improve the functioning of business models that already exist.

Many museums are already shifting from being government line departments to becoming not-for-profit institutions, with autonomous decision making and operations, as well as the requirement to generate their own revenue. Although this model may be more insecure than being assured of government subsidy, it can also be seen to enhance a museum's value proposition. As part of civil society, museums measure their worth differently than in the government and in the commercial sector, and their business models and sources of funding reflect this. Being "not-for-profit" enables museums to retain their very essence as organizations for public benefit—rather than to benefit shareholders, as with brand experiences, theme parks, or as instruments of government policy. As not-for-profit institutions, their viability and their sustainability lie in their ability to balance revenue and expenses in order to require a "manageable level of subsidy."[1]

Technology can support the four activities that generate revenue for museums—government grants, private donations, earned revenue, and investment income, and it can also support operational efficiencies in order to reduce expenses.

Evaluation and Reporting

Government grants continue to be one of the biggest, if not *the* biggest source of funding for museums around the world. Like the rest of the not-for-profit sector, long required to demonstrate their "evidence base" or "social impact," museums are required to demonstrate the impact of their grants. Private and public sector funders link the arts and culture sector to broader agendas to deliver specific economic and social outcomes—whether for urban regeneration, tourism, social cohesion, education, or health and well-being. Others reject this form of instrumentalism and seek rather to validate museums and culture for their intrinsic value and the benefits they provide for individuals.[2] In both instances, museums that can demonstrate their benefit can make a stronger case for ongoing support.

Many chapters in this book reiterate the need to establish key performance indicators on a strategic level throughout the museums. A museum's indicators or strategic objectives reflect the values of museum decision makers and, in many instances, of funders. How KPIs are assessed or evaluated can in part be tracked through data analytics if they are set up and monitored correctly—however, data will only tell half the story.

Qualitative assessment, whether to build empathy in order to design a meaningful user experience (chapter 12) or to support participant-driven learning (chapter 6) is an equally important way of measuring a museum's success. These methodologies use digital technologies in other ways—for video observation, for example, or to access social media and online museum communities. Much work within the digital humanities and in education is being done to establish standards and definitions to ensure these are rigorous and accepted as "evidence."

Whether through using data, qualitative evaluation; or, ideally, a combination of the two, assessment, evaluation, and reporting are activities that support development.

Well-designed digital tools simplify collection, analysis, and presentation of the outcomes of such evaluation, and help to make the case for continued funding. Transparency is a selling point for development programs, whether for government funders or smaller donors.

Museums can measure engagement on multiple scales, and it is now possible for everyone to understand the impact of their support. By issuing personalized reports that respond to a supporter's interests, museums can build long-term relationships where trust assists the hard work of renewals.

> **KEY PERFORMANCE INDICATORS**
>
> Examples of key performance indicators include:
>
> - Characteristics of web visitors such as unique visits, volume of target demographics, user satisfaction ("did you find what you were seeking?"), and engagement metrics such as dwell time.
> - Subscriptions to newsletters and other online campaigns.
> - Social media engagement measured by likes, friends, fans, shares, comments and other indicators.
> - Media coverage reported by absolute number of mentions, links into your digital properties, and online referrals.
> - Conversions of digital touchpoints into a user journey that deepens engagement through a visit, membership, purchase, social sharing or other museum-defined outcome.
> - Trading income that is a definitive outcome of higher engagement.
> - Retention rates of staff and volunteers measured by length of service.

Cultivating and Managing Donors

Cultivating donors requires record keeping, high levels of personal attention, and creative production of events and other donor rewards. Not-for-profits tend to be quite poor managers of donor relationships, leading to customer retention rates far below those in the commercial sector.[3] In fact, the main reasons why many donors stop giving to cultural organizations is because they were not thanked for a previous gift, were not asked to donate again, or received no or poor communication about the impact of their donation.[4] This points to a need for cultural organizations to prioritize the communication they have with their donors.

Customer Relationship Management

Customer relationship management (CRM) is a strategy and a software tool to manage all of a museums interactions and relationships with its community. CRM software stores donor and visitor identities alongside a history of their transactions, preferences, and complaints. It is therefore an extremely important tool that can be used to personalize a museum's engagement with its prospective or existing donors. It creates personal bonds by enabling staff and automated services to speak to donors and visitors about their direct concerns. It also creates efficiencies throughout museum departments to share information about individuals who want to be involved with your museum. Continuity is essential to development, and robust software provides solutions by anticipating different use cases.

CRM software can integrate data related to giving histories of individuals, donations per marketing campaign, participation in programs, visitation history, retail transactions, and special events ticket purchases in one integrated platform.

CRM applications can be server based or cloud based and are increasingly flexible to enable them to be integrated into other systems. A key aspect of CRM software is real-time reporting tools. Numbers can be quickly assembled for reports, and, in the event of turnover, new staff can easily access departmental goals and donor profiles. Development often happens spontaneously, and it is important for staff to avoid embarrassing gaps in knowledge. For instance, if a museum officer runs into a donor at a party, he or she can quickly review the donor's specifics on a smartphone during a break.

Consider the following points before introducing CRM to your museum.

- **Strategy:** CRM requires buy-in from teams across your organization.
  - What is the business justification for developing CRM within your museum?
  - Do you have a strategy and, just as important, the leadership to harmonize processes that may have been managed separately in the past?
- **Implementation:** Data is only useful when analyzed. It needs to be interpreted into patterns and trends.
  - Does your museum have someone who can interpret results into reports that inspire colleagues to take action?

- **Maintenance:** CRM applications are demanding pieces of software. Configuring data feeds and databases requires skilled administrators.

  - Does your IT department have the capacity to perform this work? If not this work can be outsourced. An outside agency can perform the work to integrate data from your website, ticketing, ecommerce, membership, and other public-facing systems into the CRM database. The CRM application itself can be hosted on an outside cloud service. However, you will still need someone in your organization who can manage outside vendors.

Understanding donor motivations is another important facet of development. Digital tools can be used to identify donor interests by cross-indexing files. Special incentives can be developed more easily, and donors with common interests can be grouped for events and other targeted campaigns.

Membership

Most museums have membership programs. CRM software can make them easier to administer by automating member privileges. Exclusive invitations, free tickets, and exhibition catalogs can be released with a few keystrokes. Member assistance can be readily offered, and issues can be flagged until resolved.

Digital CRM also lowers the threshold for adding new membership categories, incentives, and service levels. Members can be offered a degree of care previously reserved for donors. Communications can be targeted to member interests, and messaging personalized with less effort. Membership brings privileges such as early entry or members-only events, and similar incentives can be offered on digital properties.

Museums can adopt practices that have served other sectors well. Loyalty programs are well-established in airlines, hotels, and retail, and, by combining CRM with tracking, museums can reward people for engagement. This can go beyond purchases to include visits to exhibitions, lectures, and education programs. Loyalty programs offer incentives for engagement, but they also promote awareness by reminding members of their individual benefits.

Crowdsourcing

Crowdsourcing is a new form of revenue generation that is supported by digital technology, including by some CRM applications. Crowdsourced funding is when a large number of individuals donate toward a project or institution via a digital platform—such as Kickstarter, Indigogo, or Crowdfunder. The platform has a credit card processor so it can accept money directly, and a website to describe and "sell" the project. Crowdsourcing is done through campaigns that have a specific goal and duration. Individuals can track how far away the project is from reaching its goal, and in some instances, they do not have to "pay out" unless the goal is reached.

Museums have used crowdsourcing campaigns to purchase a particular item for the collections, conserve or restore an artifact or building, or fund an exhibition or public program. In some instances, corporate sponsors can be asked to provide match funding to an amount that is raised online, or a museum may use a celebrity endorsement and mainstream and social media in order to raise interest and momentum for crowdsourcing campaigns.

Crowdsourcing is an exciting new way for museums to generate funds, particularly if the following tips are followed:

- **Clear Messaging:** A crowdsourcing campaign is about connecting with members of the public to persuade to support you. A clear goal and messaging regarding the "why" of the goal is important. This may require that the marketing departments and the fundraising department work closely together to generate copy, develop video, and include appropriate imaging. Good video is essential for most crowdsourcing.

- **Adequate Resources:** Crowdsourcing is not a quick fix and requires the same resources as any other campaign. People need to be responded to quickly and efficiently; marketing needs to be consistent and plentiful. A campaign manager should be appointed to oversee the campaign.

- **Start with a Bang:** Crowdsourcing campaigns are like an opening of an exhibition or a museum. The degree to which they generate interest and excitement at the outset is the key to their success. All marketing and engagement channels should be used to generate anticipation for the launch and the campaign. Social media is particularly important in this regard.

- **Keep the Campaign Fresh with Updates:** Campaigns have peaks and lows, and it is important that momentum is sustained. Updates, new media, and new marketing pushes are essential throughout the campaign. Tracking the progress of the campaign is important so the lows can be mitigated.

- **Continue to Accept Funding Offline:** The hype of a campaign may inspire donors to contribute, but they may prefer not to do so online. The museum should be prepared for this and to continue to track such activity in their CRM.

Sponsors

Corporations are not monoliths, and they support museums for reasons that include brand identification, targeted marketing, local outreach, corporate responsibility, education, and public awareness. Each of these motivations may be handled from a different department, and several departments, each with its own agenda, may be involved with a sponsorship agreement.

> **KEY TERMS**
>
> **RETURN ON INVESTMENT**
>
> Return on investment (ROI) is a calculation of the benefits, usually financial, of the money spent on a project, staff, or other initiative.

Digital tools can help development officers manage the complexities of sponsor relations. They can automatically generate invoices, complimentary tickets, event invitations, and thank you notes. Aside from obvious functions, and the reporting features discussed above, CRM applications can also track the company's **return on investment** (ROI) on sponsored programs. By linking CRM to other databases—for example, visitor numbers—you can easily report impressions and other measures of engagement. You can also work with corporate partners to develop custom measures that meet their specific needs.

Earned Income

Every museum has unique touchpoints where it can generate revenue, but the areas given below are open to almost any institution.

Admissions and Ticketing

There is an ongoing and rigorous debate about the benefits and downfalls of charging admission. Nevertheless, for those who do charge admissions, ticketing is both an important source of earned income and a primary service channel to connect with visitors.

Admissions and ticketing is often the first point of contact between a museum and its visitor, and their first point of entry into a CRM database.

As with almost all integrated systems, admissions and ticketing systems were originally developed to serve one purpose, and other uses have been added. While there are a wide variety of reliable integrated system solutions from vendors around the world, it is noteworthy that two of the leading ticket system vendors worldwide (Skidata from Austria, and Siriusware from the United States—now part of Accesso) originated in the higher-margin ski industry, and gradually migrated to systems that may work well for a wide variety of functions, and in particular attraction/museum ticketing is now an important sales channel for both vendors.

Through industry consolidation, there are essentially two streams of system vendors that dominate the industry today: technology-driven solutions and software-driven solutions. In response to growing demand among potential clients, industry leaders from both streams have developed products and services that can serve most clients' needs, including full CRM integration and virtually every type of revenue management module, including membership, retail, and food and beverage sales, as well as web-based ticketing modules, among other functions.

Key technology-driven system attributes include built-for-purpose robust point-of-sale (POS) and printing systems that can handle high transaction volumes, as well as access control functions such as automated kiosks and turnstiles. Simplified and streamlined transaction management may allow for reduced front-of-house staff costs, freeing up the front-of-house staff to focus on serving visitors' information needs, rather than more time-consuming ticket-taking operations and direct sales/POS functions.

Conversely, software-driven systems are most often built on widely available operating system platforms such as Microsoft Windows, with some vendors now also moving to mobile platforms such as Android, the mobile platform freely licensed by Google, as new markets migrate toward a preference for app functionality over desktop/laptop-based systems and interfaces. These industry-standard platforms may allow for easier integration with legacy systems, and, for example, for smaller museum clients, multiple back-office functions can be operated on the same PC system, reducing overall hardware investment costs.

A museum or cultural destination considering moving toward an integrated digital ticketing and admissions system may be well advised to look beyond immediate solution needs to the slow and steady growth of the CRM model, and the wide variety of vendor solutions are available to ensure that virtually every key function and revenue channel can be fully integrated in planning an organization's future operations.

PACKAGING FOR TOURISM

Tourists consistently rate museums as one of the top reasons to travel, and tourist bureaus, tour operators, convention centers, and hotels are natural partners for museum outreach. Joint marketing campaigns can increase visits to a museum, and, as an added benefit, they drive digital visitors who may travel elsewhere that year. Partnerships may be managed through a variety of project management applications, and, by agreeing to common data policies, partners can generate useful data about what makes success. In order for your museum to support tourism, consider the following;

- Strong collateral drives marketing campaigns, and no one is better positioned than museums to provide it. Ensure that partners have access to high-resolution images; well-written descriptions; and short, interesting video clips about your museum.

- Supply destination marketing partners with links to independent reviews that can be embedded alongside your professional images. Feed them collateral about upcoming events with as much lead time as possible.

- Package offers make life easier for tourists and can provide additional sources of revenue. Review your ticketing systems to see if they can interoperate with partners. If so, tour operators can sell your tickets, and you could encourage uptake with packages of your own that include exhibitions guides, restaurant reservations, and other services. Operators should also have current information about the museum for distribution to their customers.

Ecommerce

Gift shops do more than generate revenue, they are an alternative entry point to your museum's collections, and they are exhibitions in their own right. The services provided by museum gift shops are underappreciated. Visitors curate their own collections in the gift shop, and they can share inspiration with others who may never visit on their own. Affordable museum reproductions let people bring great art, design, and learning into their lives.

Ecommerce extends the reach of your museum even further. Items in your online shop will appear in search results unrelated to your museum, and you can reach entirely new audiences through distribution deals. Shopping is an alternative visitor experience, but your store can build interest in collections and programs when shoppers seek to learn more about products.

Risk is omnipresent in business operations, but it can be minimized. Whether you are starting online or expanding your ambitions, find out what works before committing substantial funds. Outsource as much as possible in the beginning so you can change course. There are many outsourcing options for ecommerce, so build evidence before making capital investments.

PLANNING AN ONLINE SHOP

The rules for building an effective website hold strictly for ecommerce. Usability and responsiveness in every sense of the term are critical because losing even 1 percent of your visitors has financial impact. Some primary considerations are:

- Ensuring your UI (**user interface**) is easy to understand.
- Ensuring your UX (**user experience**) is consistent.
- Ensuring your UJ (**user journey**) ends in a purchase.

KEY TERMS

USER INTERFACE (UI)

A user interface is a control panel that enables a human to interact with a computer or other piece of machinery.

USER EXPERIENCE (UX)

User experience defines the feelings, emotions, and level of engagement provoked by a website.

USER JOURNEY (UJ)

User journey uses narrative terms to describe how a visitor passes through a website from beginning to departure.

4K

4K is an ultra-high-resolution video format that is replacing HDTV as the standard for television and exhibitions.

Invest in high-quality professional images of your products. Go well beyond what you need now. With **4K** monitors making fast inroads, standards for resolution keep improving. Follow the example of retail stores that enable customers to zoom and view images from many perspectives. Let people rotate objects in three dimensions.

Fulfillment is a critical factor in customer satisfaction. Standards for promptness, returns, and customer service are high in ecommerce, and it will be difficult for in-house staff to match the efficiency of large companies. It is almost essential to outsource management of supply chain and deliveries through a process called drop shipping. Outsourcing has the additional benefit of saving investments in stock and storage space.

ONLINE SALES STRATEGIES

Best practices in ecommerce are similar to those in physical stores and can be summarized as follows:

- It always makes sense to foreground your best sellers, but it is important to test whether online visitors have the same buying habits as visitors to your building. Iconic items in your collection have perennial interest, and these can be the basis for a range of products that can change seasonally.

- Uniqueness and authenticity can distinguish your products and also enhance your museum's brand profile. Your museum's brand itself may be marketable, and it can transform mundane items into desirable objects that spread awareness in everyday contexts.

- Exhibitions drive sales, and the online equivalent is reviews. Communications and PR departments should let the retail team know when reviews appear so they can foreground merchandise and take out advertising. Use contextual links to make sure exhibition catalogs and reproductions appear alongside each other.

- Make sure every page has sufficient information. Contextual sales tools like best sellers, related items and saved items should be available everywhere. Many people will find your website through search engines, and they should be able to engage fully wherever they land. This includes links to your main website. Many ecommerce hosts will treat your website as alien. If you outsource, find a solution that incorporates your branding, design, and navigation.

- Ticketing is another resource for contextual sales. Develop ways to work tickets, exhibition catalogs and related merchandise into your sales paths. Browsing categories should reflect the organization of the museum. Ensure, too, that shoppers can search for objects but also for results based on exhibitions and collections.

- Social media amplify any marketing effort. Standard techniques include encouraging people to announce their purchase, advertising buys and building presence directly into social networks. Best practices for social media evolve rapidly, and you should plan for a dedicated effort that is constantly revising your approach.

- Distribution deals can increase your reach considerably. Shoppers may never think of your site as a first-stop buying destination, and the marketing advantages of ecommerce sites offset the cost of retail commissions.

> **KEY TERMS**
>
> **APPLICATION PROGRAMMING INTERFACE**
>
> An application programming interface (API) is a software specification that describes how to communicate with a particular database or application. It is a powerful tool for bridging applications that would otherwise be incompatible.

INTEGRATE YOUR RETAIL PLATFORMS

It is not a given that your physical and online stores will interoperate. Bringing cohesion to your retail efforts requires foresight, planning, and technical development. However, the rise of EPOS (electronic point of sale systems) is enabling online and physical stores to share the same digital infrastructure. Combining EPOS with CRM creates the basis for flexibility, innovation, and powerful new tools for visitor engagement. It is possible to link legacy systems using **application programming interfaces** (APIs), but a growing number of multichannel retail applications are available from software vendors. Many have a modular structure that can be adapted for use in different environments.

Sophisticated EPOS brings the advantages of ecommerce in-house. Pop-up shops can be easily opened, for instance, at the exit of a blockbuster exhibition or outdoors during mild weather, and the retail potential of different areas can be tested. Advance ticket sales is one area where ecommerce supports visitation. Buyers commit to a visit, and they may spend more when they arrive because they have already absorbed the cost of the ticket. Innovative offers can be easily programmed into sales points, and the system can recognize members, donors, and concessionary groups such as students and seniors.

KEY TERMS

PCI DSS

PCI DSS is the acronym for Payment Card Industry Data Security Standards, and it refers to a code of practices mandated by major credit and debit card providers to maximize the security of financial transactions.

SECURITY

Ecommerce is a major target for cybercriminals. Theft of payment card numbers, addresses, and other sensitive information continues unabated, and the **PCI DSS** security protocols grow stricter every year. You may be fined for security breaches, and it is necessary to review all your procedures for PCI DSS compliance. (See chapter 14 for more information about security and PCI DSS standards.)

Vulnerability to cybercrime and its repercussions constitutes an important argument for outsourcing some or all of your ecommerce operations. It is important to consult your organization's Information Security Policy when planning your ecommerce operations (also in chapter 14).

Licensing

Licensing images is a time-honored way for museums to generate income. Digital technologies expand its potential by introducing efficiencies at every stage. Collections are being digitized. Publications can be reproduced as e-books or printed on demand. Artifacts and images in museums find their way into housewares, fashion, architecture, advertising, and a host of industries. With the advent of 3D printing, people can ever more easily purchase and personalize replicas of sculptures and artifacts. Everything is searchable by potential customers anywhere on the planet.

Good planning is necessary to realize the potential of digital licensing. Key considerations include:

- Collections should be digitized to the highest standards, and objects should be scanned in 3D, if possible.
- File formats should be in common use, and files should be tagged with keywords within consistent, global taxonomies.
- Databases should have APIs that make them easily accessible by partner search engines.

Rather than manage everything in house, it may make sense to assign rights to one or more clearinghouses. But bear in mind that some organizations seek to exploit rights holders as well as rights, and carefully review deals before proceeding. Future value of rights could increase considerably, and your museum should always retain ultimate control of its intellectual property.

Conclusion

Museums need to do what they can to be sustainable while preserving their not-for-profit status. They are not and should not be commercial entities, and therefore their revenue sources and targets should not be tied to market-related criteria. Educating donors about the kind of value they provide and ensuring they have measures, indicators, and robust evaluation to back this up is one of the most important challenges of the museum community. At the same time, museums need to be alert about disruption. Even if the precise value of that content is subject to debate, the fact that cultural content has value is recognized in many sectors, and disruption is as likely to come from players from media, entertainment, education, tourism, or advertising industries as it is from those already in the cultural world. Digital will almost certainly play a big part in this—and holds huge potential to completely change the business models of museums and the resources they hold. Museums that are digitally literate at the very least, and digital leaders at the most and who collaborate with others within and outside the sector have the greatest change of staying ahead of the curve.

💡 KEY TAKEAWAYS: PLANNING FOR DIGITAL REVENUES

1. Museums are using digital technologies to enhance their business models; however, innovation is still needed.

2. Evaluations and reporting are key to fundraising—whether from public or private sector. A museum's strategic objectives should be reflected in all data collection and reporting.

3. A customer relationship management system (CRM) greatly enhances the ability of museums to track, personalize, maintain, and strengthen engagement with members and donors.

4. CRM can also support ticketing, tourism, ecommerce, and licensing—which are all important options for earned revenue.

5. Crowdsourcing is a new and interesting form of revenue generation that relies on a digital platform.

Notes

1. This is the criterion that is used at consulting firm Lord Cultural Resources in preparing feasibility studies for cultural clients.

2. For an interesting discussion on cultural value see Geoffrey Crossick and Patrycja Kaszynska, *Understanding the Value of Arts and Culture: The AHRC Cultural Value Project* (Wiltshire, UK: Arts and Humanities Research Council, 2016).

3. Allyson Kapin, "Strategies to Increase Nonprofit Donor Retention Rates," accessed October 10, 2016, http://www.care2services.com/care2blog/strategies-to-increase-nonprofit-donor-retention-rates.

4. Colleen Dilenschneider, "Why Donors Stop Giving Money to Organizations," *Know Your Own Bone* (blog), accessed October 7, 2016, http://colleendilen.com/2016/04/20/why-donors-stop-giving-money-to-cultural-organizations-data/. See US data quoted within.

5. Diana Pan and Manish Engineer, "The 360-Degree View: Why an Integrated CRM Platform Is Important in Growing a Museum's Membership Program," *Museums and the Web Asia 2015*, accessed October 7, 2016, http://mwa2015.museumsandtheweb.com/paper/the-360-degree-view-why-an-integrated-crm-platform-is-important-in-growing-a-museums-membership-program/.

Afterword
Digital Placemaking

Ali Hossaini

As we invest in digital platforms, we should consider the "clicks not bricks" logic that drives investments in websites, streaming video, and social media. By pushing value into the online cloud, digital technologies flatten the competitive landscape. A flat world opens avenues to exciting new services, but the resulting ecology also removes local advantage. By lowering natural barriers to competition, efficient digital networks encourage the dominance of megabrands over small organizations that thrive locally. Amazon, Google, Facebook, and a handful of other companies are undermining the diversity of each of their sectors. Could we face a similar situation in the museum sector? Could a few "super-brands" become dominant digital destinations?

At first, museums adapted to digital technology by building websites. But the web is a big place where audiences are hard to find. Marketing imperatives are driving museum content to Google, Facebook, Twitter, and YouTube—firms driven by profit, not mission. Almost perversely, digital empowerment of individuals creates a market that favors large commercial brands. Only a few organizations have sufficient scale to push their own agenda in this environment. Social media drives aggregation, and aggregation drives consolidation. Anyone who ignores the commercial networks is left out.

How can museums benefit from digital technology? Equally important, how can museums, especially smaller museums, exercise leadership in a world of megabrands? The former rely on adaptation—a process that is underway—but the latter rely on innovation. To state the obvious, innovation is doing what has not been done before. Where can museums blaze trails—ideally through a terrain that plays to their advantage?

Three factors stand out—mobility, sociability, and place.

- Mobility is well-established, but it has far to go before innovation plateaus. By some measures, the majority of online activity is already on mobile devices. "Anywhere, anyplace" has implications far beyond what is currently available.

- Social applications underlie many disruptive technologies, and their potential for public-facing organizations is clear. Museums tend to underestimate how profoundly social experiences in their buildings can impact and be impacted by digital channels.

- Place may be the most unique strength of museums. Taken collectively the vast public investment in museums provides a counterweight to even the largest private companies.

By developing these three factors, museums could lead the next wave of convergence, and they could introduce a new medium for engaging audiences: digital placemaking.

What do we want from a digital place? Museums are beloved. They live in the centers of cities and the hearts of audiences who visit them for excellence in curation, presentation, and entertainment. Unfortunately many museums are behind the technology curve and offer digital experiences that lag behind expectations being created elsewhere. By weaving digital technologies into the experience of their buildings, exhibitions, and social opportunities, and by including visitors in the design of these experiences, museums can offer unique, leading-edge programs that play to existing and future strengths.

The ingredients for digital placemaking are already in hand. The smartphones carried by the majority of museum visitors are inherently social. Museums need to meet smartphone users halfway by engaging them in situ. Museums already possess the means to do so: public WiFi. At present WiFi is offered to visitors as a necessary free service where everyone goes their separate way.

Travelers know that airports, hotels, and trains use a WiFi splash screen, aka a captive portal, to briefly command the attention of users. Museums can adopt the same technique to address people through a channel that is both intimate and public. Give people the Internet, but let them "exit through the gift shop" by offering the best of your digital en route. Use WiFi to offer content throughout your museum, use location awareness to make sure it is relevant to the visitor's precise location, and coordinate it with monitors and digital signage. Maybe there is a deal on tickets to Cezanne, a call to share selfies with the T-Rex, or a live Q&A with the curator of Greek sculpture.

The driving imperative behind mobility, sociability, and placemaking is choice: people choose the experience they want, wherever and whenever they want it. But digital is not just about on demand content. Digital experiences can be tailored for individuals who form a relationship with the person or institution that offers specific content that makes them laugh or cry, answers questions about their interest, inspires creativity, or helps them understand their world. Museums should build on what they know about visitors to bring immediacy to the visitor experience. They should create personal, not public, interactions.

Personal means letting people control content and interactions. People typically walk into museums with companions. They speak to one another about whatever they choose, look at what interests them, eat when hungry, and rest when tired. Physical places support freedom, **bridging**, and **bonding**. They are places where you meet new people while connecting more deeply with the ones you know. Digital places should offer the same freedom.

By linking WiFi to content, collections, and relationship management systems, museums can combine the best of the physical and virtual experiences—creating flexible, interactive places that respond to people as individuals, couples and groups.

> **KEY TERMS**
>
> **BRIDGING AND BONDING**
>
> These two terms were coined by Robert Putnam in his book *Bowling Alone*. "Bridging" refers to connecting with people who are different to you (networks within a heterogeneous group), and "bonding" refers to strengthening a connection with people who are similar to you (social network of a homogenous group). Both are ways to strengthen social capital—the resources acquired through relationships with others.

But this is only the beginning. The reality is we do not know what a digital place looks like, what it will do, and what benefits it will offer. In parallel to other sectors that range from retail to government, the mature form of digital interaction is something that museum professionals and the broader world, including the visiting public, need to work out in coming years. Progress may come from unexpected quarters. A quirky game may take the world by surprise, then leave models for more serious programs in its wake.

There is little doubt that museums—and other organizations, some yet to be invented—will evolve new platforms for presenting artistic, scientific, and historical content. Smartphones are notoriously distracting, but new mobile platforms will be less intrusive, and they will co-evolve with the Internet of Things. These emerging platforms will work particularly well for museums. As objects that cannot speak for themselves are activated, people can collaborate with each other and museum experts to create new experiences—which is the essence of placemaking. Rather than play out solely online, digital leadership relies on a museum-centric strategy of *clicks and bricks* where investments align virtual spaces with physical places. As the authors of this volume strongly imply, museums should consider themselves part of networks where content generated by collections, exhibitions, researchers, educational programs, and even visitors is available globally through any digital channel. An emerging discipline of digital placemaking could provide strategic guidelines for well-defined strands of investment in cultural organizations that venture forth into the digital cloud but circle back to well-loved places within neighborhoods and communities.

By remembering the unique ingredient of place, and ensuring it drives digital strategy, museums can maintain their natural advantages in a world that offers a heady mix of disruption, misplaced optimism, and stunning opportunity.

Glossary

4K: An ultra-high resolution video format that is replacing HDTV as the standard for television and exhibitions.

access point: A WiFi transceiver that enables any enabled device to access a local network and the Internet if the local network allows.

actionable data: Information that can be viewed, interpreted, and acted upon. This is contrasted with data that is not actionable because of one of many possible reasons, such as it was collected poorly, does not answer the question it was set out to ask, or is not used due to lack of stakeholder interest.

adaptive learning: Learning . . . accomplished through "adapt[ing] the presentation of material in response to student performance. It can be embedded into a computer-based and/or online educational system that captures fine-grained data and uses learning analytics to enable human tailoring of responses."[1]

agile development: A form of project management traditionally used in software development that helps teams respond to unpredictability through incremental, iterative work cycles and empirical feedback.[2]

algorithm: A routine or process for performing a calculation that generates a change of state or result.

analytics: The discipline of gathering, interpreting, and positioning data so it offers meaningful insights into the behavior of users in a given medium.

app / application: A software program. App was initially used to describe small programs used for mobile devices, but the term is also sometimes used for larger pieces of software.

application programming interface (API): A software specification that describes how to communicate with a particular database or application. It is a powerful tool for bridging applications that would otherwise be incompatible.

augmented reality (AR): A technology that layers a digital image onto a real-world view using a mobile or other form of device.

bandwidth: The amount of information that can be carried by a digital channel or communications medium in one second.

beta: A preliminary version of a software program (or application) that is tested by users not involved in its production in order to identify potential problems.

biometrics: Technologies that measure, collect, and transmit information based on the user's physiological characteristics, such as face recognition, fingerprints, or iris scan.

Bluetooth: Radio technology that allows for communication and information to be wirelessly exchanged between devices.

born digital: Describes items or collections created in a computer or another digital format; for example, digital photographs or computer art.

bridging and bonding: These two terms were coined by Robert Putnam in his book *Bowling Alone*. Bridging refers to connecting with people who are different to you (networks within a heterogeneous group), and bonding refers to strengthening a connection with people who are similar to you (social network of a homogenous group). Both are ways to strengthen social capital—the resources acquired through relationships with others.

cache: Data stored temporarily so as to improve response time or integrity of the experience should a connection to the system be lost.

captive portal: A web page that pops up automatically when someone logs into WiFi.

Cat5 / Cat6: Cable used to transmit Ethernet signals within a facility.

change management: Methodologies for implementing organizational transition that improve the likelihood of success.

channels: A group of traffic sources of the same type. For example, the "social" channel would include Facebook, Twitter, Pinterest, and so on.

click-through rate (CTR): Percentage of people who clicked on one or more links in an email.

cloud / cloud services: Many services can be rendered over the Internet from enormous warehouses of servers. Despite their large physical size (and equally large electricity bills), these servers are invisible to end users and hence called "the Cloud."

CMS: Most commonly refers to content management system, a software application used to publish content to networks. Within the museum sector, it can also mean collections management system, which is a software application used to itemize, detail, and track collections.

constructivism and constructionism: "The word constructionism is a mnemonic for two aspects of the theory of science education underlying this project. From constructivist theories of psychology we take a view of learning as a reconstruction rather than as a transmission of knowledge. Then we extend the idea of manipulative materials to the idea that learning is most effective when part of an activity the learner experiences as constructing a meaningful product."[3]

conversion rate: The percentage of users who take a desired action; for example, visiting your website, buying a ticket, or browsing the online collection.

crowdsourcing: Crowdsourcing is a process whereby something is accomplished through outsourcing to a crowd of people. Crowdsourcing is typically supported by technology (web and social media), and can be used to expand knowledge, develop a product, or raise money—called crowdfunding.

customer relationship management (CRM): The business discipline of interacting with customers or any software application used to conduct sales and other customer interactions. It usually contains information about past transactions that can be used to ensure continuity of service with individuals.

dashboard: A visualization of the data relating to important key performance indicators (KPIs).

data: Measurements and information manipulated by computers and transmitted over networks.

data aggregation: The combining of various points of data into a single set in order to facilitate usability.

database: A digital filing system that enables data to be stored, related, manipulated, and retrieved.

deaccession: Formal removing from a collection. This may occur for a number of reasons, such as transfer to another museum or a sale, usually in exceptional circumstances.

design charrette: An intensive planning session where citizens, designers, and others collaborate on a vision for development.[4]

device: An apparatus, such as a computer, phone, or tablet, that can be used to process information or connect to a network.

digital: Electronic technology that produces, saves, and processes data according to specific standards.

digital humanities: "A diverse and still emerging field that includes the practice of humanities research in and through information technology. It also includes the development of digital educational/research/teach/archival/publishing resources for the specific use and study of the humanities and interconnected disciplines. The digital humanities is also concerned with an exploration of how humanities may evolve through their engagement with technology."[5]

disruption: Radical change in existing markets due to technologies enabled by new processes, services, or products.

educational data mining: "An emerging discipline, concerned with developing methods for exploring the unique and increasingly large-scale data that come from educational settings, and using those methods to better understand students, and the settings which they learn in."[6]

embedded assessment: "Assessment of a student's competencies and progress . . . tracked during the learning process. This kind of assessment gives both teachers and students data in real time, which can be used to gauge and further support learning. These assessments are also so well integrated into the flow of learning that oftentimes students do not even notice they are being assessed. Embedded assessments are different from typical assessments, such as quizzes, tests, and reports, because typical assessments focus mainly on what students know, whereas embedded assessments allow for teachers to gauge what students know and how students use the knowledge in action."[7]

empathy: The "effort to see the world through the eyes of others," "understand the world through their experiences," and "feel the world through their emotions."[8]

entry fields: The place in a software application where data can be inputted and reviewed.

EPOS (electronic point of sale): An electronic point of sale system is used to sell tickets, merchandise, and refreshments.

Ethernet: A digital standard that contains protocols for the transmission of data over local networks.

functionality: An operational feature of a software application.

gigabit (Gb) / gigabyte (GB): Units that describe the amount of data in a digital file or transmission.

global positioning system (GPS): A system of computers, receivers, and satellites that determine location on the Earth.

go-live: Go-live for a computer system is to literally become operational. At go-live, the system is launched into the live systems environment and will be available for use by end users (either the public or internal staff) with live data. The term launch could refer to the go-live date or could be a public/press launch, which might happen after the actual go-live for some systems.

graphical user interfaces (GUI): A video screen that enables people to interact with a computer by manipulating icons and other visual representations of data.

haptic: Digital communication through the sense of touch—that is, motions or vibrations.

hardware: The physical components of information technology such as computers, monitors, printers, and wires.

help desk: An IT support service. It can be an internal department within an organization or provided by external providers.

host: A server running a software application that is available over a network.

hotspot: A location on a digital screen that can be touched to activate a function. Also, a public space that has a wireless signal available for access to the Internet.

information communications technology (ICT) / information technology (IT): The practical application of computer science to manage data and telecommunications systems.

information technology service management (ITSM): A class of businesses that provide outsourcing services to clients.

interface design: The graphical interface a user manipulates with in order to perform functions on a system or computer.

Internet of Things (IoT): A network of physical objects connected via digital sensors, software, and the Internet to exchange and collect data.

interpretive plan: A written description of a visitor experience, including what the visitor will see, hear, and do.

IP-enabled: Allowing communication across a broad variety of devices, platforms, and networks according to Internet Protocol (IP).

key performance indicators (KPIs): A set of predetermined metrics by which a project will be judged at various stages and/or at completion.

learning analytics: "An educational application of web analytics aimed at learner profiling, a process of gathering and analyzing details of individual student interactions in online learning activities."[9]

learning objects (LOs): Learning objects is a term originating in e-learning to refer to digital content segments that can be searched through (with descriptive metadata), reused, and repurposed for different groups and lessons or courses.

learning profile: "The complete picture of [a student's] learning preferences, strengths, and challenges [which] can be shaped by categories of learning style, intelligence preference, culture, and gender."[10] Learning profiles can be developed through gathering data of students who engage in digital learning.

local area network (LAN): The ensemble of equipment that enables computers to communicate within one another in a building or other limited space.

location analytics: A method or process used to create a real-time "heat map" of people in a given area. It is a circulation management tool that can be used to increase the capacity of a building.

location awareness: Technology that uses embedded GPS (Global Positioning System) or other technology in a device to determine its spatial position.

longitudinal design: A research method involving repeated observations of a group of people over long periods of time, allowing researchers to tell the difference between short- and long-term reactions and actions. It can be used to compare the same people at different ages or life stages.

megabit (Mb) / megabyte (MB): Units that describe a measure of how much data is stored on a drive or passing through a communications medium. Megabits are usually used to measure the speed at which a file is downloaded, while megabytes refer to the size of the file.

metadata: Metadata is data that gives information about other data. Descriptive metadata is information to help discover and identify a resource. Structural metadata describes the different parts of a resource (for example title, abstract, or key words). Administrative metadata provides the information that helps to manage a resource, such as when and how it was created and who can access it.

metrics: Measurements that are used to judge performance.

minimum viable product (MVP): A version of a new product that allows a team to test various aspects of it among users and stakeholders.

mobile application (app): Software developed for smartphones, tablet computers, and other mobile devices.

multimedia: Any technology or product combining audio, video, and/or text.

multisensory: Having to do with more than one physiological sense—sight, smell, touch, taste, and sound.

natural user interface (NUI): A system for interacting with a digital device using intuitive, everyday actions, such as voice activation, gesture, or eye movement.

near-field communication (NFC): A radio protocol similar to Bluetooth that allows information to be exchanged between devices.

obsolescence: In the context of digital technology, the fall into disuse of hardware or software that is no longer wanted by an organization (usually when a more efficient system has replaced it). This impedes a museum's ability to preserve older mediums on newer technology.

open source: Describes a software application in which the source code is available for download, review, and modification by anyone.

operating system (OS): Software that enables other software to run on a computer or smartphone.

optical character recognition (OCR): A software application that detects text within an image and converts it into text that can be edited.

Payment Card Industry Data Security Standard (PCI DSS): The set of practices mandated by a consortium of payment card companies to ensure the security of financial transactions.

personalization: A system for registering a user's identity and then storing that person's preferences, characteristics, and history of interactions with an organization.

platform: A software or hardware environment that permits certain applications or functionality to operate.

point of sale: The physical place, for example—a counter—where someone buys a ticket, refreshments, or merchandise.

postmortem: A process, usually at the conclusion of a project, whereby the team evaluates the successes and unsuccessful parts of the project.

proprietary database: A database in which the underlying code is owned by an organization that licenses it for a fee.

provenance: A record of the chronology of ownership, custody, and location of a work of art or an artifact including how it came into the possession of the museum.

psychographic segmentation: Grouping users and potential users by their personality traits, lifestyle, social class, values and attitudes, interests, and others in order to provide more personalized experiences for each "segment."

reciprocal links: Mutual hyperlinks commonly between two websites in order to ensure mutual traffic. Often established using reciprocal link exchange directories, this practice can help achieve higher rankings in search engine optimization (SEO), and is one type of cross-linking used in SEO.

responsive website: A website that detects a visitor's devices and delivers content in the most suitable format.

return on investment (ROI): A calculation of the benefits, usually financial, of the money spent on a project, staff, or other initiative.

scaffolding: Scaffolding is a teaching strategy whereby facilitators provide successive level of support that help people reach increasing levels of comprehension and skill. These supports are then removed when students become more autonomous.

scenario (design or user): A scenario is a short story about a persona that imagines his or her goals and the actions he or she will take to meet them.

scrum master: The scrum master is one of the key core roles in the scrum framework for agile projects. The scrum master acts as a facilitator and lead within the development team, and is responsible for removing roadblocks that might delay the team's progress, keeping the team focused, and ensuring that the scrum framework is followed.

search engine optimization (SEO): The process through which websites maximize their number of visitors in order to ensure that the site appears high on the list of results returned by a search engine. Title tag and meta description, URL normalization, canonical link elements, 301 redirects, and cross-linking are all ways that content can be tailored to optimize results from search engine crawlers.

server: A powerful computer used to provide services over a network.

service level agreement (SLA): A contract from digital agencies that details the quality and quantity of service along with recourse for failures to provide.

social media: Sites and apps used for communication and data sharing, such as Facebook, Instagram, or Twitter.

software: The operating systems and programs that enable computers and other devices to perform complex operations.

splash screen: Also known as a captive portal, this is a window that can be programmed to open when someone logs into WiFi.

sprint: Sprints are a unit of development used in the scrum method of agile software development to refer to a regular, repeatable work cycle that iterates the product.

standard compliant format: Format that ensures the interoperability of various data and systems.

store: The physical area where items are located when not on display. This can be for short periods of time (e.g., a transit store) if awaiting imminent display or permanent areas when not in use; for example, shelves containing swords.

storyboard: A sequence of visuals accompanied by text that represents the steps of a media experience.

tagging: The practice of assigning nonhierarchical keywords or terms to a piece of information. This kind of metadata helps to describe an item and assists with browsing and searching. Tagging was popularized by websites associated with Web 2.0.

telepresence robot: A mobile robot controlled by a human who can communicate using a camera and video chat.

terabit (Tb) / terabyte (TB): A measure of data stored on a drive.

Transport Control Protocol/Internet Protocol (TCP/IP): A format that defines how computers can communicate with one another across networks.

user-centric: Describes the strategy of placing the needs and concerns of visitors, audiences, or customers at the center of organizational planning and operations.

user experience (UX): The feelings, emotions, and level of engagement provoked by a website.

user interface: A control panel that enables a human to interact with a computer or other piece of machinery.

user journey (UJ): How a visitor passes through a website from beginning to departure.

virtual reality (VR): An immersive digital experience that transports a participant into a different, artificial environment using special electronic equipment.

vision board: A visual representation of the look and feel and design approach to a media experience.

wearable technology: Electronic devices that can be worn by the user and communicate information back and forth.

wide area network (WAN): Network that enables devices to communicate over long distances by using amplification and low-loss protocols.

WiFi: Abbreviation of "wireless fidelity," the capability to connect to a network using radio-enabled computers and other devices.

wireframe: A set of diagrams that outline the step-by-step function of a digital experience.

write and read access: Specification of who can edit and make changes to a document (write) and who can merely read it (access it) and can't make changes.

Notes

1. "Adaptive Learning," *Dreambox Learning*, accessed September 23, 2016, http://www.dreambox.com/adaptive-learning.

2. "The Agile Movement," Agile Methodology, accessed October 5, 2016, http://agilemethodology.org/.

3. Seymour Papert, "Constuctionism: A New Opportunity for Elementary Science Education," National Science Foundation, http://nsf.gov/awardsearch/showAward?AWD_ID=8751190.

4. "What Is a Charrette?" The Town Paper, accessed October 5, 2016, http://www.tndtownpaper.com/what_is_charrette.htm.

5. Ernesto Priego, "How Do You Define DH?" *Day of DH 2012*, March 2012, accessed September 20, 2016, http://archive.artsrn.ualberta.ca/Day-of-DH-2012/dh/index.html#comment-94.

6. "Educational Data Mining," *International Educational Data Mining Society*, accessed September 23, 2016, http://www.educationaldatamining.org/.

7. Eliza Spang, "Embedded Assessment at Quest to Learn," *Institute of Play*, January 23, 2012, accessed September 23, 2016, http://www.instituteofplay.org/2012/01/embedded-assessment-at-quest-to-learn/.

8. Tim Brown, *Change by Design: How Design Thinking Transforms Organizations and Inspires Innovation* (New York: Harper Business, 2009), 50.

9. L. Johnson, S. Beck Adams, M. Cummins, V. Estrada, A. Freeman, and C. Hall, *NMC Horizon Report: 2016 Higher Education Edition* (Austin, TX: The New Media Consortium, 2016), 38.

10. "What Is the Best Way to Identify and Address All of My Students' Learning Profiles?" *EL Education*, accessed September 23, 2016, http://plp.eleducation.org/learning-profile/.

Bibliography

Agile Methodology. "The Agile Movement." Accessed October 5, 2016. http://agilemethodology.org/.

Allen-Griel, Dana. "Silvia Filippini-Fanoni, Director of Interpretation, Media, and Evaluation at the Indianapolis." *Musete.ch*, September 14, 2013. Accessed September 20, 2016. http://www.musete.ch/2013/09/14/silvia-filippini-fantoni-director-of-interpretation-media-and-evaluation-at-the-indianapolis-museum-of-art/.

Anderson, Maxwell L. "Metrics of Success in Art Museums." *The Getty Leadership Institute*. Los Angeles: The Getty Leadership Institute, 2004.

Association for Project Management. *APM Body of Knowledge*. Buckinghamshire, UK: Association for Project Management, 2012.

Association for Project Management. "Quality Management." *APM Body of Knowledge*. Accessed July 31, 2016. http://knowledge.apm.org.uk/bok/quality-management.

Barabasi, Albert-Laszlo. *Linked: How Everything Is Connected to Everything Else and What It Means for Business, Science, and Everyday Life.* New York: Basic Books, 2014.

Barabasi, Albert-Laszlo. *Network Science.* Cambridge: Cambridge University Press, 2016. PDF at http://barabasi.com/book/network-science.

Bautista, Susana, and Anne Balsamo. "Understanding the Distributed Museum: Mapping the Spaces of Museology in Contemporary Culture." In *Museums and the Web 2011: Proceedings*, edited by J. Trant and D. Bearman. Toronto: Archives & Museum Informatics, 2011. Accessed October 7, 2016. http://conference.archimuse.com/mw2011/papers/understanding_distributed_museum.

Beck, Kent, et al. *Manifesto for Agile Software Development*, 2006. Accessed July 31, 2016. www.agilemanifesto.org.

Biotopia. "Discover Uppland with Biotopia." Accessed September 16, 2016. http://www.biotopia.nu/besok-oss/in-english/.

Blankenberg, Ngaire. "Learning for Change." In *The Manual of Museum Learning*, edited by Brad King and Barry Lord, 29–52. Lanham, MD: Rowman & Littlefield, 2016.

Brown, Tim. *Change by Design: How Design Thinking Transforms Organizations and Inspires Innovation.* New York: Harper Business, 2009.

Clifton, Brian. *Advanced Web Metrics with Google Analytics.* Indianapolis, IN: John Wiley & Sons, 2012.

Clifton, Brian. *Successful Analytics: Gain Business Insights by Managing Google Analytics.* Burgess Hill, UK: Advanced Web Metrics, 2015.

Cogapp. *Agile for Museums and Cultural Organisations.* Accessed July 31, 2016. www.cogapp.com/agile.

Connected Learning. "Connected Learning Principles." Accessed September 9, 2016. http://connectedlearning.tv/connected-learning-principles.

Connexity. "Understand How Your Customers Use the Web." Accessed September 22, 2016. http://connexity.com/gb/hitwise/online-intelligence.

Cooper Hewitt. "Meet the Staff: Sebastian Chan," September 9, 2013. Accessed September 20, 2016. http://www.cooperhewitt.org/2013/09/09/meet-the-staff-sebastian-chan/.

Crabtree, Andrew, Mark Rouncefield, and Peter Tolmie. "Design Ethnography in a Nutshell." In *Doing Design Ethnography*, 183–205. London: Springer, 2012.

Csikszentmihalyi, Mihaly. *Flow: The Psychology of Optimal Experience.* New York: Harper & Row, 1990.

Curedale, Robert. *Design Thinking: Process and Methods Manual.* Topanga, CA: Design Community College, 2013.

Cushing, Annie. "The Definitive Guide to Campaign Tagging in Google Analytics." *Annielytics.* Accessed September 22, 2016. https://www.annielytics.com/guides/definitive-guide-campaign-tagging-google-analytics.

Davachi, Lila, Tobias Kiefer, David Rock, and Lisa Rock. "Learning That Lasts Through AGES." *NeuroLeadership Journal* 3 (2010): 1–11.

Davis, Josh, Maite Balda, David Rock, Pail McGinniss, and Lila Davachi, "The Science of Making Learning Stick: An Update to the AGES Model." *NeuroLeadership Journal* 5 (2014): 1–15.

Dilenschneider, Colleen. "Why Donors Stop Giving Money to Organizations." *Know Your Own Bone* (blog), accessed October 7, 2016. http://colleendilen.com/2016/04/20/why-donors-stop-giving-money-to-cultural-organizations-data/.

DMAdashboard. "Dashboard." Accessed October 7, 2016. https://dashboard.dma.org/.

Downes, Stephen. "What Connectivism Is." *Half an Hour* (blog), February 3, 2007. http://halfanhour.blogspot.com.br/2007/02/what-connectivism-is.html.

Dreambox Learning. "Adaptive Learning." Accessed September 23, 2016. http://www.dreambox.com/adaptive-learning.

BIBLIOGRAPHY

Dreambox Learning. *Intelligent Adaptive Learning: An Essential Element of 21st Century Teaching and Learning*, 2014. http://www2.dreambox.com/e/14872/lligent-adaptive-learning-21st/bd367/606617662.

Easley, David, and Jon Kleinberg. *Networks, Crowds, and Markets: Reasoning about a Highly Connected World.* New York: Cambridge University Press, 2010.

EdutTech Wiki. "Learning Object." Last modified December 3, 2010. Accessed September 19, 2016. http://edutechwiki.unige.ch/en/Learning_object.

Ellis, David, Gavin Foster, Ray Shah, and Petar Bjkov. "The Service Oriented Museum Web." *Museums and the Web 2007*. Accessed September 28, 2016. http://www.museumsandtheweb.com/mw2007/papers/ellis-d/ellis-d.html.

Espinós, Alex. "Do Museums Worldwide Form a True Community on Twitter? Some Insights on the Museum Twitter Ecosystem through Social Network Analysis and Network Science." *Museums and the Web 2014.*

Espinós, Alex. "Museums on Social Media: Analyzing Growth through Case Studies." *MW2016: Museums and the Web 2016*, January 31, 2016. Accessed September 26, 2016. http://mw2016.museumsandtheweb.com/paper/museums-on-social-media-analyzing-growth-through-case-studies/.

Espinós, Alex. "Museums on Twitter: Three Case Studies of the Relationship between a Museum and Its Environment. Victoria & Albert, Palazzo Madama, CCCB." *Museums and the Web 2015.*

Falk, John. *Identity and the Museum Visitor Experience.* Walnut Creek, CA: Left Coast Press, 2009.

Fiorina, Carly. "Information: The Currency of the Digital Age." *HP*. Accessed September 22, 2016. http://www.hp.com/hpinfo/execteam/speeches/fiorina/04openworld.html.

Fortune, Stephen. "The Arts Organization as System: An Interview with Paul Bennum." *Digital R&D Fund for the Arts*, June 26, 2013. Accessed October 7, 2016. http://artsdigitalrnd.org.uk/features/the-arts-organisation-as-system-an-interview-with-paul-bennun/.

The Franklin Institute. *Field Trip Planner 2016–2017.* Accessed October 6, 2016. https://www.fi.edu/sites/default/files/FieldTripPlanner_TFI_FieldTripPlanner_2016.pdf.

Fusion Research & Analytics. *Mobile Survey May 2012: Museums Association*. Accessed October 7, 2016. https://www.museumsassociation.org/download?id=731198.

Fusion Research & Analytics. *Natural History Museum: Understanding the Mobile Visitor*, July 2013. Accessed October 7, 2016. http://www.nhm.ac.uk/resources-rx/files/nhm-mobile-report-july-2013-127910.pdf.

Fusion Research & Analytics LLC and Frankly, Green + Webb Ltd. *Understanding the Mobile V&A Visitor: Autumn 2012.* Accessed October 7, 2016. https://www.vam.ac.uk/__data/assets/pdf_file/0009/236439/Visitor_Use_Mobile_Devices.pdf.

Gantt.com. "What Is a Gantt Chart?" Accessed July 31, 2016. www.gantt.com.

Golbeck, Jennifer. *Analyzing the Social Web*. Amsterdam: Elsevier, 2013.

Google. "About Dashboards." Accessed September 22, 2016. https://support.google.com/analytics/answer/1068216?hl=en.

Google. "About Demographics and Interests." Accessed September 22, 2016. https://support.google.com/analytics/answer/2799357?hl=en.

Google. "About Goals: Use Goals To Measure How Often Users Complete Specific Actions." Accessed September 22, 2016. https://support.google.com/analytics/answer/1012040?hl=en&ref_topic=6150889.

Google. "Analytics Help." Accessed September 22, 2016. https://support.google.com/analytics.

Google. "Create and Manage View Filters." Accessed September 22, 2016. https://support.google.com/analytics/answer/1034823?hl=en.

Google. "Custom Campaigns." Accessed September 22, 2016. https://support.google.com/analytics/answer/1033863?hl=en.

Google. "Enable Demographics and Interests Reports." Accessed September 22, 2016. https://support.google.com/analytics/answer/2819948?hl=en&ref_topic=2799375.

Google. "Google Tag Manager: Overview." Accessed September 22, 2016. https://www.google.co.uk/analytics/tag-manager.

Granovetter, Mark. "The Strength of Weak Ties." *The American Journal of Sociology* 78, no. 6 (1973): 1360–80.

Granovetter, Mark. "The Strength of Weak Ties: A Network Theory Revisited." *Sociological Theory* 1 (1983): 201–33.

Gulbahce, N., and S. Lehmann. "The Art of Community Detection." *BioEssays* 30, no. 10 (2008): 934–38.

Haughey, Duncan. "A Brief History of Smart Goals." *Project Smart* (blog), December 13, 2014. Accessed September 22, 2016. https://www.projectsmart.co.uk/brief-history-of-smart-goals.php.

Interconnections. *Interconnections: The IMLS National Study on the Use of Libraries, Museums and the Internet*, February 28, 2008. Accessed October 6, 2016. http://interconnectionsreport.org/presentations/IMLSConclusionsOverview022708.ppt.

International Educational Data Mining Society. "Educational Data Mining." Accessed September 23, 2016. http://www.educationaldatamining.org/.

Jeong, H., Z. Neda, and A. L. Barabasi. "Measuring Preferential Attachment in Evolving Networks." *Europhysics Letter* 61, no. 4 (2003): 567–72.

Johnson, L., S. Beck Adams, M. Cummins, V. Estrada, A. Freeman, and C. Hall. *NMC Horizon Report: 2016 Higher Education Edition*. Austin, TX: The New Media Consortium, 2016.

Kaushik, Avinash. *Ocam's Razor* (blog), Accessed October 7, 2016. http://www.kaushik.net/avinash./.

Klein, Gary. "Performing a Project Premortem." *Harvard Business Review*, September 2007.

Kniberg, Henrik. "Making Sense of MVP (Minimum Viable Product)." *Crisp's Blog*, January 25, 2016. Accessed July 31, 2016. http://blog.crisp.se/2016/01/25/henrikkniberg/making-sense-of-mvp.

Kvale, Steiner. *Doing Interviews*. London: Sage, 2007.

Lemke, Jay, Robert Lecusay, Michael Cole, and Vera Michalchik. *Documenting and Assessing Learning in Informal and Media-Rich Environments*. Cambridge, MA: MIT Press, 2015.

LunaMetrics. *LunaMetrics* (blog). Accessed October 7, 2016. http://www.lunametrics.com/blog/.

Martin, Bella, and Bruce M. Hanington, *Universal Methods of Design: 100 Ways to Research Complex Problems, Develop Innovative Ideas, and Design Effective Solution*. Beverly, MA: Rockport Publishers, 2012.

McCarthy, John. "Learning Profile Cards." *Opening Paths*, January 15, 2014. Accessed September 10, 2016. http://openingpaths.org/blog/2014/01/learning-profile-cards/.

Merritt, Elizabeth. "Museum Design 2034: The Distributed Museum." *Center for the Future of Museums* (blog), March 12, 2010. Accessed October 7, 2016. http://futureofmuseums.blogspot.com.es/2010/03/museum-design-2034-distributed-museum.html.

Mountain Goat Software. *Scrum*. Accessed July 31, 2016. www.mountaingoatsoftware.com/agile/scrum.

National Archives. "Archives.gov Metrics Dashboard." Accessed October 7, 2016. https://www.archives.gov/metrics/.

The New London Group. "A Pedagogy of Multiliteracies: Designing Social Futures." *Harvard Educational Review* 66, no 1 (Spring 1996): 60–93.

Newman, Mark. *Networks: An Introduction*. New York: Oxford University Press, 2010.

Office of Government Commerce. *Managing Successful Projects with PRINCE2*. London: TSO, 2009.

Onnela, J.-P., J. Saramäki, J. Hyvönen, G. Szabó, M. A. de Menezes, K. Kaski, A.-L. Barabási, and J. Kertész. "Analysis of a Large-Scale Weighted Network of One-to-One Human Communication." *New Journal of Physics* 9 (2007): 1–27.

Opperman, Amanda. "Embedded Assessment Upgrades Personalized Learning for the 21st Century." *Association for Talent Development*, March 27, 2015. Accessed September 10, 2016. https://www.td.org/Publications/Blogs/Science-of-Learning-Blog/2015/03/Embedded-Assessment-Upgrades-Personalized-Learning.

Pan, Diana, and Manish Engineer. "The 360-Degree View: Why an Integrated CRM Platform Is Important in Growing a Museum's Membership Program." *Museums and the Web Asia 2015*. Accessed October 7, 2016. http://mwa2015.museumsandtheweb.com/paper/the-360-degree-view-why-an-integrated-crm-platform-is-important-in-growing-a-museums-membership-program/.

Pantoja, Javier, Javier Docampo, Ana Martin, Ricardo Alonso Maturana, and Carlos Navalon. "The New Prado Museum Website: A (Semantic) Challenge." *MW2016: Museums and the Web 2016*, January 28, 2016. Accessed September 19, 2016. http://mw2016.museumsandtheweb.com/paper/the-new-prado-museum-website-a-semantic-challenge/.

Papert, Seymour. *Constuctionism: A New Opportunity for Elementary Science Education.* Accessed October 5, 2016. http://nsf.gov/awardsearch/showAward?AWD_ID=8751190.

Parity Solutions. *Summary of PRINCE2.* London: Parity Solutions, 2012.

Penuel, Bill, Jean Rhodes, Julian Sefton-Green, Juliet Schor, Katie Salen, Kris Gutiarrez, Mizuko Ito, Sonia Livingstone, and S. Craig Watkins. *Connected Learning: An Agenda for Research and Design.* Irvine, CA: Digital Media and Learning Research Hub, 2013.

Priego, Ernesto. "How Do You Define DH?" *Day of DH 2012*, March 2012. Accessed September 20, 2016. http://archive.artsrn.ualberta.ca/Day-of-DH-2012/dh/index.html#comment-94.

Priozic, Ursa. "Using Electronic Paper for Museum Labels." *Museum Next*, August 26, 2016. Accessed September 20, 2016. http://www.museumnext.com/conference/using-electronic-paper-museum-labels/.

Project Management Institute. *A Guide to the Project Management Body of Knowledge (PMBOK® Guide).* Newtown Square, PA: Project Management Institute, 2013.

Ries, Eric. *The Lean Startup: How Today's Entrepreneurs Use Continuous Innovation to Create Radically Successful Businesses.* New York: Crown Business, 2011.

Rijksmueum. "RijksStudio." Accessed September 20, 2016. https://www.rijksmuseum.nl/en/rijksstudio.

Saffer, Dan. *Designing for Interaction: Creating Innovative Applications and Devices.* Berkeley, CA: New Riders, 2010.

Science Museum. "InfoAge+." Accessed September 27, 2016. http://www.sciencemuseum.org.uk/educators/things-to-do/activitysheets-trails-apps/info-age-app.

Sclater, Niall, Alice Peasgood, and Joel Mullan. *Learning Analytics in Higher Education: A Review of UK and International Practice Full Report*, April 19, 2016. https://www.jisc.ac.uk/sites/default/files/learning-analytics-in-he-v3.pdf.

Sharples, Mike, Anne Adams, Nonya Alozie, Rebecca Ferguson, Elizabeth FitzGerald, Mark Gaved, Patrick McAndrew, Barbara Means, Julie Remold, Bar Rienties, Jeremy Roschelle, Kea Vogt, Denise Whitelock, and Louise Yarnall. *Innovating Pedagogy 2015: Open University Innovation Report 4.* Milton Keynes, UK: Open University, 2015. https://www.sri.com/sites/default/files/publications/innovating_pedagogy_2015.pdf.

Shum, Simon Buckingham, and Rebecca Ferguson. "Social Learning Analytics." *Educational Technology & Society* 15, no. 3 (2012): 3–26.

Slater, Niall, Alice Peasgood, and Joel Mullan. "Learning Analytics in Higher Education a Review of UK and International Practice." *Jisc*, April 19, 2016. Accessed September 10, 2016. https://www.jisc.ac.uk/reports/learning-analytics-in-higher-education.

Smithsonian. "Smithsonian Dashboard." Accessed October 7, 2016. http://dashboard.si.edu/digital.

Smithsonian Center for Education Museum Studies, Navigation North Learning Solutions, LLC, Cross & Joftus, LLC. *Smithsonian Center for Education and Museum Studies: Digital Learning Resources Project, Volume V, Final Report*. Washington, DC: 2012. Accessed October 6, 2016. https://smithsonian-digital-learning.wikispaces.com/file/view/DLRP_Volume-5_Final-Report.pdf.

Spang, Eliza. "Embedded Assessment at Quest to Learn." *Institute of Play*, January 23, 2012. Accessed September 23, 2016. http://www.instituteofplay.org/2012/01/embedded-assessment-at-quest-to-learn/.

Successful Projects. *PM Methodologies*. Accessed July 31, 2016. www.successfulprojects.com/PM-Topics/Introduction-to-Project-Management/PM-Methodologies.

Sullivan, Ben. "Museum Collections at the Core of Learning," *SlideShare*, slide 18. Accessed October 5, 2016. http://www.slideshare.net/BenSullivan5/museum-collections-at-the-core-of-learning.

Tate. "Digital Metrics." Accessed October 7, 2016. http://www.tate.org.uk/about/our-work/digital/digital-metrics.

Tate. "Learning Spaces." Accessed September 16, 2016. http://www.tate.org.uk/about/projects/tate-modern-project/learning-spaces.

The Town Paper. "What Is a Charrette?" Accessed October 5, 2016. http://www.tndtownpaper.com/what_is_charrette.htm.

Twitter. (n.d.b). "About Twitter's Suggestions for Who to Follow." Available at https://support.twitter.com/articles/227220.

Twitter. (n.d.a). "FAQs about Tailored Suggestions." Available at https://support.twitter.com/articles/20169941?lang=en.

Walker, Steve, and Linda Creanor. "The STIN in the Tale: A Socio-Technical Interaction Perspective on Networked Learning." *Educational Technology & Society* 12, no. 4 (2009): 305–16.

Warren, Lee. "Managing Hot Moments in the Classroom." *The Derek Bok Center for Learning and Teaching at Harvard University* (blog). Accessed September 20, 2016. http://bokcenter.harvard.edu/managing-hot-moments-classroom.

Index

3-Legged Dog Art and Technology Center, 332

acoustics, 337
access control, 159, 188–89, 192, 323
access point, 302–6
accessibility, xix, xxi, xxiii, 15, 20, 36, 47, 55, 79–80, 87, 93–97, 103–5, 110, 113, 116, 128, 134, 138, 144, 178–81, 200, 284, 308
actionable data, 87
activity worksheet, 92
adaptive learning, 86
admin privileges, 65
admissions, 148, 347–48
AGES model, 83
agile, 17, 32, 205, 215–16, 228, 239–41, 247, 275–77;
algorithm, xix, xx, 49, 53–55, 57, 59; definition, 359
analytics, 21–22, 51, 53, 61–76, 110, 135, 281, 326–27, 343; learning, 86–89; reporting software, 71. *See also* location analytics
analytics and evaluation manager, 281
annotation, 97, 143
application programming interface (API), 74, 107, 169, 177, 180, 187, 193, 196, 200, 351–52; definition, 49, 359
assessment, 85-86, 103, 114, 116, 277; embedded, 87–88, 90, 95; financial, 208
audience, 45–59, 115, 125, 164, 355
audience research, xix, 39, 46, 54–59, 88, 112, 135, 248, 250, 253; ethical concerns and privacy, 87

augmented reality (AR), 90, 110, 112, 115, 137, 139, 141–43, 171, 254
average session duration, 62

bandwidth, 150, 279, 291, 306, 308, 310, 317; assessing need, 157, 208, 223, 295–96; definition, 360; router selection, 312
baseline: data, 37; project schedule, 218
blended learning, 93
blog, 72, 94, 96, 99, 116, 126, 144, 145, 150, 224, 225, 234, 280
bookings manager, 282
bounce rate, 66
bridging and bonding, 357
bring your own device (BYOD), 110
Bristol Museums, Galleries, and Archives, 71
British Museum, 3–11
budgeting, 17, 58, 71, 78, 114, 128, 157, 159, 164, 238, 242, 280, 285; content, 145–48; control, 120; evaluation, 19, 55, 117–19; infrastructure, 335–37; network administration, 281, 290, 302, 309, 320, 324, 326; project, 201, 203, 206, 208, 209–13, 222–27, 282; software, 316
business case, 206–8, 237, 320

cache, 167
campaign, 34, 48, 55, 63, 72, 74, 76, 224, 275, 283, 284, 343–48; capital, 333; crowdsourcing, xxi, 52, 275; email, 150; membership, 16; tagging, 67–68; Twitter, 50–51, 58–59
Canadian Museum for Human Rights, 110, 161–64

377

captive portal, 21, 256
Cat5/Cat6 cable, 302; definition, 360
cataloging, 163, 196, 171, 173, 182–83, 187, 189, 192
Chan, Seb, 6
change management, 226–27, 276–77, 320
charging stations, 309
chief digital officer, 280–81
chief information officer, 281
circulation management, 22–23, 149, 309, 309, 326–27, 364
citizen science, xxi, 52
Cleveland Museum of Art, 111, 121
click-through rate, 64
Clicky, 64
cloud services, 19, 225, 280, 296, 300, 302, 316, 318–19, 325, 338, 344–45; definition, 360; pros and cons, 290–92
collaboration, 7, 52, 119, 191, 196, 206, 216, 220, 247, 266, 277, 279, 286, 287
collection information manager, 283
collections management system (CMS), 18, 20, 138, 153, 175–99, 201, 310; definition, 360
collections steering committee, 181
color, 82, 261
communication, 204, 215, 277, 278
competitions, 52–53
connected devices, 309, 317–18
connected learning, 78
connectivity, 17–18, 223, 295–307, 323–25
constructivist, 83, 93
content audit, 137, 145, 147, 159
content development, 171
content guidelines for digital experience, 255
content manager, 281
content management system (CMS), 96, 149, 161–73, 255, 285; planning, 151–53, 155, 157–59; definition, 360
content distribution network (CDN), 151, 159
content producer, 284
content strategy, 133
conversion, 68–69, 72, 343; conversion rate, 66, 361
cooling options, 301
Cooper Hewitt Smithsonian Design Museum, 113, 121

copyright management, 169
Creative Commons, 151
crowdsourcing, 52, 59, 134, 178, 193, 197, 273–74; definition, 361; for revenues, 345–46
Csikszentmihalyi, Mihaly, 83
customer-centrism. *See* user-centrism
customer relationship management (CRM), 155, 168, 229, 283, 302, 307, 314, 318, 327, 351, 353; definition, 361; revenue planning, 344–48
Cyfe, 71

dashboard, 52, 69, 72–74, 87; definition, 361; example, 70
data backup, 181, 225, 301, 314, 325–26, 328
database, 115, 155, 195, 296, 297, 306, 311, 314, 318, 323, 329, 338, 345, 347, 351, 352, 359, 361, 365; collections, 176, 177, 178, 180–83, 185, 191, 200; content, 151, 153, 157, 159; educational, 89, 99, 144; management of, 281, 282, 285; proprietary, 14–15, specification of, 24, 168; visitor, 74
database manager, 282
data collection, 39, 74, 85–87, 144, 353
datacom center, 281, 293, 299, 300, 301, 306, 314, 331
data migration, 180, 223, 232–33, 235
data mining, 86–87
data protocols, 304
deaccession, 185
demarcation point, 299
design framework, 256–61
design requirements, 250, 252, 254, 264
design charrette, 247; definition, 361
digital archivist, 283
digital art, 140–41, 159
digital asset management (DAM), 168, 169, 173, 177, 187
digital assets, 133, 136–37, 141, 144, 153, 169, 283
digital cinema protocol (DCP) files, 308
digital content manager, 281
digital content producer, 284
digital development, 136, 205, 215, 242
digital divide, 279
digital learning programs manager, 284

digital project manager, 282
digital projects. *See* project documentation; project management
digital rights management (DRM), 187, 194
digital signage, 133, 145, 150–52, 160, 163, 169, 285, 292, 308, 356
digitization, 137–40, 143, 160, 178, 180, 187, 192–95, 197, 200, 281, 341
disaster recovery, 325–26
discoverability, 96, 143
disintermediation, 8–9, 11
disruption (digital), 14, 15, 17, 141, 274, 358; definition, 362
diversity, 57, 246, 265, 355
documentation: collections, xviii, xxi, 137, 139, 140, 159, 168, 179, 182, 186, 194, 226; IT management, 290, 322; learning, 85, 99, 143; manager, 181, 215, 190; project, 153, 204, 206–16, 236–38, 277; video, 87–88, 104
donors, 181, 188, 283, 318; cultivating, 343–46, 352–53
Dropbox, 296
DuckDuckGo, 149

ecommerce, 63, 148, 158, 208, 228–29, 273, 285, 302, 312, 345, 349–53
ecommerce manager, 285
ecommerce test plan, 229
educational data mining, 86
electronic point of sale (EPOS), 307–8, 328, 351
email marketing manager, 283
embedded assessment, 90
emotional journey maps, 254
empathy, 246
empathy maps, 254
encryption, 319, 329
enterprise content management system, xxi, 161–74
entry documentation, 182
entry fields, 176
Ethernet, 302–9, 313, 329, 338, 360
ethnographic research, 251
evaluation manager, 281
event tracking, 66–68, 114, 283, 345
Excel. *See* Microsoft Excel

exhibition media, xviii, 137, 144, 159
experimentation, 13, 16, 17, 81, 83, 98, 142, 248, 275, 279–80, 287, 291, 338

Facebook, xx, 29, 283, 295, 355; audience development, 55, 58, 126, 136; as content channel, 45–50, 65, 67, 72, 146, 151, 163; Insights, 64; value of, 61, 69
facilitators, 83, 93, 104
fiber to the premises (FTTP), 298
Filippini-Fantoni, Silvia, 5
fire codes, 301
firewall, 310–13
flowchart, 260
functional requirements, 153–55, 186; design, 255–56
fundraising, 286, 343–46, 353

games, 137, 147, 245, 254, 357; exhibition, 110–12, 114–15, 118, 128, 144; learning, 81, 87–88, 92, 104–5, 143
Gantt chart, 219–21
go-live, 253
gradualism, xxiii, 133, 143, 151, 271–77, 287
graphical user interface (GUI), 172, 177, 180, 200, 362
graphic designer, 285
Google, 295, 348, 355; Analytics, 62–69, 72, 74, 88, 110, 139; Apps (Google Suite); 296; Art Project, 20, 97, 139; docs, 75; Drive, 217, 296; glossary, 48; Maps, 136; SEO, 149

hashtag, 48, 50–52, 59. *See also* Twitter
head of technology, 281
heat and humidity standards, 301
help desk, 321, 324; definition, 363
Hitwise, 63
holographic projection,
Hootsuite, 64
HTML5, 150, 151

Iconosquare, 64
IMAX, 297, 308, 338.
 Also see DCP files
immersive: experiences, 90, 112, 163, 190, 332; research, 86; video, 141, 336, 338

Indianapolis Museum of Art, 6
infographic, 73, 82, 261
informalization, 8–11
Instagram, xix, xxiv, 47, 48, 49, 64, 72, 126, 136, 283
Institute of Electronics and Electrical Engineers (IEEE), 304
interaction design, 83
interactives, 109, 122–24, 135; embedded assessment, 93; design of, 245–65; for learning, 81, 88, 89–90, 93, 143; job description, 284; planning, 332–38; project management, 201, 208
interest report, 67
interface layout, 261–63
Internet of Things (IoT), 14, 15, 128, 309, 318, 363
Internet Protocol (IP), 149, 292, 295, 311–13, 318, 363, 367
Internet Service Provider (ISP), 294–95, 297–99
interpretive plan, 114, 118–19, 128, 249, 252, 254, 258, 266; definition, 363
iterative development, xxii, 32, 39, 123, 205, 275
IT service management, 19, 320

key performance indicator (KPI), 53, 62–63, 68–69, 75, 86, 104, 281, 286, 343; definition, 363
    linking to mission, 35–38
kickoff, 205–6, 214, 242
knowledge sharing, 280

language, 10, 51, 57, 90, 101, 255, 278
Lean Startup (Ries), 6
learning analytics, 86
learning for change, 79–80
learning network, 100
learning object, 89, 97, 107; definition, 363
learning profile, 88; definition, 363
learning programs manager, 284
learning resource, 88–89, 104
licenses, 23, 141, 151, 225
LinkedIn, 46, 47, 55, 56
live streaming, 8–9, 15, 48, 50–51, 59, 82, 90, 134, 151,

loan management, 178, 182, 185–86, 190, 285, 329
local area network (LAN), 281, 282, 296, 308, 316–20, 325, 329, 338; definition, 292, 363; logical configuration, 310–13; physical configuration, 301–6. *See also* VLAN
location analytics, 21–22, 326–27; definition, 364
location awareness, 21, 22, 25, 145, 149, 309, 356; definition, 364
logical topology, 294, 310, 320
longitudinal design, 86
look and feel requirements, 256

MAC address, 313, 317
MacGregor, Neil, 4
managing change, 274–75
massive open online course (MOOC), 93, 151
media literacy, 80–82
media writer, 285
membership, 16, 23, 34, 87, 147, 152, 239, 241, 283, 285, 307, 328, 343, 345, 348. *See also* campaign
membership and development manager, 283
metadata, 69, 141, 143, 148–49, 168, 176, 283, 284; in collections, 187, 191, 195–96, 200; definition, 89, 363; use in learning, 89, 93, 95, 97
methodologies: ECMS design principles, 165; museum learning, 101;
Project Management Body of Knowledge (PMBOK), 205;
Projects in Controlled Environments (PRINCE2), 205; website development, 158. *See also* agile; scrum; waterfall
metrics, 5, 33, 35, 37, 40, 46, 53–54, 62, 65, 68–72, 76, 78, 111, 156–60, 207, 281, 327, 343, 363, 364
Metropolitan Museum of Art, 239
Microsoft Excel, 69, 71–75, 176,
Microsoft OneDrive, 296
Microsoft Power BI, 71
Microsoft Project, 220
millennials, xix, 10, 46, 136
minimum viable product (MVP), xxii, 221, 237, 241, 274, 364
mission statement, 18, 175

INDEX

mobile, 14, 15, 22, 23, 25, 357; analytics, 67; app, xviii, 87, 110, 114, 118, 143, 163, 166, 167, 248, 254, 110, 128, 169, 359; development, 81, 96, 114, 118, 120, 126, 135, 163, 166, 167, 169, 245, 248, 251, 254; engagement, xx, 45, 59, 82, 90, 94, 103, 110, 136, 143, 149, 207, 307, 309, 356; games, 112, 137; infrastructure, 291, 303, 348; management, 281, 283; sales, 239, 317; tracking, 88

modularity, xxi, 165, 167, 174

mood board, 119, 248, 256

movement control, 184, 200

multiliteracies, 80, 82

multimedia, 87, 89, 90, 145, 163, 252, 358; definition, 364; producer job description, 284; hardware requirements, 324; writer job description, 285

naming conventions, 188–89

National Museums of Scotland, 197

natural user interface (NUI), 111

network administrators, 298, 318, 320–22

network manager, 282

network storage, 314, 325

network termination device, 324

network topology, 310, 320

New London Group, 82

new media literacies, 80

object exit, 185

obsolescence, 140, 195, 274, 276, 364

Office 365, 296

omnichannel, xviii, xix, xxiv, 14–25, 46, 133–37, 145, 149, 152–154, 159, 272, 277, 286, 287, 342

online sales, 350

online shop, 349

OODA loop, 31–32, 36, 38, 39

open source, 14, 97, 98, 140–42, 150, 169

operating costs, 225

optical character recognition (OCR), 138–39; definition, 365

organizational structure, 78, 275

organogram, 272–73

outsourcing, 19, 289, 290–292, 319, 338, 349–52. See also cloud services

participation, 8–11, 30, 34, 39, 46, 52, 78, 86, 88, 101, 104, 115, 118, 128, 165, 247, 284, 344

patch panel, 299–300, 303, 321, 327

payment card, 158, 296, 317–18, 328–29, 338, 352, 365

Payment Card Industry Data Security Standard (PCI DSS), 334–35, 356, 365

pay-to-play, xx, 58

pedagogies, xx, 78, 83

performance plan, 156–59

persona, 253; definition, 365

personalization, xix, xxi, 18, 22, 90, 95, 105, 143, 149, 159, 197, 328; definition, 365; experiences, 115

pervasive media, 21–22

photographer job description, 284

physical topology, 294, 310, 320

photography, 144, 150, 223, 279, 283; archive, 52, 138, 139, 140, 176, 186, 187, 188, 191, 194; digital asset, 143, 169, 171; job description, 284; learning, 83; visitor, 23

Pinterest, 48, 49, 60, 65, 146, 283, 386; analytics, 64

placemaking, 23, 355–57

policy, 77, 256, 321–28, 330

postmortem, 236, 277; definition, 365

Power over Ethernet (PoE), 304–6

privacy, 23, 87, 95, 110, 111, 117, 328

profiles, 50, 111, 337; administrative, 323; brand, 350; donor, 344; learner, 87–88, 106; Twitter, 55; user/visitor, 15, 58, 135, 136, 143, 147, 154, 167, 307

project documentation, 206; archiving, 179, 236; business case, 206–7; project aim, 207; project charter, 209; project initiation document, 209; tools, 217; version control, 179, 204, 217. See also project management

project management, 205; budget management, 222; change, 226; measuring success, 237; methodologies, 205; project costs, 225; project roles, 212; project stakeholders, 213; project team, 211; quality management, 227–28; risk management, 225; schedules, 218; triple constraint, 203. See also methodologies

project phases, 216, 219; go-live, 227; planning, 235; post-live, 236; testing, 230. See also project management

proprietary: database, 15, 169, 391; digital signage, 150; software, xxiii, 332–34, 338
prototype, 123–25, 219, 247–49, 255, 261–65
psychographics, 135, 365
public participation officer, 284

qualitative methods, 39–40
quality management, 227; test plan, 228; test script, 229–31; user acceptance testing (UAT), 228–32. *See also* project management
quality of service (QoS), 296–97
quantitative research methods, 39–40, 62, 86, 135, 250, 281. *See also* metrics

rack server, 315
regulatory compliance, 207, 320
responsive, 49, 53, 134, 159, 207; definition, 149
organization, xiv, xix, xxiii, 15–16, 25, 274, 278; website, 136, 146, 149, 154, 283, 349
retail, 13–15, 18, 25, 71, 72, 272, 338, 341, 344–48, 350–51, 357
return on investment (ROI), 159, 347, 365
retweet, 55, 56, 68
Ries, Eric, 6
rights and reproductions coordinator, 285
risk log entry, 226
RJ-45, 302–4
robotics, 113, 139
roles in digital organization, 211, 212, 280–285
router, 282, 299, 302, 305, 310, 310–13, 317, 329

scanning, 138, 194–95, 264; 3D, 139
scaffolding, 95
school visitors, xx, 36, 73, 85, 99, 103, 113, 136, 172, 196, 282, 284
scrum, 205, 228, 240–43, 366, 367
search engine optimization (SEO), 94–95, 148–49, 159, 365
security, 22, 65, 99, 111, 133, 149, 158, 281, 299, 304, 307, 310–12, 338; collections, 180–88, 191, 194–95; compliance, 317, 329, 352; online, 23, 155, 177, 316–17; policy, 167, 316–23, 325–30, 352

segmentation, 58, 135, 282–83, 365
server, 155–58, 181, 187, 188, 223, 282, 290, 292, 294, 299–302, 305, 314–16, 318, 323–25, 331, 338, 344, 365
server rack standards, 300; heat and humidity, 301
SMART objectives, 63
smartphone, 8, 21–23, 25, 45–47, 96, 97, 103, 110, 136, 142, 145, 149–50, 175, 194, 278, 279, 292, 308–9, 317–18, 325, 327, 344, 356–57
Snapchat, xx, 47, 48, 49
social media, 8–10, 11, 15–16, 45–60, 62–75, 84, 87, 88, 90, 91, 96–99, 133–36, 143, 145, 150, 152, 157, 160, 163, 175, 234, 274, 278, 279–86, 343, 346, 351, 355, 361, 367
social media manager, 283
sociotechnical interaction network (STIN), 85
Software as a Service (SaaS), 238
software development. *See* digital development
splash screen. *See* captive portal
sponsorship, 148, 346–47
sprint, 32, 205, 228, 367
Sprout Social, 64
stakeholder, xxii, 16, 18; analytics, 62–63, 69; collections management, 177, 187, 194, 200; digital content, 145, 147, 157, 159, 171; ECMS, 171; museum learning, 89; museum organization, 274, 278; project management, 202, 204, 206–10, 213, 216, 218, 221, 227, 238–39; visitor experience design, 252, 256, 264, 265
standards compliance, xxi, 165, 167–68, 174, 329
storage, 137, 187, 194, 196, 200; digital, 223, 225, 314, 316, 325, 350
storyboard, 119, 121, 248, 252, 257–58, 266, 367
strategic plan, 18, 158, 179
style guide, 207, 228, 261, 285
success metrics, 62–63, 207
SumAll, 64, 71
SurveyMonkey, 75
sustainability, 10, 27, 29, 199, 209, 238, 290, 329, 331, 339, 342

INDEX

switch, 282, 299, 301–6, 312–13, 316–17, 324, 325, 329, 338

tags, 67–68, 94–95, 328, 367
teacher guides, 92
teaching networks, 98–99
teaching skills, 36, 39, 77, 82, 88, 143
technology plan, 153–56
temperature control, 299, 331
test plan, 228
test script, 229–31
ticketing, 21, 110, 133, 155–58, 296, 297, 302, 307, 314, 318, 322, 328, 345, 347–49, 351, 353
touchscreen, 109, 114, 125, 126, 177
tourism, 10, 134, 135, 151, 242, 348–49, 379
tours, 8, 10, 21, 50, 72, 82, 95, 99; audio, xix, 110, 118, 146, 254, 285; Braille, 97; mobile, 166, 254, 308; personalized, 115; virtual, 90, 113
training, 39, 121, 159, 211, 233–34; collections management, 180, 187; IT management, 290, 304, 310, 331, 334; organizational change, 278, 280; project management, 224, 233–34, 241, 242; volunteers, 198–99
Transmission Control Protocol/Internet Protocol (TCP/IP), 292
treasure hunt, 92, 105
triadic closure, 55, 57
triple constraint, 203
Twitter, 46, 72, 136, 283, 355; analytics, 64; building community, xix, , 54–58, 136; as content channel, 47, 48, 50, 146, 163, 280; cost of new users, 58; glossary, 48; Periscope, 8; value of, 61, 64–66, 72

uninterruptable power supply (UPS), 300
use case, 136, 158, 227, 307
user acceptance testing, 232
user-centrism, 3–7, 11, 13 14, 26, 69, 71, 92, 134, 159, 246, 271–72, 278, 287, 367
user experience, 5, 153, 156–57, 202, 207, 222–23, 245–66, 343, 349–50, 357, 367
user-generated content, 126, 148, 225
user interface, 111, 118, 155, 172, 176–77, 181, 200, 257, 264–65, 285, 349, 364, 367
user journey, 157–58, 237, 343, 349–50, 367
user manual, 192

user permissions, 179, 183, 188, 189, 233, 285, 323
user profiles, 136
user requirements, 165

video mapping, 334
Vimeo, 151, 154
virtualization, 141, 280, 290–91, 294, 307, 316
virtual local area network (VLAN), 308, 316–17, 328, 329
virtual private network (VPN), 319
virtual reality (VR), 15, 22–23, 90, 111–12, 128, 139, 141–42, 197, 245, 291, 295, 367
visitor-centrism. *See* user-centrism
visitor experience (VX) design, 245–49, 266
visitor motivations, 254
visitor research. *See* audience research
visualization, 62, 69, 82, 88, 247, 256, 266, 294
Voice over Internet Protocol (VoIP), 297, 317, 320

waterfall method, 215–16
wearable, 111, 367
web and digital media developer, 285
website, 20, 21, 52, 107, 112, 115, 145, 233, 341, 349–51, 355; 3D objects, 139; accessibility, 97, 228; analytics, 61–67, 69, 71–75, 88; content plan, 146; development, 71, 135–36, 148, 158–60, 163, 166–69, 193, 196, 201–2; display of digital art, 140; ecommerce, 229; licenses, 225; maintenance, 281, 285, 286, 345; management, 63; mobile, 126; performance, 157–58, 207–9; promotion, 234, 366; search, 89, 94–95; user experience, 367
WhatsApp, 45
WiFi, 14–15, 21–25, 45, 95, 96, 110, 113, 115, 136, 145, 149, 152, 160, 164, 223, 255, 256, 279, 285, 291, 296–97, 302–10, 312, 326, 327, 338, 341, 356–66
wireframe, 367
workflow, 190
working conditions, 277

Yahoo, 149
YouTube, 10, 47, 50, 151, 154, 163, 342, 355; analytics, 64

About the Authors

Pam Babes is the collections information manager for National Museums Scotland, where she manages a team of information and photography professionals. She is responsible for managing and providing access to information about the museum's diverse collections and their digitization. Pam also has overall responsibility for the development, management, and training provision for the museum's collections information system. She has worked at National Museums Scotland since 1988 as a documentation and information specialist and has gained extensive skills and knowledge in collections management, particularly around policy and procedures, information management and standards, collections information systems, digitization and digital asset management, IPR, volunteer and intern management, and the museums accreditation scheme. Recently Pam has project managed an upgrade of the museum's collections information system with the successful migration of over three-quarters of a million database records. She was chair of the Scottish Collections Managers Forum for a number of years and delivered documentation training and knowledge sharing for MDA and National Museums Scotland. Prior to working at the museum Pam worked in electronics in the private sector and in the Royal Air Force.

Jake Barton is principal and founder of Local Projects, a media and physical design firm that creates groundbreaking experiences. Credits include landmark projects like the 9/11 Memorial Museum, the Cooper-Hewitt Smithsonian Design Museum, and the Cleveland Museum of Art. Local Projects has won every major award including the National Design Awards and Cannes Lions, for work that focuses on retail, including Open House for Target, storytelling with StoryCorps, and education with a suite of Noticing Tools for the Gates Foundation. Jake's TED talk has nearly one million views, and he is on *Fast Company* magazine's list of top fifty designers.

Ngaire Blankenberg is internationally recognized for her work planning innovative museums and revitalizing urban spaces. She is coauthor, with Gail Lord, of *Cities, Museums and Soft Power* (2015), which urges museums to play a more vital role in creating equitable, inclusive and empowering cities. As European director and principal consultant at Lord Cultural Resources, the world's largest museum and cultural professional practice, Ngaire advises museums, the private sector, and governments throughout the world on ways to develop their cultural assets for public benefit. She is cofounder, with Stephanie Nolen, of the Museum of AIDS in Africa.

Gloria Castellví is a web and social media analyst at LaMagnética, a Barcelona-based cultural consultancy. She graduated in mathematics from the Polytechnic University of Catalonia.

Kevin Cunningham is an award-winning New York–based artist and entrepreneur. He is the founder and executive artistic director of 3-Legged Dog Media and Theater Group and 3LD Art & Technology Center, 3-Legged Dog's multi-venue high-tech development studio in Lower Manhattan. He is known for artistic and technological innovation as well as business innovation in the not-for-profit arts. His artistic focus over the last thirty years has been on the creation of large-scale interdisciplinary artwork of all kinds and on the creation of artists' tools that enable intuitive manipulation of time-based and sensory elements. Awards and honors include two Rockefeller Foundation residencies in Bellagio, Italy, Edward F. Albee Foundation residency, selection for the Venice Biennale 2004 and 2008 for interactive media design, 2007 American Theater Wing Hewes Design Award, and a Hewes Nomination in 2008. Two of his works have been selected for the prestigious Prague Quadrennial of Performance Design 2011 and official selection for the 2013 Sundance, American Film Institute, New York, and Hamptons International Film festivals, as well as CPH:DOX. He has twice been awarded the Rockefeller Foundation Cultural Innovation Fund Grant. In 2016 he was nominated for two Drama Desk Awards.

Jessica Doig is the vice president and executive producer of NGX Interactive, an award-winning technology firm that is driven by meaningful, inspirational, and educational exhibits. NGX creates digital interactive storytelling experiences for museums, science centers, and cultural destinations. Armed with her PMP Certification and a UBC Science Degree, Jessica's formal credentials belie her passion for creativity and education through nontraditional means. Jessica leads the visitor experience strategy for her projects through a convergence of educational objectives, interpretive storytelling, audience profiles, and smart use of technology.

Alex Espinós founded LaMagnética in 2009, a Barcelona-based online consulting agency that works mainly for museums and tourism authorities. The company focuses on digital strategy, social network analysis, website analytics, and competitive intelligence. Alex studied philosophy and mathematics at the University of Barcelona, where he completed the doctoral courses in logic and philosophy of language. During four years he worked as a researcher and assistant professor at the University of Barcelona. He also teaches in several postgraduate programs.

Ali Hossaini works at the cutting edge of art, technology, and business. Having collaborated with talent ranging from Robert Wilson to Brad Pitt, his productions have shown in museums, performing arts centers, galleries, and festivals around the world, winning acclaim from *Vanity Fair*, *Cool Hunting*, and others, including the *New York Times*, which calls him "a biochemist turned philosopher turned television producer turned visual poet." He speaks, works, and exhibits globally, and he is CEO of Cinema Arts Network, a consortium of UK arts venues. Currently he is an associate of Lord Cultural Resources, research fellow in the Department of Informatics, King's College London, research fellow in museum studies at National Taipei Education University, and a fellow of the Royal Society of Arts. He received his PhD in philosophy of science from the University of Texas at Austin.

Barry Lord is internationally known as one of the world's leading museum planners. He and Gail Lord founded Lord Cultural Resources in 1981. Dedicated, thorough and knowledgeable, Barry brings over fifty years of experience in the management and planning of museums, galleries, and historic sites. He has particular expertise in facility planning, having developed a unique approach to zoning museum spaces and a comprehensive, systematic approach to space planning and functional requirements for museums. He has also directed hundreds of master plans; feasibility studies; collection analyses; and exhibition planning, design, and installation projects for museums around the world ranging from a focus on marine archaeology to industrial technology and from heritage villages to the complex stories of a nation.

Barry is an esteemed author and speaker. Books include *Art and Energy: How Culture Changes* (2014), *Artists, Patrons, and the Public: Why Culture Changes*, with Gail Lord (AltaMira Press, 2010); *Manual of Museum Learning*, 2nd edition, with Brad King (Rowman & Littlefield, 2016); *Manual of Museum Exhibitions*, now in 2nd edition, with Maria Piacente (Rowman & Littlefield, 2014); *Manual of Museum Planning*, with Gail Lord and Lindsay Martin (now in 3rd edition, AltaMira Press, 2012); and *Manual of Museum Management*, with Gail Lord, now in 2nd edition (AltaMira Press, 2009). As an author and editor, Barry was originally known for *artscanada* magazine (1967) and for *The History of Painting in Canada: Toward a People's Art* (1974).

Gail Dexter Lord is cofounder and copresident of Lord Cultural Resources. With Barry Lord, she is coeditor of *The Manual of Museum Planning* (1991, 1999, 2012), coauthor of

The Manual of Museum Management (1997 and 2009), and with Kate Markert the first edition of the *Manual of Strategic Planning for Museums* (2007). Gail's most recent book is *Cities, Museums and Soft Power* (coauthored with Ngaire Blankenberg in 2015). Gail has collaborated with museums and cities to create new kinds of institutions such as the Museum of the African Diaspora in San Francisco, the Foundling Museum in London, and the Canadian Museum for Human Rights in Winnipeg. Gail is a Member of the Order of Canada (2016), and Officier de l'Ordre des Arts et des Lettres de France (2014). In 2016 she was awarded an Honorary Doctor of Letters, by McMaster University.

Marco Mason has a PhD in design and is a researcher at the School of Museum Studies at the University of Leicester UK. For the second time he has been awarded with one of the most prestigious European research fundings, a Marie Curie fellowship to carry on research that aims to investigate design theory and practices of digital media for museums. The first Marie Curie research project—titled "Digital Media for Heritage: Refocusing Design from the Technology to the Visitor Experience" FP7 2012-2015—investigated the phenomenon of digital media design in the museum context by analyzing and interpreting existing design practices. The project was conjunctly conducted with the Program in Science, Technology and Society at the Massachusetts Institute of Technology and the School of Museum Studies at the University of Leicester UK. The current Marie Curie project—titled "Design Thinking for Digital Heritage: Developing Communities of Design Practice for Visitor Experience H2020," 2016–2018—aims to advance design research by conducting a systematic analysis of design thinking culture in the particular domain of museums engaged in digital heritage projects. It is conjunctly conducted with the School of Museum Studies and the University of Cambridge Fitzwilliam Museum. Marco obtained his master's degree in Architecture at Iuav University of Venice, Italy. At the Faculty of Architecture he conducted practice-led research and teaching activities before moving to the Faculty of Arts and Design, where he obtained his doctoral degree in design sciences in 2012.

Chris Michaels is head of Digital and Publishing at The British Museum in London. His role is to create and deliver the Museum's digital strategy—a five-year program of transformation that ties the possibilities of digital culture to the Museum's enlightenment ideals. He joined the Museum in 2014, having previously worked in tech startups, in TV, publishing, and advertising. He has a PhD in literature from Bristol University.

Katie Moffat is an experienced consultant, trainer and digital specialist. Currently head of digital at The Audience Agency, Katie has been working in the digital arena for over sixteen years. In the early 2000s she was a digital project manager, responsible for the development of first-stage websites and CD-ROMs. Following that she spent many years as an independent consultant, advising companies and charities on their digital strategy.

At The Audience Agency Katie consults with arts, culture, museums and heritage organizations, helping them to better understand and reach their online audiences. She often works alongside the research team, using a variety of different methodologies. Katie is a mentor on the Arts Marketing Association's Digital Academy and a frequent speaker at conferences. She has written for many publications and websites including *.net magazine*, *CreativeBloq* and *The Next Web*. She is @katiemoffat on Twitter.

Adam Padron just marked ten years at the Metropolitan Museum of Art and has spent the majority of his time driving transformational projects, building highly functioning teams and implementing sustainable technology as a member of the Information Systems and Technology department. Most recently Adam has led the completion of a multiyear enhancement of all of the Met's revenue systems, focusing on implementing a centralized transaction and CRM system, extending sales and service capabilities by developing the museum's first sales kiosks and mobile sales tablets, and reorganizing his organization to support these areas into the years to come. In addition, he's driven initiatives to eliminate paper-based and informal workflows by leveraging Jira, SharePoint, and other tools to meet the needs of Met staff from departments ranging from IT and Digital to Facilities and Objects Conservation. The technology solutions that Adam and his team have implemented are used by tens of thousands of museum visitors and hundreds of staff each day. Outside of his work at the Met, Adam provides consulting services to other large institutions in the New York area, primarily focusing on revenue systems, workflow transformation, and implementation of agile scrum practices.

Mark Pajak heads up the digital team for Bristol Culture, driving digital development across Bristol Museums and Archives. He has a background in digital analytics, having previously worked as a consultant for analytical database platforms in the marketing sector. His current focus is harnessing new technologies to increase digital engagement with collections as well as streamlining business processes.

Edward Purvis is head of collections services at the National Portrait Gallery, London. At the Gallery he leads the collections management, conservation, and art-handling teams. He also oversees the rolling displays schedule and manages the strategic development of objects in external storage and on display at regional partners around the UK. Before joining the Gallery, he was collections standards and care manager at the National Army Museum, London. He was responsible for one million collection items at the museum's off-site store and also project managed the move of over one hundred thousand objects into new storage. Other roles at the museum included registrar, with responsibility for loans and the strategic development of the collections management system. Before that he was a curator in the Department of Exhibits, responsible for the cataloging of weapons, equipment, vehicles, uniforms, badges, and medals. He began his career in 2002, when he assisted the Duchy of Lancaster with recording old title deeds. After that he volunteered in a number of local and independent museums, including the Museum of Lancashire and Beamish Museum. He is also Museum Mentor for the Musical Museum, London, where he advises on collections management strategies. He has a BA (Hons) degree in ancient history and an MA in museum and artifact studies, both from Durham University. He was awarded the Associateship of the Museums Association (AMA) in 2014.

Robert Stein is a museum leader, technology expert, and strategist with deep experience in the museum field heading up innovative projects and diverse teams. In April 2016, Rob joined the American Alliance of Museums as the executive vice president and chief program officer to lead the organization's programming efforts in service to both national and global audiences. In that role, Stein is responsible for key strategic initiatives including the expansion of the Alliance's role as a thought leader, content provider, and global catalyst for excellence in the field of museums.

Rob is a sought-after author, speaker, and consultant, focusing on the impact museums can have in their community, how technology efforts can change the dynamic of museum innovation, and how metrics and measurement can drive continuous improvement for the practice of museums. Stein is active in service to the museum field having served as a board member of the Museum Computer Network, an active member of the International Program Committee of Museums and the Web, and as a national advisor to the Education Committee of AAM. He is currently a senior advisor to the National Center for Arts Research at Southern Methodist University.

Corey Timpson is responsible for the direction and oversight of all exhibition programs; research and curation; design and production across all media, digital platforms, and transmedia storytelling; and collections-based initiatives at the Canadian Museum for Human Rights (CMHR). As vice president of exhibition, research, and design, Corey is also a member of the CMHR executive leadership, charged with the fulfillment of the CMHR's national mandate. Corey's primary focus at the CMHR is to facilitate interactive and dialogic experiences between and among visitors (on-site and online) through the use of mixed media, digital technology, and immersive environmental design, relying on sustainable, scalable, and efficient data and interaction models. Corey has a BA in law from Carleton University and a postgraduate diploma in interactive multimedia from Algonquin College of Applied Arts and Technology. Joining the Canadian Museum for Human Rights in September 2009, he was the first experienced museum professional on staff. Prior to accepting his role at the CMHR, Corey spent eight years at the Canadian Heritage Information Network and the Virtual Museum of Canada, where he led the interface and creative design, information architecture, and web management teams, working with a large number of Canada's three thousand museums on digital innovation projects. Published by ACM SIGGRAPH and MIT, among many others, and sitting on multiple national and international cultural committees, Corey is an active collaborator in experience design and digital media discourses within the cultural domain.

Rachel Clements Walker has worked at the intersection between the arts, technology, and commerce for the past eight years. Specializing in ecommerce, Rachel has substantial experience in leading innovative digital projects, and exploring new areas for revenue generation in the cultural sector. Rachel is currently senior manager of ecommerce and systems at the Metropolitan Museum of Art. In this capacity she leads the development of new digital commercial platforms as they emerge in the marketplace, and oversees the day-to-day operations of the ecommerce website and back-end retail systems.

Rachel began her training in digital retail systems as an IT graduate trainee with John Lewis department stores, and has since worked for various cultural organizations including the British Museum, Royal Academy of Arts, and Imperial War Museums. Rachel is a PRINCE2-trained project manager and a graduate of the University of Cambridge. She has an MA in innovation management from Central Saint Martins, where she specialized in success and innovation in the creative industries. Rachel has spoken at digital conferences internationally, including Museums on the Web, and is a coauthor of the 2012 Culture24 Let's Get Real report, a unique collaborative-action research project with a range of cultural sector organizations to help them define and measure their success online.

Eileen Willis has worked in the visual and performing arts world in New York for fifteen years, developing, publishing, and managing editorial content for both print and digital channels. She has extensive experience managing internal and external stakeholders on complex, large-scale projects. She is currently the editorial director for Lincoln Center for the Performing Arts, where she oversees content development and strategy for web and print. In previous roles she managed digital content projects for the Metropolitan Museum of Art, the International Center of Photography, and the Brooklyn Museum.

Eileen graduated with honors from Wellesley College, where she majored in Italian language and literature.

Lisa Wright is a senior consultant in exhibitions and events at Lord Cultural Resources. She is responsible for exhibition planning and development for a range of cultural institutions, including research, content development, interpretive planning, coordination, and project management. Lisa holds a bachelor of arts (Honours) degree in history from Queen's University and a master's degree in museum studies from the University of Toronto. Lisa helps her clients develop stimulating and innovative exhibitions to engage a range of audiences with diverse backgrounds, interests, and learning styles.